D1611587

Promoting Social Justice
in the Multigroup Society

PROMOTING SOCIAL JUSTICE in the MULTIGROUP SOCIETY

A Casebook for Group Relations Practitioners

JACK ROTHMAN, Editor

ASSOCIATION PRESS

published in cooperation with
Council on Social Work Education
NEW YORK

PROMOTING SOCIAL JUSTICE
IN THE MULTIGROUP SOCIETY

———

Copyright © 1971 by Association Press
291 Broadway, New York, N. Y. 10007

———

International Standard Book Number: 0-8096-1804-4
Library of Congress Catalog Card Number: 73-167687

Printed in the United States of America

Foreword

The United States was built by and consists of people from many nations, religions, and cultures. Many groups in American society, however, have not yet received the full measure of their rights nor have they been accepted in the mainstream of the life of America. Social work and social workers have a special role to play in helping these groups to share in the opportunities afforded the larger population in this country. This is a difficult task in these critical times and one which requires knowledge and skill as well as commitment.

The selections in this book cover numerous approaches to group relations. The situations described range from problems in state and local agencies, to group attitudes of various minorities, to individual experiences in specific communities. Through this publication, the Council on Social Work Education (CSWE) hopes to enrich the social work curriculum, to heighten the social work students' awareness of group relations, and to increase the knowledge and competence of future social workers in the area of group relations. It is also hoped that those already involved in this crucial field will find further ideas and experiences which are applicable to their own work.

Our thanks are due to Jack Rothman, professor of social work at the University of Michigan School of Social Work, for his efforts in compiling and organizing this collection and to the Advisory Committee which helped guide the conception of this volume and the identification and selection of appropriate content.

The preparation and publication of this volume has been made possible by the generosity of the Slawson Fund of the American Jewish Committee and especially through the personal interest of Dr. John Slawson, of New York City, the executive vice-president emeritus of the American Jewish Committee.

ARNULF M. PINS
Executive Director
Council on Social Work Education

April, 1971

Contents

As a further help to the reader, the units of the book are here listed by Social Groups and by Problem-Program Areas. Numbers refer to the units as they appear in the Table of Contents.

Introduction

This volume represents a modest effort to meet a large problem. There is a critical need for teaching materials of all sorts relating to work with racial and ethnic groups, both in social work and other human service professions. As the context of group relations in our society has shifted and the urgency of making significant adjustments become increasingly manifest, the inadequacy and obsolescence of existing curriculum is painfully apparent.

The approach taken here is to produce a range of source materials which illustrate and illuminate aspects of group relations practice. Such a source book, composed of cases, documents, episodes of practice, agency reports, etc., is intended to highlight issues and techniques and to provoke systematic analysis relative to this area of practice. Its purpose is both to teach and to stimulate further conceptualization concerning this very important field of work. In this sense, the source book means to open up issues and lines of inquiry rather than to settle or close them.

The Council on Social Work Education has found in the past that the issuance of a casebook for classroom teaching is a useful impetus for further curriculum development in a content area. We could have elected to produce a textbook, a theoretical statement, or a book of substantive readings. The case book route is quicker (it took slightly over one year from inception to the finished manuscript) and perhaps more developmental in its impact on curriculum. This publication is only the first step in unfolding a major program in the area of race, ethnic and other group relations. Other source books are being planned by the Council for each of the major ethnic groups.

As the reader will see, the framework concerning group relations practice which is reflected in the book is broad and eclectic. The book attempts to capture the empirical reality of what is actually happening operationally in the field without becoming ideologically aligned with any one approach. Rather it views all alike from a discerning analytic posture. We define the field in terms of a series of functions designated *Group Rights* (gaining civil and other rights), *Group Solidarity and Power* (gaining political, economic and cultural strength), *Intergroup Attitudes and Relationships* (mediating conflicts), and *Group Welfare* (giving supportive services to individuals). We have attempted to gather source material which gives adequate coverage to each of these functions and at the same time highlights some of the major issues that are reverberating in the field. The stance that was set down in the original prospectus prepared by the Council and which we attempted to implement was stated as follows:

> In general, it might be said that the approach that is being considered for a format is one of variation and flexibility. The source book should be lively, interesting, current and diverse. There should be long cases and short ones. Some that follow a process through longitudinally and some that delve into a single episode or document. Actual agency documents should be used to the degree possible. Dialogues with the practitioner should be included where useful and possible. Professional material written by practitioners should be included as well as more popular pieces written by newspaper reporters or clients. We should avoid a drab pattern of consistency and strive for diversity that engages the reader's interest.

The casebook will not restrict itself to the tried-and-true process case record which has for so long dominated the social work profession's orientation to teaching materials.

We have used the term "group relations" to describe intervention in the ethnic and racial field and in other group relations areas. The previously prevalent term "inter-group relations" has come to be associated with a consensus, status-quo, attitude-change mode of action. In encompassing a wider spectrum of strategies and techniques, it seemed wise to utilize a different terminology in order to avoid semantic booby traps.

As the reader will see, we have attempted to include material on a wide range of American groups: American Indians, blacks, Chicanos (Mexican Americans), Puerto Ricans; Catholics, Jews, Protestants, whites in the suburbs, blue-collar ethnic nationalities, and women (although the latter have not been typically included in group relations writings). While aiming at breadth of coverage, we have not given "equal time" to each of these groups in a mechanistic way. Discussion of black issues has considerable weight, in part because the majority of students and readers of this book in all likelihood will be confronted with these issues in urban centers on both coasts. In addition, selections were influenced simply by the availability of suitable descriptive narratives. In the end, judgment was exercised regarding the matter of scope, relevance, suitability, and emphasis, a judgment for which the editor assumes responsibility.

We have refrained from using the term "minority groups" because of our view of the dynamics of group relations in American society. While group relations practice was previously viewed as activity aimed at improvement for minority groups, the minority group term might not, in the current era, be serviceable. Racial, ethnic, religious, and nationality groups, including blacks, Chicanos (Mexican Americans), American Indians, Puerto Ricans, and others no longer picture themselves as long-suffering victims, but as assertive and dignified social entities articulating legitimate aspirations and making a fully significant cultural contribution to the society. Rather than conceiving beleaguered minorities grappling with a unitary superordinate majority, it might be better to think of a pattern of complex social relations in a pluralistic, multigroup society, involving shifting configurations of group accommodation or adjustment on the one hand or conflict and rearrangement of power and status on the other. We are thus concerned generally with matters of group aspiration, status, identity, conflict, power relations, and accommodations. This perspective has been articulated well by Tom Wicker in a discussion of the Nixon Administration:

> There remains a real danger for a government based too strongly upon identification with a majority united primarily in bitterness, mistrust, fear and anger. The danger is that those who seek the favor and support of such a majority may encourage, and themselves emulate, these qualities, rather than trying to build, too, upon those other strains of generosity and courage that many a President has found not lacking in the American people.
>
> If the Nixon Administration defies classification, after all, how much more do the times and "the people"! Not just the Forgotten Man—himself a none too well-known quantity, a flesh-and-blood human rather than a polltaker's cipher—but the blacks, the students, the liberals of Park Avenue, the Chicanos, the intellectuals, the businessmen, the affluent suburbanites, the welfare recipients, the old, the young, the Appalachian poor—all the infinite variety of a continental democracy in ferment and turmoil, caught in the explosive change of the Twentieth Century. It would be a curious political view that saw some static majority, fixed and definable, dominating all these other forces even for one Presidential term, let alone a new political era.[1]

Hence minority-majority designations conceptually leave much to be desired. For convenience in discourse we will use these terms occasionally but sparingly, "minority" implying an ethnic or racial group singled out for discussion, "majority" implying the over-all national cultural configuration.

Social workers have a deep involvement in matters pertaining to ethnic and racial groups. In part, this is so because discrimination and prejudice create or exacerbate many of the problems with which social workers contend professionally day by day in their practice—poverty, crime, family breakdown, dependency. On a more fundamental level, the profession should strike out ideologically and behaviorally against racial and ethnic oppression simply because it embodies the evil of social injustice. Historically the profession has recurrently combated social injustice, championing such causes as the rights of children, social security, workmen's compensation, and the like. The reluctance to grapple with race and ethnic matters with equal vigor reflects a peculiar narrowness and parochialism—a tendency to avoid controversy, an overconcern with technique and status, a clouded social perspective. The Kerner Commission has described America as a white racist society. Perhaps the profession's limited performance in the past can best be understood by viewing it as an institutional arm, or form of expression, of that society. It is more than time to make vigorous thrusts on behalf of justice and equality. This book may be viewed as a vehicle to promote such endeavor.

[1]Tom Wicker, "Nixon's First Year," *The New Republic,* January 24, 1970, p. 20.

The Group Relations Field:
A Conceptual Overview

by Jack Rothman and Richard A. English

The nation is in the midst of a great social revolution. Black Americans are in a dramatic and sometimes explosive battle to achieve full citizenship. Simultaneously, other ethnic and cultural groups are engaged in efforts to eliminate the onerous burdens of discrimination and social injustice which afflict them.

Agencies concerned with group relations are involved in this significant movement on two levels. Some are in the forefront as combatants in the struggle for equal rights. Others serve an ameliorative function, attempting to moderate the potential and actual violence inherent in the contending forces involved in such a struggle and, thus, to minimize lasting damage to the social system.

Given the increasing tempo of group relations developments and the concomitant difficulties (increasing militancy, civic disorder, polarized "backlash" reactions, marginal position of the white liberal and radical), it is apparent that the need for skillful practice in this field will be both persistent and mounting.

In addition to involvement with problems of discrimination, group relations agencies are concerned with and related to problems of poverty. Minority status and poverty are very much intertwined in the United States. All informed commentators and minority groups, as well as the President of the United States, have recognized that equal rights in poverty are not rights at all; that the quest for group rights must take into account the problem of poverty which so disproportionately affects minority groups. Group relations agencies are in a strategic position relative to poverty in the United States because poverty is to such a large extent an integral element—as consequence and cause—of minority status.

Despite the growing and changing role of group relations agencies, or perhaps because of it, there is no general agreement about the knowledge and skill required of its practitioners, the nature of the field, or the type of professional preparation which is most desirable and effective. Nevertheless, it is likely that a substantial number of social workers and other professionals and activists will be engaged in this work increasingly, often in leadership positions. Furthermore, social workers and other professionals, regardless of setting, need to know more about group relations problems and issues and methods of intervention in this area in order to gear their work to this perhaps most important social development in contemporary America.

All of which, of course, lends impetus to the development of teaching materials such as this casebook, aimed at the enhancement of practice competence. In this introductory statement, we will attempt to sketch a picture of the group relations field in order to construct some framework through which to examine modes and issues of relevant practice. We recognize that this is a somewhat hazardous undertaking at this period of time, both because of the rapidly changing character of the field and because of the sharp and emotional differences of opinion which exist regarding its nature. Nevertheless, a conceptual scheme, even if tentative, is necessary in order to provide a basis for ordering the content of this volume.

At the end of this introductory conceptual statement will be found a review of literature indicating previous efforts to define the field. This literature review will be provided in the form of an addendum in order to facilitate the reader's engagement with our conceptual formulation.

Preliminary Considerations—Some Dimensions of Group Relations Work

Let us examine some dimensions of group relations work as a way of moving toward a useful conceptualization. In the past, little attention has been given to intervention strategies, diagnosis and planning as informed by sociological and social psychological theory and research, for dealing with group relations problems. In the field of what has been called group relations, the term has come to mean those relations among social categories that are primarily defined by racial, ethnic, and religious distinctions. From the perspective of group relations practice, the domain of interests has been those collectivities subject to stereotypic labeling, effective-evaluational criteria, and recipients of discrimination and segregation. It has been concerned with issues and problems of black-white relations; racial, ethnic, and religious discrimination in housing, employment, education, public accommodations, recreational facilities, and transportation; deprivation of rights through unequal administration of justice; acts of violence and incidents of vandalism, intimidation, and terrorism against minority group members.

Aside from ignoring definitional problems of the concept "group," group relations experts have paid scant attention to group structures and processes—leadership opportunities, social pressures toward conformity, control of deviance, social power, and the like—important phenomena for analysis and understanding of group conditions, problems, and directions for social change.

Robin Williams has suggested that it would be preferable to speak of "intercategory or intercollectivity relations, were it not that 'intergroup' is so widely embedded in current usage."[1] Group relations work for the most part incorporates a strong psychological bias or line of vision. Until recently, community organization, a logical method of practice for group relations, had often been construed in psychological terms. The process focus of working with groups in the community rather than on substantive problems or social need and organizing to deal with them is an example of this orientation. This approach was principally represented in the conceptualization of community organization as "intergroup" work rather than "community."[2]

[1] Robin M. Williams, *Strangers Next Door, Ethnic Relations in American Communities* (Englewood Cliffs, New Jersey: Prentice-Hall, 1964), 354.

[2] Wilber I. Newstetter, "The Social Intergroup Work Process," *Proceedings of the National Conference of Social Work* (New York: Columbia University Press, 1948), 205-217; Helen D. Green, *Social Work Practice in Community Organization* (New York: Whiteside, Inc. and William Morris, 1954).

Group relations work involves three systems of human social interaction: *Culture, personality,* and the *social system.* The cultural level involves systems of beliefs, values, norms and behaviors. Personality systems consider properties of individuals such as attitudes, needs, traits, and feelings, as well as processes of learning or perceptions. The social system focuses on relations among persons as may be influenced by social power complexes, group structures and properties, social stratification systems, and so on. Personality is related to both cultural content and social interaction, thus they are interdependent and interpenetrating even though they each may be viewed independently. Notwithstanding, there has been a tendency to interpret group relations exclusively in either cultural, psychological, or sociological terms.

All three systems of interaction are essential for an adequate understanding of group relations. As Robin Williams points out, "to treat whole systems of discriminatory behavior—in all their extensiveness, complexity, regularity, and historical persistence—as if they were solely the outcome of the spontaneous express of stereotyped beliefs and hostile feelings of separate individuals—this is now manifestly an untenable approach."[3] Moreover, as Williams points out, it is likewise erroneous to treat prejudice as if it were an automatic response to collective or societal structures and processes. The psychological explanation gives too little place to the pervading influences of group properties and systemic effects, while the sociological perspective fails to consider the imperatives of psyche and organism.[4]

Only recently has the research on prejudice and discrimination shifted from a concern with cognitions and feelings to a concern with behavior, power complexes, and conflict.[5] Such research has identified several clusters of variables that are related to intergroup contact and interaction and to cooperation and conflict. Williams has classified these variables into the following categories:

1. Status attributes of individual persons—age, sex, education, generalized prestige ranking.

2. Cultural values held by individuals—universalistic evaluations of competence in technical tasks.

3. Stereotypes and prejudices—definitions of ethnic objects.

4. Personality structure and dynamics of individuals—sources of psychological energy.

5. Characteristics of the situation of contact—nature of collective goals, if any; presence and role of third parties; number of participants and proportion of each significant social category represented; relative power.

6. Collective properties emerging from interaction—awareness of attitudes shared with others; sense of group position; patterns of concerted action (sit-ins, lynchings, passive resistance, boycotts); group cohesion.[6]

[3]Williams, *Ibid.,* 360.

[4]Williams, *Ibid.,* 360.

[5]Hubert M. Blalock, Jr., *Toward a Theory of Minority-Group Relations* (New York: John Wiley, Inc., 1967); H. M. Blalock, "A Power Analysis of Racial Discrimination," *Social Forces,* 39, No. 1 (October, 1960); Don J. Hager, "Housing Discrimination, Social Conflict, and the Law," *Social Problems,* 7, No. 1 (Summer, 1960), 80-87.

[6]Williams, *Ibid.,* 360-361.

From this categorization one may see that it is not easy to treat one factor or any set of factors while ignoring others. Moreover, any one set of factors might be expected to vary according to its relationships with other factors. Thus, any sovereign, mono-causal explanation of group relations is patently untenable.

Related to the theoretical understanding of group relations are the approaches and strategies utilized to effect change in these areas. Consensus strategies of social change and action have been employed more widely than strategies which stress the elements of power and conflict. The latter perspective, referred to as the dialectic approach in sociological literature, views society as one of dissension, conflict, and disequilibrium. The consensus or functionalists' model of society is one of consensus, stability, and harmony. Some sociologists have indicated that a true picture of a social system must incorporate both sides of the coin—thus synthesizing the functionalist and dialectic models into an empirical model of society.[7]

Consensus approaches to group relations took the individual as the unit of analysis and concentrated on programs designed to change attitudes and opinions, thereby changing behaviors. Efforts to change minority group members were designed to make them more acceptable to majority group members. Some of the basic assumptions underlying these approaches included ideas of gradualism and tokenism with the view that social change must be slow yet with "all deliberate speed" so as not to be disruptive to the larger society. Social psychological evidence has demonstrated the very nebulous relationship between opinions and attitudes as measured by interviews and questionnaires, and subsequent behavior with respect to the objects of these opinions and attitudes. For example, in the case of racial desegregation of public schools, slightly less than one-third of the white population in border states that had desegregated their school system endorsed desegregation. Yet desegregation of the schools had been accomplished without social upheaval, violence or disorder.[8]

In the sections to follow, we intend to take into account this broad, multivariant view of group relations work and to illustrate its utility in conceptualizing the types of agencies and functions comprising the group relations field.

The Group Relations Agency Network: Domain and Functions

Most group relations practice has been organized along racial, ethnic, and religious bases. The organizational network of group relations practice can be divided into several different categories: *voluntary* agencies, both national and local, sponsored by some particular ethnic, racial, or religious group; *public* agencies, federal, state, municipal, established by legislation, and those appointed by mayors, governors, or the President; *host agencies* having *some other primary purpose,* such as unions, colleges and universities, schools, churches, and social welfare agencies. Among the national voluntary agencies are: The American Friends Service Committee, the American Jewish Committee, the American Jewish Congress, the Anti-Defamation League of B'nai B'rith, the Association on American Indian Affairs, the Black

[7]Pierre Van Den Berghe, "Dialectic and Functionalism: Toward a Theoretical Synthesis," *American Sociological Review,* 28 (October, 1963), 695-705; Alvin L. Bertrand, "The Stress-Strain Element of Social Systems: A Micro Theory of Conflict and Change," *Social Forces,* 42 (October, 1963), 1-9.

[8]H. H. Hyman and P. B. Sheatsley, "Attitudes Toward Desegregation," *Scientific American* (1956), 35-39.

Panthers, the Congress of Racial Equality, the Japanese-American Citizens League, the Jewish Labor Committee, the NAACP, the National Association for Puerto Rican Civil Rights, the National Urban League, and the Southern Christian Leadership Conference. Religious agencies with race relations departments or commissions on social justice include the National Catholic Welfare Conference, the National Council of the Churches of Christ in the United States of America, various Protestant denominational groups, the Synagogue Council of America, and others. Nonsectarian agencies interested in some special area of group relations include the American Civil Liberties Union, the National Conference of Christians and Jews, and the Southern Regional Council.

Not only does the field contain this stated range but, as suggested earlier, it is also in a state of great flux and transformation. Old ideas concerning methods and values have come up for serious question and re-evaluation, which makes the problem of classification and boundary definition exceedingly difficult.

Because group relations practice is in such a fluid state it is not fruitful to spend great energy and time in defining the field in detail and for all time. We do need, however, some rough boundaries and categories on the basis of which we can view practice and select or reject source materials illustrating practice problems. An attempt will be made here to sketch such boundaries. The approach to categorization that we will use relies on capturing the varieties, contexts, and methods which are found to exist empirically in the real world of practice and action as determined by a process of interviews and reading of pertinent literature. It will also be informed by the previous discussion concerning the inclusion of cultural, sociological, and psychological variables. We will attempt to formulate an embracing framework which will take into account as many of the modes of practice which actually exist in the field without prejudgment of their validity or legitimacy. The approach is essentially empirical, pragmatic and eclectic.

In our view a useful way to conceptualize the field is in terms of functions of group relations agencies. Taking this approach, agencies and programs can be seen as pursuing programs aimed at: 1. Group Rights; 2. Group Solidarity and Power; 3. Intergroup Attitudes and Relationships; 4. Group Welfare.

To elaborate on the scheme, agencies and programs may be viewed as follows:

Group Rights. Programs which are geared to securing civil rights for members of disadvantaged groups and the elimination of discrimination in areas such as employment, housing, and education. Much of this work has a legal and judicial character involving the enforcement of law and administrative directives and is often carried out by Federal or state antidiscrimination agencies such as the Federal Civil Rights Commission. On the other hand, voluntary pressure groups such as NAACP or SCLC, and the "Civil Rights Movement" more generally make their major contribution here. Involved are mass political and social agitation, advocacy, litigation, and legislative campaigns.

Group Solidarity and Power. Programs are most frequently conducted by locally based racial and ethnic groups. The approach involves the accumulation of resources and influence which raises the status and position of the group in the society through increasing its political or economic power or its role in national or community decision making. Fostering ingroup identity through building a sense of a common history, culture, and destiny may accompany this work. Self-help and co-operative ventures, such as black capitalism programs, also pertain. The contemporary Black Power, Brown Power, Red Power and Women's Liberation movements in this country embody this approach.

Intergroup Attitudes and Relationships.   This is the area that in the past has often been at the heart of "group relations" or "human relations" work. One dimension of it has to do with improving the attitudes of some groups (often "majority groups") toward other groups (often "minority groups"). A wide variety of techniques have been employed toward this end—human relations workshops, encounter groups, mass media educational campaigns, personal contact activities, and the like. Another dimension pertains to conflict management through such programs as riot prevention, rumor control centers, etc. The National Conference of Christians and Jews has historically symbolized certain aspects of this approach. Municipal human relations agencies also "fit" here.

Group Welfare.   Assuming that citizens who experience disadvantage or injustice do indeed sometimes suffer personal damage and require special individualized supports, some organizations provide a variety of services aimed at personal upgrading or advancement. These include vocational guidance, job training, scholarships, dissemination of information about community resources, and the provision of casework or group work services. In the past, the National Urban League has been identified with a variety of such programs.

These four categories are not viewed as mutually exclusive. They overlap and interact with one another. Some agencies devote their entire resources exclusively to one of these functions. Other agencies pursue several simultaneously. For example, an agency with a function of group welfare might also have functions of group rights as well as solidarity. Similarly, group rights agencies might have group welfare functions and so on. As with most organizations, group relations agencies on the one hand have multiple goals and on the other will set different goal priorities at different stages of their work or in response to differing social circumstances. Moreover, such organizations have functions which are neither intended nor recognized.

We underline, then, that we are talking about *emphases* by certain agencies or programs, not with a rigid construct. The scheme is necessarily arbitrary, but has the advantage of being convenient for analytical purposes. By abstracting from the swirling, pulsating world of practice it attempts to reduce and simplify a highly complex, dynamic phenomenon to a level that makes it manageable for analysis.

It would perhaps be of interest to the reader to view these four functional areas in terms of a number of factors related to practice. For this purpose the following factors have been singled out as potentially useful:

1. Problem Area Focus
2. Assumptions Concerning Causes of Problems
3. Targets of Change Effort
4. Value Stance
5. Goals of Change Effort
6. Modal Strategies of Change
7. Typical Programs

In Chart I there is a paradigm describing dimensions of group relations work for each of the functional areas according to the enumerated factors in practice.

One is tempted to elaborate on this chart with a fuller narrative commentary for each functional area. Space precludes this step. Instead we will develop one functional area illustratively in order to demonstrate the general utility of the scheme. Because of its current prominence and contemporaneity we will select the area of

CHART I

	Group Rights	Group Solidarity and Power	Intergroup Attitudes	Group Welfare
(1) Problem Focus	Legal inequities, public discrimination in social institutions	Low self-esteem in minority group, low organizational and psychological cohesion in group; low minority group power in control of or representation in political and social institutions	Inimical attitudes in majority (prejudice, religious defamation); intergroup tensions and hostile relations; violence-riots extremism	Limitations in skills, resources or cultural forms (family structure) in minority group members, limited opportunities resulting in social, economic, educational disadvantage
(2) Assumptions on Causes of Problems	Discrimination and injustice by majority group causing legal inequities and limited opportunities	Lack of group identity, solidarity or power within minority group; political and economic weakness; majority group exploitation	Inappropriate, distorted majority group attitudes; minority group overreaction	Inadequate training or socialization in minority group membership; limited opportunities given by majority group
(3) Targets of Change	Majority social institutions —legal structure in particular	Minority group individuals, institutions and communities; the over-all community system and its distribution of power and status	Majority group members, majority institutions; minority group individuals and organizations	Minority group members; some majority institutions
(4) Values Assumptions Regarding Society	Social institutions are flexible and responsive to democratic public pressure	Social structures and institutions are rigid; institutionalized racism will only respond to extreme pressure and new power alignments	Individuals and society can change if provided appropriate information and values on racial and ethnic matters	Individuals need aid to change so they can be more acceptable to majority or at least cope better in an unfavorable milieu

(5) Goals of Change Effort	System change, middle range change or social reform in institutions	Redistribution of power and status in society; restructuring of institutions; elimination of institutionalized racism	Create positive image of minority group members; quell disturbances and avert hostilities; social integration	Changed minority group persons; new policies and opportunities in majority institutions.
(6) Strategies	Legislative action, administrative compliance machinery, litigation, conventional legal and political activism; nonviolent pressure tactics generally	Mass grass-roots organizing, use of conflict (protest, militant confrontation, violence); establishing minority institutions; training for local community leadership roles	Consensus (persuasion, mediation, educational impacts) using small groups and mass media; mediation and intergroup contact; use of workshops, conferences, institutes, mass media, written word; conjoint community problem-solving structures	Consensual approaches stressing services and expanded opportunities; education and training of minority members; persuasive interaction with target systems (industries, schools, etc.); development of technical and social skills
(7) Typical Programs	Enacting fair housing ordinances, antidiscrimination laws; compliance programs re above; school desegregation policies and programs; voter registration programs, etc.	Establishing local mass minority group organization, usually issue oriented—local control of schools, welfare, etc.; training for local control, school board membership; voter registration and political participation campaigns; formation of local business, co-ops, other institutions; ethnic identity and cultural expression programs; dealing with local utilities, banks, businesses to make them more responsive to local people	Human relations workshops and other programs—sensitivity training; work with whites in suburbs, with blue-collar ethnic groups, with extremist groups (Birch Society, etc.); minority ethnic coalitions, Jewish-black relations, black anti-Semitism, social mediator and negotiator roles in extreme conflict situations; interreligious programs; violence prevention, control, management in ghettos, high schools, colleges; police-community relations programs; dealing with black militant groups at colleges, high schools, communities	Employment counseling and educational guidance programs; education of the disadvantaged child; training programs for foremen, teachers, social workers to give better services and treatment; work with employers re-hiring, training, promotions

solidarity and power for expanded treatment. In addition, we will concentrate on the Black Power movement in order to develop the general theme.

1. Problem Focus

The concept of group solidarity and power, in this instance Black Power, symbolizes the view that the social structure and problems of the black community are unique with distinctive historical antecedents.[9] These unique characteristics and problems demand immediate attention and action and must be explicitly recognized, setting aside elements common to the majority culture.[10] The black community has been placed in a position of inequity and disadvantage because of exploitation by white society, resulting in low esteem, inadequate organizational cohesion, little power and control of societal resources, and under-representation in political and social institutions. The quest for greater equality and opportunities require major structural changes in American society. Such changes exceed matters of prejudice, correctable by widespread attitudinal changes. No racial barriers to social mobility exist for white people. While there are common problems peculiar to the economic underclass, middle-class blacks are confronted with restrictions in social mobility, social contacts with other groups, and many other barriers preventing the realization of life goals.[11] To state the issue differently, the social dynamics of American society generate and perpetuate unequal separation of races and ethnic groupings and maintain various forms of institutional racism which are both disjunctive and discriminatory.

2. Causes

While the basic cause of the problem stems from institutional white racism, in multiple forms, more immediate problem circumstances reside in the minority community. The black ghetto is a compact center of social interaction isolated from social life in the larger community.[12] Consequently, the ghetto tends on the one

[9]Donald I. Warren, "Social Structural Processes Related to the Negro Ghetto: Research Design and Preliminary Findings," unpublished paper, 10/2/67; Raymond J. Murphy and James M. Watson, "The Structure of Discontent: The Relationship Between Social Structure, Grievance, and Support for the Los Angeles Riot," Department of Sociology, University of California, Institute of Government and Public Affairs, 1967; William Brink and Louis Harris, *Black and White* (New York: Simon & Schuster, 1966); Seymour Parker and Robert J. Kleiner, *Mental Illness in the Urban Negro Community* (New York: The Free Press, 1966); Karl E. Taeuber and Alma F. Taeuber, *Negroes in Cities* (Chicago: Aldine Pub. Company, 1963); Nathan Glazer and Daniel P. Moynihan, *Beyond the Melting Pot* (Cambridge: Massachusetts Institute of Technology Press, 1963); E. Franklin Frazier, *Black Bourgeosie* (Glencoe: The Free Press, 1957).

[10]U.S. Riot Commission Report, *Report of the National Advisory Commission on Civil Disorders* (New York: Bantam Books, 1968).

[11]Donald I. Warren, "Race and Middle-Income Status in Detroit," Detroit Urban League, 1968, in press. These data show, for example that one in ten whites have informal contacts with blacks compared with three in five blacks having such contacts with whites; Peter M. Blau and Otis Dudley Duncan, *The American Occupational Structure* (New York: John Wiley & Sons, 1967); James S. Coleman, *Equality of Educational Opportunity* (Washington: U.S. Government Printing Office, 1966); Bullough, Bonnie, "Alienation in the Ghetto," *American Journal of Sociology,* 72 (March, 1967), 469-78.

[12]Kenneth Clark, *Dark Ghetto* (New York: Harper, 1965); Gilbert Okofsky, *The Making of a Ghetto* (New York: Harper, 1966); *Youth in the Ghetto: A Study of the Consequences of Powerlessness and a Blueprint for Change* (New York: Harlem Youth Opportunities Unlimited, 1964); Robert C. Weaver, *The Negro Ghetto* (New York: Harcourt, Brace, 1948); Karl Taeuber and Alma Taeuber, *Negroes in Cities, op. cit.*

hand to magnify problems of social deviance, personal pathology, and social disorganization and to block opportunities for anticipatory socialization with external secondary groups. On the other hand, the ghetto tends to exacerbate the problems of those blacks who remain in it despite the achievement of some social status through occupation, income, or education. Such problems include status inconsistency, value conflicts, invidious characterizations due to class differences, as well as the development of attitudes and behaviors indicative of social alienation.[13] Despite these oppressive obstacles a viable cultural form, including language, art, custom, etc., has emerged in black communities and is beginning to flower.

The over-all political and economic level of the ghetto remains low, making it an ineffective instrumentality for gaining resources for its members. Even those blacks who have escaped the ghetto are confronted with considerable problems. Aside from problems of ethnic inconsistency, they are likely to encounter whites who do not have accurate anticipatory knowledge of their behavior, to confront problems of ambiguous and conflicting role expectations, to experience a loss of "psychological safety," and to find themselves alienated from other blacks.

3. Targets

As implied, the *immediate* or proximate target of change effort is the black community itself. In an earlier period, even Booker T. Washington stressed the fact that only through self-help and racial solidarity could blacks achieve acceptance and respect in America. The cohesion of the black community is seen as an end in its own right by certain separatists and as the only instrumental means of making powerful demands for change on the wider society by other supporters of this approach.

4. Value Stance

Black Power may perhaps be usefully described as a cultural phenomenon, probably best represented in the term "*la negritude,*" as developed principally among the poets of African descent writing in the French language. It is cultural in the sense that it calls for a recognition of "art forms indigenous to American blacks . . . such as habits of dress, diet, personal adornment, sometimes religious practices and specific interpretations of religious ritual, dogma, and paraphernalia."[14] Indigenous norms, values, symbols, and belief systems encompass ". . . . its devotees in a kind of *mood ebony* which intensify self-appreciation and the sense of belonging to an intimate society of black men who, like their white counterparts, may have an exaggerated sense of their own racial destiny."[15]

In its most profound sense Black Power emerges as a critical judgment about the quality of life in the United States. This judgment is represented in the widely disseminated statistics about the present position of black America as compared with white America: shorter life expectancy; higher infant and maternal mortality; lower

---

[13]Seymour Parker and Robert Kleiner, *Mental Illness in the Urban Negro Community* (New York: The Free Press, 1966); Elton Jackson, "Status Consistency and Symptoms of Stress," *American Sociological Review*, 27 (August, 1962), 469-580.

[14]C. Eric Lincoln, "The Black Revolution in Cultural Perspective," unpublished manuscript, 1968.

[15]*Ibid.,* 9.

number of school years completed, particularly for black males; high per cent of unemployment and underemployment; lower incomes; higher incidence of homicides and deaths from diseases; and the like.[16] National recognition and legitimation was given this judgment by the black militant minority in the President's Commission on Civil Disorders, which described America as a white racist society.[17]

5. Goals

At the political level, Black Power means independent action and influence building. This is black control of the political power of the black ghettos and its deliberate use to improve slum conditions. A "political modernization" is in prospect in which the base of political participation is broadened and new and different forms of political structures are developed to attack the critical problems of racial discrimination in employment, housing, and education. At the community level, local control of schools and other local institutions is sought.

In economic terms, it means the development of independent, self-supporting black businesses, the encouragement of black entrepreneurs, and the formation of black cooperatives.

In those urban centers where black social work associations have been organized, the primary goal is to establish social agencies to provide services for residents of the black ghetto.[18] Their rationale is based on the premise (and evidence) that such services have not been forthcoming from existing social agencies as well as the assertion that, when such services were available, they have been demeaning and degrading without an understanding of the peculiar problems and social dynamics of the black community.[19]

6. Strategies and Programs

The basic strategies of the mode of action have been implicit in what has been previously suggested—mass organization of black communities on a political and cultural level; training for local leadership roles; establishing local institutions in the political, economic, and social scene; employing various forms of social conflict to coerce the larger society to make concessions and shift resources and power. The use of confrontations and the heightening of ingroup hostility toward the outgroup may also be used as a technique for increasing internal cohesion. Confrontation

---

[16]Rashi Fein, "An Economic and Social Profile of The American Negro," in Talcott Parsons and Kenneth B. Clark (eds.), The Negro American (Boston: Beacon Press, 1965), 102-133; Manpower Report of The President, March, 1965; Karl E. Taeuber and Alma F. Taeuber, Negroes in Cities (Chicago: Aldine Publishing Co., 1965).

[17]U.S. Riot Commission Report, Report of the National Advisory Commission on Civil Disorders (New York: Bantam Books, 1968).

[18]Organizing efforts for such agencies are being made by the Association of Black Social Workers in Detroit, Chicago, and New York.

[19]Henry Miller, "Value Dilemmas in Social Casework," Social Work, Vol. 13, No. 1 (January, 1968), 27-33; David Wellman, "The Wrong Way to Find Jobs for Negroes," Transaction, Vol. 5 (April, 1968), 9-18; Richard A. Cloward and Irwin Epstein, "Private Social Welfare's Disengagement from the Poor: The Case of Family Adjustment Agencies," in The Adjustment of Social Welfare to Social Change, State University of New York at Buffalo, School of Social Welfare-Social Work Alumni, Eighth Annual Social Work Day, May 12, 1965.

also serves the purpose of dramatizing social injustice and intensifying white guilt. A similar analysis may be performed for each of the other functions specified.

Issues in Group Relations Practice

As one moves toward action in the group relations field a number of compelling issues immediately surface. We will mention here only a limited number of issues most of which have been pointed to as the more important or prominent by practitioners themselves.[20] These issues reverberate throughout the grid in Chart I.

1. The role of official agencies—how practitioners can support militant movements while operating under governmental or other establishment sponsorship.
2. Preferential treatment vs. equality of opportunity.
3. The question of integration vs. local community control.
4. The value and utility of judicial-administrative-compliance procedures in furthering group justice.
5. Political discrimination and bigotry—how to deal with it.
6. The role of the white worker in the black (brown, red) community—relevance of ethnicity in professional relationships.
7. The place of coalitions in racial and ethnic group power-oriented movements.
8. The place of confrontation in group relations.
9. The utility of the "black capitalism" concept in achieving racial justice.
10. The role of OEO, Model Cities, and other governmental programs in facilitating racial and ethnic power—cooling out vs. tooling up.
11. The place of local community control in the social work system.
12. Women's liberation as a group relations area.
13. How to deal with white racism in middle-class suburbs.
14. The white backlash reaction among ethnic nationality groups or institutions.
15. Dealing with youth conflicts in the schools.
16. The danger of a punitive or retaliatory police response to civic disorder.
17. The effects of programs involving cross-group contacts.
18. Mediating conflicting interests among minority groups.
19. The effects of educational programs.
20. Improving or helping the minority group individual vs. institutional change in society.
21. Values and problems in compensatory educational programs.
22. Cultural factors in group relations work.
23. Saliency or nonsaliency of group relations work in an organization's work.

We intend to delve into these issues in the sections which follow. Illustrative source material revealing programs, activities, and strategies will be presented to reflect various aspects of the issues raised. Introductory comments will be made to bring out some of the major points of interest or controversy regarding the issues. While a given illustration may be placed under one or another of the functional

[20]"The 'Big Think' Conference—A Working Conference of Intergroup Practitioners and Social Scientists," sponsored by the National Association of Intergroup Relations Officials with the Community Relations Service of the United States Department of Justice, Foodergong Lodge, Ephrata, Pa., May 17-19, 1968; Alex Rosen and Barbara Mogalesco, "Some Basic Strategy and Social Policy Dilemmas Facing the Intergroup Relations Practitioners: A Report Summarizing and Assessing Questionnaire Findings," presented to Conference sponsored by the National Association of Intergroup Relations Officials, Foodergong Lodge, Ephrata, Pa., May 17, 1968.

areas and may embody a position on the particular issue, this is not to support that position or to indicate the editor's point of view. The position reflected in the illustrative piece is meant to convey to the reader what implemental action looks like if approached in a particular way. Thus, each illustration is meant to open up further deliberation and discussion, rather than to resolve the issue and bring closure.

We have, of course, not attempted to exhaust all issues or forces impinging on group relations practice. Among other matters that might be considered are the structure of a given community (economic, political, cultural); its racial and ethnic composition; the type of power structure in existence; the types of group relations agencies and organizations and their strength; existing and potential community linkages and coalitions; the pattern of community leadership; number and density of voluntary associations; the extent of inequality, deprivation, and discrimination which prevails; amount of general community resources; extent and rate of population shifts including immigration; cultural variables related to the subgroups involved; and the particular historical development within the community. National politics, policies, and programs are also of vital significance. These matters and others will likely arise in an informed and intelligent discussion of the illustrative materials which are presented.

It would not be inappropriate to conclude by expressing a point of view regarding the pattern and impact of group relations practice. We view group relations not so much as a profession, but rather as a "field of practice" or arena of action, not unlike, for example, community mental health. There one finds a multiplicity of professional groups—medical, psychological, social work, psychiatric, occupational therapy, nursing, etc.—in a collaborative set of actions or roles oriented toward dealing with a given substantive problem area. In a similar vein one can visualize group relations practice as encompassing the collective input of various professional actors and tasks—social workers, educators, lawyers, public relations specialists, researchers, administrators; and nonprofessionals—politicians, militants, civic leaders, racial and ethnic leaders, etc. The focus is problem solving and social change on the part of this configuration of individuals and organizations with respect to the problem of racial and ethnic discrimination, disadvantage and injustice.

While we have said that our approach here is to provide a reflection of the empirical world of action in this "field of practice," the stance taken reveals more than a bent toward sociological realism and objectivity. The functional areas we have delineated, it seems to us, suggest important and valid dimensions of dealing with over-all problems of group inequity and injustice (incorporating social, psychological, and cultural factors). *Group rights* to rectify unfair laws and practices within the legal and social framework of the existing community system. *Group solidarity and power* to strengthen the cultural, organizational, and political fabric of racial and ethnic groups so as to enhance internal strength and dignity and at the same time change status and power relationships among groups. These shifting relationships imply changes in the social order itself and the modification or elimination of institutional forms or practices which foster racism or other modes of injustice. *Intergroup attitudes and relationships* to change detrimental attitudes, foster favorable associations, and mitigate tensions or disruptions that may be intrinsically harmful to all on either a short-term or a long-term basis. *Group welfare* to provide support and guidance to individuals who are suffering personally from the effects of the system, while broader and more long-range legal and institutional changes are being acted upon. While these functions are often viewed as contradictory or conflictual by partisans of organizations employing them, from a broader systemic perspective they may be seen as potentially complementary and mutually reinforcing.

For example, there has always been a duality in the goals of the black liberation movement. During periods of defeat and pervasive oppression and white resistance, black Americans have turned from the more pervasive and persistent goal of integration to that of racial solidarity, self-help, and development of separate institutions. In some instances it has meant emigration, as witnessed in the back-to-Africa movements, the colonies of black American artists and writers in many western European cities, and the proposals for a black state within the geographic boundaries of the United States.

Duality in the black protest movement is a *strength,* not a *weakness.* It would be advantageous to strengthen black institutions as well as support integration, and consequently it is imperative that efforts be directed on both these fronts. The effort presents an opportunity for the utilization of resources that both blacks and whites can contribute to a full realization of the "moral integration" of American society.

It is difficult to predict the racial and ethnic shape of America in the period ahead. Because of the rapidly changing character of the social scene, it is not possible to forecast confidently avenues of opportunity and forward movement and sources of resistance and repression. Whether a strategy of integration or of separatism will be most fruitful for the nation and its constituent groups is an open question. Therefore it seems logical to hold strategic and organizational options also open and fluid. The conception we have suggested, it seems to us, provides the range and flexibility necessary to cope rationally and advantageously with the accelerating social drama of America as it unfolds.

Some Previous Efforts—A Literature Review

There is no one established definition of the group relations field or even agreement concerning its nomenclature. The area has been referred to variously as group relations, civil rights, race relations, community relations, minority group relations, and the like. Writers have approached the area somewhat differently and have given differing emphases and interpretations to the practice.[21]

[21] Arnold Aronson, "Organization of the Community Relations Field," *Journal of Intergroup Relations* (Spring, 1960), 18-32; Nathan E. Cohen, "Is Community Relations a Profession?" Community Relations Paper No. 5, Association of Jewish Community Relations Workers (July, 1952); Frances R. Cousens and John G. Field, "Some Observations on the Nature and Scope of Intergroup Relations," *Journal of Intergroup Relations* (1958), 83-93; George W. Culbertson, "Intergroup Relations and Community Welfare Planning," *Community Organization 1961* (New York: Columbia University Press, 1961); John P. Dean and Alex Rosen, *A Manual of Intergroup Relations* (Chicago: University of Chicago Press, 1955); Joseph H. Douglass, "Intergroup Relations in the Federal Services," *Journal of Intergroup Relations* (1960), 37-48; John G. Field, "The Emerging Intergroup Profession," *Journal of Intergroup Relations,* 1 (1960), 61-65; John G. Field, "Nature and Scope of Intergroup Relations"; Charles Livermore, "Scope and Function of Intergroup Relations Work"; Alexander Allen, "Professionalization of Intergroup Relations Work and Workers"; George Schermer, "Professionalism and the Intergroup Worker," *Journal of Intergroup Relations,* 1 (Spring, 1960); Charles S. Johnson, "National Organizations in the Field of Race Relations," *The Annals,* 244 (1946), 117; Robert B. Johnson, "Value Dilemmas in the Profession of Intergroup Relations," Association of Jewish Community Relations Workers, Paper No. 5 (July, 1952); John Slawson, "An Examination of Some Basic Assumptions Underlying Jewish Community Relations Programs," *Journal of Jewish Communal Service,* 36 (December, 1959), 111-119; Whitney Young, "Intergroup Relations and Social Work Practice," *The Social Welfare Forum* (New York: Columbia University Press, 1960), 146-153; "The 'Big Think' Conference: A Working Conference of Intergroup Relations Practitioners and Social Scientists," sponsored by the National Association of Intergroup Relations Officials in cooperation with the Community Relations Service of the Department of Justice, Foodergong Lodge, Ephrata, Pa., May 17-19, 1968. Mimeographed by NAIRO.

Robin Williams, in his excellent survey of research related to the reduction of group tensions, was led to conclude that a "dearth of appropriate research and consequent lack of a proven base for action is one of the most conspicuous features of existing intergroup programs. . . . The working assumptions of action programs are subject to definition and specification, but these assumptions generally have not been validated by research. In particular, the possibilities and limits of given methods of control have not been scientifically delimited; and the comparative effectiveness of various actual and potential approaches to the control of intergroup relations is unknown."[22] While this statement was written in 1947, it is equally and uncomfortably descriptive of the field at this time. Indeed, two important agencies existing then and devoted to the production of group relations research (the Commission on Community Interrelationships of the American Jewish Congress and the American Council on Race Relations) are no longer operative in this connection.

In surveying the literature pertaining to this area, one finds a number of descriptive and analytical essays and volumes concerning minority group problems and ameliorative agencies.[23] In addition, there are several directories which describe group relations agencies, their objectives, methods, and programs.[24] Cousens and Field have done a modest analysis based on the 1959 Directory prepared by the National Association of Intergroup Relations Officials[25] and Charles S. Johnson analyzed the activities of seventy-five agencies operating on the national level.[26] In addition to general overviews of the field, there has been some analysis of interrelationships among agencies or studies of a specific agency.[27] There have been some statements suggesting standards of professional performance with regard to qualifications or required skills of the practitioner.[28] In some instances there have been more empirical studies in this area, such as Chworowsky's survey of the

[22]Robin M. Williams, Jr., *The Reduction of Intergroup Tensions* (New York: Social Science Research Council, 1947), 8 and 105.

[23]Robert M. MacIver, *The More Perfect Union* (New York: The Macmillan Company, 1948); Walter A. Luria, "Intergroup Relations," in *Social Work Yearbook* (New York: National Association of Social Workers, 1957), 302-311; George E. Simpson and Milton Yinger, *Racial and Cultural Minorities: An Analysis of Prejudice and Discrimination* (New York: Harper and Brothers, 1953); and *Conference on Group Life in America* (New York: American Jewish Committee, 1956).

[24]*Directory of Intergroup Relations Agencies* (New York: Brotherhood-in-Action in cooperation with the National Association of Intergroup Relations Officials, 1969); *Directory of Agencies in Intergroup Relations: National, Regional, State and Local* (Chicago: American Council on Race Relations, 1948); *Directory of Agencies in Race Relations* (Chicago: Julius Rosenwald Fund, 1945), 123 national private agencies; and *Public Human Relations Agencies (State, County, City)* (New York: Anti-Defamation League in Cooperation with National Association of Intergroup Relations Officials, 1947).

[25]Frances R. Cousens and John G. Field, "Some Observations on the Nature and Scope of Intergroup Relations," *Journal of Intergroup Relations,* 1 (1958), 83-93.

[26]Charles S. Johnson, "National Organizations in the Field of Race Relations," *The Annals,* 244 (1946), 117.

[27]Robert J. Green, "Some Proposals Looking Toward Cooperation Among Public and Private Intergroup Relations Agencies," *Journal of Intergroup Relations,* 3 (1962), 21-27; Charlotte Epstein, "A Plan for Coordination of Intergroup Relations Service," *Journal of Intergroup Relations,* 1 (1960), 32-36; and Robert B. Johnson, *In the House of the Friends, A Study of Race Relations Work of the American Friends Service Committee,* sponsored by Russell Sage Foundation, unpublished, 1955.

[28]Association of Jewish Community Relations Workers, "A Statement of Qualifications for Jewish Community Relations Workers," October, 1956; and Association of Jewish Community Relations Workers, "The Skills of the Jewish Community Relations Workers," statement adopted at the Tenth Annual Meeting, Pittsburgh, Pa., May, 1959.

opinions of executives regarding qualifications for entry level positions.[29] Several writers have discussed the relationship of the group relations field to the profession of social work.[30]

One has the impression that with the advent of Black Power in the mid-'60's, and the concomitant intensification and politicization of the field, professional writings, more exactly writings on professional aspects of the field, have been much reduced in volume. The virtual demise of the *Journal of Intergroup Relations* in this more recent period has been an additional impediment to the production and diffusion of professional writings. While the literature concerning the professional character of group relations has been almost entirely expository, consideration of strategies and techniques has been more empirical in form. For example, Goodwin Watson, on the basis of a survey of group relations agencies conducted for the Commission on Community Interrelations, concluded that action approaches employed by these organizations can be classified into seven categories—exhortation, education, participation, revelation, negotiation, contention, and prevention.[31] Gordon Allport drew upon existing research studies to specify several action approaches which he referred to as the research approach, educational curricula, contact and acquaintance, group retraining, mass media, legislation, and individual therapy.[32] Allport suggests conditions under which each of these may be used and develops a frame of reference which is eclectic. Perhaps the most comprehensive and useful statement is the volume prepared by Robin Williams under the sponsorship of the Social Science Research Council.[33] In this thoughtful work, Williams develops 102 propositions concerning the reduction of intergroup hostility and conflict based on a rather thorough survey of the then existing research literature. Williams recognized the speculative nature of his propositions, referring to them as "educated guesses." The *Manual of Intergroup Relations* by Dean and Rosen is based on observation of and interviews with practitioners.[34] This work suggests twenty-seven propositions concerning appropriate practice approaches. The *Manual*, like other major works in this area, is somewhat dated as circumstances shift rapidly (although it has recently been reissued with a new preface) and in some quarters it has come under severe criticism concerning some of its major premises relative to appropriate strategies.[35]

While there has been no over-all study of the organization of group relations

[29]Martin P. Chworowsky, *How Public Intergroup Agency Executives Perceive Qualifications for Entry Level Professional Workers* (Philadelphia: Albert M. Greenfield Center for Human Relations of the University of Pennsylvania, 1963).

[30]John Slawson, "Intergroup Relations in Social Work Education," in *Education for Social Work, Proceedings of the Sixth Annual Program Meeting* (New York: Council on Social Work Education, 1958); John C. Kidneigh, "Intergroup Relations and Social Work," *Journal of Intergroup Relations* (Spring, 1961); and Walter Zand, "An Approach to Training for Intergroup Relations Work," *Journal of Intergroup Relations,* 2 (Winter, 1961-62), 45-54.

[31]Goodwin Watson, *Action for Unity* (New York: Harper and Brothers, 1946).

[32]Gordon W. Allport, "The Resolution of Intergroup Tensions," An Intergroup Education Pamphlet, National Conference of Christians and Jews, 1952.

[33]Robin Williams, *The Reduction of Intergroup Tensions* (New York: Social Science Research Council, 1947).

[34]John P. Dean and Alex Rosen, *A Manual of Intergroup Relations* (Chicago: University of Chicago Press, 1955).

[35]James B. McKee, "Community Power and Strategies in Race Relations," *Social Problems,* Vol. 6, No. 3 (Winter, 1958-59).

practice in the United States, there have been various studies of delimited portions of the field such as local Jewish community relations councils, local official municipal agencies, Federal agencies, and church groups.[36] By the same token, there have been studies and analyses of particularized problem areas within group relations such as housing, employment, renewal, and education.[37] Likewise, there have been descriptions and evaluations of the utilization of various intervention techniques such as the mass media, education approaches, conferences, personal contacts, law, sit-ins, quotas, neighborhood organization, planning councils, and commissions.[38]

The picture then is one of numerous studies and writings, fragmentary in pattern, with little coherence characterizing the research, the theoretical literature, or conceptualizations of the arena of practice—creating a serious handicap for the practitioner and educator.

[36]See, for example, Alvin I. Mellman, "A Survey of Jewish Community Relations Councils," master's thesis, University of Pittsburgh, 1961; Jack Rothman, "A Study of Local Official Intergroup Relations Agencies in the United States," master's thesis, Ohio State University, 1951; Joseph H. Douglass, "Intergroup Relations in the Federal Services," *Journal of Intergroup Relations*, 1 (1960), 41-46.

[37]M. Deutsch and M. E. Collins, *Interracial Housing: A Psychological Evaluation of a Social Experiment* (Minneapolis: University of Minnesota Press, 1951); John Hope II, "Equal Employment Opportunity: Changing Problem, Changing Techniques," *Journal of Intergroup Relations*, 4 (Winter, 1962-63), 29-36; Dennis Clark, "Urban Renewal and Intergroup Relations," *Journal of Intergroup Relations*, 2 (1960), 68-78; and NAIRO Reports on Education, Special Report by NAIRO Commission on Education (New York: NAIRO, 1955).

[38]Burton I. Gordin, "The Mass Media and Intergroup Relations," *Journal of Intergroup Relations*, 3 (1961), 205-212; B. Samuelson, "Does Education Diminish Prejudices?" *Journal of Social Issues*, 2 (1945), 22-23; Arthur W. Chickering and Thelma W. Babbitt, "The Conference as a Race Relations Resource," *Journal of Intergroup Relations*, Winter, 1961-62; B. MacKenzie, "The Importance of Contact in Determining Attitudes Towards Negroes," *Journal of Abnormal and Social Psychology*, 43 (1948), 417-447; *The Uses of Law for the Advancement of Community Relations*, A Report of the Special Committee on Reassessment of the National Community Relations Council, 1955; Margaret Price, *Toward a Solution of the Sit-in Controversy* (Atlanta: Southern Regional Council, 1960), mimeographed; Dan W. Dodson, "Can Intergroup Quotas be Benign?" *Journal of Intergroup Relations*, 1 (1960), 12-17; Michael G. Iskander, "The Neighborhood Approach," *Journal of Intergroup Relations*, 3 (1962), 80-86; and Richard Robbins, "Local Strategy in Race Relations: The Illinois Experience With Community Human Relations Commissions and Councils," *Journal of Intergroup Relations*, 4 (1961), 311-324.

PART I

GROUP RIGHTS

Protecting Civil Rights and Combating Discrimination

UNIT 1.

The Role of Established Agencies in Militant Movements: A State Civil Rights Commission Advocates Tenants' Rights

Group relations agencies have in the past been associated typically with tactics and strategies that may be characterized as generally moderate. Practitioners who are employed in governmental civil rights and antidiscrimination agencies consequently have frequently found themselves in an awkward position. On the one hand their employing agency provides a variety of resources—a base of operations, legal or administrative machinery, manpower, program tools, etc., as well as, importantly, a livelihood. On the other hand, because of the attachment of such an agency to "the establishment" and its location in a web of traditional political interrelationships the practitioner has been constrained in his activities. Thus, the governmental agency offers both a set of opportunities represented by its resources and a set of restraints represented by its political sponsorship and alignments.

The practitioner is faced with the dilemma in the first place of whether to work for such an organization or not. If he chooses not to, he may be disregarding some of the very limited resources available for dealing with group relations problems. Also some of the positions in governmental service are among the more stable (and well-paying). If he chooses to be employed by such an agency, can he do any good? Perhaps a better way of asking the question is how may he maximize the opportunities while at the same time minimizing the restraints? Is it possible for the practitioner in such a role to relate to the more militant movements in race and ethnic relations and to channel the agency's resources in such a way as to reinforce their efforts? Does the provision of such support necessarily mean the practitioner comes into direct conflict with the "powers that be," leading to the jeopardy or termination of his job? Or can the practitioner, through tactical skill and selection of circumstances, play a role which permits him to keep one foot in an establishment agency and the other in militant grass-roots organizations?

In the case study which follows, a state Civil Rights Commission worker is portrayed playing an advocacy role in a local community dispute. The disagreement here is between a black low-income housing community and a public housing authority, with racial attitudes of housing commissions and inadequate responsiveness to tenants' complaints constituting central issues. The practitioner's advocacy

31

posture in this instance is in an extra-legal civil rights context. A range of community variables are highlighted, including the key position of the mayor.

Even were it not for its historical significance as the first low-income public housing project wherein tenants have gained control over policy-making decisions affecting their lives, the resolution of the East Park Tenants' Organization rent strike against the City of Muskegon Heights Public Housing Authority merits the professional intergroup official's attention for several reasons: (1) Unlike the physical sciences, intergroup situations requiring crisis intervention never afford an exact duplication of a previous situation as controlled laboratory experiments can. In the East Park Manor Tenants' strike, many "constants" were involved in the second crisis—the strike from July 2, 1968, to October 3, 1968—which were present in the first strike—February 3, 1967, to August 21, 1967. These were: (a) the same tenants' organization versus the same five member public housing commissioners; (b) the same law firm rendering legal aid to the tenants and the same city attorney advising the PHA; (c) Michigan Civil Rights Commission involvement; (d) the same mayor in office. (2) Therefore, the situation offers a very close approximation of the first rent strike which permits a clear comparison of intervention differences. Yet while certain constants were present in the second rent strike, certain variables had changed. The president of the Tenants' Organization had changed since the first strike. (The new president was involved in the first rent strike as a member.) The legal adviser to the Tenants' Organization had been involved "behind the scenes" in the first strike while another firm member was in the public eye as adviser. There was a new District Executive of the Muskegon District Office, Michigan Civil Rights Commission, who had arrived in Muskegon Heights the last week in July, about four weeks after the second strike had begun.

Although it would be an oversimplification to state these were the only variables which had changed, a comparison of the differences in decision-making behavior with the behavior of persons occupying the same positions in the first rent strike is instructive. (3) For those intergroup specialists who are interested in the social psychological phenomena of the development of "we-ness" with its concomitant awareness of fate control, this situation offers much data.

For the purpose of this paper, this case history will be presented with an emphasis upon the role of the intergroup specialist's role as a change agent, with particular attention to the crisis interventions which appeared to be the effective "turning points" leading to conflict resolution.

It is important to note that the first rent strike provided useful insights regarding strategic decisions in the second rent strike which were a decided advantage in its conclusion. The agents in the first rent strike did not have such an advantage. Therefore, it must be underlined that whatever success was achieved in the second strike was based upon the work done in the first one.

In fact, in order to grasp the stratagems of the second strike, it is important to know a little about the community in which East Park Manor is located, how the East Park Manor Tenants' Organization was formed, and the events of the first strike.

"East Park Manor Rent Strike." State of Michigan Civil Rights Commission. A Community Services Report by George V. Neagu, District Executive Muskegon District Office, 1968. Mimeographed.

The Community

Muskegon Heights, Michigan, is a small community of about 25,000 population with a 52 per cent Negro ratio. It has one low-income public housing project—East Park Manor—which was built in the early '60's. There are 200 units in East Park proper and 17 in Fairview Homes nearby, both of which are managed by the PHA. Fairview Homes is rapidly deteriorating war housing scheduled for demolition when all the tenants move out.

Muskegon Heights has a city manager form of government with a mayor who receives only a nominal salary for his services.

East Park Manor Tenants' Organization

The East Park Manor Tenants' Organization was organized by a tenant, who is now an aide with the Community Action Against Poverty program. She knew there was widespread frustration and dissatisfaction with the physical conditions in East Park and the management of it. Basements flooded after each rain and sewage backed up; whenever police were called to a unit it was reported to management and, regardless of reasons, if police came a third time to the same unit, the tenant had to move. These were just a few of the unsatisfactory conditions. Efforts to remedy the problems through the project director, who was white, not only were fruitless but led to a feeling on the part of the tenants that he was unconcerned about them. Efforts to involve the city councilmen were unsuccessful. Letters to the mayor were unanswered. Faced with institutional indifference, a meeting was called at the Catholic Information Center. Nine persons attended. The director of the center provided the place because the group could not meet at the project's Administration Building. The basic organizational plan of the group was to hold a meeting on each block in East Park. Only those blocks with more than half of the block in attendance could elect a block captain and be eligible for membership in the Tenants' Organization.

On November 16, 1965, the first large organizational meeting was held and officers were elected. This time the meeting was held at the Administration Building. In addition to the Executive Committee, each block captain was a member of the Steering Committee.

One of their first acts was to formally draw up a list of 15 grievances to present to the Public Housing Commission. When they were refused a meeting with the commissioners, they contacted HUD's Chicago Regional Office. Chicago sent a representative to meet with the group. He stated he could not commit himself to any particular course of action but promised something would be done in 30 days. After six months of waiting, without any remedial action evidenced, the tenants became restive and East Park Manor Tenants' Organization Steering Committee made a private decision to have a rent strike six months prior to the first rent strike. However, they did not know whether they could gain widespread support for it and felt their first goal must be to achieve formal official recognition as the sole representative group of the tenants from the Housing Commission.

Early in January, 1967, a meeting was called at the Administration Building by the Tenants' Organization. The PHA director also sent out notices of the meeting. The meeting was held to determine by vote of the commissioners whether the Tenants' Organization would be recognized officially as the tenants' representative group. Three of the five Public Housing Commissioners, including the only Negro, voted for reorganizing the Tenants' Organization. During the meeting a petition was presented by a rival group, allegedly organized by the Muskegon Area Development Council (local Chamber of Commerce), to neutralize the Tenants' Organization. The Tenants' Organization believed that the director was in collusion with this and that the commissioners voted favorably for the Tenants' Organization because they had heard of the strike talk and felt they could avoid a strike by official recognition of the group. The official recognition of the Tenants' Organization was later included in a new lease which was issued.

Following this meeting, the Tenants' Organization Steering Committee divided responsibility for "selling" the rent strike to tenants. They went door-to-door, day after day, and held innumerable small home meetings. They encountered fear of eviction and even suspicion. Finally, a meeting was called in the latter part of January, 1967, at the Administration Building and a unanimous strike vote was taken.

First Tenants' Strike

The first tenants' strike began February 3, 1967. This was the date the first monies collected were placed in escrow with the National Lumberman's Bank Company. It was also the date the first pickets appeared around the Administration Building to stand from 9 A.M. to 5 P.M. on an eight degrees below zero day. (The group picketed every Friday for the length of the strike.) A local attorney served as legal adviser to the tenants and the MCRC Muskegon District Executive served as consultant. The PHA director reacted almost immediately by announcing on television that the tenants on strike would be evicted on February 21. The tenants increased their demands to include the ouster of the five commissioners. The greatest difficulty for the Tenants' Organization was convincing some members that they should not simply withhold rental payments but put them in escrow. One hundred and thirty-five tenants placed money in escrow.

Talk of violence to certain commissioners and the director was not infrequent by some of the tenants.

The Tenants' Organization was supported by the local branch of the NAACP, Inter-faith Council on Human Rights, and other groups.

A Judgment of Eviction was ordered by the Circuit Court Commissioner against the 135 tenants. On February 14, 1967, a meeting was called by Mayor Kenneth Heineman which was attended by over 150 tenants, three city councilmen, and the Public Housing Commission. A resolution resulted in a moratorium being called until March 21, 1967, to discuss grievances. During this time, tenants who withheld rent payments were immune from eviction. The purpose of the moratorium was to attempt to resolve grievances. At this point the mayor's role was that of a liaison person. He carefully avoided becoming centrally involved by not committing himself on the Public Housing Commission's jurisdiction. When the moratorium deadline arrived, grievances were still unsettled. The PHA director announced that if rents were not paid in seven days tenants would face eviction.

The tenants' legal adviser decided to appeal the evictions. At a hearing in Circuit Court on April 11, 1967, the judge announced, after conferring privately with attorneys for the tenants and City of Muskegon Heights, that he would mediate the dispute. Both sides agreed to this, pending approval by the city's Public Housing Commission, which was subsequently given.

In May, 1967, the judge announced that an agreement was approved by the Public Housing Commission and tenants' representatives and that a special meeting would be held in the courtroom at which time a vote would be taken by the East Park Manor Tenants' Organization to accept or reject the agreement. The Tenants' Organization accepted the agreement which was molded into a new lease for tenants and the commission and then sent to Federal authorities for sanction. The lease included the aforementioned recognition clause, an altered rent schedule, a four-step grievance procedure, orders to repair defects in structures, and a clause keeping the lease in effect until January 31, 1968. The latter was included because tenants planned to test the lease for six months; they stressed another rent strike could develop if the lease failed to work properly. The Federal Government, however, did not approve the historic agreement until several weeks later, but on August 21, 1967, $50,119.85, which included late fees and court costs, was turned over to the housing commission by the East Park Tenants' Organization, thus concluding the first strike. Not included in the officially publicized agreement between tenants and housing commission was a compromise to the demand that the commissioners be ousted. According to the tenants an agreement was reached in January, 1968, whereby a black director would replace the white man who had held the job.

Evaluation 1

In order to render more clearly the behavioral options open in both strikes, and for comparison's sake, it is useful to review the situation up to this point.

One can see that the unresponsiveness of the Public Housing Commission, the PHA director, the City Council, and HUD's Chicago regional office, contributed to the organization and cohesiveness of the tenants' group. This cohesiveness was cemented when the PHA director over-reacted by immediately announcing, via television, the eviction deadline for tenants once the strike began.

One can segmentalize the movements of the strike: (1) moratorium on evictions brought about by the mayor; (2) renewal of threat of evictions following the moratorium after abortive efforts to resolve grievances; (3) decision by tenants' legal counsel to appeal evictions; (4) circuit court judge's offer to mediate issues by agreement of tenants' leadership and attorney and all other parties concerned—an agreement made in private; (5) an acceptance of the terms of agreement by all parties and a decision on tenants' part to accept a change in PHA directors rather than removal of commissioners.

It is interesting to note that, despite the prior institutional indifference, there was an apparent readiness to trust the judge's conciliatory efforts. Also, at this point, the Tenants' Organization would appear not to have been heavily invested in the removal of the commissioners. They were willing to settle for the replacement of the PHA's director, which meant that the mayor, who appoints commissioners, was not seen as central in pursuit of their goals at this time.

Second Tenant Strike

Almost a year following the resolution of the first strike, very few of the physical repairs agreed upon were completed. In early April, 1968, a strike vote was taken scheduled to begin on May 1, 1968. The president of the Muskegon Branch of the NAACP contacted the Tenants' Organization on April 17, 1968, and asked that the new PHA director be given 60 days without a strike to produce a new contract and remedy problems. The Tenants' Organization agreed, as the NAACP had supported it in the first strike and they did not want to embarrass the director. At the end of the 60 days, he presented a list of 15 *Modernization Work Items* which constituted a proposal he wanted to submit to HUD for the Tenants' Organization's approval. As this was essentially the same list included in the grievances presented by the tenants a year earlier, the tenants were disappointed and decided to pursue the strike. At this point, a new legal counsel was retained. The strike began on July 2, 1968. Unlike the first strike, the East Park Manor Tenants' Organization stood virtually alone. The director was either related to or good friends with most of the leadership in the area. In fact, most of the civil rights groups and black councilmen disapproved of the strike.

The pattern of picketing was the same as in the first strike. The tenants' distrust of governmental institutions was very deep. From the outset it was the strategy of the East Park Manor Tenants' Organization to demand the ouster of all five commissioners. Toward the end of July, the Tenants' Organization leadership began to hold daily meetings with the MCRC Muskegon District Director. It was clear that the situation was at an impasse as the Public Housing Commission had not initiated any meetings and the mayor was maintaining a policy of noninvolvement. Rapport with the tenant leadership was maintained by providing the group information received through the MCRC Housing Division and by checking with this division on strategic decisions. The mere fact of MCRC's lending its resources to aid the tenants cannot be underestimated in the re-establishment of institutional trust.

From the outset, MCRC's contact with HUD's Chicago regional office was similar to that of the tenants. For example, when the Muskegon District Executive called Chicago to introduce himself and interpret the gravity of the East Park Manor situation, the HUD representative asked, "What business is it of yours?" The executive had to explain that the crisis involved racial tension. The HUD representative stated the project "was beautiful and I saw nothing wrong for tenants to complain about."

As the MCRC Muskegon District Executive became acquainted with the tenants' leadership, he recognized a great sense of responsibility in their efforts. In discussion it was decided by the group that the basic issue should be removal of the commissioners. They related paternalistic and racist comments allegedly made by commissioners to the tenants. It was apparent that the communications problem between the Public Housing Commission and the tenants was beyond repair.

In the early part of August, the Tenants' Organization sent letters to the mayor and the director formally requesting the removal of all five commissioners. At this point, although the Tenants' Organization had about 117 members, money in escrow had dropped toward the middle of August.

In an evaluation of the situation, an important strategic decision was made to involve the mayor and, hopefully, to bring him into a central position in the dispute.

On August 23, 1968, the MCRC District Executive held a lengthy meeting with the mayor, carefully interpreting his role as concern for the potential racially explosive situation in East Park Manor and a desire to be of assistance to all sides to resolve the situation. However, although respectful of the various "sides," he stressed to the mayor the growing emphasis upon tenant participation in the context, especially, of the desire for more voice in the control of their own fate on the part of black people and the poor. The mayor showed an understanding of this desire and asked for his help in resolving this matter. The District Executive indicated the mayor's role and understanding was crucial in opening the way for communication as he seemed to have the sensitivity the commissioners were alleged to lack. The mayor indicated he absolutely refused to remove all five commissioners because he felt someone with experience must remain on the commission for continuity of experience. At the suggestion of the MCRC District Executive, he agreed to meet with the Tenants' Organization leadership the following Monday at a luncheon meeting. He stated he had already called for a public airing of the Park Manor situation for Monday night at the regular Council meeting when all sides could be heard: he wanted the councilmen to hear the facts directly and to dispel rumors. The MCRC District Executive, however, suggested such a public meeting could only be injurious and cause greater unpleasantness. However, it was too late to cancel it.

Over the weekend, the MCRC District Executive received the approval of the tenant leadership for the meeting with the mayor.

During the Monday luncheon meeting, which was extremely important as it set the climate for the subsequent resolution of the conflict, the only ground rules set were: (1) parties involved would not publicize whatever was said, and (2) no commitments would be made by anyone.

During this exploratory meeting, several distinct suggestions emerged. Some of these suggestions were: (1) An end to the rent strike for four to six months during which time the mayor would "moderate" or work closely with PHA to insure better human relations. If the Public Housing Commission failed to improve following the mayor's personal appeal to them to shape up in the vital area of attitudes, he would remove them instantly. (2) Two tenants would be named as commissioners when openings occurred. (3) An HUD Training Program would be embarked upon in the near future which would include PHA-tenant participation aimed toward improving tenant relations and decision making. (4) A five-member group composed of tenants would meet in an advisory committee with PHA at its meetings. Other important ideas were discussed, but it can be seen that the flow of communication was opening up and the mayor was committing himself to a more central role in the dispute. Before the meeting ended, all had agreed not to allow the Council meeting that evening to become too abrasive in order to enhance the opportunity for resolution of the controversy.

At a packed meeting in the Common Council, the mayor played a strong role as chairman in preventing the housing commission or anyone else from becoming too abusive.

The day after the two meetings, the MCRC District Executive sent the mayor a letter providing him with personal reactions to the effect that the group left feeling the meeting was a worthwhile and fruitful discussion of the issues. It was the first time optimism was evidenced that the strike could move beyond its impasse. The letter also summarized eight distinct suggestions offered in the meeting on a possible basis for resolving the problems.

Unfortunately, at the very time that the mayor was meeting with the tenants' leaderships, the PHA director had issued 94 seven-day eviction notices. The tenants were furious and their leadership was puzzled, angry and hurt.

The mayor issued a public statement claiming he had found out about the eviction notices only after the meeting with the leadership. He stressed the bad timing involved in issuing them. A spirit of cooperation was salvaged and a regular meeting of the Tenants' Organization called at which time the mayor, the Public Housing Commission, and PHA director would be present. (A hearing the day after the issuance of the notices before the Circuit Court Commissioner temporarily blocked until the next Friday the processing of further action on the eviction notices pending the possibility of ironing out differences at the Thursday night meeting.)

At this point, the press played up the mayor's assumption of responsibility for resolving the strike. He was finally not only centrally involved in private negotiations, but publicly as well.

Prior to the Thursday night meeting, the MCRC District Executive was able to persuade the Tenants' Organization to modify the demand for the ouster of the entire commission to only three.

He felt that the mayor would never accede to the demand for the removal of all five for two reasons: (1) he was firmly convinced continuity of experience had to be maintained, and (2) the demand had been given him in a way which had racial overtones and, politically, with an eye on next year's election, he felt such a complete concession would destroy him. The Tenants' Organization decided to allow the retention of one black person and one white person and demand the removal of the other three white members.

At the Thursday night meeting, grievances were discussed point by point. The mayor was extremely sincere in his efforts to respond fully and accurately to each question but also quick to admit what he did not know. Finally, the tenants opened up with their charges that the three commissioners were paternalistic and racist. They recounted remark after remark made by each commissioner to them to substantiate their accusations. One of the accused commissioners began to laugh out loud. The mayor made no effort to defend the commissioners but he did urge settlement and gave a "let's go on from here" type speech. The mayor suggested that all the points in MCRC Executive's letter, which he had read to the group (and which had been sent to the tenants also), be used as a basis for improving communication and resolving problems. The tenants were unmoved and narrowed their demands to one demand—the removal of the three commissioners.

Efforts to settle the strike by the mayor had failed.

On Monday, September 16, 1968, Circuit Court Commissioner Kuck rendered a judgment for possession in favor of the housing commission. Under the law, the Tenants' Organization had ten days to appeal or face mass eviction on September 26, 1968. At this point 89 tenants were under threat of eviction.

Prior to the regular weekly meeting of the tenants, the Tenants' Organization leadership, using the MCRC District Executive as a sounding board, made the decision to recommend to the membership that it vote not to appeal. In effect, at a dramatic meeting of the group on September 12, 1968, in anticipation of Kuck's action, the group unanimously decided it would to to jail rather than return the monies held in escrow.

Several moves were made during the Detroit Staff Meeting beginning on September 16, 1968. A member of the MCRC Housing Division secured the support of a newly formed state housing group, the Michigan Housing Federation, which issued a news release deploring the eviction process as a method for solving social problems. It also sent a telegram to the mayor offering its services to help resolve the matter.

In discussion with a field representative of the MCRC Housing Division, it was decided to ask the Executive Director of the MCRC, who was to attend the Michigan Conference on Mayors that week, to contact the mayor. The purpose of this contact would be: (1) To informally open the discussion with the mayor and reinforce as much as possible the concept of tenant participation. It was felt the Executive Director's status used in this direction might make the mayor feel more comfortable about the idea of removal of commissioners. Later in the week, the Executive Director stated the mayor agreed to removal of the three commissioners on a "phase-out" basis—one every two months—and appointment of three new commissioners from a list of 15 drawn up by the tenants. He resisted efforts of the mayor to secure MCRC's cooperation as an arbitrator in the situation. The mayor at this point was clearly feeling the pressure and wanted a "face-saving" vehicle. He had hoped that the MCRC would serve as a fact-finding body for him and recommend to him the removal of the three commissioners so he would not be centrally responsible. The Executive Director sidestepped this invitation although he offered to come to Muskegon Heights at any time to help in the crisis. The MCRC District Executive contacted the mayor and repeated this offer as well as checking the new terms of agreement which the mayor proffered.

On September 19, 1968, there was an overflow attendance at the Tenants' Organization meeting. A popular local minister, in a stirring speech, pledged his support. Another group, Blacks for Immediate Action (BFIA), offered to go to jail with the tenants. The telegram from the Michigan Housing Federation was read.

On September 23, 1968, the MCRC District Office Executive met with the mayor privately. He stressed that tension was extremely high due to the eviction deadline. He suggested that community harmony was the mayor's responsibility and asked him to weigh seriously whether retaining the three commissioners was worth the tension. Also, he pointed out our nation moves by pressure groups . . . except that when blacks pressure, such a move is categorized as "difficult." He also pointed out the demands of a thousand whites at a nearby community who were demanding removal of school board members. This persuasive effort was necessary as the mayor was wavering in his resolve to remove the commissioners. They spoke for three hours. At the end of this time the mayor agreed to another meeting on September 26—the date of the evictions—with the tenants' leadership.

During the week the District Executive met with the Tenants' Organization leadership to invite them to the meeting and to persuade them that, in his judgment, the mayor had reached his final concession. He also met nearly all night with the legal counsel to evaluate the situation. The legal counsel agreed that maximum expectations would be realized from this strike should the mayor hold to his agreement.

On September 26, 1968, the community and the press were braced for a mass jailing.

The tenants' leadership met with the mayor. The mayor agreed to the following terms: (1) He would immediately stay the evictions. (2) He would find a way to pay for the late fees which had been incurred by the tenants. (3) He agreed to call the three commissioners on the meeting date and request their resignations. (4) He would issue a news release on the same day stating a resolution of the rent strike was imminent. (5) He proposed that one of the three commissioners would be "phased out" every two months and that the three new commissioners would have to be approved by the Tenants' Organization. (6) The first newly selected commissioner would be selected by the Tenants' Organization and accepted unconditionally by the mayor. (7) The first commissioner to be removed would be the one most objectionable to the tenants. (8) He would work toward recommendations listed in the letter to him and the tenants. In addition: (1) The tenants' leadership agreed to call a meeting on September 30, 1968, to vote on the agreement. (2) It was proposed by both the mayor and the Tenants' Organization that the MCRC Executive Director participate in the Tenants' Organization's regular meeting on October 3, 1968, when the mayor would publicly present his terms. (3) On the following day a joint press release approved by both parties would be released announcing the end of the strike and escrow monies would be reimbursed to PHA.

That evening the East Park Manor Tenants' Organization voted unanimously to accept the terms and to return escrow monies, provided some arrangement could be made regarding court costs and late fees.

The following day the District Office submitted a complete report to the MCRC Executive Director and suggested his role would be: (1) at the mayor's request, to stress the strong trends implicit in Federal guidelines and Michigan Tenants' Rights laws; (2) to assume a posture emphasizing the significance of the decision reached and statesmanship exercised by the parties involved in reaching such a decision; and (3) to point to the importance of all parties involved to work together to build a model community. The Executive Director concurred and agreed to participate. Actually, his presence was also a strategic move as it not only made the mayor and Tenants' Organization feel supported but also served as an implicit reinforcement of the commitment the mayor was to make publicly.

The District Executive invited the Tenants' Organization leader, the mayor, the Executive Director of the MCRC, and the Housing Division Director of MCRC for a meeting at the district office prior to the public meeting. The format of the meeting and the roles each would play were frankly discussed. The thorny question of penalty payments for nonpayment of rent and court costs would be negotiated between the tenants' legal counsel and the Public Housing Commission. No one wanted this issue to become a last-minute "bottleneck" to the settlement. A news release was prepared incorporating the agreement terms and statements from each of the leading figures in the meeting—the mayor, the Tenants' Organization president, and the MCRC District Executive.

The public meeting went off as planned and the rent strike was concluded. The Executive Director expressed the feelings of all when he congratulated the Tenants' Organization and the City of Muskegon Heights for converting what could have become a destructive situation into a significant and creative settlement.

Evaluation 2

The major strategic differences and a comparison of behavioral options affecting the course and outcomes of the two strikes may now be clarified. The same options existed in the second strike as in the first: Should the tenants emphasize the physical conditions in the demands or the removal of housing commissioners? Should they deal with the housing commission or involve the mayor centrally in the negotiations? Should they file for appeal, or not and risk a direct confrontation? Should they deal with the problem of the war housing—Fairview Homes—together with East Park Manor or treat them separately? (This was treated separately in the second strike.) Should they make private agreements without tenants' participation or should participant democratic methods be the guiding principle?

In evaluating the options selected in the second strike with the tenants' leadership and their legal counsel, there is agreement that there were several major stratagems: (1) the concentration of demands for the ouster of the commissioners and the shift from the ouster of all of them to three; (2) the moves made to involve the mayor centrally as a primary agent in the rent strike resolution; and (3) the decision not to appeal the evictions.

The first stratagem was based upon the realization that a real solution to the physical and communications problems would not be resolved but only postponed further unless more sensitive, concerned individuals replaced the three commissioners. The second was based upon the recognition that to achieve the objective the mayor had to assume responsibility for the exercise of his power. The third was a calculated risk that the social problems involved in jailing eighty-nine families would be too great for a community to tolerate and that a direct confrontation would move the situation beyond an impasse.

Other characteristics of the second strike which catalyzed the movement were: (1) The intensive involvement of the MCRC Muskegon District Executive, who was able to maintain a trusting, consultative relationship with the mayor, and the tenants' leadership. At no time did he pretend nonpartisanship with the mayor yet theirs was always a relationship of mutual respect. (2) In an era of extensive disillusionment with the rigidity of governmental systems, the responsiveness and vertical fluidity of MCRC's services from the district to the divisional and executive level was executed in a timely and effective manner.

Author's Note: Since the above case study was written, the mayor has replaced three public housing commissioners with three persons chosen from a list provided by the East Park Manor Tenants' Organization. The first new appointment to the public housing commission was the president of the Tenants' Organization. It seems, to the author, in an era of great disillusionment and distrust on the part of the poor and, especially, poor blacks, this historic rent strike settlement, in which the Michigan Civil Rights Commission was privileged to play a part, is an important record that the credibility gap between governmental services and the "grass roots" need not exist.

UNIT 2.
Equality of Opportunity vs. Preferential Treatment: Discrimination in Public Employment—The Police

Group relations agencies have generally taken a strong civil libertarian stance on matters pertaining to rights and responsibilities. A philosophy of equality of opportunity was a benchmark of the field. Issues were settled on the basis of the merits of the particular case in question. In more recent years "preferential treatment" has emerged as a competing point of view, with its emphasis on "unequal" treatment or opportunity in favor of disadvantaged groups as a way of compensating for past injustice and deprivation. This has been declared by critics to represent a position of discrimination in reverse, since an individual with equal or better qualifications for a job, for example, might be bypassed in favor of a less qualified ethnic group member. The more qualified person, it is said, has his civil rights abused in this process because, as an individual, he is blameless for the over-all state of society and because, through hard work in education or previous employment, he has earned favorable consideration. In addition, this type of competition may embitter individuals who are bypassed in this way, contributing to a polarized "backlash" climate in the country. Some commentators feel that the preferential treatment procedure is a bad precedent to set and maintain because, in the long run, it is more likely to be used against rather than for ethnic minorities as these groups hold less power and influence. The rejoinder, of course, is that without such compensatory weighting, ethnic groups may never or only over many additional generations be able to overcome the debilitating scars of disadvantage, in particular those of slavery.

While the use of unfair employment practices is a central concern of group relations agencies, discrimination in public employment is especially odious and objectionable. Municipal governments, ideally representative of all the people and receiving financial support from all segments of the population, have neither explicit nor implicit justification for discriminatory hiring practices. Yet a recent report of the United States Commission on Civil Rights indicates a considerable amount of inequity in state and local government employment. Police departments were especially prone to place blocks in the way of equal employment opportunity, despite the critical nature of present-day relations between the police and racial and ethnic communities.

In this section on police departments from the Federal Civil Rights Commission Report, a number of issues relevant to employment practices are covered. The na-

42

ture of the problem is discussed as well as recommendations for action or policy. The point of view expressed here invites re-examination in terms of the equal opportunity-preferential treatment issue.

Barriers and obstacles to equal employment opportunity for minority group members were greater among uniformed policemen and firemen than in any other area of state and local government. . . . The employment records of police and fire departments consistently showed less Negro representation in these departments than in nearly any other department of government.

The belated admission of any minority group members to these occupations accounts, in part, for this situation. Atlanta and Memphis had never hired Negro policemen until 1948; Baton Rouge not until 1963. The city of Philadelphia, which had a substantially better record of minority employment on the police force than any of the other central cities studied, made no major effort to recruit Negro policemen until about 10 years ago. The city of Oakland had Negroes on its police force at least as early as the 1940's, but according to one respondent, the 21 Negro policemen currently employed represent only a few more than were on the force more than 20 years ago. (But between 1940 and 1965 the Negro population of Oakland increased from 3 per cent to an estimated 31 per cent of the total.)

Police and fire departments are similar in many respects. Each has a uniformed force, with a formal semimilitary chain of command. They are the most widely visible manifestations of local government operating throughout the community. Each is charged with protecting life and property; each exposes its men to danger in the course of their duties; and each stresses discipline and team spirit. Both promote entirely from within, requiring each applicant to begin as a recruit irrespective of his background or experience. In most cities both departments have the same general entry requirements and salary ranges. There are, however, important differences between the two protective services which are reflected in the relationships of the two to the minority community, the minority applicant, and the minority member on the force.

One of the more significant differences lies in the fact that police departments across the country are understaffed, some substantially below authorized strength, while for the most part fire departments are not.

Police Recruitment

In every central city studied, the police force was under its authorized strength, ranging from a deficit of 23 positions in San Francisco to a deficit of 767 positions in Houston. In Baton Rouge, Detroit, Houston, Memphis, and Oakland, the number of vacancies exceeded the number of minority group members on the force. It was estimated that in 1967 increases in police departments' authorized forces and normal turnover created a national need for 50,000 new policemen. In contrast, the number of new firemen needed each year across the country has been estimated to be only 6,000 to 7,000.

The police departments studied have conducted vigorous recruitment programs, many of which have included specific attempts to recruit members of minority

From *For All the People . . . By All The People: A Report on Equal Opportunity in State and Local Government Employment.* A Report of the United States Commission on Civil Rights, U. S. Government Printing Office, Washington, D. C. 20402, 1969.

groups. For the most part these efforts have not been notably successful either in satisfying the departments' overall manpower needs or in substantially increasing the number of minority group members on the forces. One commentator has stated: "There is no such thing as a successful police recruitment drive in our large cities; there are just varying degrees of failure."

The tension, suspicion, and hostility which exist between the Negro community and the police department are obstacles to the recruitment of black policemen, officials in many of the cities studied told Commission staff. The Michigan State Civil Right Commission concluded in its recent study of recruitment efforts in six large cities:

> The Departments that are making the greatest headway in obtaining minority group applicants are those that have made headway in *reversing* their image in the minority community. The programs that most of these departments have, go beyond mere dialogue between citizens' groups and command officers. The departments have actually involved themselves in programs designed to assist citizens. . . . These departments also have clearly spelled out policies in citizens' complaints against the department, the behavior expected of an individual patrolman, etc. (Emphasis added.)

The police departments in the central cities studied availed themselves of all the recruiting techniques used by other units of city government to attract minority applicants. In addition, some departments initiated special methods to reach minority groups. Both the Philadelphia and the Oakland Police Departments used mobile vans for recruitment in ghetto areas. Applicants for police jobs in Philadelphia were given written examinations in the recruiting van as well as at precinct stations and at the civil service office. An applicant who failed the examination was permitted to retake it within 30 days. Philadelphia also uses the life-size figure of a Negro police sergeant—a former Olympic star—to help recruit prospective policemen. In addition, Philadelphia policemen recruit from door-to-door and all members of the force are encouraged to recruit among their friends and neighbors.

The city of Detroit has benefited from a statewide recruitment program initiated by the Michigan Civil Rights Commission and supported by a grant from the U. S. Department of Justice. The objective of the program was to obtain 500 white and 500 black recruits to serve on police forces at the city, county, and State levels. A corporation was formed, the Police Recruitment Project of Michigan, Inc., to conduct the campaign. The campaign was publicized by advertising on radio and television, and in buses, post offices, and office buildings. National television personalities—Negro and white—participated in the effort.

The Memphis Police Department assigned a white lieutenant to recruit in community centers and neighborhood shopping centers. When it became obvious that Negroes were reluctant to talk with a white police officer, a Negro patrolman was assigned to accompany him. This integrated team also manned a booth at the Mid-South Fair in Memphis.

Most of these efforts were followed by an increase in the number of black patrolmen on the force. The campaign of the Police Recruitment Project of Michigan in 1967, for example, helped produce 4,122 applications for the Detroit Police Department; 47 per cent were from Negroes. The attrition rate among applicants during the various phases of the screening process was so great, however, that only 323 recruits were ultimately hired. Of these, 71 or 22 per cent were Negroes, the largest number and proportion of Negroes ever hired to date by the department in a single year. Similarly, efforts by the Oakland Police Department resulted in a class of recruits in 1967 which was 50 per cent Negro, a proportion large enough to double the number of black patrolmen on the force. The Memphis recruitment efforts produced seven Negroes in a class of 46.

Obstacles to Minority Hiring

Among those Negroes who are recruited and do apply, the proportion which finally is accepted for the force is usually quite small. This is true, although to a lesser degree, for white applicants. The screening process for police applicants is similar to that used for regular civil service jobs although in many respects it is more stringent. Applicants face a number of hurdles which may include a written examination, an oral examination, a physical proficiency test, a medical examination, a psychological examination, a polygraph test, and a background and character check. They must also get clearance on the departments' requirements concerning citizenship, residency, arrests, and convictions. Accordingly, if there are even fewer Negro applicants, the high attrition rate will result in even fewer Negroes actually being accepted for the force.

Written Tests

Minority group applicants may encounter difficulty in passing though any of the various points in the screening process. One particular point of difficulty is the written test. The written examination for both firemen and policemen in San Francisco was characterized by one informant as one which a recent high school graduate could pass, but which a "C" student out of high school for a few years and not employed in a job requiring word usage, arithmetical reasoning, and wide vocabulary would fail. Since 21 years is the minimum age for policemen in San Francisco, few recent high school graduates take the test. In Detroit in 1967, 50 per cent of the Negroes and 17 per cent of the whites taking the written examination failed it.

In many ways the problem of written tests for policemen is comparable to that encountered with regular civil service examinations. The tests used have not been validated so there is little if any evidence of a clear relationship between ability to pass the test and ability to perform well as a patrolman. As an example of this, a Georgia legislator cited the case of several Negroes who failed the examination for State patrolmen even though they had served on the Atlanta police force for years.

In Detroit, the mayor's special task force on police recruiting and hiring has replaced the routine 2½ hour written test with the Wonderlich test, a 12-minute general intelligence test judged to be just as good until a better examination can be located or developed.

The supervisor of police community relations for the Michigan State Civil Rights Commission said that he was told by a former supervisory officer of a university which recruits and trains its own campus police force that the university administers a standard test developed for police applicants together with a routine clerical test. The supervisory officer found by checking the personnel records of officers that there was a higher correlation between job performance and scores on the clerical test than between performance and scores on the test designed specifically to select individuals with a high potential for police work.

Despite the adverse effect of the written examination, training programs can improve test performance significantly. For example, in an effort to increase the number of Puerto Ricans on the force, the Philadelphia Police Department designed a recruitment campaign which included a follow-through effort to assist applicants in negotiating the screening process. The basic recruiting techniques were contacts with the clergy, house-to-house recruiting, and advertising in Spanish news media. These efforts produced 40 candidates.

The police department reached an agreement with the city civil service commission by which the written test was to be administered in Spanish. The translation took culture as well as language into account. The school board provided a 12-week, 23-hour-a-week course through its school extension program to prepare the candidates for the written examination. Of the original 40 candidates, 35 took the course, 30 completed it, and 11 passed the examination. One of the 11 men who passed the written examination subsequently failed the physical examination because he did not meet the 5'7" minimum height requirement. The course was conducted a second time with 30 candidates, nine of whom eventually passed the written examination.

The successful candidates were assigned to areas with sizable Puerto Rican populations and the police department feels that relations between the department and the Puerto Rican community are improving. The chief inspector considers the program a success and plans to continue it as long as necessary.

In another training effort in Baton Rouge in 1963 four Negro leaders conducted an informal class to prepare a group of young men for the police examinations. Six of their students passed the test and became the first Negro policemen on the Baton Rouge force. This experience appears to hold true for fire departments as well. The first Negro employed by the Oakland Fire Department tutored many Negroes on his own initiative and time over a period of more than 20 years to prepare them for the written fire department examination. As a result of his efforts, 25 Negroes have been hired by the department. In the spring of 1967, the city of Oakland reported to the Commission that 26 of its 651 uniformed firemen were Negroes.

Physical Qualifications

Police and fire departments have more rigid requirements concerning age, weight, height, and vision than other departments of city government generally have. Yet, despite their rigidity, these standards vary from department to department and even have been altered within departments with no adverse results. In the police departments studied by the Commission, minimum age ranged from 19 years in Houston to 21 years in most other places; maximum age, from 29 years in Oakland to 36 years for the Texas State Patrol. Height requirements are similarly variable. As part of an intensive campaign to recruit more Negro officers for the police force, Detroit has recently liberalized its age, height, and vision requirements.

A recent study showed that several large cities have lowered their height requirements to 5'7" as a result of pressures from their Spanish-speaking populations. Both San Francisco and Oakland, however, have a minimum height requirement of 5'9" which has been cited as an impediment for Oriental Americans. The 5'9" requirement of the California Highway Patrol also has been cited as a factor in eliminating Oriental Americans.

Arrests and Convictions

Police departments put more emphasis on the background, character, and reputation of an applicant than do other agencies of government. Consequently, they are more stringent in their treatment of arrest and conviction records. In each of the police departments supplying information to the Commission, a felony conviction automatically disqualified an applicant. Frequently this prohibition was required by law and therefore not subject to modification by the police department. In several jurisdictions studied, convictions for lesser offenses also automatically disqualified an applicant. The city of Memphis will not employ anyone as a policeman or fire-man who has been guilty of a "crime involving infamous or notoriously disgraceful conduct." The Philadelphia Police Department will not employ anyone convicted of a misdemeanor, nor will it employ any applicant who fails to report an arrest or a conviction. Applicants are not informed, however, of the different treatment ac-corded reported and unreported arrests. Several jurisdictions will not employ ap-plicants convicted of various traffic violations. The Shelby County Sheriff's De-partment will not employ anyone *arrested* for any offense other than a traffic vio-lation.

The treatment of juvenile records by police departments varies. Most police de-partments reported to the Commission that they were more lenient in considering juvenile offenses than those committed as an adult. The California State Police De-partment, for example, does not consider offenses committed before the applicant's 21st birthday. On the whole, however, police departments appear to evaluate juve-nile offenses more carefully than do civil service systems. The Atlanta Police De-partment treats all offenses rigidly because it does not want anyone on the force who "has any kind of a record."

The California State Police Department is the only police agency surveyed by the Commission which does not request information about arrests on the employ-ment questionnaire, although it does require information on most, but not all, con-victions. The Detroit Police Department, which is prevented by the city charter only from hiring persons with felony convictions, asks the following comprehensive ques-tion on its application for policemen:

"Have you ever been arrested, accused of breaking a law, taken into a police sta-tion for investigation or fingerprinted because of suspicion in any place at any time in your life as a juvenile or adult?"

No police departments studied, however, relies on the information furnished by the applicant concerning his arrest and conviction record. All departments rou-tinely make an independent police record check. These frequently are checked against FBI records as well as state and local records. In addition, many departments investigate the background and character of the applicant. This is most commonly done by police officers, but the city of Atlanta uses private detectives for this purpose.

The Background Check and Oral Interview

The great emphasis placed on the background and character of the applicant is reflected in the Detroit police application forms in such questions as: "Were you ever guilty of and/or charged with being the father of a child born out of wedlock?" "Have you ever been widowed, separated or divorced? If . . . 'yes' explain." "List all past and present creditors giving name, address, account number and amount due." "Have you ever been involved in any matter pertaining to an unpaid debt or . . . taxes?" "List all checking and savings accounts you have in banks, savings and loan associations, credit unions, etc." The signature of the applicant on the form must be notarized.

Although no other police department studied elicits as much personal information on the application, many make similar inquiries during the oral interview and background investigation. The Philadelphia Police Department investigates an applicant during visits to five houses in his immediate neighborhood. The Memphis Police Department checks into the candidate's family relationships and his civic and religious activities.

Because the presence of minority members on the police force is limited, most oral interviews and background checks on minority applicants are conducted by white policemen. The oral examination and the background check have been characterized as two elements in the screening process in which subjective opinions are critical. It has also been pointed out that because police departments, unlike most other departments of State and local government, do their own recruiting, screening, and hiring, policemen may consciously or unconsciously seek applicants who are like themselves; the applicant whose background and character is most acceptable may often be the one whose background and character most closely resemble that of the investigating officer.

The Commission found few clear-cut cases of intentional discrimination during the oral interview and background investigation. These do, however, offer many opportunities for discrimination to occur. Separate studies have shown a high degree of racial prejudice among white policemen. The Commission also found considerable evidence of discriminatory behavior and treatment in other aspects of the day-to-day operations of the police forces studied. Therefore, it is reasonable to surmise that it occurs in these two areas as well. Statistics collected by the Detroit Police Department indicate that 49 per cent of the Negro applicants who made it to the preliminary oral examination were disqualified during the oral examination and background investigation as compared to only 22 per cent of the whites.

The following examples of the conduct of the background investigation illustrate the extent to which the opportunity for prejudice exists in the examination and screening processes. The instructions for the field investigation of potential troopers in the State of Michigan call for the investigating officer to give specific attention to home conditions: specifically, "neighborhood, dwellings, applicants' position in dwelling, condition of home, number of occupants, etc."

The Michigan Civil Rights Commission characterized the screening process used by the Michigan State Police Department as one which provides several opportunities for persons harboring racial prejudice (consciously or unconsciously) to exercise personal choice and thereby possible discrimination. The Commission added that during an 8-month period, seven black candidates for jobs as state troopers passed the written examination, but five of these were eliminated during the course of the field examination. "In at least one case, there is a serious question regarding the manner in which the applicant's credit record was evaluated by the investigating trooper and approved by the Civil Service Commission."

A member of the San Francisco City and County Civil Service Commission told Commission staff that some San Francisco police investigators were hypercritical during security checks of black candidates, digging into past criminal records, common law marriages, and other related matters in meticulous detail; he also reported that they usually recommended against appointment of persons with the slightest blemish on their record. He cited a case in which a Negro police applicant had been rejected because of a juvenile arrest for stealing a jar of hair oil, even though he had never been sentenced.

Detroit police check the background and character of all relatives who live in the applicant's home. A Michigan Civil Right Commission staff member said that such a procedure adversely affects black candidates who, more than white candidates, are likely to have relatives living with them who have been involved with the police. The staff member added that she felt that the character investigations were conducted objectively but that the material gathered was reviewed by the oral board in an extremely subjective manner.

Members of panels conducting the oral examination frequently have not had adequate preparation for the task. The supervisor of police-community relations for the Michigan Civil Rights Commission told Commission staff that oral board members often are selected by going through the office at police headquarters and "collecting" any three command officers who are available at the time. A white policemen characterized as a "known bigot," because of his involvement in a racial incident which caused his picture to be published in the newspapers, sat on an oral board for minority group applicants on at least one occasion. A 21-year-old Negro applicant in Detroit was rejected by an all-white board because the board alleged "he looked immature." Since the charge was based on the *appearance* of immaturity *per se,* the applicant appealed his rejection to the Michigan Civil Rights Commission. Before the Michigan commission had proceeded beyond preliminary investigations, the young man was hired.

Psychological Screening

Several of the police departments studied make psychological evaluations of the applicants through written tests or by psychiatric examinations while others use the oral interview to appraise the psychological fitness of the individual. The city of Detroit used a psychological test at one time, but found it so unsatisfactory that it was discontinued. At the time of this study the city was again considering the possibility of psychological evaluation of prospective recruits as well as the possibility of employing a psychiatrist on a regular basis for men on the force because of a significant increase in mental disorders among patrolmen. Recruiting is becoming more difficult, the department believes, apparently because of the strain of a policeman's job.

The supervisor of police-community relations for the Michigan Civil Rights Commission told Commission staff that there really is no adequate test for mental and emotional suitability for police work. He added that the general goal of such tests is to find out if the individual is aggressive enough to be a good policeman, but not overly aggressive, whether he has sadistic tendencies that will surface when he begins to exercise authority, and to determine whether or not he is overly enamored of firearms. He knew of no cases where psychological examinations had been used to test applicants for attitudes of hostility toward minorities which might affect the performance of their duties. A few Michigan police departments use polygraph tests as their "psychological test" but cursory attention only is paid to the subjects of racial prejudice and discrimination.

Selection

The selection process for police and fire departments is similar to that for civil service systems and the same opportunity for discrimination usually exists. Applicants who have passed all phases of the examination process are placed on a register from which they are selected, usually by the rule of three. The Oakland Fire Department and both the Atlanta Police and Fire Departments, in order to avoid charges of discrimination, officials said, always select the top man on the list, although they are permitted to select from among the top three.

Discrimination on the Job

Reports of discriminatory treatment in work assignments, promotions, and in personal interaction were more frequent in the police and fire departments than in any other area of government studied by the Commission. The effect of these practices probably was the most significant factor in increasing the difficulty of recruiting minority group members for jobs on the force.

The area of promotions was a subject of concern in every department studied where more than a handful of Negro policemen were employed. Statistics indicate that minority group members were rarely found in the upper ranks of the police departments studied. The promotion system for police departments resembles that of a typical civil service system, except that it is likely to be more formal. Typically, a policeman is promoted on the basis of his seniority, his proficiency rating, and his score on a promotional examination, which sometimes includes an oral as well as a written test. The weight given to each of these components varies from jurisdiction to jurisdiction.

Sometimes seniority is not given a specific weight, but a minimum requirement for promotion. For example, Memphis policemen are not eligible for promotion until they have been on the force for 5 years. On the other hand, seniority is no guarantee of promotion. A Negro, formerly on the Memphis force, told Commission interviewers that although 13 Negroes were hired by the Memphis department in 1948, no black policeman was promoted to the rank of lieutenant until 15 years later. Furthermore, many white precinct chiefs had less seniority than some black patrolmen. He added that: "Negro policemen took a lot of chances, but got no credit."

Proficiency ratings by supervisors also were charged with being discriminatory. Two staff members of the Michigan Civil Rights Commission told Commission staff that they had personal knowledge of cases in which a black policeman's proficiency rating was lowered as he became eligible for promotion. Each claimed that he had seen this happen often enough to believe that it was a deliberate pattern.

The assistant chief of police in Memphis told Commission staff that most Negroes ranked no higher than patrolman because they lacked seniority, could not pass the test, or were satisfied with remaining patrolmen. The city director of personnel, when interviewed by Commission staff, stated that both police and fire promotions rely heavily on performance rating by supervisors, that the rule of three applies, and that there is no protection against discrimination in promotion.

The police chief in Houston told a Commission interviewer that most of the charges of discrimination leveled at the police department were based on the complaint that Negroes weren't promoted, especially to supervisory positions. He added, however, that the police department promotes strictly on merit.

It is common practice for a promotion register to be established similar to that used for entrance into the force. Policemen who have met all the requirements for promotion are placed on the list according to their overall scores and are then selected for promotion from the list. Frequently, departments have a choice from among the top two or three. When this is the case, as the personnel director for the city of Memphis pointed out, there is no protection for the individual from discrimination by the selecting official.

Discriminatory treatment and work assignments are closely related to the problems of promotion in the uniformed forces. A black fireman, discussing supervisor ratings in Memphis, said that leadership was one of the items on which the men were rated. He then asked how black firemen could be rated on leadership when they were never given the chance to lead.

Discriminatory assignments appeared to be a greater problem in the southern cities investigated than in the northern ones. The president of the Baton Rouge Branch of the National Association for the Advancement of Colored People stated that the nine black policemen employed by Baton Rouge were assigned exclusively to Negro areas and were not allowed to give so much as a traffic ticket to a white person. The chief of police in Baton Rouge denied the allegation. He told Commission interviewers that under the former chief of police, Negro policemen were not allowed to carry traffic ticket books or to intervene in matters other than those involving Negroes. He said he had changed that policy when he took office in 1965. His present policy, he explained, is to fire a Negro policeman who is present when a white person commits a crime if he does not arrest the offender without regard to his race. The chief added, however, that he does not advertise this arrangement because the public would vigorously disapprove if they discovered he had eliminated the restrictions. At the same time, he did confirm that Negro patrol cars were limited to patrolling Negro areas of the city.

At the time Commission interviewers visited Baton Rouge, the question of integrating police patrol cars was an issue of considerable controversy. In early August 1967 the mayor of Baton Rouge ordered the chief of police to integrate the patrol cars and the chief prepared to implement the order. He was met with a threat of mass resignation by white policemen on Sunday, August 20, 1967, the day when rallies of Negro organizations and the Ku Klux Klan were scheduled at the State Capitol. The mayor rescinded his order. When interviewed by Commission staff in September 1967, the chairman of the Baton Rouge Community Relations Committee said he felt that the order would be reissued in 30 to 60 days. In May 1968 the executive director of the Louisiana Council on Human Relations said that, although she had raised the matter with the mayor, the patrol cars still were not integrated.

The Baton Rouge Chief of Police told Commission staff that he felt the best way to integrate police patrol cars was on a volunteer basis. The two volunteers, since they could not be expected to enter a restaurant together, would frequent take-out counters of drive-in restaurants and eat their meals in their patrol car. He felt that gradual implementation of this approach would be acceptable to the community.

In Memphis, Negro policemen were restricted to Negro areas and segregated in car patrols until 1967. Then the police department integrated some of the cars and put them in integrated neighborhoods and the downtown business district as well as the black neighborhoods. At the time of the Commission's field investigations, however, there were still no Negro policemen assigned to white areas.

In San Francisco, only two Negroes were assigned to the motorcycle division which is considered a prestigious assignment. These two policemen had had this assignment for 3 years at the time of the Commission's investigation. Allegations were made that they had been exposed to hostile and derogatory treatment by their white fellow policemen. Commission interviewers also were told that no Negro policemen in San Francisco were assigned to the homicide or burglary squads, although such experience would be useful in obtaining promotions. The Wayne County Sheriff's Department was charged by an employee with assigning Negroes to units which offered the least desirable positions. For example, no Negroes were assigned to the racket squad except when an "undercover Negro" was needed.

Frequently the attitudes and atmosphere in a police department can be such as to make the minority policeman feel uncomfortable and unwelcome. The San Francisco Police Department was characterized as an Irish-Italian "closed society" by several officials interviewed by Commission staff. An official in the San Francisco civil service system said that higher level officers in the police department were intolerant and that their attitudes encourages expressions of hostility at lower levels. He added that he personally knew of cases in which white policemen used racial slurs in the presence of Negro policemen and where derogatory notes had been pasted on the lockers of Negro policemen. Another respondent in San Francisco told of Negro policemen constantly finding that their lockers had been moved in front of the toilets. Charges such as these were by no means limited to San Francisco. In most cities studied by the Commission, prejudice on the part of white policemen toward their black colleagues was considered a problem by persons interviewed.

Cases of known or alleged brutality against the Negro community on the part of white policemen also had a demoralizing effect on Negro policemen and were a strong deterrent to potential Negro applicants.

RECOMMENDATIONS
Action Needed to Achieve Equality in State and
Local Government Employment

A. Every State and local government should adopt and maintain a program of employment equality adequate to fulfill its obligation under the equal protection clause of the 14th Amendment to assure
  —that current employment practices are nondiscriminatory; and
  —that the continuing effects of past discriminatory practices are undone.

This report has found that state and local government employment is pervaded by a wide range of discriminatory practices. These practices violate the requirements of the equal protection clause of the 14th Amendment and accordingly must be eliminated. Unconstitutional practices include not only those which are purposefully discriminatory, but also those which have the effect of creating or reinforcing barriers to equal employment opportunity. Such barriers will persist until affirmative action is taken to overcome the. For this reason, a public employer can assure that its employment practices are nondiscriminatory only if it maintains a comprehensive, well-planned program of equal employment opportunity.

The following are examples of discriminatory barriers to equality in public employment which may arise in the absence of an effective program of employment equality. Evidence of the effects of many of these discriminatory barriers may be found in the pages of this report.

a. Recruitment through schools or colleges with a predominantly nonminority makeup discriminates against minorities wherever comparable recruitment is not done at predominantly minority institutions.

b. Unless special precautions are taken, use of recruitment sources such as private employment agencies, informal community contacts, or other sources, may incorporate into the employer's recruitment system the discriminatory practices or prejudices of the sources used.

c. Wherever a work force, or significant levels or components of it, is predominantly nonminority in makeup, recruitment practices which rely upon employee "word-of-mouth" contact for new applicants may discriminatorily perpetuate the majority predominance.

d. Unless special precautions are taken, a past history of overt discrimination may continue to deter minority applications for employment or advancement, particularly with respect to positions which have not traditionally been held by minority persons. Such a history also may signal to outside employment sources that the employer does not welcome minority referrals, at least for nontraditional positions.

e. Unless special precautions are taken, harassment or unfair treatment by nonminority supervisors or co-workers, or other discrimination not countenanced by the employer, may discourage minority applications for employment or advancement.

f. Where minority persons have less access than nonminority persons to informal networks of employment information—such as through present employees or officials—relating to such matters as available openings, hiring procedure, or the basis for rejection or other action taken with respect to applications, this may impede access of minorities to available opportunities.

g. Since minority persons, competing for positions at the entry level or elsewhere in the work force, frequently may have limited education or job experience, the employer may unfairly penalize minority applicants wherever he imposes qualifications not likely to be possessed by minority applicants and not substantially related to the needs of the job.

h. Selection standards may be applied reasonably to nonminority applicants, but unfair if extended on the same terms to minority persons. For example, the level of academic achievement—such as the level of verbal skill—may be one measure of an applicant's native ability, but when applied on the same basis to a group whose schools afford a markedly inferior education, it may cease to be a fair and equal measure of ability.

In the case of many state and local governments, such discriminatory barriers, or other discriminatory practices, have given rise to patterns of minority underutilization, including concentration of minority employees at lower job levels.

Such discriminatory patterns of minority underutilization themselves give rise to denial of the 14th Amendment right to equal protection of the laws. Such patterns, for example, mean unequal enjoyment by minorities of those public funds which are paid as salaries to public employees. Also, since public employees shape the conduct of their government, discriminatorily created underutilization of minorities in public employment weakens the ability of government to reflect equally the interests of all segments of the governed. Finally, as shown in this report, discriminatorily created patterns of minority underutilization tend to be self-reinforcing and self-perpetuating; for this reason such patterns themselves constitute vehicles of discrimination which must be corrected.

Accordingly, wherever in public employment discriminatorily created patterns persist, the Constitution requires that they be remedied by measures aimed at giving the work force the shape it presently would have were it not for such past discrimination. It should be recognized that such measures are not a "preference" but rather a restoration of equality; one can see inequality in such remedies only by being blind to the past injustices which they cure.

B. Though the programs of employment equality adopted by individual State and local governments will vary widely with the particular needs and problems of each, all such programs should include the following three elements:

1. An evaluation of employment practices and employee utilization patterns adequate to show the nature and extent of barriers to equal opportunity for minorities and of any discriminatory underutilization of minorities.

The first step in the program of employment equality is an assessment of needs and problems. This requires a thorough evaluation by the state or local government of the employment practices of each of its constituent agencies, to determine the effect of its practices on utilization of minorities. Though the principal aim is to identify barriers to equal opportunity, the evaluation also should make note, for continuation and strengthening, of those policies which have the positive effect of overcoming such barriers.

In order to make this assessment, and identify patterns of minority underutilization, the state or local government will need to gather and review comprehensive information, by nonminority-minority classification, on employee distribution among the various agency components, job levels and locations, as well as data on referrals, applications, acceptances, promotions, and other personnel action.

This initial evaluation should culminate in a written analysis of discriminatory barriers to equal employment opportunity in the state or local government, as well as an analysis of any patterns of minority underutilization which have resulted from the operation of such discriminatory barriers.

2. Preparation and implementation of a program of action which is calculated
   —to eliminate or neutralize all discriminatory barriers to equal employment opportunity; and
   —to undo any patterns of minority underutilization which have been brought about by past discrimination.

Having evaluated employment practices and assessed patterns of minority underutilization, the next step is to formulate a program which will overcome barriers to equal employment opportunity and, in addition, will bring about whatever changes in minority utilization are necessary to undo the effects of past discrimination. Where patterns of minority utilization are to be changed, the program should include specific goals, or estimates, to be achieved within a specified period of time.

Even in those cases where evaluation has disclosed that the present employment practices of a government or of one of its component agencies fully overcome all barriers to equal employment opportunity and that no pattern of discriminatorily created underutilization of minorities is present, formulation of relevant practices into a program is still desirable in order to help assure that nondiscriminatory practices continue to be followed.

Affirmative programs should be developed in a form which makes clear the obligations of each component agency of the government. Programs should be put in writing and made available upon request to public employees, minority leaders, and others with a legitimate interest in the status of minorities in public employment. Staff responsibilities for implementing the program should be allocated clearly, and employees informed of the program and of their rights, duties, and obligations under it.

The adoption of affirmative programs by state and local governments may be subject to limitations imposed by statute, state constitution, city charter, or the like, which inflexibly mandate that certain employment policies be followed. Similar limitations may be created by the amount or terms of budgetary allocations made to governments or to their component agencies.

Questions of the right or duty of individual public agencies or officials faced with such restrictions can be resolved only on a case by case basis. However, inherent in the supremacy clause of the Constitution is the requirement that state and local governments must alter any laws, regulations, or practices which stand in the way of achieving the quality in public employment which is required by the equal protection clause of the 14th Amendment.

There follows a sampling of the kind of actions which state and local governments will need to include in programs of employment equality. Use to some degree of most of these techniques will be necessary to assure that all barriers to equal employment opportunity are eliminated. In addition, public employers with discriminatorily created patterns of employee utilization should use the techniques to a degree sufficient to undo the effects of past discrimination.

Recruitment

a. Maintain consistent continuing communication with the state employment service and schools, colleges, community agencies, community leaders, minority organizations, publications, and other sources affording contact with potential minority applicants in the job area.

b. Thoroughly and continually inform sources affording contact with potential minority applicants about current openings, about the employer's recruiting and selection procedures, and about the positions (together with personnel specifications) for which applications may be made.

c. Inform all applicant sources, both generally and each time a specific request for referral is made, that minority applicants are welcome and that discrimination in referrals will not be tolerated.

d. Fully inform each applicant of the basis for all action taken on his or her application. Supply in detail the basis for rejection, including evaluation of tests and interviews. Suggest to rejected minority applicants possible methods for remedying disqualifying factors.

e. Make data on minority employment status available on request to employees, to minority leaders in the job area, and to others with a legitimate interest in non-discrimination by the employer.

f. Invite minority persons to visit state and local government facilities; explain employment opportunities and the equal opportunity program in effect.

g. Have minority persons among those who deal with persons applying for employment, with clientele, or with other members of the public, in order to communicate the fact of minority equal opportunity.

h. Coordinate the employment and placement activities of the various components of the state or local government, at least for the purpose of facilitating minority applications or requests for transfer. To the same end, maintain minority applications or transfer requests on an active basis for a substantial period of time.

i. Participate in Neighborhood Youth Corps, New Careers, other Federal job training or employment programs, or similar state or local programs. In connection with such programs, or otherwise, make a particular effort to structure work in a way which gives rise to jobs which are suitable for minority persons who are available for employment.

j. Independent of outside training programs, institute on-the-job training or work-study plans, in which persons are employed part-time while studying or otherwise seeking to satisfy employment requirements; this may include summertime employment for persons in school.

k. Solicit cooperation of academic and vocational schools to establish curricula which will provide minority candidates with the skills and education necessary to fulfill manpower requirements.

Selection

a. Take steps to assure that tests used for the purpose of selecting or placing applicants are demonstrated to be valid in forecasting the job performance of minority applicants.

b. Pending validation, discontinue or modify the use of tests, minimum academic achievement, or other criteria which screen out a disproportionate number of minority applicants.

c. Do not in all cases give preference to nonminority applicants on the basis of higher performance on tests or other hiring criteria, as long as it is apparent that competing minority applicants, especially where they have waiting list seniority, are qualified to do the job.

d. Where tests are used, employ them as a guide to placement rather than as the determinant of whether an applicant is to be hired.

e. Make increased use of tests comprised of a sampling of work to be performed on the job.

f. Make increased use of the probationary period, affording an opportunity for on-the-job training and enabling the applicant's ability to be judged on the basis of job performance.

Placement and Promotion

a. Make available to minority applicants and to present minority employees a complete description of positions for which they may be eligible to apply.

b. In the initial placement of newly hired employees, wherever possible place minority employees in positions or areas with low minority representation.

c. Broaden job experience and facilitate transfers of minority employees by creating a system of temporary work experience assignments in other positions or areas of work. Such a system may include temporary assignment between jurisdictions, such as a suburban-inner-city interchange.

d. Individually appraise the promotion potential and training needs of minority employees, and take action necessary to permit advancement.

e. Announce all position openings on a basis which brings them to the attention of minority employees and makes clear that minority persons are eligible and encouraged to apply.

Discipline

a. Formulate disciplinary standards and procedures in writing, and distribute them to all employees.

b. In case of proposed disciplinary action, inform the employee of the infraction alleged and afford an opportunity for rebuttal. If the rebuttal is deemed unsatisfactory, clearly state the reasons why.

Facilities

Assure that facilities, including all work-related facilities and those used in employer-sponsored recreational or similar activities, are not subject to segregated use, whether by official policy or by employee practice.

3. A continuing review of employment practices and of the status of minority persons in employment.

This third step of the program responds to the need for a continuing review of employment practices—particularly those related to the affirmative program—and of their effect upon minority persons. Such a review requires the regular collection and evaluation of data on employee disbribution and personnel actions, such as that described under paragraph 1, above.

These data afford an important measure of the effectiveness of steps taken to overcome barriers to minority employment, by showing the actual impact of employment practices on minorities; the data may indicate points at which changes are needed in the affirmative program to make it more effective. Similarly, where patterns of minority underutilization which arose from past discrimination are being corrected, such comparative nonminority-minority data show the extent to which required changes in minority utilization are in fact being made.

Like the affirmative program itself, current data on minority employment should be made available to persons and groups with a legitimate interest in the status of minorities in public employment.

The following are illustrations of the steps necessary for an effective continuing review by state and local governments of their employment practices and of the status of minorities in employment.

a. Maintain records containing for the period covered, and indicating nonminority-minority classifications and the positions involved, complete data on inquiries, applications, acceptances, rejections, promotions, terminations, and other personnel actions, as well as data as of the end of the period, by nonminority-minority classification, on employee distribution within the work force.

b. Maintain for a reasonable period of time, with nonminority-minority classification, a file on each applicant (including those listed on a civil service register) adequate to document the specific grounds for rejection or passing over of the applicant.

c. Maintain a record, with nonminority-minority classification, of applicants by job source, to facilitate review of the impact of each source upon minority utilization.

d. Where there are a substantial number of separate components within the state or local government, make periodic inspection and review of employment practices and minority status in the various component agencies.

e. Regularly interview minority employees upon termination to determine whether discriminatory acts or policies played a role in the termination.

Integration vs. Local Community Control in Education: Desegregation in Berkeley

The historic Brown vs. Board of Education decision gave momentum to school desegregation programs in communities across the country—north and south. In 1969 the "all deliberate speed" doctrine was overthrown in favor of what might be termed "integration now." Schools have a central place in liberation movements by racial and ethnic groups, as these groups give high priority to equality as well as quality in education. The question of how the right to a decent education may be achieved has become caught up in a philosophical and strategic controversy concerning the advantages of desegregation efforts vs. local community control of the schools. This question is, in turn, related to the growing Black Power, Brown Power, and Red Power movements in this country and to the degree that separatism or growing ethnic unity is seen as a useful development for racial and ethnic groups and to the nation as a whole.

It would be useful here to introduce comments from the Foodergong Conference of NAIRO (National Association of Intergroup Relations Officials):

> Professional Intergroup Relations workers must distinguish between those who advocate black power and those who advocate black separatism; while all who advocate black separatism advocate black power, not all who advocate black power advocate black separatism; while there is overlap the two are not identical. Also, there are those who see separatism as a means to an end and not an end in itself; one may see it as a temporary step through which the black community can gain cohesion and during which black institutions may be strengthened—so that the black community can gain sufficient strength that it can deal with the general community on an equal status basis. Then, and only then, it is held that the black man may enter into the main stream of American life and society....
>
> There has been increasing discussion among Intergroup Relations professionals, city planners and Negro leadership as to whether the ghetto should be dispersed or enriched. Too often, the wishes of the ghetto residents are not considered in these discussions; it is the height of presumption to discuss or—worse—plan the future of a neighborhood without providing a decisive role for the residents in the decision-making process. Those who advocate dispersing the ghetto so so, for the most part, because they believe in an integrated and open society; a few advocate dispersal because they fear the potential political muscle of large

58

concentrations of black people. Those who advocate building up the ghetto are not so easily categorized. Some favor enriching the ghetto and its institutions so that blacks might compete with whites on an equal status basis and, thus, move into the main stream of American life. Others want to build up the ghetto as a power base and as a separatist community. Yet others primarily wish to improve the institutions and facilities of their neighborhood. Realistically, it would be very difficult and highly costly to disperse the ghetto; equally realistically the current situation in the ghetto and the forces which maintain it are an affront to human dignity. . . .

Most of what has been said of the ghetto is also true of the barrio; there are some significant differences. The barrio is more self-imposed than is the ghetto; for cultural, language and religious reasons Mexican-Americans have tended to gather together in neighborhoods. They are more free to leave the barrio than is the black to leave the ghetto. The barrio has more control over its internal affairs and institutions than does the ghetto. The barrio, like the ghetto, is in urgent need of vastly improved schools, housing and employment opportunities.

While the issue of segregation-local community control is being fought out in rhetoric and politics, group relations practitioners are involved programmatically in both types of developments. Persuasive advocates promote local community control. Meanwhile, the desegregation movement continues and even accelerates, buttressed by increased determination by the Supreme Court to remove all remaining obstacles to this process. One of the more imaginative approaches to desegregation has been promulgated by the Berkeley, California, School Board. The story of that effort is recounted below. (An illustration of local community control in social work will be found in Unit 11. This illustration affords an opportunity to examine necessary ingredients for successful integration, assuming one chooses that course.)

On September 10, 1968, the buses rolled. The buses not only rolled, they rolled in both directions, carrying some 3,500 of Berkeley's 8,700 elementary school children to new schools outside their traditional neighborhoods. Kindergarten through third-grade students living in west Berkeley were transported to schools in the central and eastern parts of the city. Fourth, fifth and sixth graders living in the latter areas were transported to schools in west Berkeley. This move was made specifically for the purpose of desegregating the elementary schools.

The inauguration of the new plan was a history-making event. Since Berkeley has only one senior high school and since the junior high schools had been desegregated four years earlier, September 10, 1968, marked the completion of the total desegregation of all Berkeley schools. With this step, Berkeley became the first city of over 100,000 containing a substantial minority population to desegregate its schools through an equitable two-way busing program.

What lessons were learned from the long struggle in Berkeley, culminating on September 10? What implications does Berkeley's experience have for other districts which are, or should be, facing this same issue? The primary purpose of this article will be to discuss these lessons and implications rather than to present a detailed chronological account of the Berkeley experience. However, it is first necessary to provide the background of Berkeley's experience to serve as the basis for discussion.

"Desegregation in Berkeley: Some Applicable Lessons," by Thomas D. Wogaman. From *The Urban Review*, a publication of the Center for Urban Education, Vol. 3, no. 5, April 1969, pp. 13-16.

Background in Berkeley

The City

Berkeley is a cosmopolitan city of 120,000 population located on the east side of San Francisco Bay. Although best known for its University of California campus, Berkeley also contains a substantial industrial complex and is the site of many state and Federal governmental offices. Like most Northern and Western cities, Berkeley has a tradition of segregated housing. Most of the Negroes live in the western and southern parts of the city, with most of the Caucasians living to the north and east. Orientals reside mainly near the center.

Politically the city tends to be slightly more liberal than most comparable communities, although a wide range of opinion is represented. Each shade on the opinion spectrum contains highly articulate spokesmen who don't hesitate putting their verbal skills to use. This makes Berkeley an exciting city, one used to facing problems and discussing new ideas.

The School District

The Berkeley Unified School District is conterminous with the city. The K-12 enrollment of approximately 16,000 students contains the broad range of racial and ethnic groups found in the population at large. A recently completed student census revealed the racial makeup to be 49.6 per cent Caucasian; 42.8 per cent Negro; 7.5 per cent Oriental; and .1 per cent American Indian. The Caucasian enrollment includes approximately 3 per cent classified as "Spanish Surname."

In the twenty years following World War II, Berkeley schools experienced a growing Negro population and a declining Caucasian enrollment. Since 1965, however, this trend has not continued. The last four annual student racial censuses have resulted in approximately the same racial balance. This is interesting in view of the continuing flight to the suburbs experienced in many cities and the oft-heard threat that integration would accelerate this flight. The residential segregation described above resulted in de facto segregation of the junior high schools up until 1964 and in the elementary schools until 1968.

Berkeley's move toward desegregating its schools came in three major steps. In 1964, following a year and a half of study, first by a citizens committee of thirty-six people (appointed by the board of education at the request of CORE), then by various staff and community groups, the school board adopted a new organizational plan for the junior high schools that eliminated de facto segregation at that level.

In taking this action, the board had to withstand intense community pressures, including an effort by opponents to remove them from office in a recall election. This recall attempt was not successful and the pro-integration board was sustained by the community.

Late in 1965 the board adopted, as part of its ESEA's Title I Project, a plan that would bus about 240 elementary students from predominantly Negro schools in west Berkeley to predominantly Caucasian schools having room for them in other areas of the city. This was done to reduce pupil-teacher ratios in the target-area schools and was not treated as the district's answer to the segregation problem. However, the success of this project provided an important introduction to elementary school integration. Incidentally, the children chosen were not skimmed off the top of their classes; they represented a cross section, ranging from low-average through the top.

In spring 1967 the board adopted a policy committing it to completing elementary school integration and established September 1968 as the target deadline. The balance of 1967 was spent in developing and refining the plan to implement this desegregation commitment. This process included massive involvement of staff and concerned lay citizens. The plan emerging from this process was adopted on January 16, 1968. Its implementation on September 10 ended de facto school segregation in Berkeley.

Lessons Learned

The experience of Berkeley moving toward integration provides many lessons which are, in fact, interrelated but, for purposes of discussion, are here divided into distinct categories.

Lesson One—It can be done

The most important lesson from the Berkeley experience is that the schools of a city of this size, with a substantial minority population, can be desegregated through a large-scale two-way busing program. There never has been any doubt that desegregation was possible logistically. After all, over 16,500,000 American school children board about 225,000 buses every school day. Furthermore, existing school facilities, with slight renovations, were adequate to house the new program. School desegregation is not basically a question of logistics, although it is frequently debated in those terms.

The real issue in Berkeley was whether the community would accept this kind of change. A few communities have permitted minority students to enroll in predominantly Caucasian schools where space permitted. Usually such action has been taken in the name of relieving overcrowded ghetto schools, rather than to achieve integration *per se*. Even this minimal effort has generally met with controversy and open resistance from Caucasians. In some instances this hostility has been sufficient to stop the program altogether.

Other cities have been successful in achieving total desegregation (for example, Riverside, California) through a one-way busing program. The minority schools were closed or put to a different use, and the minority students were bused to predominantly Caucasian schools in the city. In certain smaller communities (for example, Greenburgh, New York, and Sausalito, California) busing was two-way with Caucasians spending part of their school years in minority areas as well as vice versa. Berkeley demonstrated that two-way busing can also be accomplished in a city of over 100,000 population.

Lesson Two—The predicted dire consequences did not materialize

During all three major periods of community discussion of integration (junior high, limited ESEA busing program, and full-scale elementary school integration), various threats and negative predictions were made regarding what would happen in and to the city if the proposed action were taken. These predictions included a large-scale flight of teachers, mass exodus of Caucasian students, defeat for future tax or bond measures, and overthrow of the board itself.

These negative consequences simply did not happen. There was no mass flight of teachers. In fact, the teacher turnover rate for the school district has been cut in half since the first step toward integration was taken in 1964. Furthermore, the two teacher organizations (one affiliated with the National Education Association, the other with the American Federation of Teachers) have become staunch advocates of integration. Their members have worked unstintingly to bring it about and to make it successful. Nor has there been an exodus of Caucasian students. This stability, moreover, has been achieved during the very period in which integration was being discussed and implemented. This indicates that the topic can be faced and resolved without accelerating Caucasian exodus from the city.

The threat of financial defeat likewise proved to be spurious. In June 1966, Berkeley citizens were asked to approve an increase of nearly 50 per cent in the school tax ceiling. Although similar tax proposals were being roundly defeated in other districts, both in California and across the nation, the Berkeley tax proposal was carried by more than a 60-40 per cent margin, a distinct vote of confidence in the school system.

An interesting sidelight to this election was the pattern of voting. In the predominantly Negro areas of the city not only was the vote favorable, but the voters turned out in substantial numbers. This can be interpreted as recognition that the schools belong to them, too. The progress of the city toward desegregation could well have been a major factor in bringing about this assumption by minority citizens of financial responsibility for the system's welfare.

The most serious threat to stop integration occurred in connection with the 1964 desegregation of the junior high schools. At that time the Parents Association for Neighborhood Schools was formed to block desegregation or, failing that, to recall board members who voted for it. The board unanimously voted in favor of desegregation in spite of threats from this group.

The group was strong enough to obtain enough signatures on petitions to force a recall election. However, in the recall election the board was sustained by a vote of approximately 23,000 to 15,000—a substantial victory for school integration. This victory meant courageous board members would stay in office, that the junior high desegregation program would have a chance to develop and succeed. More important, it demonstrated that a board of education could move toward integration—not because it was forced to, but because it was right!—and still remain in office.

In spite of threats and negative predictions, the board insisted on facing issues squarely and moved step by step in the direction of integration. The failure of dire predictions to materialize vindicates the board's judgment.

Lesson Three—The policy commitment and its timing are crucial

It is obvious that no school district will desegregate its schools without the board of education at some point formally adopting a policy commitment to that goal. Not all policy commitments, however, are realized in practice. Many school districts have excellent policy statements about the value of integrated education and commitment to move in the direction of achieving as much integration as possible. Yet most districts have taken only a token step at best, in the direction of policy implementation. Several features about policy commitment are crucial, if it is to be more than just a policy statement. Berkeley's experience with the elementary integration issue illustrates this point.

In April 1967 the board was approached by both teacher organizations with the suggestion that it was time to get on with the task of completing school integration. A board member read a suggested motion to renew the board's commitment to the integration of all Berkeley schools with all deliberate speed.

Superintendent Neil Sullivan quickly pointed out that the words "with all deliberate speed" represented an excellent sentiment which had lost something in translation since first used in connection with the *Brown vs. Board of Education of Topeka* case in 1954. At his suggestion the motion was amended to provide a specific deadline for implementation: namely, September 1968. This deadline, in effect, made a commitment of what otherwise could have been simply another nice-sounding statement of goal.

The policy statement as ultimately adopted provided that integration take place in the context of "continued quality education" and that plans be developed with widespread community participation. Both of these provisos, when utilized by a strong and committed administration, resulted in development of a plan for implementation that was stronger and more easily sold to the community than would otherwise have been the case.

It is important that policy precede development of the plan. During the period between adoption of the policy and formulation of the plan, discussion is focused on integration *per se*. Opponents do not have the opportunity to mask their opposition to integration behind some alleged weakness of a given plan. During that interim the only thing that has been adopted is the policy itself, so opponents must either come to grips with that or maintain their silence. Many people find it much tougher to oppose integration in principle than to oppose a particular plan to bring it about. If their real opposition is to integration, they should have to say so, rather than hide behind defects of any particular plan.

Furthermore, this interim period between policy and plan is a chance to line up community endorsement. In Berkeley these endorsements came from the city council, the PTA and a host of civic, religious, and socially oriented groups. This timing permitted people to endorse integration in principle without committing themselves to any particular plan of implementation. By the time the plan was presented in October, the policy question was so thoroughly accepted in the community that the plan itself could then be studied on its own merits.

Placing policy resolution before development of the plan is important for another reason. People who honestly favor integration, but who have reservations about certain plans, are able to make their ideas, suggestions, and constructive criticism known during development of the plan. They are not placed in the position of having to withhold constructive criticism for fear that it will be interpreted as opposing integration itself. The plan of integration, as finally adopted in Berkeley, was greatly strengthened by the fact that its development had included give-and-take discussion and debate among people who, while committed to integration in principle, differed as to how it should be brought about.

Lesson Four—The plan and its development will determine whether or not the program will be successfully implemented

The logistical plans used to implement each stage of Berkeley's desegregation were "made in Berkeley." Information was gathered from other cities making progress in race relations, and occasional visitors gave helpful counsel, but Berkeley's integration, first of the secondary and then the elementary schools, evolved through devoted efforts of many Berkeley citizens and school staff members. This involvement, in addition to generating many valuable suggestions, furnished a substantial base of support for the program, once the final plans had been developed.

During the summer and fall of 1967. as logistical plans for desegregating the elementary schools were being developed, the school administration took great care to provide channels for participation by staff members and lay citizens. Every elementary school faculty was given released time for discussion and suggestions. Letters were written to sixty civic, educational and religious groups in the city inviting their counsel and suggestions. The public at large was invited to submit proposals.

By early summer, over forty different proposals had been submitted. These were carefully analyzed by a staff task group and narrowed to five prototypes involving various grade-level configurations. When school opened in the fall, these five prototypes were referred to school faculties and the public for their reaction. During the last week of September, some thirty staff members, representing a cross section of the total school staff, hammered out the formal proposal which was presented to the board early in October.

Community reaction to the proposed plan was invited and was forthcoming during the ensuing three or four months. Valuable suggestions and constructive criticisms were received, resulting in several alterations prior to the board's final adoption of the plan on January 16, 1968.

Throughout this period of discussion the school administration demonstrated willingness to compromise on details and to encourage widespread involvement in mapping the plan itself. There were, of course, areas not open to compromise. These included the requirement that the plan must actually accomplish integration, that it must involve the entire city, and that it must be fair to both sides of town.

Tactical factors were taken into account. Special efforts were made to avoid false handles for opposition arguments, to anticipate features of any proposal that could be used as a red herring, or serve as a vehicle for arguments against integration itself. Those involved in developing the plan were determined it should be logistically and educationally sound and salable to the community as being such.

Lesson Five—The campaign to win public acceptance of the integration plan cannot be left to chance

From the 1964 recall election to the present, there has been a loosely knit network of supporters of the board and administration and of the integration concept. Although not formally organized, this network of people actively supported the board elections, as well as the 1966 election to raise the school tax ceiling, and has been a ready source of speakers for community meetings on the subject of integration.

The proponents of integration in Berkeley had long since learned certain techniques necessary to win this type of campaign. These techniques include checking ground rules of all nonschool-sponsored meetings to which school speakers are invited, scheduling sufficient supportive speakers in public forums, and arranging for adequate attendance of pro-integration people at public meetings, so that the "applause meter" will not be overbalanced in the wrong direction. Appropriate tactics will, of course, vary from situation to situation, but they do require planning.

Lesson Six—Adequate attention must be given to preparation of staff and community

Berkeley was not altogether successful in this dimension in the first stage of its desegregation: the junior high school plan of 1964. The plan was adopted in May for implementation the following September. This barely left time for necessary transfer of equipment, minor facility alterations, assignment of teachers, etc. Insufficient attention was given to preparing staff members, particularly those not sympathetic to the new organization. This became apparent during the early months of the plan, especially at the junior high school regarded as a "prestige" school under the old order. Integration was complicated by other problems at that school: for instance, overcrowding, and lack of enthusiasm for the new program among a number of staff members. This problem was ultimately solved by meeting their legitimate needs (e.g., providing extra staff), and many improvements were made. However, initial experience with the junior high school reorganization underscored the need to prepare the staff more adequately.

Preparation of staff and community for elementary school integration was both organized and effective. During 1967-68, prior to implementation, substitute teachers were employed to rotate among elementary schools to release every teacher for one week of service on the opposite side of the city. During that week the teacher would both visit and teach in the host school. Seminars were then held so teachers could discuss their new experiences. This helped remove fear of the unknown from teachers who had remained in the same kind of teaching position for many years. At several workshops, teachers received specific training to prepare them for working with wider ranges of ability found in more heterogeneous classrooms.

For the community, several forums were held to provide information about the new plan. People from both sides of the city were invited to a series of living-room meetings. Schools had open house for parents of children who would attend the following year. Two attractive news reports were mailed to every home in Berkeley. These tabloids provided comprehensive information about the integration program, including bus routes, stops, schedules, as well as safe walking routes to and from neighborhood schools.

As fast as rumors developed, they were met head-on. Every effort was made to keep the community informed. Many Berkeleyans, including this writer, attribute the lack of hostility and the remarkable degree of community acceptance which the elementary school program has received, to involvement of staff and community in development of plans and to the extensive steps taken in preparing community and staff for implementation of the plans.

Lesson Seven—*Desegregation does not complete the job*

What Berkeley has accomplished so far is *desegregation* of its schools: that is, a racial balance at each local school. The real *integration*—development of positive attitudes and meaningful relationships among members of differing racial groups— has not been achieved in Berkeley or in any other city. This is a long-range effort toward which desegregation is an important step.

Following desegregation of its schools, Berkeley, along with other neighboring districts, had its confrontations with the Black Student Union and other militant groups. Demands included an increase in black counselors and teachers, more black studies, "soul food" occasionally in the cafeteria, in-service training in minority history and culture for certified staff members, etc. Most of these demands were readily acceptable. In fact, the school district had already taken major steps in regard to some of them.

This black militant confrontation was relatively calm compared to the extremes in other districts. None of our schools was shut down. However, the situation served notice that no district, including one that had just made a giant step forward in de-segregation, could rest on its laurels. After segregation among schools has been re-moved, there remains the task of building genuine integration within each school. Berkeley continues to address itself to that task.

Implications for Other Districts

Just how far is the experience of Berkeley and the lessons learned in that city rel-evant to other communities facing the problem of de facto segregation? This is dif-ficult to determine and doubtless will vary from city to city. Cities such as New York and Washington, D.C., certainly have situations far different from Berkeley's.

The popular stereotype of Berkeley as a "liberal" city has been used by some people to indicate that Berkeley's experience is irrelevant to other communities. However, this alleged uniqueness of Berkeley is not totally valid. Although Berkeley has become a city more liberal than the average, liberalism has not always been characteristic. Not until 1961 did Berkeley elect its first Negro representatives to the city council and the board of education.

The fact that Berkeley today is more in sympathy with integration than the aver-age city should not be interpreted as a reason integration won't work in other cities. Rather, it should be viewed as an example of what a city can become when it genuinely faces this issue and marshals its resources, material and human, to over-come the problem. The success of Berkeley in achieving desegregation should stim-ulate and encourage other communities to face conscientiously the problem of seg-regation. Even the giant cities, whose logistical problems would dwarf those of Berkeley, could do much more if they were to address themselves to the task.

Each city must develop its own plan to meet its own needs, taking into account its geography, investments in existing buildings, and residential patterns. While the Berkeley plan is not exportable, elements of it could be used in many communities.

However, the *procedure* used in Berkeley can be used anywhere. (1) Recognize the problem and determine to resolve it; (2) organize community resources toward the task of finding a solution; (3) develop the solution; and (4) implement the new program.

Any community using this approach can develop a plan to fulfill its own needs. Regardless of the logistical obstacles found in certain communities, any city consci-entiously facing the problem can develop a program that will represent a decided improvement over present practice. In fact, most communities could totally deseg-regate if they were determined to do so. Developing commitment to integration is the toughest part of the problem. A way can be found, once that commitment has been achieved.

The overriding lesson from Berkeley is that IT CAN BE DONE! Furthermore, it can be done without the dire consequences generally predicted for communities that face honestly the segregation problem.

UNIT **4.**

The Place of Administrative Compliance / Quasi-judicial Procedures: A Public Hearing on Discrimination in Education for Chicanos

Governmental group relations agencies because of legal statutes, linkage to the political structure, or legitimacy attached to them, potentially possess considerable power to influence events and practices. At the same time such agencies are subject to suspicion and criticism on the part of minorities because they fail to utilize this power to its maximum. For example, agencies become bogged down in individual complaints, struggling to keep up with civil rights violations one by one, without attempting at the same time to change general patterns through initiating more comprehensive affirmative action. Should the agency be merely responsive, processing complaints as they are received, or aggressive in encouraging complaints, or taking class action aimed at eliminating the abuses? Is it possible to distinguish between significant precedent or pattern-setting cases or situations as opposed to limited-value ones? Can investigative procedures be used to shake up and expose as well as to calm down and cover up? Can public hearings open up neglected areas of injustice and incite civic action or must they be routine, bland, and mesmerizing in effect?

These procedures are tools and like all instruments can be used in varying ways, with diverse consequences. It is no doubt the skill of the practitioner in utilizing the tool that makes the difference in the product that is shaped. This is not to say that there are not boundaries which are imposed on the practitioner by the agency and community context. But there is reason to believe that there are possibilities for maneuver and impact within the confines of such boundaries.

One long-established administrative device for advancement in the civil rights arena has been the public hearing, which is intended to reveal and dramatize abuses, and at the same time to provide factual information and guidelines to action. The Federal Civil Rights Commission through its State Advisory Committees has made extensive use of this medium. We are reproducing below portions of a report of hearings on education of the Mexican-American community held in Los Angeles County in June, 1967. The reader may want to ponder ways of maximizing the impact of a hearing such as this.

67

The United States Commission on Civil Rights is an independent agency of the Executive Branch of the Federal Government created by the Civil Rights Act of 1957. By the terms of that Act, as amended by the Civil Rights Act of 1960 and 1964, the Commission is charged with the following duties: investigation of individual discriminatory denials of the right to vote; study of legal developments with respect to denials of equal protection of the law; maintenance of a national clearinghouse for information respecting denials of the equal protection of the law; and investigation of patterns or practices of fraud or discrimination in the conduct of Federal elections. The Commission is also required to submit reports to the President and the Congress at such times as the Commission, the Congress, or the President shall deem desirable.

An Advisory Committee to the United States Commission on Civil Rights has been established in each of the 50 States and the District of Columbia pursuant to section 105(c) of the Civil Rights Act of 1957 as amended. The Committees are made up of knowledgeable persons who serve without compensation. Their functions under their mandate from the Commission are to: advise the Commission of all relevant information concerning their respective States on matters within the jurisdiction of the Commission; advise the Commission upon matters of mutual concern in the preparation of reports of the Commission to the President and the Congress; receive reports, suggestions, and recommendations from individuals, public and private organizations, and public officials upon matters pertinent to inquiries conducted by the State Committee; initiate and forward advice and recommendations to the Commission upon matters which the State Committee has studied; assist the Commission in matters which the Commission shall request the assistance of the State Committee; and attend, as observers, any open hearing or conference which the Commission may hold within the State.

This report was submitted to the United States Commission on Civil Rights by the California State Advisory Committee. The conclusions and recommendations are based upon the Advisory Committee's evaluation of information received at two days of meetings held in East Los Angeles on June 8 and 9, 1967. This report has been received by the Commission and will be considered by it in making its report and recommendations to the President and the Congress.

Introduction

The California State Advisory Committee to the U.S. Commission on Civil Rights conducted a two-day meeting at La Casa del Mexicano in East Los Angeles in June, 1967, to collect information about civil rights problems in the Mexican-American community.

More than 40 persons who live and work in the barrio—the Mexican-American section—of East Los Angeles expressed their views about the opportunities open to them in employment and education. Representatives of public and private agencies described their existing programs and future plans.

The information gathered during those two days, the discouragement and hopelessness in the face of constant struggles with poverty and discrimination disclosed by speaker after speaker, vividly portrayed to the Committee the difficulties the Mexican-American faces in a Los Angeles barrio.

From "Education and the Mexican-American Community in Los Angeles County." A Report of the California State Advisory Committee for the U. S. Commission on Civil Rights, Los Angeles, April, 1968.

This report concentrates on the issue of education which recently has been the cause of major disruptions in the East Los Angeles schools and community. In early March, 1968, thousands of students staged walkouts in five predominantly Mexican-American Eastside schools; student-police clashes, arrests, mass demonstrations, and sit-ins followed.

The conditions of a year ago summarized here clearly have not been resolved and perhaps have been compounded. But it is hoped that this report will increase public awareness and understanding, and in turn, result in constructive action at the Federal, state, and local levels to deal with the problems in the barrio schools effectively and promptly.

Overview

"Civil rights," as generally defined and interpreted in the United States, is a phrase of vague implications to the Mexican-American who is aware that the nation offers less of its prosperity to him than it does to others. But he is inclined to blame himself for any failure to gain an equal share of that prosperity.

His experience in this country does not provide the basis for the belief that he can attain first-class citizenship. His tradition stresses one's intrinsic worth, as opposed to the esteem one must fight to obtain from others.

This attitude, however, does not change the reality. There are 5,000,000 Mexican-Americans in the Southwest who have problems with education and employment, more serious in some cases than those suffered by Negroes. It is evident that various forms of discrimination are major causes of these problems.

In recent years, many Mexican-Americans have become more vocal in defining the problems and demanding that society act responsibly toward all its citizens. Understandably, much of the current discussion about Mexican-American problems emanates from metropolitan Los Angeles where the largest concentration of Mexican-Americans within the United States resides.

The 1960 census reported that more than 6,000,000 persons lived in Los Angeles County and at that time the Spanish surname population was the largest minority group with about 10 per cent of the total. In East Los Angeles, the Spanish surname population was 70,802 or 67.1 per cent. This group has continued to grow as shown by the Special Census in 1965; in East Los Angeles 76 of every 100 residents in 1965 were Mexican-American. The Mexican-American population of East Los Angeles advanced by 6 per cent between 1960 and 1965, while the area's total population declined by 8 per cent.

Approximately one-fourth to one-third of the total population is Mexican-American in 11 areas outside East Los Angeles: San Fernando, Pacoima, Wilmington, University, Wholesale, Elysian Park, Mount Washington, La Puente, Pico Rivera, Montebello, and Terminal Island. Seven of these areas are close to the East Los Angeles region. In spite of these concentrations, the Mexican-American population is widely distributed throughout the county; in 23 areas surveyed in the county, the Spanish surname population accounts for 10 to 20 per cent of the total. In 29 additional areas it is 5 to 9 per cent of the total. There is no area from which Spanish surname people are completely absent and only 12 areas where they account for less than 2 per cent of the total.

According to the 1960 census, the Spanish surname population ranked below the county averages in many socioeconomic characteristics, such as income, employment, housing, and education. Median family income was $5,762 as compared to

$7,287 for other whites. Twenty-five per cent of all families had an annual income below $4,000; slightly less than 10 per cent had incomes below $2,000 a year. The 1965 unemployment rate for males was 7.6 per cent, about two percentage points higher than the county average. Fewer than half of all Spanish surname families owned their own homes in 1960. Median value of these owner-occupied homes was $13,000, $2,900 below the county average of $15,900. More than half, 54.6 per cent, of all units occupied by Spanish surname families and individuals were built before 1950 and one-fifth were classified as dilapidated or deteriorated.

The 1960 census also reported comparative scholastic achievement for persons over twenty-five years old. In California, the median school years completed for Spanish surname persons was 8.6; the comparative figure for Anglo Americans was 12.1 and for nonwhites, 10.5.

According to California's first public school racial census, released in March, 1967, by the State Department of Education, 57 per cent of the Spanish surname students in districts with more than 50,000 enrollment attended "minority schools." The Department defined a minority school as one which fails to come within 15 per cent of matching the proportion of minority students in the school district as a whole. For example, if a school district has a total minority student enrollment of 35 per cent, a school in that district with more than 50 per cent minority students would be considered a "minority school."

In East Los Angeles where more than 76 per cent of the population is Mexican-American, approximately 7 per cent, according to the 1960 census, had no schooling at all and less than 9 per cent had completed even one year of college.

According to a 1965-66 survey undertaken by the Los Angeles City School System, the two high schools with the highest dropout rates were the predominantly Mexican-American schools—Garfield, where the dropout rate was 53.8 per cent, and Roosevelt, with a 47.5 per cent dropout rate. In contrast, two Westside schools, Palisades and Monroe, had dropout rates of 3.1 per cent and 2.6 per cent respectively.

Mexican-American enrollment in California colleges is extremely low. At the University of California at Los Angeles there were fewer Mexican-Americans enrolled in 1967—less than 70—then there were ten years before despite the huge enrollment increase. At the University of California at Berkeley there were approximately 70 Mexican-American students in a student body of more than 25,000. Even at California State College at Los Angeles, in the heart of the nation's largest Mexican-American community, there were only 200 Spanish-speaking students out of a student population of 22,000. While Mexican-American students comprise 13.6 per cent of California's public school population, they comprise less than one per cent of its college student population.

Summary

During the open meeting, the Committee heard many parents, students, and community leaders complain about the inadequacies of the public schools.

Lack of knowledge and concern about the Mexican-American stifled effective communication between the school system and its minority constituency, the Committee learned.

Administrators claimed that parents do not care and parents claimed that they are not properly informed or involved. In spite of some recent progress, there are still schools that do not provide staff capable of communicating with non-English-speaking parents. Because of this, communication between parents and schools is minimal.

Community leaders stressed the fact that students were frustrated by the apparent indifference of administrators and teachers. Parents claimed that the schools were staffed by poorly qualified teachers who rejected and made no effort to understand their children.

The curriculum was considered inadequate for job preparation and irrelevant to the needs of the students. It was charged that disproportionate numbers of Mexican-Americans are placed in classes for the mentally retarded because they could not cope with the placement tests given in English; textbooks fail to represent the positive contributions Spanish surname citizens have made to our society. Frustrated and misunderstood, Mexican-American children are rushed through, pushed out, or drop out.

With the exception of Head Start, all special programs operating to assist the Mexican-American are directly controlled by the school system. Since most of these programs such as English as a Second Language and New Horizons use Federal and state funds rather than general operating funds, their expansion and continuity depend on efforts or funding outside the school system. In other words, the local school system makes no plans to support these special programs should outside funding fail, nor are any efforts made beyond minimal Federally funded demonstration programs. Few as they are, the most encouraging programs are those which encourage parent and student participation in planning and implementation.

The Committee was told that the education problems of Mexican-Americans and their solutions have only recently been of concern to school policy makers and administrators. In fact, the parents and community leaders have only recently recognized that the public schools are failing to provide adequate education for the Mexican-American child.

Marcus de Leon, president of the Association of Mexican-American Educators, summarized the position of Mexican-American teachers and parents: "We can no longer stand by and accept the point of view that considers this population as culturally deprived or disadvantaged simply because its value system and language are different."

Recommendations

The following recommendations to the U.S. Commission on Civil Rights are based on the findings in this report as well as additional information gathered by Committee members subsequent to the open meeting.

The recent passage of the Bilingual Education Act—Title VII of the Elementary and Secondary Education Amendments of 1967—has added a new dimension to the opportunities of the Mexican-American community in the area of bilingual, bicultural education. Bilingual education measures have also been enacted in California. These developments call for an in-depth reconsideration of the role of the school system, the parent, the community, and the student in the educational process of bilingual, bicultural students, and the development and implementation of new and comprehensive programs.

Although the recommendations are directed to the Federal Government, the Committee feels that a major responsibility for alleviating many of the legitimate problems described in this report rests fundamentally with the citizens and school and government officials of the State of California and especially with those of the

County of Los Angeles. Therefore, the Committee has included Suggestions for Action for consideration by state and local authorities.

The California State Advisory Committee recommends that the U.S. Commission on Civil Rights:

1. Recommend to the President and the Congress that adequate appropriations under Title VII of the Elementary and Secondary Education Amendments of 1967 be provided for programs to study the implications of the bilingual, bicultural approach to education methods and techniques.

   a) That the results of such research be made immediately available to policy makers at the Federal, state, and local levels so that they will be in a better position to understand the special needs of Mexican-Americans.
   b) That the implications of such a study be incorporated into federally sponsored pre-service and in-service training programs for teachers and counselors.
   c) That the developments of curriculum materials based on the bilingual concept be supported with Federal funds.

2. Recommend to the Department of Health, Education, and Welfare, Office of Education:

   a) That existing programs be monitored to assure that they are:
      1) meaningfully combating the problems;
      2) reaching the designated target group; and
      3) involving the community in decision making on educational policy.
   b) That federally sponsored teacher-training programs encourage the recruitment of Mexican-Americans by offering incentives for bilingual abilities.
   c) That an education program for administrators, teachers, and community members be developed to show the damage resulting from isolated education and the advantages for all groups of integrated education.
   d) That national, standardized testing instruments be re-examined for cultural bias and that the development of bilingual, bicultural tests be sponsored by Federal contract.
   e) That current vocational education programs re-evaluate their curricula and methods to meet the special needs of Mexican-Americans, especially the potential dropouts.
   f) That the U.S. Office of Education, Mexican-American Unit, and the regional laboratories in the Southwest be given the authority and funds to explore and develop the above recommendations.

Suggestions for State and Local Action

The California State Advisory Committee offers the following suggestions for the consideration of state and local authorities:

1. Acquire textbooks and supplementary materials which portray a positive and truthful image of the Mexican-American, his history, and his contributions to American culture.

2. Increase the number of bilingual and English as a Second Language (ESL) programs and encourage the involvement of both Mexican-Americans and Anglos in the bilingual efforts.

3. Re-evaluate the qualification and certification requirements at the state and local levels and at the state universities and colleges, and include the following provisions:

a) A complete re-evaluation of teacher preparation should be made with special emphasis on preparation for teaching in disadvantaged areas.

b) Make incentives available to encourage more Mexican-Americans to complete higher education and join the teaching profession.

c) Grant credits toward certification for bilingual abilities and salary incentives for all teachers with bilingual ability.

d) Make bilingual ability a mandatory requirement for teachers and counselors working in schools with a large bilingual and non-English-speaking student body.

4. Because of the widespread concern in Southern California with the indiscriminate placement of Mexican-American children in educable mentally retarded classes, the Advisory Committee feels that this valid concern must be dealt with and recommends that there be a re-evaluation of the testing instruments and the placement procedures of students in the special education and the educable mentally retarded classes. The content and methods used in these classes should also be re-evaluated.

5. Seek adequate funds from the California Legislature to finance the recently enacted bilingual bill, including a study of its impact to determine whether local school districts are improving their ability to teach Spanish-speaking students.

6. Establish at the state level an analytical apparatus to explore the cultural isolation of the Mexican-American and the implications of this isolation for his survival in the education system. (This activity might be related to the state's annual racial census data currently being collected.)

7. The Committee, recognizing that the schools are not relating to the communities which they are supposed to serve, recommends that joint planning seminars and community meetings be instituted to bridge the gap between the schools and the community. Such seminars would enable parents and community residents to discuss education problems and concerns with school personnel and would encourage communication and combat the cultural isolation of the Mexican-American in the barrio.

8. Stimulate greater parent and community participation through such devices as paraprofessionals, teachers' aides, adult education programs, and community meetings. Each school should form a Community Advisory Committee which would represent the total ethnic and socioeconomic composition of the student body. In schools with Spanish-speaking students, the Community Advisory Committee should have bilingual representation.

Political Bigotry and Discrimination: Crisis in Suburbia— A Case of Political Anti-Semitism

While racial issues, particularly those involving the black community, have dominated the national scene, inter-religious difficulties have also been of concern to group relations agencies and practitioners, as have problems of specific religious groups. Professionals ask themselves whether the problem of anti-Semitism has been eliminated in this country or whether it has merely receded into the background, to emerge in full virulence at a more opportune time. Political anti-Semitism, a long-standing phenomenon, has erupted sporadically in various communities over the past several years. There is the question of how to deal with outbreaks of anti-Semitism—whether one should fight fire with fire by exposing the bigots, or quarantine and isolate them in order to block out their influence.

Does the rising socio-economic status of the American Jew make his position in American society more or less secure? Does his consistent liberal position on political and social issues make him particularly vulnerable to attack from the right? Does the recent conflict between Jew and black, typified by the teachers' strike in New York City and the pressure on the Jewish ghetto merchant, weaken Jewish support and give fuel to the fire of anti-Semitism? Whose responsibility is it to act on these matters?

Safeguarding the rights and prerogatives of religious minorities has been a continuing responsibility of group relations agencies. Interreligious problems involve such matters as Bible reading in the schools, birth control policies, use of public school funds and facilities for religious education, Christmas celebrations in the schools and other public institutions, service in the armed forces for religious pacifists, etc. Political anti-Semitism, a peculiar form of religious discrimination, is reflected in the account which follows. The authors glean a lesson from the incident. Some readers may perhaps draw a different one.

* * *

School board elections are normally the dullest, least publicized, and most uncontested elections in American politics. Rarely do more than the most dedicated voters appear at the polls. Yet, in February, 1967, such an election in the previously obscure township of Wayne, New Jersey, suddenly attracted nationwide news coverage. A responsible public official had transformed a typical humdrum campaign into the first significant outbreak of overt anti-Semitic electioneering in America for some years.

In the Wayne election, five candidates were running for three vacancies on the school board. Two of the candidates were Jews, one of whom was an incumbent. One week before the election, both Jewish candidates were singled out for attack in a newspaper interview by Newton Miller, school board vice-president:

"Most Jewish people are liberals, especially when it comes to spending for education. If Kraus and Mandell are elected . . . and Fred Lafer [a Jewish board member not up for election] is in for two more years, that's a three-to-six vote. It would only take two more votes for a majority, and Wayne would be in real financial trouble.

"Two more votes and we lose what is left of Christ in our Christmas celebrations in our schools. Think of it."

During the last week of the campaign, despite a furor which included his censure by both the school board and the township council, the publication of dozens of sharp protests by officials and clergymen, and coverage by national press and network television, Miller apologized but refused to retract his statement.

On Election Day public leaders and officials in Wayne, Jewish and Christian alike, were confident that the injection of prejudice would be overwhelmingly repudiated at the polls. "Open political anti-Semitism simply is no longer tolerated in American life," was the way one observer put it. It seemed a reasonable judgment.

But when the votes were counted the two Jewish candidates had been buried under a landslide as had the proposed school budget. And so this rapidly growing bedroom community of more than 45,000 people, only twenty miles from New York City, raised once more the specter of political anti-Semitism in America. It couldn't happen here, but it did. Could it happen elsewhere?

The authors, both of whom are participating in the University of California Five-Year Study of Anti-Semitism, immediately went to Wayne to see if there was any clear answer to this question. After talking to leaders, officials, clergymen, teachers, and knocking on doors and interviewing voters, a coherent picture began to emerge. The factors which led to the anti-Jewish voting in Wayne were neither bizarre nor altogether idiosyncratic. Perhaps a similar event could not occur everywhere, but it seems very probably that it could occur in any of the hundreds of American towns that are much like Wayne. This makes the lesson of Wayne extremely important, if future Waynes are to be prevented.

To account for what happened in Wayne, three classes of factors must be isolated, understood, and assembled:

1. The historical and structural strains present in the community;
2. The actual precipitating events;
3. The process by which various sectors of the community came to form conflicting definitions of the situation.

From *It DID Happen Here, An Investigation of Political Anti-Semitism: Wayne, New Jersey, 1967,* by Rodney Stark and Stephen Steinberg. A pamphlet published by the Anti-Defamation League of B'nai B'rith, New York, 1967.

The Precipitating Events

The Courts Break the Covenant

In retrospect, the first precipitating event of the Wayne affair came in the late spring of 1966, when the New Jersey courts invalidated restrictive covenants in Packanack Lake, one of the two lake communities. Suit was initiated by two Protestant residents. The case for the plaintiffs revealed the elaborate mechanisms by which the "wrong" people were systematically excluded from either joining the club or buying property in the surrounding area.

The reaction of residents within their lake sanctuaries was strong and fearful. The fear was partly economic. Housing values in these communities are reputed to be considerably above the actual physical worth of the homes. Some portion of this inflation is based on the intangibles of exclusiveness and fashionableness, which are a direct function of the discrimination practiced.

The court action was regarded as a threat to this inflation. This threat was especially acute because it raised more than the specter of paper devaluation. Local consensus is that the lake community dwellings change hands once every five years. For such transients, changes in the resale prices of homes represent a tangible economic fact.

It is hard to determine whether anxiety over the loss of the covenant influenced the way lake community residents responded to the dispute over anti-Semitism in the school election. That they were fearful and upset by the court decision was reflected in their community newsletters at the time, but these sentiments may have played no direct role in the subsequent voting. Still it seems reasonable to assume that it did at least make them a bit less willing to oppose anti-Semitism. It seems revealing that while Jack Mandell ran a stronger race in Packanack Lake than in other districts when he was first elected to the school board, he was overwhelmingly rejected by this same district in the most recent election. He was a Jew both times.

Christmas Carols

A slight misunderstanding over Christmas carols in the schools seems to have played only a very minor role in shaping Wayne public opinion, but it perhaps played a major role in prompting Newton Miller's anti-Semitic statement.

Shortly before Christmas the local rabbi met with the Superintendent of Schools to discuss the kinds of Christmas carols appropriate for classroom singing. The fact of their meeting leaked to a local reporter and appeared in the paper giving the impression that there was a dispute going on over Christmas carols. Subsequently, the purpose of the meeting was clarified by the paper and the matter apparently ended.

When questioned later few residents of Wayne recalled that there had been such an event—the circulation of the paper in which the story appeared is not high—and the affair probably had very little impact except among those especially informed about school activities. However, the misunderstanding did appear to disturb Newton Miller at the time. He is reported to have wondered whether there would be any further difficulties over religion in the schools. One can only conjecture whether this event had some effect on him two months later when he drafted his gratuitous and now notorious statement mentioning a Jewish threat to Christ in Christmas.

The School Campaign

Newton Miller was engaged in a typical one-man stand against the rest of the school board over the proposed budget as 1967 began. Furthermore, although more than 100 of Wayne's teachers had threatened resignation this spring unless their pay was made comparable with that of surrounding communities, Miller demanded substantial cuts in faculty salaries. In his years on the board, the forty-seven-year-old Bell Telephone employee has conducted a personal crusade to slash spending to the bone. For nearly two years he singlehandedly blocked construction of a new high school. He has also conducted an unsuccessful campaign for teacher loyalty oaths. Several years ago, his behavior and statements provoked the school board to censure him.

All other members of the board, and all candidates save one, favored this year's $8½-million budget proposal. Considering Wayne's phenomenal student explosion and the fact that the community spends proportionately less on education than do surrounding towns, this near unanimity suggests, if anything, a modest budget proposal.

Of the five candidates for the three school board vacancies, only Jack McLaughlin opposed the budget. McLaughlin once served on the board, but had been defeated in each of the past two years in efforts to regain his seat. In past elections he had experimented with several different images. This time he was running as a fiscal conservative. But it was hard to tell that he was running at all.

School board and budget elections in Wayne are fought out at dozens of coffee parties held day and night during the weeks before the voting. It is customary for all candidates to appear at each of these coffee hours, in homes throughout the community, and explain their ideas for education in Wayne. In this campaign all went pretty much as usual except that while four of the five candidates regularly attended these meeting, Jack McLaughlin chose to keep out of sight. This tactic drew considerable criticism from the community and earned him ridicule in the local paper. One letter to the editor referred to him as the "phantom candidate."

The campaign for the school budget began in deep trouble. Despite nearly universal support from community leaders, the mood in Wayne was anti-spending and the public disputes between the school and the teachers over pay demands added to voter discontent. But according to experienced officials, who fight a campaign like this at least once a year, the budget was beginning to gather support as the campaign progressed. In the past ten years school budgets have been beaten only once (by a narrow margin in 1965) and it began to seem that once again the budget might pass.

A week before the election, with the budget gaining and the conservative candidate behind, Newton Miller intervened. On Monday evening, February 6, he phoned a local columnist and told her he had some thoughts on the campaign that she might want for the paper. As he began to enunciate this concern about Jewish candidates, the columnist grew uneasy. She asked him if he had his remarks written down. Miller said he did, but not typed. She replied that she would come over and pick them up.

The scene that followed, according to the columnist who is a longtime resident of one of the restricted lake communities, would have caused many men to have second thoughts about making such a statement public. But not Miller. She finally asked him to sign his statement, which he did willingly, and then she took it back to the paper. Tuesday morning she dumped the whole thing on her editor's desk. He immediately recognized the sensational possibilities of the story and Miller's remarks were splashed across page one of the newspaper that afternoon, under the headline: "MILLER WARNS: DON't PUT MANDELL, KRAUS ON BOARD."

The Reaction

The next day, Wednesday, brought an avalanche of reaction. With one voice, responsible civic and religious leaders deplored Miller's remarks as anti-Semitic, and many called for his immediate resignation. The newspaper filled Pages One and Two with the denunciations, giving only scant space to a major local blizzard that had brought twelve inches of snow the preceding day. Some typical examples were:

"Mr. Miller has gone off the deep end this time . . . [his statements] are so far off base that they are impossible to give credence to. They are ridiculous and shameless." George Schroeder, president of the school board.

"It's despicable." David Caliri, incumbent school board candidate.

"I deplore this kind of statement. There is no place for an appeal to prejudice." Richard Davis, candidate for the school board.

"These comments are uncalled for." Leonard Pine, councilman.

"I cannot put into words my reaction to this statement by Newton Miller. . . . I am sick over this. I cannot understand bringing religion into this." Andrew Militello, president of the Wayne P.T.A.

Miller, in the face of the potent condemnation that greeted his original statement, tried to call the whole thing misquotation and misunderstanding. Yet, when asked, he reaffirmed the truth of his statements.

By Thursday the national press began to staff the story and the tranquility of the local neighborhoods was interrupted by prowling reporters and television crews. Reactions deploring Miller's remarks began to pour in from farther away, from U.S. Senators Clifford Case and Harrison Williams, and from other political and religious leaders.

That night a dramatic scene unfolded at an emergency school board meeting. Before an emotional crowd of more than 500 townspeople, and the national press corps (while three network television crews filmed the meeting), the school board voted 8 to 1 to "censure Mr. Miller's appeal to bigotry" and called for his resignation. Miller himself cast the lone vote against censure and refused to resign, but rather promised to "serve out my term and do the job I was elected to do for the people of Wayne."

Following the vote, obviously shaken and mystified by the widespread condemnation, Miller rose to deny that he was prejudiced or that his press release had appealed to anti-Semitism. He said he was "truly sorry for the incident," and declared he was prepared to eat "humble crow" [sic]. Yet he refused to retract his original statement. Instead he repeatedly defended it as true, but misinterpreted. To demonstrate his lack of prejudice, he pointed to the fact that he had good friends who were Jews. As evidence he repeatedly referred to his friendship with fellow board member Jack Mandell, one of the two he had attacked in his statement.

Finally, Mandell could endure it no longer. Speaking up for the first time, he turned to Miller, seated next to him, and said quietly, "Newt, you're right. We have been friends. But it grieves me to tell you that you are an anti-Semite and a bigot."

The crowd applauded, while Mrs. Carl Yoder, a board member, wept silently.

Later, Mandell recalled that he had meant to keep silent because he felt that basically anti-Semitism "is a Christian problem," and it was up to the Christians to oppose it. But Miller's performance changed that. "I knew when I spoke that I well may have been jeopardizing my candidacy. But the eyes and ears of the nation were literally upon us and bigger issues were involved. This man had to be told that simply having friendly relations with a few Jews did not exonerate him."

Outside the hall a local history teacher walked a one-man picket line with a placard: "REPUDIATE ANTI-SEMITISM." A few others circulated a petition asking Governor Richard Hughes to take whatever steps he could to remove Miller from office.

As the meeting broke up, Miller continued to deny that he had meant to cause trouble or to imply anti-Semitism. But he still insisted that his statements were essentially accurate if "correctly understood."

From then on through election night the public outcry increased. The newsmen and TV crews continued to roam the city, and more and more public leaders issued statements decrying bigotry. Wayne had become a seven-day wonder. Each morning residents read new dispatches about their town in the New York as well as local papers and in the evening they watched reports from Wayne on nationwide television news programs.

The town was turning bright red in the glare of press exposure. And it hurt. "My God, they are making a wonderful town sound like Germany, it'll never get its good name back," one resident complained.

The Vote

Condemnations of Miller continued to pour in. In the face of this swift and uniform response by civic and religious leaders, both from Wayne and elsewhere, the outcome of the election seemed certain. As one veteran local observer put it: "Frankly, from the moment I heard about it until the votes were in, I was absolutely certain the Jewish candidates would be elected and that the budget would be a shoo-in. I said to myself, 'Newt has just done the budget the biggest possible favor.' I also thought Miller had committed political suicide. I was sure that you just can't get away with open political anti-Semitism in America anymore." No one, including the Jewish candidates, questioned his logic.

But the voters turned this universal confidence among civic leaders into a shambles. The two Jewish candidates were overwhelmingly defeated, while Jack McLaughlin and two pro-budget candidates were swept in. The school budget lost by a three-to-one margin.

An analysis of the returns makes it clear that the voting singled out the Jews and could not be attributed to a taxpayers' rebellion.

There were apparently three main patterns of voting. A small proportion of voters obviously voted only for the fiscal conservative. But the rest voted for three candidates. A minority cast their ballots for the two Jewish candidates and for David Caliri, a liberal incumbent. A much larger bloc voted for the three non-Jewish candidates: McLaughlin, Davis, and Caliri. Caliri received the most votes because, as one local observer commented, "He was everyone's third man."

How can one be sure that the voting was anti-Jewish? Recall that Jack McLaughlin had not attended the normal campaign functions. His candidacy, which had failed in each of the past two years, was considered a joke before the crisis over anti-Semitism occurred. Yet, he was number two behind Caliri. Richard Davis, the third candidate elected, had also been considered out of the running. He had failed to create any significant public image, though he had favored the school budget.

The fact that his own children attended parochial schools created questions in the minds of many voters as to why he wanted to be an overseer of the public school system. This was perhaps another sympton of Wayne's underlying religious prejudice.

Prior to the crisis, the local consensus was that the two Jews and David Caliri were overwhelming favorites. But when the votes were counted it was not even close. The two Jewish candidates trailed the field by a better than two-to-one margin.

Why were the election forecasts of the civic leaders, the candidates, the press, and school officials dead wrong? Were the people of Wayne undeterred, indeed attracted, by open anti-Semitism despite unanimous condemnation by their leaders? Is the veneer of public tolerance so thin that the slightest public provocation releases an uncontrollable backlash? Just what did Wayne voters have in mind when they cast their ballots?

The answers to these questions seem relatively clear, but not simple. They are intimately connected with the complex character of contemporary American attitudes toward Jews and to differences in public conceptions of what anti-Semitism *is*.

What Should Have Been Done?

Much of what happened in Wayne was the result of an inability of people to know anti-Semitism when they saw it. As a result they saw Miller as a victim. Had Newton Miller's statement been ignored little might have happened in the election.

However, let no one assume that for this reason it should have been ignored. It would have been utterly foolish to have let the matter pass unprotested. We have moved from a norm of dark gray to light gray anti-Semitism in America precisely because prejudice has been hotly opposed and identified as evil. Thirty years ago polls showed that a substantial number of Americans were attracted to a political candidate who proposed to "do something about the Jews." Today, very few Americans find this attractive.

Had Newton Miller merely been some local citizen with a preoccupation about Jews, he could have, and probably would have, been ignored. But when men holding elective office make such remarks they must be opposed lest prejudice become socially acceptable once more. For progress in human relations depends not upon "peace in our time," but on protest. Indeed, part of the inability of the people of Wayne to detect the anti-Semitism in Miller's statement stems from the fact that past incidents and the open sore of discrimination had not been sufficiently protested. Consequently, the people of Wayne had not previously been forced to ask themselves about prejudice and its implications.

But protest is useless if it does not educate, and when it finally came in Wayne it did not. The leaders who spoke out against Newton Miller were insensitive to the fact that neither the general public nor Miller himself recognized the anti-Semitism in his charges. Thus, the reaction assumed that anyone who denied the anti-Semitism in Miller's remarks, including Miller, must in his heart be a bigot. As a result the attack on Miller was both harsh and unenlightening, and the citizens of Wayne were angered rather than educated.

The lesson of Wayne, in our judgment, is that the widely used techniques for opposing prejudice have been made obsolete to some extent by their own past success. Until recently, outbreaks of anti-Semitism in America were virtually always of the black or at least dark gray variety. We have learned to deal effectively with such episodes and it is probably the case that today any public figure who engages in virulent prejudice insures his own immediate ruin. Indeed, had Newton Miller spoken like a true hate merchant the people in Wayne would almost certainly have risen up in wrath against him.

But Miller is not a hate merchant, and the Wayne affair was not an outbreak of virulent anti-Semitism. The methods which in the past have been so effective in opposing virulence, and which have greatly helped to eliminate black and dark gray anti-Semitism from political life, are probably self-defeating when applied to incidents of light gray anti-Semitism.

The response of public spokesmen to Newton Miller was ineffective because it was inappropriate. Instead of an attack upon Miller, the reactions should have tried to inform and educate both Miller and the people of Wayne. It was essential to help people understand why these statements were prejudiced, and why such charges are intolerable in American politics. Newton Miller's outburst could perhaps have been deactivated, and made into an important lesson for the general public, by dispassionate analysis, firm, but not angry. Instead, Miller was inadvertently made into a folk hero through condemnation and outrage.

If a similar situation arises in other towns like Wayne, and if the response is again one of outrage that does not inform, the same tragedy will be re-enacted. Unless we learn from Wayne, it can happen again.

PART II

GROUP IDENTITY
AND POWER

*Fostering the Growth of Resources, Power
and Self-Identity Among Ethnic
Communities*

The Role of the White Worker in the Ethnic Community: The Relationship of the White Worker to the Black Power Movement

With increasing frequency the question has been asked, "What should be the role of the white worker in the "ghetto" or in the "barrio" or on the reservation. During the heyday of the civil rights movement of the 1950's and early 1960's, whites were welcomed into black organizations and indeed gave leadership in many. As the Black Power theme became more prominent, there was a trend to dismiss whites as an inhibiting factor in the development of black self-assertion and self-reliance. A number of perplexing issues come to light concerning this question. Should whites be excluded altogether or should they be used in limited, specialized roles? While whites may be counterproductive in leadership roles or in directing organizational drives, they do represent needed manpower resources and might be utilized productively in supportive roles, behind the scenes, and in technical assistance and advisory capacities. Indeed, it may not be the role which one plays but the sensitivity and conviction with which it is performed. Do specific circumstances or programs signify when whites should or should not be involved? Does the exclusion of whites in certain ethnic and racial movements represent a general principle or does it apply to certain stages of development through which these groups are passing?

The narrative below follows the career of a young social worker who enters a somewhat disorganized ghetto community and begins to organize for Black Power. His activities and the stages through which he passed are highly instructive for examining the issue at hand. Would the possibility of his success have been different if he had performed in a different way?

Is there a role in the black ghetto for a white community organizer? Two years ago, Don Roose, former executive director of the Robert Wade Neighborhood House in Chester, said Yes. Today, No.

From an unpublished manuscript by Joseph R. Zelnik on the activities of Don and Barbara Roose in Chester, Pa. Used by permission.

What, then, for a young man, thirty-one, who had decided to dedicate his life to freeing the oppressed? Roose is not sure. But at this moment, he is in Bolivia working for an international child welfare agency, seeking to create opportunities for young people with limited life chances.

Roose put twenty-six months of his life into Chester, a city of 60,000—50 per cent black—repeatedly called "a microcosm of the nation's urban ills." The same problems which seem to defy solution in Philadelphia, New York, Cleveland, Chicago, and almost every urban area in the country, exist in Chester.

Roose had some successes and some failures. But in the end, his ultimate achievement was that the city's black leaders wanted to take over their own programs, without any help from a white man. In a sense, Roose was a victim of his own "success."

Roose's dilemma from the start was that if he did not speak out on social issues, no one would. But when he did, there was always the danger that he was holding back the black residents who should have been taking the lead.

When, in the summer of 1968, the Black Power movement finally bore fruit in Chester, Roose could claim to welcome it and point to his accomplishments at Wade House as part of the new movement.

Besides, after twenty-six months of crisis, confrontation, criticism, and controversy—always controversy—Don Roose was lonely. Chester's black ghetto today can be a lonely place for a white man—friend as well as foe.

In his classes at the Graduate School of Social Work of the University of Michigan, Roose heard of Chester, Pennsylvania, six months before he would see it. One of the required readings was an analysis of the role the Students for a Democratic Society (SDS) at Swarthmore College played in Chester's school demonstrations of 1963-64, led by Stanley Branche's Committee for Freedom Now. In May of 1966, Roose received his master's degree in social work and placed a "Situation Wanted" ad in the *National Association of Social Workers Personnel Information*.

The spring of 1966 was a bad time for the United States, but a good time for job-hunting social workers. Roose received twenty-four replies to his ad and narrowed them to Yonkers, N.Y., and Chester, Pa.

On May 22, his twenty-ninth birthday, Roose flew to Chester for the weekend. He stayed with Alan Hunt of Swarthmore, prominent Quaker, chairman of the Civil Liberties Committee of the Philadelphia Yearly Meeting of the Religious Society of Friends, and Wade House chairman. Wade House officials gave Roose a quick automobile tour of Chester, then took him back to stately Swarthmore. The next day, Roose returned to the city on his own. "Chester was obviously sick," recollects Roose, "which meant it was a good town to organize." Before Roose would accept the position of executive director, Roose wanted his wife to see the community. He and Barbara returned in mid-June. Roose toured the agencies that should have been involved. He found CFN relatively inactive, the NAACP and CORE stagnant, and the Chester Home Improvement Project (CHIP) dealing in nothing more than clean-up, paint-up, fix-up projects.

Roose explained to the Wade House board that he believed in the "strategy of conflict" as opposed to consensus. "I laid it on the table," he said. "My wife and I were pretty radical at that point. I made it clear to the board that there would be many controversial issues on which I would have to take a stand." Some board members may have been nervous, but Wade House hired him.

Robert Wade Neighborhood House in Chester was a little-noted institution in Chester in the summer of 1966. The hiring of Roose did not even warrant a news item in the local newspaper, the Delaware County *Daily Times*. Twenty-two months later, on May 22, 1968—Roose's birthday again—the paper's publisher would forbid him from ever entering the Times building.

But only the sharp-eyed in the community would hear about Roose until more than a month after he began his new job. Only those who read the letters column in the *Daily Times* would have learned that a young man who would become the city's most controversial figure was on his way. Roose had subscribed to the paper from Toledo, Ohio, in order to become acquainted with the community. On July 2, 1966, a short letter to the editor from Roose commented on a *Daily Times* story which compared school facilities in the city's white and nonwhite schools.

"As a professional social worker," wrote Roose, "who will, by choice, soon move into the city of Chester to live, work and become part of the community, this type of responsible news coverage is to be commended." A typographical error resulted in the signature being "Dan" D. Roose. It was probably the last time anyone in Chester would mistake his name.

Robert Wade Neighborhood House had been a safe, noncontroversial settlement house known primarily for its excellent day care center. It was named for Robert Wade, a Quaker who came from England to Upland in 1675. The story has it that William Penn, who made his first landing in Pennsylvania in 1682 at what was to be Chester, "proceeded to the house of Robert Wade, the hospital Friend, and attended a meeting for worship there." The first Society of Friends meeting house was built on Market Street in Chester in 1736. The building endured, but the neighborhood went downhill and in the 1940's was part of the infamous Bethel Court, internationally known red light district. The Chester Meeting of Friends moved to its more desirable location at 24th and Chestnut and converted the Market Street structure into the Robert Wade Neighborhood House in 1942. Its purpose was "to promote leisure time activities for all age groups and both sexes in Chester." The programs included Golden Agers, a mothers' club and scouting. But the building fell victim in 1961 to the city's first urban renewal project. So the Friends purchased the Franklin Fire House at 217 Concord Avenue and it became the new Robert Wade Neighborhood House. A charter from the county attempted to minimize any religious connotations. It identified Wade as "a neighborhood settlement house." But the programs continued to be such safe offerings as baskets for the needy and basketballs for the youth. Any doubts as to whether Roose would continue this type of operation should have been settled in those first days when Roose moved in. A 2-foot-by-3-foot photo of Malcolm X was hung in his office, clearly dominating the scene.

Although Roose was to affect Wade House programs significantly, his key impact on the day care program was to integrate it—his youngest son, Daniel, would attend two days a week, the only white among fifty-five children.

The Rooses moved in August—sight unseen (Hunt's wife, Margot, had found them the house) into a duplex at 22 W. Elkington in the predominantly white First Ward. They were adjacent to the Chester Park and almost across the street from Mrs. Frances P. Donahoo, Republican committeewoman and former school board director for whom the city school directors were to name the unbuilt new high school twenty-two months later, a decision which caused considerable furor. The Rooses' first reaction to the pleasant neighborhood was astonishment at the number of large dogs—many of them police dogs—which the Rooses interpreted as a sign of fear in the community.

Within a month, two events within two days would bring Roose into the public eye, a position in which he would remain.

A *Daily Times* article of September 10, complete with a picture of a smiling, bearded, pipe-smoking Roose in front of Wade House, told the community exactly what Roose was doing there.

And a fire September 12 burned to death a sixty-two-year-old black woman living in an old garage at 212 W. Mary Street, 30 feet from Roose's office. The dwelling had been ordered vacated almost three months earlier, in June. Yet rent had been collected through August 31 by the landlord, Mrs. Sadie Pileggi, an aunt of school board member Francis F. Pileggi. It was the third fatal fire in the ghetto that year and was to be the catharsis that would infuriate the black community and start a new era for Wade House and CHIP.

The September 10 *Daily Times* article by Jack Hopkins laid it on the line for those who would never enter Roose's office and see the portrait of Malcolm. Roose, it reported, was a community organizer who opposed the war in Vietnam and endorsed Black Power. Neither of those positions, although acceptable in many places today, depending on one's definition of Black Power, was calculated to impress Chester's establishment in September, 1966.

In the article, Roose announced his opposition to violence and riots, on everyone's mind at the time, but charged "society" was responsible for them and "at least" they pointed out the inequalities suffered by the poor.

"We are organizing for power," he said. "And by power I mean that the residents as groups, block clubs or larger organizations should have a real gut voice in decision making in all areas that affect their lives, that they have a voice in the decision making when it comes to housing conditions, educational services in the city, public and private agencies . . . everything."

He did not limit his campaign to blacks: "The Negro poor people and the white poor people can work together," he said. "There are issues that affect them both. I believe 100 per cent in Black Power and 100 per cent in poor power. The poor have been denied everything and then the white power structure is upset by two words—Black Power—said by one guy, Stokely Carmichael."

Roose offered what he called "participatory democracy" as an answer to urban disorders. "The alternative [to riots] is organizing the poor. But who will organize them? Civil Rights? The Communists? Democrats? Republicans? Maybe the poor themselves. That's why I'm here. Let the poor get organized themselves. If we must have an 'ism,' let's have 'poorism.'"

Roose indicated at that time that he did not believe being white would hamper his efforts. "Whether you are black or white or purple, as a community organizer the residents discover very quickly if you are for real or if you are a fake. That's the key criteria—not the color of your skin."

Only two days later, "the residents"—and the city—had the opportunity to determine if Roose was a fake. The flames that burned Mrs. Pearl Anderson ignited a reaction that spread through the black community. Her death precipitated a citizens' protest that threatened to rival the demonstrations of 1963-64. Civil Rights leader Stanley Branche would speak at Mrs. Anderson's funeral services and charge, "The system killed her." A street rally was planned by militants. Roose conferred with Richard James, CHIP staff worker. CHIP had been formed in 1964. It had been concerned with weekend work camps, clean-up, fix-up, etc. Its only previous link with Wade House had been some financial assistance. But the coordination of the two groups in this crisis were to result in formal ties which would last almost two years.

Fearing that a street rally could lead to rioting, it was decided to take over the gathering and bring it inside Wade House. But there was to be no mitigating the seriousness of the charges. The Wade House-produced leaflets announcing the meeting were headlined: "Another Chester Black Murdered by Slum Housing." They were distributed house to house that afternoon. Shortly before five, Roose received a phone call from Andrew J. Schroder 2nd, president of the United Community Fund of Chester and Vicinity (UCF). Schroder was then a director and executive vice president of the Scott Paper Co. For the Wade House leaflets to get to his desk at Scott's administration building adjacent to the Philadelphia International Airport, by then was at least fast service.

"Welcome to Chester," said Schroder to Roose, who had been there for a month. He got quickly to the point. He understood Wade House was to hold a rally? "We," he said, speaking for UCF, "feel it would be very unfortunate for this to be held under the auspices of Wade House." It was not necessary to point out that $26,000 of the Wade House budget, the major share, came from the UCF. Schroder explained that he feared the gathering could spill over into violence. Roose explained this was exactly the reason it was being moved indoors. Schroder was adamant. He said Wade House would proceed "at its own risk."

If Roose were to copy Richard Nixon and write a book on his "Six Crises," this would have to be one of them. On the job for only a month, he faced a potential riot situation, and a threat from his agency's key financial supporter. Roose called Hunt and an emergency board of directors meeting was scheduled for that night. It was to be the turning point for Robert Wade Neighborhood House. Roose defended his point of view. He said grievances would have to be heard and petitions circulated and delivered to the proper city officials. "This is what community organization is all about," he told the board. The members, acknowledging this could mean the end of UCF assistance, gave him overwhelming support.

The rally was anticlimactic compared the hubbub that preceded it. One hundred attended. There was no violence. The voices were high, but the demands were minimal. They called for enforcement of the city's housing code and demolition of five unsafe houses in the 500 block of W. 2nd Street. The demands were taken to city council. The city agreed to demolish the buildings within ten days. Actual demolition started within thirty days. Seldom has Chester moved so fast on anything. The enforcement of the city's housing code, however, remains an issue to this day.

But Roose had his first success, and it was a significant one. Equally important, the formal alliance of Wade House and CHIP followed, bringing the two organizations into a whole new program of communtiy organization. Finally, the incident was to cost Wade House its UCF support, a blow that would be greeted with mixed emotions.

True to its threat, UCF started an investigation of Wade House that was to last more than six months. Significantly, the allotment committee became a special investigating committee. Roose claims the group never contacted the Wade House board, Wade House staff, or ghetto residents. UCF officials suggested that Wade House disaffiliate with CHIP and that Roose, whom they felt was the major problem, stay with CHIP. The UCF money could continue to go to Wade House, they suggested. The Wade House board declined the offer. Several more meetings in the next month ironed out a compromise. Wade House, marking its twenty-fifth year in the community, and CHIP would be out of UCF, but the Wade House day care center, renamed the Concord Day Care Center, could remain in UCF and receive appropriations equal to what Wade House had received. One of the reasons UCF offered the compromise was to avoid a public fight threatened by Wade House. So, in June, the UCF announced that Wade House was being expelled because it did not "come up to the standards" of the fund. Neither side would comment further. The public could only guess at the behind-the-scenes controversy.

In retrospect, Wade House officials looked at the loss of UCF support as a mixed blessing. First, it was no longer handicapped by affiliation with a major money source which demanded safe programs. Second, when the day care center broke away in January, 1968, a half dozen of Wade House's more conservative directors left Wade House for the Day Care Center Board, resulting in a more radical Wade House board lineup. Finally, the dollars and cents question was not as bleak as might be imagined. True, Wade House lost a $26,900 appropriation. But the day care center program had cost some $21,000 of that (its budget had totaled $31,000, of which $10,000 was raised by fees) so that the true loss to Wade House was less than $7,000.

Nevertheless, Wade House looked ahead to a January, 1968, financial situation that was not encouraging. In addition to UCF, its major money sources in 1967 had been only some $10,000 from foundations and $3,000 in individual donations.

Roose did two things. First, he went out to the light blue Wade House book bus and changed its lettering. It had read: "A Chester United Fund Agency Working." Roose painted out the "United Fund" with two red streaks that left it clearly legible, then painted the word "ACTION" about it. This five-minute job brought newspaper publicity (including a picture) and let the public know in no uncertain terms that UCF was no longer assisting. Several phone calls to Roose from UCF officials were made to request the "United Fund" be painted out a little more thoroughly, but Roose was "too busy" to get to that for several months.

This was followed by a financial "appeal" to Wade House "friends." It described the UCF action as "a friendly separation." But it reported that the split of the day care center from Wade House was necessary to save the UCF allotment for the center and still permit Wade House "to continue the kind of direct involvement in gut community issues to which the United Fund took exception. . . ." Wade House pledged "programs that go to the heart of a number of urban ills which we all know to be our country's major domestic problems. The result of a failure to solve these problems will be a national disaster."

Individual donors to Wade House apparently got the message. Their 1968 contributions climbed from a previous $3,000 to $13,000.

For the second source of funds, foundations, Roose sat down at his typewriter and prepared a 68-page proposal. He described what Wade House and CHIP wanted to do, documenting the need for an annual budget of $171,000. Key foundations support had come in the past from the Philadelphia Foundation, and three others. This had totaled some $10,000 in 1967. In 1968, it would go to $18,000.

But new money still had to be found. Roose made the rounds of major foundations and hit pay dirt in New York. The Interreligious Foundation for Community Organization (IFCO), an eight-month-old fondation financed by the Episcopal, Presbyterian, Methodist and American Baptist denominations, awarded CHIP a $56,309 grant to run from May, 1968, to May, 1969. And there was the hint that two more years of similar funding would follow if IFCO was satisfied with the results. IFCO's major previous allocation had gone to Operation Exodus, a project to bus Boston's ghetto children to the suburbs. The IFCO grant to CHIP specified that it was to be used "to develop a community organization program within the ghetto areas of Chester, to realistically deal with neighborhood issues through block clubs and neighborhood councils, and to expand participatory democracy for low-income residents." The words could have been written by Roose himself. Wade House and

CHIP were jubilant. They had come out of the UCF controversy with twice as big a budget as previously. What made Wade House and CHIP happy, of course, was not likely to do the same to Chester's establishment.

Roose, who had come to be synonymous with Wade House and CHIP, had been attacking most of Chester's institutions: city hall, the police, schools.

In November of 1966 he had gone to city council to support a pay boost for police —to the embarrassment of the police—and to urge a police-community relations board to investigate charges of police brutality. He also asked for more housing inspectors and demolition of substandard homes.

By February of 1968, CHIP had eight predominantly Negro block clubs working for housing improvements and one—the Park Terrace Civic Improvement Committee—made up mostly of white families in a lower-middle-class area.

Roose became practically a shadow for John Fitzgerald, director of Chester's urban renewal program. Every time Fitzgerald stood up to explain his program, Roose was there to ask where Fitzgerald intended to relocate those who would be displaced by urban renewal. It was not an easy question to answer. Fitzgerald, one of Mayor James Gorbey's most qualified appointments, could take a half dozen maps and a pointer and by talking very fast, make everything come out just about right. New construction of housing in some areas would come through just in time to accommodate persons being removed from others. Fitzgerald undoubtedly believes this, but even he will admit that the line between success and failure is thin in a city like Chester with an acute shortage of decent housing, especially for low-income blacks with large families.

After Roose asked the same questions enough times, even the Federal Government began asking them. The result was that the city's application for $598,000 in survey and planning funds for the $16,500,000 Waterfront Industrial Urban Renewal Project, an integral part of the over-all program, was rejected in February, 1967, by the Housing and Urban Development Department because of failure to show sufficient relocation. That project would have displaced 620 families.

One of Roose's more interesting controversies with the city came in the summer of 1967 when he demanded that Mayor Gorbey appoint Wade House or CHIP to memberships on the Citizens Council for Urban Renewal (CCUR) and the Demonstration Cities Coordinating Committee (DCCC), the organization planning the city's Federal model cities application. This was right up Roose's alley—the key issue of participation by those involved.

Gorbey ignored several communications from CHIP. Finally when the press got wind of the controversy, the mayor said that, first, he didn't appoint to the boards, just recommend; and second, neither board had any vacancies.

Roose fired back that the mayor's reply was filled with "serious inaccuracies." Actually, neither of the mayor's statements was precisely true. In fact, the mayor's "recommendations" were always accepted. Besides, neither board had a set number of members; others could be added at any time.

The mayor's determination to keep Wade House-CHIP off those boards was made clear days later when a Negro member of CCUR, Rev. J. Pius Barbour, pastor of Calvary Baptist Church, offered to resign his post to facilitate the appointment of Roose. Gorbey, who had said only a few days earlier that he had "no absolute power" over the boards, refused to accept Barbour's resignation.

Roose's statement of June 29 was typical of the kind of charges that so upset the city's establishment.

"They are playing with dynamite," he said, "in not only not encouraging participation of the poor on important city committees, but in fact discouraging participation of the poor on these committees.

"In the year that I have worked and lived in Chester, it is clear that there has been and is now either an overt or covert plan to keep the poor in their place and to prevent the voices of low-income residents from being heard on those decisions which affect their lives.

"The time has come for all those people who agree with this point of view to demand that the poor not only have a voice, but a majority decision-making role on those policy-making boards and committees of programs which are supposed to be for the poor. Specifically, I demand that those citizens of Chester who live in the demonstration city area sit and be a majority on the Chester city-wide model cities committee (DCCC).

"What the mayor is saying is that he is not going to make any appointments until the decisions are made. Are we so deaf in Chester we can't hear the cries of the low-income residents who say they want a decision-making voice in the programs before the decisions are made? We are not asking removal of all the politicians, bankers and industrialists from these city boards. They are part of the community and make valuable contributions and should be represented. But at the same time, if we cruelly co-opt our participation of one-third of Chester's citizens, we can expect continued protest by the low-income community over its powerlessness and the fact that its voice is not being heard."

Gorbey defended the makeup of the committees by pointing out that representatives of the Greater Chester Movement served on both. As for Roose, the mayor, seldom one to hide his feelings, said: "I think his statements are completely irresponsible and more stupid than I gave him credit for. We don't want his recommendations. I think he is here as an agitator. He's completely irresponsible."

Roose indicated he accepted the "agitator" label.

"Agitator" Roose did not limit his agitation to the Chester establishment. Possessing seemingly limitless energy, he also took out after the Greater Chester Movement, Michigan Governor George Romney, the Vietnam war and those who oppressed seasonal farm laborers, not necessarily in that order.

The Rooses' antiwar protests were usually good for newspaper headlines, often pictures. But Roose was always careful to make clear that he acted from conscience and as an individual with no connection to Wade House. For example, when a *Daily Times* story on the PMC penal discussion identified Roose as Wade House director, he wrote a letter to the editor pointing out he attended as a "private citizen."

In retrospect, Roose concedes that his peace activities "turned off Ward One [Chester's predominantly white ward] and also some professional and bourgeois blacks." But both Rooses felt they had no alternative but to speak out on what they considered a vital issue. "How could we talk of domestic social change without relating to the programs being curtailed by the war?" asked Mrs. Roose.

Some members of the public mistakenly assumed war protest to be a normal extra effort by a Quaker-sponsored agency like Wade House. Actually, although a majority of the Wade House board are Quakers, this was not a sign of their approval of Roose's position. As a matter of fact, adverse publicity after the Rooses marched in March, 1967, in support of the Quaker ship *Phoenix,* which had taken medical supplies to North and South Vietnam, caused an emergency meeting of the Wade House board. It agreed that Roose's antiwar activities on his own time were his own business.

The reaction of Roose's neighbors, however, was more typical of Chester as a whole. One neighbor displayed in his window a picture of a sinking sailboat with the caption BOMB THE PHOENIX. Across the street, another neighbor put in his front window the sign: SINK THOSE DRAFT DODGERS.

The Rooses prefer not to talk about the all-white First Ward neighborhood where they lived during their first year in Chester. But they felt no regrets when their lease expired August 1, 1967, and the landlord refused to renew it. The Rooses hoped for an integrated neighborhood, but the critical housing shortage in the city, plus the fact that many realtors looked upon the Rooses as being as undesirable as blacks, made the search difficult. When a row house in the heart of the black community at 419 Jeffrey was found, they quickly took it. It was a move they never regretted. They found a warmth in clear contrast to the attitudes at 22 W. Elkington.

"It was the first time in Chester I really felt at home," said Barbara Roose. "There was more warmth, more spirit of sharing. The moment we moved in, neighbors brought us some plants. Another invited us to go to church with them. They shared their garden crops."

But there were disadvantages—minor ones like the sporadic garbage pickup, compared to prompt service in the First Ward; and the lack of equipment in Veterans Memorial Park, a half block from the Jeffrey Street home, compared with Chester Park in the First Ward which had considerable equipment.

And then there was the day eight-year-old Stephen was awakened to a new concept of the police. Stephen, his mother points out, came to Chester with the typical, middle-class impression of police—the fellows you go to if you're lost. One day, Stephen was playing outside with a group of black boys. Someone threw a rock at a passing police cruiser. The car stopped and a policeman jumped out, grabbed Stephen and shook him. He rushed into the house, sobbing: "I thought you told me police were supposed to protect you."

A high mark of sorts came in the summer of 1968, even though Roose was already privately making plans to leave.

The state Human Relations Commission, concerned about "tension" in the city, came to Chester for a series of nine investigatory hearings that would run from July 17 to September 11. The sessions started at the community colleges, but were moved to Wade House to be more accessible to ghetto residents. Roose was undeniably one of the factors in bringing about the investigation. He also was a witness on several separate occasions. He still has hopes that the HRC's recommendations, not yet made, will bring some change to Chester. Certainly under the incisive probing of HRC general counsel Nathan Agran, duly reported by the local press, the public became more aware of intolerable conditions in Chester. And, at the insistence and prodding of Agran, city officials promised numerous efforts to alleviate these conditions.

Mayor John H. Nacrelli testified July 29. Nacrelli, former city councilman and finance director, had succeeded Gorbey, who was appointed a county judge in January. Roose, who considered Nacrelli a considerable improvement over Gorbey, had had few clashes with the new mayor.

"I submit," said Mayor Narcelli, "that when a person wants to stop the urban renewal program, the industrial highway, the Housing Development Corporation of Chester and the Model Cities program, he's not interested in curing the problems. He's only interested in creating social unrest through half-truths. As soon as another project starts, Roose organizes another committee to oppose it."

In the interest of avoiding half-truths, the facts were that Roose did not oppose the Housing Development Corporation, he had suggested something like it a year before it was formed; he did not oppose the Model Cities program, only urged more participation by those affected; and he did not oppose urban renewal or the proposed widening of Second Street (the "industrial highway"), he merely demanded assurance that no people would be relocated without having adequate places to go.

Roose's decision to leave Wade House brought curious reactions. Many of the same people who wondered why he had come in the first place ("What's your angle, going to write a book?") now wondered why he would resign a position in which he had achieved so many successes ("Got a good deal someplace else, huh?"). In fact, he had not come to write a book, and he was not leaving for a "good deal." He was leaving without even having another job to go to. Even his friends found that hard to believe.

"We had achieved a radical change at Wade House," Roose explained. "Many of the things I had thought would take three to four years were accomplished in two. The goals and values of the agency were changed to social issues. The agency changed its focus. I think it will continue to increase in social relevancy. I was hired to try to make Wade House more relevant to the people it served and the needs of the community, to organize the poor. I felt I succeeded.

"But the pressure of the black movement necessitated that I get out. We were a very black agency in a very black ghetto. It was obvious I had to leave. The only question was when."

Roose says he had decided to leave six months before his July 23 notice. He was searching for a competent black man to take over. He found Granville Lash in April, working as a counselor at GCM. Lash joined Wade House in May as program and recreation director, the agency's number two position. This was a turning point. The more Lash developed, the readier Roose was to turn over the position to him. This was probably a key factor in Roose's decision to leave. But it ignores a young man named Charles Brewer and the Wade House-CHIP split.

Brewer, twenty-eight, came to CHIP on June 3, 1968, from Buffalo, N.Y., where he had been an organizer for Saul Alinsky's BUILD—Build Unity, Integrity, Liberty and Dignity. He seemed to have the experience needed by CHIP—fourteen months with BUILD, sixteen months prior to that as a social worker and organizer for Friendship House in Lackawanna, outside Buffalo. He had completed two years of work at the State University of New York at Buffalo. He was black, and a past chairman of the Buffalo chapter of CORE. CHIP hired Brewer upon the recommendation of Roose. Six weeks later, again on the recommendation of Roose, CHIP's executive committee let Brewer go. Infighting followed. Ten days later, at the regular CHIP board meeting of July 24, Brewer was rehired.

The next step came at CHIP's next regular board meeting on August 21. Because of a lack of a quorum (the board had twenty-one members), Chairman Paul Thomas canceled the meeting. Then Thomas, Brewer, Roose, a representative of IFCO, the foundation which was giving CHIP the bulk of its money, and five CHIP directors went to Thomas's home to discuss problems. "It ended up being a kangaroo court," claims Roose. What was shown at the meeting was CHIP resentment at Wade House control, real or imagined. What came out of the meeting was a vote to split from Wade House, an improper vote since it was not taken at an official meeting or with a quorum. The vote apparently was never taken to the full CHIP board for ratification. But it was taken to the Wade House monthly meeting the following night and made final.

Roose could hardly oppose a CHIP desire for independence and autonomy. He had been urging that on the black community for two years. But he claims more than that lay beneath the surface. He says Wade House had offered to merge the CHIP and Wade House boards with black Chester residents making up 60 per cent of the single board. CHIP refused.

"I found the split sad and tragic," said Roose. "We had schisms where we needed coalition." He agreed the loss of CHIP was "a tremendous personal blow."

With CHIP went the IFCO grant of $56,000, but, more important, many of the agency's most successful projects. Four VISTA (Volunteers in Service to America) workers had been assigned to CHIP, the first in Dealware County. Three were white. With CHIP emphasizing blackness, the three straggled off before their terms ended.

The Concerned Residents of Second Street (CRSS), an organization formed to delay a state Highways Department widening of Second Street until adequate relocation was available, had achieved success in the summer. Their demands brought a survey of residents and a promise the project would be delayed until relocation was available. The organization hasn't been heard from in months.

The Welfare Rights Organization was organized largely through the efforts of VISTA workers assigned to CHIP. An integrated group, it has chosen not to remain with CHIP.

It would be wrong to suggest the black emphasis has had nothing but negative results. One of the more successful achievements was the formation during the summer of the Awakening Conference of Parents (ACP) to fight for better school conditions. When demands were ignored by the school board in its usual fashion, ACP sponsored a student boycott centered in the black elementary schools. It achieved some success, opening on September 9 with 1,893 pupils absent of a total of 11,696. ACP ran freedom schools for the boycotting pupils. By the close of the boycott on September 24, the number had dwindled, but ACP received enough of its demands to claim victory. The sweet smell of success brought representatives of practically every black group in the city (even Stanley Branche showed up) to several unity meetings. A permanent umbrella-type organization has resulted. It is called the Committee for Chester Affairs. It claims to be putting together a new approach in dealing with the city's racial ills, uniting all blacks for the common goal of equality. It is loosely knit, de-emphasizes "leaders" and publicity. It calls for individual organizations to deal with problems in their own special fields; CHIP with housing, for example, Wade House with recreation. Nine groups were represented at a November 2 meeting: CHIP, Wade House, the Friends Project House, Consumers Education and Protection Association, Shipyard Workers Association, Fifth United Presbyterian Church, ACP, Concerned Residents of Second Street, and the Chester Black Unity Movement.

But there does not seem to be any meaningful role for whites. During ACP's boycott, Roose and his wife volunteered their assistance. Their credentials were good. They had fought the school board single-handed for many months. They probably knew more about the city's school problems than most other citizens in the community. The Rooses were told they could make sandwiches for the freedom schools. They declined.

Roose, out of Wade House permanently, out of Chester temporarily, and perhaps out of the black rebellion too, harbors no resentment.

"I'm not condemning or judging Chester's black community," says Roose. "I am merely realizing and acknowledging the mood, right now, of the black movement for social justice in Chester."

He concedes he is disappointed in the city's black leadership, in "Uncle Tom" ministers, in those he feels were "bought off" by GCM, and in silence from much of the community.

But he is much more dissatisfied with Chester's white community. "Chester's whites haven't spoken out," he said. "Fundamentally, they are racists. If not individual racists, then they have knuckled under to institutional racism. For example, not one white church in Chester gives a damn. Through all the issues, all the problems, all the crises, I cannot remember a single white Chester professional person speaking out. There are many committed suburban whites, but they are all outside Chester. That's really sad. That's one of the reasons Chester is in the sad shape it's in. Their silence is deafening to my ears."

W. H. Ferry wrote in "Farewell to Integration" in the March issue of *The Center Magazine*, publication of the Center for the Study of Democratic Institutions, that racial integration is impossible. And "the efforts of the tough and high-minded who are giving their lives in the urban bearpits of America?" "Ultimate zero," he replies.

Roose would not agree with that. He would look back at the defeats (the biggest one being that "nothing really significant changed in the school system") and the victories (a new awareness, Welfare Rights, VISTA workers, no half-day sessions, rent-in-escrow under study, MACE withdrawn, code enforcement, unfit houses demolished, Second Street widening postponed, Park Terrace Civic Improvement, Granny Lash, and, most important, the new Wade House, and he could not agree that all was for an "ultimate zero."

Even those who hated Roose most would have to concede some things changed while he was in Chester. When he came to town, in August, 1966, he and Wade House were little noted. When he left, in October, 1968, that could not be said of Wade House or his successor, Lash. When Roose arrived the official attitude was that there was not really much wrong with Chester. Two months before he left, city officials not only conceded "social problems" at the Human Relations Commission hearings, but blamed Roose for them.

Roose has a theory that Chester's "black power," like everything else in the city, is at least two years behind the times. He feels the separatist mood is only temporary and that the next emphasis will be renewed cooperation—on an equal basis—between blacks and whites. He points, for example, to the candidates of the Peace and Freedom Party: black Eldridge Cleaver for President and white Peggy Taylor for Vice President. Their appeal was to black militants and white New Leftists.

"An increasing number of people are saying that it is oppressed versus oppressor, friend versus foe, color regardless," said Roose. "It is what Malcolm X said in the last six months of his life, in the last three chapters of his autobiography."

Malcolm remains one of Roose's prophets. When he left Wade House, he took that 2-foot-by-3-foot portrait of Malcolm with him.

Coalitions—If and When: The Puerto Rican Movement in New York City

Since ethnic and racial groups generally are low in power and influence, they have often found it necessary to form alliances and coalitions with other groups in order to increase their strength. While coalitions can bring increased resources from other parties, there are certain risks and potential losses involved. For one, the group entering a coalition must ordinarily give up one thing to gain another, thus its freedom of action and options may become reduced. Secondly, some of the group's autonomy in the sense of doing for itself or shaping its own destiny is sacrificed. For racial and ethnic minorities this may be a vital forfeit since the group may already have a low level of self-confidence and group self-assertiveness may in itself be a necessary or at least favorable objective. Alliances with more powerful units often entail linkages with groups that are closer to the establishment or more conservative in orientation. Thus groups concerned with building ingroup solidarity and power may find that they are obliged to reduce their militancy or self-oriented programs in order to enter into alliances.

The question of coalitions then becomes a highly important and complex strategic matter. Under what circumstances is it appropriate to form such linkages and when is it inadvisable? What are the gains and losses in any given coalition and how does one decide on an acceptable balance? Should coalitions be "ad hoc" or continuing, formal or informal, single issue or multi-issue, and with what kinds of groups?

The Puerto Rican group in New York City experiences a number of dilemmas in its assertive organizational trust, particularly with respect to the matter of coalitions. The group is quite dispersed geographically, making it difficult to accumulate a viable nucleus of power in any one location. A natural ally is the growing Black Power movement in the city. However, certain divergences in group interest and assumptions about the saliency of racial considerations cloud the potentiality of productive coalition ventures. Developments in the Puerto Rican drive in New York are sketched in the following article.

"I'm not black; I'm not white; I'm not in-between. I'm Puerto Rican."

Few other words strike more powerfully to the core of the peculiar situation of the mainland puertorriqueño. The words of the "Newyorican," a current phrase for the New York Puerto Rican, can tell America many things about the political and philosophical aberrations stemming from its color blindspot.

The Newyorican was saying that race and color don't matter, that personal identity does—at least for him. On the basis of being puertorriqueño, no more, no less, there is developing slowly, sometimes dramatically, a special vision among Puerto Ricans of what they stand for on the U.S. mainland.

Caught in the middle of the white and black extremes of society, the Puerto Rican strives to maintain his personal equilibrium based on cultural or ethnic identity which accepts the diversity of skin color or other features among his own people. He is aware of other factors of class and wealth which create formidable barriers within the group. But he must insist on his own personality, on his peculiar identity, which he considers not only unique but essential to his existence.

In early September, about 2,000 Puerto Rican people demonstrated before City Hall in New York City demanding that a manpower program of the Puerto Rican Community Development Project be maintained at the proposed funding level of $815,000. The Manpower Commission had been contemplating a cut of $215,000 but as a result of the puertorriqueño showing, the PRCDP program was given a respite. The project director, Mrs. Amalia Betanzos, and its board chairman, Rev. Ruben Dario Colon, and other board members met with Cyril Tyson, director of the Manpower Commission, who assured the group that the program funding would be reconsidered. However, only a few days later, the Commission announced that a $155,000 cutback had been ordered.

In no small way, such a demonstration illustrates the practical aspects of a growing activism and militancy among Puerto Rican individuals and organizations. Among the placard carriers were State Senator Robert Garcia and Assemblyman Armando Montano of South Bronx, the Puerto Rican community's sole representatives in the state legislature. Puerto Ricans themselves give ample reasons for their mounting concern and personal involvement. Many suggest that little is being done to offset the kind of street confrontation with city hall which took place in September; that, in fact, more overt acts of frustration and dissatisfaction can be expected. In at least four Puerto Rican neighborhoods last summer, tense encounters with police took place.

Puerto Ricans are acutely aware that on every count—housing, education, employment, income, welfare—the puertorriqueño ranks last in comparison to other groups comparable or larger in size in New York City. Scattered about the five New York boroughs are 841,000 Puerto Ricans, or *boricuas* (a term of self-identification that recalls very early Indian roots on the island of Puerto Rico). The figure increases daily. New York City's Puerto Rican population, in fact, is twice that of San Juan, the largest city in Puerto Rico. Commonwealth office estimates indicate a new migration annually for the past two years of about 30,000.

Some data are available which lend credence to the arguments and demands of Puerto Rican leaders. A recent study by Leonard S. Kogan and Morey J. Wantman of City University of New York reported that Puerto Rican family income was lowest among the three major groups in the city: $3,949 compared to $4,754 for nonwhites and $7,635 for whites. Puerto Ricans had made a gain of only $49 in the past two years in contrast to white gains of more than $900.

Employment trends among Puerto Ricans showed a decrease from 17 to 12 per

"El Puertorriqueño: No More, No Less." From *The Civil Rights Digest,* Fall, 1968, pp. 27-35.

cent in white-collar fields while women's employment increased from 18.7 to 24.9 per cent between 1960 and 1965. Unemployment rates in three densely puertorriqueño districts, East Harlem, South Bronx, and South Brooklyn, reached 12 per cent, three times the national rate.

But even these figures and statistics cannot begin to tell the story of "el barrio." "There is only one 'el barrio,' " a young boricua explained as he leaned against a car parked not far from the subway entrance at Lexington Avenue and 103rd Street. Coming out of the subway into the streets of el barrio after being in downtown Manhattan is like stepping into another world. A senses-offending squalor is first apparent after the tall, glass and steel cityscape, a contrast suddenly sprawling before the eyes of squat three- and four-story tenements littering the streets. It is hard to judge which is more disturbing—the suddenness of the climb up the subway stairs or the abruptness of East 96th Street which runs like an invisible Berlin Wall between affluent Manhattanites and East Harlem puertorriqueños and Harlem blacks.

This might be the initial impression of el barrio or of most of the other slum neighborhoods in which thousands of human beings are compressed. Beyond that first jar, however, one can begin to sense the living that is going on there, to feel that very little goes on in those streets with which everyone is not familiar or involved. Life during the summer, of course, is conducted as much on the streets as possible. Poorly ventilated apartments are extremely close; the smell of sweat and refuse of generations is stifling. Most of the dwellings are privately owned (few by Puerto Ricans themselves), and in final stages of dilapidation; most of the buildings, which house many times the occupants they were meant to house, were built before the First World War.

In 1962, representatives from a number of Puerto Rican organizations formed the Puerto Rican Citizens Committee on Housing to investigate the effects of housing and city planning in the Latin community. Their report cites a "conscious effort to remove the Puerto Rican from the so-called prime real estate in Manhattan," that urban renewal programs had "uprooted and destroyed established Puerto Rican communities," and called for a voice in the housing and planning agencies.

The particular area studied by the committee was West Side Manhattan, a ghetto romanticized in the Broadway musical *West Side Story,* above 79th Street to 125th Street. According to residents and community workers in the area, things haven't changed much since the citizens' group study. In fact, the decision of the Housing and Development Administration to construct two middle-income projects as part of the West Side Urban Renewal Area (87th to 97th between Central Park West and Amsterdam Avenue) has been vigorously disputed by community groups and leaders who consider it a threat to some 6,000 present tenants who might not be adequately relocated and regard it as an act of economic discrimination; monthly rents in the 325 apartments to be built will run between $48.61 and $50.64 per room.

The solutions to such a complex issue will not come easily. In el barrio, the concept of private, minority group control of low-income housing is being tested by the East Harlem Redevelopment Corp., in a project codenamed "Pilot Block." The objective of Pilot Block, which evolved from the groundwork of the East Harlem Redevelopment Council, itself the offspring of a tenants' council, is to place the ownership and management of housing in the hands of former tenants. The block selected for the project, 122nd-123rd Streets between 2nd and 3rd Avenues, consists of several family residences, a handful of single-occupant rooming houses, and, the source of greatest local resistance to the project, according to Pilot Block staff people, long-established furniture and clothing stores.

There has been one major obstacle in the more than a year and a half negotiations in which Pilot Block promoters have been engaged: The city has not condemned the site for clearance and transferral to the East Harlem citizens' group. During the past six months, there have been at least two major confrontations with "city hall," a demonstration in front of Gracie Mansion, the Mayor's residence, and a presentation before a city housing commission meeting of six demands made by the tenants' council. The project was approved by the Department of Housing and Urban Development more than twenty months ago but still awaits city action on condemnation.

A much-repeated theme among recognized Puerto Rican spokesmen and young activists was evident in the comments of the tenants' council and Pilot Block staff such as Rene Rodriguez, Tony Santos, and Bobby Azevedo. They conceived of their work as stemming essentially from the need for social change. "The Pilot Block means political power; it means that the politicians would have to give up some of their control over people," one of them said. Tenants—and first chance would be given to those people already living on the pilot location—would elect their own representatives to the management board of the four-building complex of high-rise apartments, medical, educational, and recreational facilities to be provided on the site. "It is also a social thing," another said, referring to the obstacles barring the progress of Pilot Block. "People on the outside don't want to give us middle-class, material things."

Local community control is not an issue solely in the area of housing. Long-standing disputes between local school officials and community leaders erupted on the scheduled first day of school in a major teachers' strike which closed down all but one district, the Ocean Hill-Brownsville School District, an area about two-thirds black and one-third Puerto Rican. The district is an experimental one, testing the decentralization concept under Ford Foundation funding. The district's governing board demanded that it have the right to choose its teachers without interference from the central Board of Education. (It was earlier this year that the first Puerto Rican, Hector I. Vasquez, head of the Puerto Rican Forum, was named to the Board of Education.)

An important facet of this issue is the fact that although the eventual capitulation to the city school board by the local governing board seemed inevitable, the coalition of black and Puerto Rican parents managed to keep the school doors open. In so doing, the parents proved something to the city and to themselves. The struggle in the cities has always been between those who have power and those who don't. Blacks and Puerto Ricans clearly demonstrated that alliances have a greater impact on a recalcitrant opposition, whether it is a city administration or a 40-thousand-member teachers' union.

To a great degree, the confrontation between the Puerto Rican Community Development Project supporters and the city administration presents another aspect of the problems facing the Puerto Rican because he is the last minority to enter New York. Mrs. Betanzos, PRCDP director, frames the issue in this way:

"The blacks want us to be black and the whites want us to be white because they both want to use us. In terms of issues, I would have to side with the blacks—but I'm a Puerto Rican and no one has the right to tell me or want me to be black or white.

"In the poverty program, black organizations have not wanted Puerto Rican groups funded. This is unfortunate because they have been using the same arguments that the whites have," she contends. "They say that the Puerto Ricans cannot run their own programs." She points out that the scattering of the Puerto Rican population has led several groups to seek anti-poverty funding on an at-large basis, that is, taking in an entire borough or even all five boroughs. This conflicts with the concept of geographic representation inherent in the makeup of the poverty program governing board, which consists of representatives of 26 geographic areas.

Mrs. Betanzos, a native New Yorker, notes that under this system Puerto Ricans control only one area, the Hunts Point district in South Bronx, while the black community, which is much more "homogeneous" in the various geographic regions, virtually controls the poverty board. "The Puerto Ricans must have citywide programs," insists the Project director, who is also chairman of the National Association for Puerto Rican Civil Rights. At present, the Project and three other groups, ASPIRA, an education-oriented program, the Puerto Rican Forum, a young activist business development group of professionals, and the Puerto Rican Family Institute, concerned with family social services, operate citywide programs.

A Puerto Rican who can observe the difficulties of the puertorriqueño community from two angles, as a member of the community and as a city official, is Manny Diaz, deputy commissioner in charge of the Manpower and Career Development Agency. His agency coordinates Neighborhood Youth Corps, Concentrated Employment Programs, and other manpower and training contracts with community groups.

A study of three areas, Harlem, East Harlem, and Bedford-Stuyvesant in Brooklyn, released in late September by the regional office of the Bureau of Labor Statistics, disclosed that: Puerto Ricans were unemployed or underemployed (working less than full time or earning no more than the minimum wage) at a rate higher than the over-all rate in two of the three areas—36.0 per cent to 33.1 per cent in East Harlem and 29.7 per cent to 27.6 per cent in Bedford-Stuyvesant. The data indicate that one out of every three Puerto Ricans has a serious job problem and that Puerto Ricans in general fare worse than Negroes in the job market.

Employment was just one of many areas which Diaz cited as critical to the general well-being of the Puerto Rican community. "Puerto Ricans are far behind in voting, 20 per cent behind the blacks in voter registration, worse off in terms of housing and in education," he said.

But what is most crucial to the present status of the Puerto Rican, is involvement in the political process. There has been a gradual development since the early 1940's of different levels of organizations, from the first services or social oriented groups such as hometown clubs through the mid-1950's when the first wave of young, second-generation puertorriqueños began to develop issue-oriented organizations. Now in the 1960's, organizations have taken entirely new forms as tenants' councils, Pilot Blocks, community development agencies, professional and youth activist groups, coalescing various groups into single bodies, and developing coalitions around basic problems of the poor. The objective is political muscle. With the election of Mayor Robert Wagner in 1960, the patronage of jobs in city administration and other areas, which had passed by the Puerto Ricans, began to fall to el barrio as the Puerto Ricans started to make their ethnic vote count. And because, as observers of New York have pointed out, at least five general ethnic or racial groups vie for political attention—the Irish, the Italians, the Jews, the Negroes, and the Puerto Ricans—the latter is last not only alphabetically; he is literally the fifth community, the last minority.

The shape and scope of the Puerto Rican's coming to terms with the necessity for political push and pull, for "clout," is in great flux.

The problem basic to the Puerto Rican's future political life and of course to every other phase of his existence is again twofold: he must develop a personal and group awareness built on self-identity as a Puerto Rican, yet he must also adjust to political realities which demand certain compromises or rationales for coalition in order to achieve certain goals. As to the latter, the Ocean Hill-Brownsville issue comes to mind and, not as recently, the participation of 2,000 Newyoricans in the March on Washington in 1963, and of 5,000 puertorriqueños in a weekend march on Washington to support the Poor People's Campaign.

Gilberto Gerena-Valentin, director of the Puerto Rican-Hispanic Division of the city Commission on Human Rights, offered this view of the problem: "New York like any big city is a close-ended city. Politically, the machines have worked out the deals and will not give anything to the Puerto Rican. If we had a ghetto, we could elect our own representatives, but we have only one Assemblyman [of 68] from the five boroughs. Where we are densely concentrated, we're not registered because of the literacy test. [New York State requires a person to write and speak English or have a sixth-grade education.] This situation will be hard to change because the political powers want to keep the status quo."

Reflecting a very common view, Gerena-Valentin, who has sought election as councilman-at-large, added, "Many answers to the problems of the Puerto Ricans lie in gaining political strength. But in terms of political participation, the Puerto Rican has a different concept of the social dynamics involved. He identifies with the desire of black people for self-determination. But," in relation to the racial attitudes of America, "he comes in between the black and white, but he is neither. He experiences a psychological impact because he is the majority in Puerto Rico but here a minority." The racism in American society, he stresses, divides the Puerto Rican family because in its economic and social struggles, white society favors certain of the children on the basis of their skin color.

He abhors the idea of a fight between blacks and Puerto Ricans, Gerena-Valentin says, because, "Both are impoverished. We should join our power and demand more. The Puerto Rican is beginning to learn the value of direct action. If the white power structure doesn't want to give up some power," he said, "we are learning to take power another way. We are going beyond getting political appointments in terms of solving any problems. As long as we are lowest on the totem pole, none of us is safe."

Monserrat, a member of the New York State Advisory Committee to the U.S. Commission on Civil Rights, points out that Puerto Rican reaction to civil rights issues is not the same as for other groups. "We do not accept the color value of either the black or majority group. Thus we are way ahead of both on this—to accept either would be to create a racism in us and that would be a tremendous step back. This is a major contribution which we as a people, from our history, our experience, our conditioning, can make.

"The Puerto Rican has always possessed basic civil rights. He has always seen himself as the whole and as part of the whole in Puerto Rico." His experience in the United States, Monserrat describes, has been generally negative, tending to cause rejection of the Puerto Rican identity (dropping out or passing into white society) or immersing oneself in the culture, to escape from the reality of a sometimes perverse environment. "The most significant aspect of our struggle," he believes, "is also one of our biggest problems: whether we will be able to make the contribution which we can make by being and remaining Puerto Rican. There is a great gap between third and fourth generation groups and ours which hardly has a second generation. We have upward mobility but the rate and spread depends on what is happening now, and what is happening doesn't promise much for the great number of the people."

A former director of the PRCDP, Jose Morales, brought up a significant new factor in the political thinking of puertorriqueños. A great many Puerto Ricans, he believes, have withdrawn from "politics" because of the assassination of Robert F. Kennedy. They have given up on political involvement, he says, but the full effect may only appear following the November elections.

Direct confrontation and organizational skill are the two sides of a double-edged sword being honed by young activists such as Jack Agueros, currently working for a private firm concerned with business development and chairman of a new group called Puerto Rican Institute for Democratic Education. Last June 30, Agueros began a five-day fast in his office when he was deputy commissioner of the city Community Development Agency. He sought a number of specific changes by his fast, that a Puerto Rican be named to the Board of Education, that city colleges and universities alter their policies toward minority students, and, his major objective, that Puerto Ricans be included at the decision-making levels throughout the city administration.

"I want a better economic situation for the Puerto Rican," he says. "I want for him to come out of an invisible category, to be considered and consulted with in city, state, and Federal programs. The answer to our problems is political—when we can sit on the policy-making bodies, everything else will fall into place."

Political withdrawal, growing group identity, overwhelming social problems, new organizations and coalitions, devastating physical needs—a complex and perplexing picture of el barrio. And what of the threat of violence in this picture? No one denied that violence could occur. When asked about the prospect of barrio violence, most persons suggested that the points most in question were the time and place of street disorders. The subject usually evoked cautiously phrased responses.

Mrs. Betanzos remarked that Puerto Ricans "have tried to resolve problems in a law-abiding way, but they're getting the impression that the only way they will be resolved will be by militant, non-law-abiding action."

Few if any Puerto Ricans talk of riot as inevitable or desirable. Among the youth, there was always talk of working out answers some way, of aggressively strengthening the sense of unity by building on the fact of being puertorriqueño. A young community organizer hopes to institute television and radio programs aimed at developing cultural and group awareness among boricua youth. Or, a few young Puerto Ricans block traffic at a bridge entrance to get funds for a poverty program, and succeed. The trend is to reject "the racist bag." Besides, one young puertorriqueño said, "There's always the temptation to cut out of the barrio but luckily someone will ask you, are you Spanish—with that sickly smile—they won't let you forget."

It seemed obvious that Puerto Rican activists were optimistic in seeking solutions through political, democratic methods and that all other alternatives to violence simply have not been eliminated. Also, goals are generally short-range so they seem more attainable. No one plans more than fifteen years ahead, a young community leader in his mid-twenties commented, because "that's all anyone can see ahead."

The Puerto Rican people are also struggling to "make it" on their own terms. They are striving to resist the pressures of the dominant elements of the society which threaten to suppress to disperse them. For they realize that only by being and remaining Puerto Ricans can they truly enhance the quality of life in the nation. Indeed, if they and their way of life were to be disintegrated, the loss in the end would be America's.

Tactics of Confrontation:
A Welfare Rights Group Wins a Victory

In the past, highly militant, confrontational tactics were seen as anathema by group relations professionals. Such tactics, it was asserted, split the community and fire the flames of mutual antagonism. At this time some practitioners are apt to assert that it is only through confrontations that injustices and implicit "de facto" conflicts can be surfaced and concessions granted, because those with privilege in the white power structure will only give up that which they are forced to relinquish. Groups seeking to enhance their position of power have tended to use conflict as a necessary tool. A number of tactical questions immediately arise. When may such initiatives be used with success and when may they lead to failure? Are there accordingly special conditional factors or internal organizational variables which should be taken into account in planning confrontations? What resources or support in the form of allies are necessary to sustain a confrontation? Are there ethical considerations or factors related to general community welfare that must be weighed?

The Welfare Rights Movement has been a vehicle for the development of power, particularly in the poor black community. This movement has not avoided the use of conflict tactics when these seemed necessary to achieve its goals. In the case record that follows, a local chapter in a middle-sized university community conducts a campaign for increased clothing allowances. A group of social work students act and learn as they support the welfare mothers. Issues related to confrontation tactics become illuminated in the process.

Having spent the summer of 1968 on a block placement as an organizer for the National Welfare Rights Organization (NWRO), I returned to the Midland School of Social Work eager to test out some of the organizing and benefit-producing tactics which had been successful around the country. My "home" community—Green City—is made up of about 110,000 people, of whom some 20,000 are connected with the local State University. Most of the county's recipient population

---

"Welfare Rights: A Study in the Tactics of Confrontation," John L. Erlich, School of Social Work, University of Michigan, August 21, 1969. The author has condensed events and roles of various practitioners to facilitate this presentation.

(about 500 families) are concentrated in Green City and nearby Howell. Having been informally related to the local welfare rights groups over the previous academic year, I was in an excellent position to make contact with recipient leaders when I arrived in Green City. The following is an account of a rather successful school clothing drive in which I participated as an organizer—on my own time.

Humanizing Existing Welfare (HEW), the Green City group of local welfare recipients, had not called a meeting since the spring of 1968. In April a drive by Helen Smith, chairman of HEW, for a position on the County Board of Supervisors was defeated by a narrow margin, and a summer "Black Forum" program aimed at the broad problems confronting blacks in Green City had drained the resources of the group, and reduced the energy which could have been spent on welfare issues. Although there had been strong local support for the Poor Peoples' Campaign and about fifteen people from Green City had participated in the campaign, for all practical purposes HEW was a nonfunctioning group during the summer of 1968 and up until the fall clothing drive.

In relation to the NWRO, HEW had a fluid status; it was not a legitimate affiliate although possessing ten of the necessary twenty-five members.

In addition to HEW, there was one other active welfare rights organization in the county. The Howell group, Howell Welfare Action, had more capable leadership and broader membership support. Mrs. Sylvia Willis, chairman of the group, was strongly supported by two vigorous and articulate young mothers. The group had paid their $25 fee and had the twenty-five required names into the NWRO prior to the clothing drive. While Sylvia Willis manned the information booth at Resurrection City, other ladies along on the trip recognized that organizing locally was one way to learn some useful skills and gain some prestige.

At the July State Welfare Rights Meeting, Sylvia was elected the state secretary. Plans for a school clothing drive were first discussed during this gathering, and were carried back by the various representatives to their local groups. Thus, by the end of the summer the Howell groups had a more coherent conceptualization of what a welfare rights group could do than their Green City counterparts, and had a membership ready and willing to move into action.

My discussion with organizers in New York and Boston provided strategy and endouragement for a clothing drive. The basic tool for welfare rights organizing in New York City was the minimum standards form. Minimum standards forms list clothing, household furnishings, appliances and other items which each recipient has a right to under law. Everything from window curtains to a fruit reamer is listed along with suggested prices. Of course, the Welfare Department doesn't tell the clients what they are entitled to. Instead, the welfare rights group contacts a mother, has her fill out a form and then goes with her to the welfare office to demand the items listed. It is possible for a new "recruit" to walk out of the welfare office with up to $1,000 in a special needs grant.

Green City and Indian County had been a typical example of a situation with good potential but no significant organizing tool. The possibility of a school clothing drive turned out to be just such a tool. With my help, the mothers interested in a clothing campaign had contacted at least eighty others, fifteen of whom had promised to attend a meeting scheduled with Miss Stanton, director of the County Social Services Office. At my suggestion, other social work students contacted Sylvia Willis and offered their help as staff for the group.

Seven mothers and three students met with Miss Stanton at the County Department of Social Services on Thursday, August 22. The mothers from Green City did not attend because they feared being arrested or intimidated. In addition, many

Howell mothers were more fearful of retaliation than convinced that they could obtain money for childrens' school clothing. Previously, Mrs. Willis, leader of the Howell group, had told the ladies she planned to remain at the office until their demands were met.

Because Mr. Dale (county director of the Social Services Department) and several members of the County Social Services Board were not available that first Thursday, the ladies conveyed to Miss Stanton an over-all picture of their concerns. Clothing needs were their first priority.

Although the ladies requested an immediate meeting with the County Social Services Board that following Friday, they were informed that they would have to wait until Tuesday (27th) when the Board could be formally convened. A meeting was planned for 10:00 A.M. with the stipulation that Miss Stanton would contact Mrs. Willis to confirm the date and time. However, the Board refused to meet on such short notice.

At this point, the group decided that a sit-in was inadvisable for two basic reasons: (1) the individuals with decision-making power were not readily available, and (2) the mothers did not have enough "troops" at that time for an effective confrontation. However, we students made plans with the mothers to draw up a minimum standards form with the New York form as a model. Two mothers and I designed the form.

The mothers from Howell were determined but their numbers were small. The Green City leadership wasn't unified enough to bring their own numbers out, let alone rapidly attract a larger membership.

The Department of Social Services position was far from liberal. They could have chosen to deal with the first group of seven mothers who came in to satisfy their needs and thereby perhaps co-opt the organization's leadership. The department, however, placed a higher priority on saving money than on playing politics (let alone meeting needs). A Social Services Board meeting was finally set for September 3.

We went to work. After the minimum standards forms were run off and collated, the mothers whose names had been compiled by a small group of recipients were contacted. Student and mother manpower were concentrated in Howell where most of the county's recipients were located. In three days, over seventy forms were filled out. (This constituted contact with approximately 18 per cent of local recipient families.)

On Monday, September 2, a meeting was called for all those who had filled out forms. Over thirty people turned out—including both old members and new (potential) members. The regional coordinator of NWRO spoke to the ladies and prepared them to fight for their children by comparing how Moses had led his people out of bondage to the mothers' responsibility for their children. There was a risk that the speaker's militancy could have confused and upset those attending the meeting; instead, it brought them all back the following morning with their completed minimum standards list.

The legitimacy of the forms was a point which we student organizers questioned. The mothers who filled out the forms had been told that the only way they could get the items they had checked would be to pressure the Department in large numbers. We explained that the present system did not guarantee the items checked. There were strong misgivings about raising people's hopes and expectations. I drove two mothers and their seven children to the County Building. They exemplified the feelings of the mothers; they were silent and seemed somewhat fearful.

The form showed clearly and concretely what people needed to clothe their children, served as a basis from which negotiations could begin, and acted to raise the expectations of the mothers by focusing on the difference between their needs and the amount of their grants. The distinction between a flat grant and the basic concept of individual need was emphasized to give the mothers a more solid sense of their rights.

The strategy which the mothers agreed upon for the Social Services Board meeting was quite simple. The ladies would meet with the Board, give them the forms, demand immediate action and stay until they got some satisfaction. In consultation with Professor Miller of the School of Social Work, I decided not to contact potential middle-class support groups to ask for a show of strength at the meeting. Our feeling was to let the mothers initiate the action so that they would get credit and not have to share it with a broad nonrecipient coalition. Offers of support did come from leaders of SDS and from Citizens for New Politics who visited during the Tuesday afternoon confrontation to see if the mothers needed reinforcements. At that time the mothers stood pat on their decision to keep the action as *their own* without the help of outside organizations.

Going into the meeting, the mothers determined to stay until they got their school clothes. We discussed what to do with the secretaries and caseworkers. It was decided that they should be made uncomfortable and, depending on what happened, perhaps forced to stay. There were two general goals for the action at the Social Services Board office: (1) to obtain the school clothing demanded; (2) help the ladies develop confidence in their ability to handle bureaucrats and make tactical decisions on the spot. The county's reactions were hard to predict and thus confidence in the mothers' ability to make quick decisions was significant. Moreover, Indian County is known for its "buck passing" orientation in matters involving the needs of people who are poor—especially if they are also black.

The expectation was that the County Social Services Board (three members) would be able to meet the group's clothing demands or at least agree to make a positive recommendation to the Board of Supervisors. The ladies and organizers anticipated that the county would be expected to pay 100 per cent of the money out of direct relief funds. Therefore, the Board would be asked to make this appropriation immediately. It was expected that Mr. Dale (county director) would raise the objection that direct relief was already budgeted and was insufficient to pay the extra amount requested. The other ploy which might be used was to say that the Welfare Department did not have the necessary authority to make the decision.

Some of the mothers were emotionally prepared to take any means necessary to get clothing for their children. However, there was a serious tactical split between advocates of violence and nonviolence, and it was personified in the leadership which was more militant than the majority of the group. About one-third of the group was ready to fight, one-third was nonviolent yet persistent, and the remainder had no consistent philosophy but would make their decisions in accord with the circumstances. While the ladies were prepared psychologically, they had made no physical plans to remain in the welfare office. We had not thought to furnish such necessary items as food, blankets, or to provide care for the children who accompanied their mothers to the welfare office. (Question might be raised about the degree to which this was my responsibility.)

The social work students who assisted the mothers worked with them in partnership with mutual goals. While this "staff" was somewhat more militant than the mothers (in part because they had less at stake), they were willing to abide by the mothers' chosen actions. At the same time, the mothers looked to the students for strategy ideas and to help in decision making. On several occasions the mothers were more persistent with their demands than we would have been. Aside from my-self and two other social work students, the involvement of the university com-munity was minimal in the early stages of organization.

The decision as to what would constitute a victory for the group was influenced by a power allocation theory. The mothers determined to shift some measure of power from the Department of Social Services to themselves. It would be necessary to use conflict (and also, the threat of future conflict) as well as demand pressure to get the Board to arrive at the desired decision.

The mass media were contacted. The intent was that media coverage would aid in widely publicizing the issue, thus stimulating outside pressure and enhancing the chances of achieving a victory.

The significance of allocating heavy student (and mother) resources to media coverage was pointed up by the response which was given to the group's actions by the press. The press was informed of a major confrontation which was to take place at the County Building. This approach aroused their interest. When the *Howell Press* refused to cover the story the first day, the city editor was given Sylvia Willis' phone number. The excellent, detailed story which resulted from this first contact is evidence of the necessity of obtaining press coverage and spending time with the media.

It was not until late Monday evening that Miss Stanton notified Mrs. Willis that the Social Services Board meeting had been arranged as agreed. Arriving down-stairs in the County Building at the Social Services Department for the meeting (about fifty people in total, including children and students), the mothers found Mr. Dale assuming a belligerent stance, asking for token (three) representation by the mothers (as he had done in negotiating with them in the past). His rationale was that so many people would disrupt his office, the secretaries, and the orderly process of "doing business." He alternated between demanding that the mothers leave and suggesting that the Social Services Board make that decision. Mr. Wren, a member of the three-man Board, made the determination that the group could stay. The Board initially intimidated the students by asking whether they were mothers—this type of harassment became an undercurrent throughout the crisis. The problem clearly points out a certain lack of role legitimacy with which the commu-nity organizer is faced.

By ignoring Dale the mother set the stage for the confrontations which were to follow. Dale was defined as the enemy, he was not asked for cooperation but was rather personally threatened and humiliated by being backed down in his stance in front of the Board and his employees. Throughout the dealings which the mothers had with Mr. Dale in past years, the ladies had determined that he would give noth-ing unless he was under direct pressure.

Once inside the meeting room, the mothers dealt directly with the Social Services Board and Dale was treated as an errand boy. The mothers' refusal to compromise on numbers helped to strengthen the group and to increase their recognition of their bargaining power. By disregarding Mr. Dale's protocol, the mothers turned what was a theoretical clothing emergency into a real (physical) emergency situation. Mr. Dale then attempted to regain control of the situation by closing down the Social Services office. The Board began to leave the conference room. Mr. Apple was the first to reach the door. When Mrs. Willis and I grabbed him, he "decided" to stay in the meeting. The three-member Board, along with Miss Stanton, were held "captive" in the conference room. Meanwhile, mothers in the outer office blockaded the main office door.

Mr. Dale, meanwhile, had left to consult with the Ways and Means Committee of the County Board of Supervisors. The mothers were awaiting his return. They stated that they wanted to speak with whoever had decision-making power, whether that was the Social Services Board or the Ways and Means Committee of the Board of Supervisors. They had also decided to detain the Social Services Board members and Miss Stanton until Mr. Dale returned.

The ladies had not discussed keeping hostages in their strategy planning, their assumption being that the Ways and Means Committee would meet with them when they were made aware that their colleagues were being inconvenienced.

During this period a local black militant leader arrived at the meeting and began to contribute to the dialogue and continuing pressure. He stuck with the mothers throughout the crisis and played an important role as adviser, supporter, and liaison with the student organizers and supporting students and community groups.

Mr. Hanson, chairman of the County Board of Supervisors, came down as soon as he heard about the lock-in. He listened to the demands and seemed receptive to them. He recommended that the ladies bring their problems to a meeting which would be scheduled for the next day between the mothers, the Ways and Means Committee and the Social Services Board. This was the first time that the group had been informed of the proposed meeting. The next day was not soon enough for the mothers. Not yet convinced of the mothers' determination, Hanson refused to budge and stated that twelve hours was the necessary interim before another meeting could be called. Hanson advised the group that Sheriff Stoner was aware of the situation inside the welfare office and was "itching" to come down.

Stoner, true to this threat, burst into the office about fifteen minutes later in spite of the ladies blocking the door. About twenty of his deputies entered the outer office and allowed the secretaries and other staff to leave. Hanson, Stanton, and the Social Services Board voluntarily stayed with the mothers.

At this point, the sheriff called a special meeting with two leaders of the mothers' group. Stoner's threats to arrest the women and children—in front of the entire group—visibly shook the mothers, along with the fact that his men arrived in riot helmets and full "battle" gear. Although in tears and outraged at the sheriff's style of threatening them, the ladies were determined to remain. This was a good example for the supporting social work students of real determination and courage.

The stalemate was settled and arrests averted by the chairman of the local Anti-Poverty Board who helped to convince Hanson to call a special session of the County Board of Supervisors and to arrange for the withdrawal of the sheriff's "troops."

Following testimony and discussion at the special Board of Supervisor's meeting, a "gentleman's agreement" was settled upon: the ladies present were to have their forms processed by the Social Services Department beginning at 8:00 A.M. the following morning when that office opened. Hanson wisely did not call for a vote of the Board. He was aware that he would lose and that this would anger the mothers. Thus, he directed Dale to start processing the forms as the ladies prepared them. One supervisor questioned whether a special meeting would be necessary to appropriate the needed funds. Hanson replied that Dale had enough money in his direct relief fund to deal with the present emergency and that when this source was drained the county could allocate supplemental funds to the Social Services Department. Mr. Dale, however, did not choose to hear Mr. Hanson. Mr. Dale closed the meeting by saying that he wouldn't be too optimistic about having the needs of these mothers met in the morning. Dale obviously had no intention of carrying out Mr. Hanson's orders.

The mothers arrived early Wednesday morning and expected to obtain the clothing vouchers promised them the night before. Instead, they were locked out of the Social Services office. Intake had been moved by Mr. Dale from the interior offices to an office on the main hall, and the waiting room had been moved outside the offices of the secretaries, or specifically, into the hall.

The ladies determined to let Mrs. Minns be a test case in the processing. If she obtained satisfaction of the needs she listed, then other would follow her. It soon became clear that Dale's instructions to his workers were to circumvent the Board's directive and that the Department would not be giving out any money that day. The mothers stopped meetings with their caseworkers and, to emphasize the shoddy treatment which they had received, barricaded the office door.

Sheriff Stoner arrived at this point to warn the ladies, but was deluged by their questions. His helmeted deputies then came in and formed a double column along both sides of the door, thus freeing the caseworkers who were being detained inside their offices. By tough-minded persuasion from the black men who had served as their advocates, the ladies were convinced to leave the building. The mothers were fed up with fruitless meetings, they had been given the bureaucratic runaround long enough and had seen enough red tape to know that there were just too many dead-end channels for them to go through. From this point on, the County Building became an armed camp with deputies placed at all entrances of the building.

By the late afternoon a meeting was arranged with representatives of the Social Service Board, Dale, the Ways and Means Committee of the Indian County Board of Supervisors, and over thirty mothers. Three black men attended as the mothers' advocates and spokesmen.

Each mother came to the front of the room and gave a brief statement of her need. It was a moving documentary. Some were brief, saying things like, "I have four kids and I need help right now." Some were demanding, "I'm full up to here. When are you going to give us our clothes and stop asking questions?" Others were righteously angry, "We will die for our kids and what we believe in." Some mothers were cynical, "You don't know what it is like, how could you cope with this problem? Would you have been so civilized? If the police are here to protect citizens, I guess that means we aren't citizens." In addition, the concept of minimum standards and individual needs was emphasized.

In response, Mr. Wren was "very sympathetic" to the ladies' problems and "aware of the acuteness of their distress." He said that caseworkers had been unable to go over the forms and make recommendations because of the morning's confusion. As a result, the Social Services Board was prepared to recommend a $40 allotment per child. Thus, with 1,200 children in the county, the cost would be over $50,000. The program would be administered through vouchers, first to the welfare rights members and then to other recipients in alphabetical order.

This "$40 solution" was totally unacceptable to the mothers. First of all, they wanted an individual needs determination. The mothers caucused, then came up with a four-point position:

1. The principle of individual evaluation of need.
2. Determination to receive the full amount of need as listed on the minimum needs form.
3. Agreement that processing be started immediately with Mr. Dale calling back all his caseworkers to work until all applicants had achieved full satisfaction.
4. Method of payment: vouchers should be a last resort.

Following this position statement, Chairman Brody adjourned the meeting in spite of the mothers' very vocal protest. The committee finally agreed that the mothers would present their proposal to a small committee which immediately convened across the hall. The mothers' first demand in the special session was that the sheriff's deputies leave the County Building. The Board used the intransigence of the mothers on this issue as a pretext for adjourning the meeting and left.

Earlier that day a student editor of the *University Chronicle*—covering the welfare story—was beaten and arrested. The threat of violence and force used laid the groundwork for the conflict which ensued in the days that followed between the police and the welfare rights advocates.

Stoner's decision to harass the mothers' advocates, student leaders, organizers and student press was further evidenced in his refusal to admit a *University Chronicle* reporter to the negotiations, although representatives of every other press and media agency had been admitted. Not only was the second-floor corridor outside the Board meeting room then cleared, but sheriff's deputies were then posted in front of the meeting room and deployed around the second floor. Guards were also placed at the entrances of the building to "keep objectionable persons from entering the building." This meant that those unaware of the order who came to see what was happening at the meeting were verbally harassed or physically carried off the premises. These people, mainly students, were directed to stay off county property. What this action accomplished was a polarization with sheriff's deputies on one side and the mothers, their supporters, organizers and advocates on the other side.

Discrimination against student organizers, against the *Chronicle* and against supporters by Stoner and the sheriff's department crystallized strong resentment in the university student body. At the same time, the move may have been designed politically to gain the support of the essentially conservative Indian County citizenry which had recently supported Stoner in his party primary and would later vote him back into office. It is significant to note that those treated as the "niggers-of-the-day" were not the supervisors, not black people, recipients or the media people in general, but very clearly the students and student-run organizations.

A student march to the County Jail that night was a reaction to the reporter's beating and arrest. The general tone of the march was nonviolent but concerned. The Welfare Rights Regional Coordinator suggested to the crowd (of over 300) assembled at the parking lot across from the County Jail the paradox of symbolic *vs.* real protest. He pointed out that if one really chose to be involved in this issue, he should return the next day to support the mothers.

At noon on Thursday a campus rally was held to mobilize people to march directly on the County Building. Again, the regional coordinator was the primary speaker who gave legitimacy to student participation. The call to action given by him would have been considered "revolutionary" had it been articulated by an SDS member. He was able to cut through their apathy and give the students a sense of helping poor people in a real way.

More than 400 marchers arrived at the County Building before the scheduled 1:30 P.M. meeting. The tone of the negotiating team was optimistic. Hanson had called the state capitol to say that the Board of Supervisors was negotiating under duress. He also suggested the removal of Dale. In addition, there was news that the state would match county resources with 40 per cent matching funds. Nevertheless, after the mothers explained their four-point proposal, Mr. Dale explained the impossibility of implementing such a proposal. The Ways and Means Committee came back with a $60 offer which was clearly based upon a recent settlement in a nearby county. This proposal would mean that $72,000 would have to be made available. The mothers were clear that they would not accept a flat grant and adamant in their emphasis on individual needs.

New points of strength had developed at the beginning of the negotiations. Besides the mothers and those outside the County Building, there were finally some 500 marchers present. This show of support was enhanced by the mothers' refusal to being at the meeting without their spokesmen or to compromise over the admittance of the press.

The "$60 grant" was obviously a politically symbolic issue; the money was not the primary concern of those in power, although it was their basic bargaining point. A $70 grant would have cost the county the same as the original $40 offer would because of the attorney general's ruling on the appropriation by the state of the needed matching funds. Yet, $60 was an acceptable figure, and $70 was fought hard. Clearly, substantial measures of power were at stake. When the Ways and Means Committee returned from a long caucus which lasted until 5:00 P.M., their final offer was still $60. The ladies refused the offer and Brody dismissed the meeting with the understanding that the negotiations would recommence at 1:30 P.M. on Friday.

By 5:00 P.M. the numbers of supporters had dwindled to 100 and the number of photographers, newsmen and police had increased. Tense students, ADC mothers and children quietly filed past the guarded doors to the hallway outside the second-floor meeting room.

Two mothers spoke to the remainder of the crowd. They announced that the supervisors had reneged on their previous acceptance of the need principle by placing a ceiling on the proposed grants, and that the mothers had decided to remain in the building until the next day when negotiations were to continue. Their supporters (about 100) responded by sitting down in the hall with the mothers and linking arms. We felt there should be no need to leave the building until our demands were met, and we were willing to stay as long as necessary to achieve them. Hanson, Sheriff Stoner and the prosecuting attorney decided to enforce an administrative provision of the Board of Supervisors (not a law) that the building should close at 5:30 P.M. and open again the next morning at 7:30 A.M. Stoner read out an arrest warrant which he said would go into effect in five minutes if the demonstrators were not out of the building. Fifty-two adults and about fifteen children remained seated on the floor, singing and clapping as Stoner stepped out to call up his forces.

First the men were dragged out (by two policemen each) and then they started with the women. The protesters sang "We Shall Overcome" and "Freedom, Freedom" while they were dragged down the steps and outside to be thrown in waiting paddy wagons. Even though most of the demonstrators "went limp" and did not physically resist being dragged and shoved, many had bruises on their arms or bodies from being held and pulled along the ground. The protesters' anger and frustration were further provoked in the course of the dehumanizing jailing and booking procedures.

At the County Legal Aid Clinic, funds were raised for bail which Hanson set at $25 per person. Phone calls were made to liberal faculty and community members, receipts for contributions were given out and the whole office took on the air of a bank in its daily transactions. By 8:30 P.M. they began letting people out of jail. A crowd of 200 waited outside. By midnight all but two of the fifty-two had been released on bail.

The response of the mothers who were arrested to the events of Thursday could be characterized as a strengthening of their determination to carry their fight through to the end. In addition to pride in their own courage, the mothers were also buoyed up by the manifestation of commitment on the part of the students who had been working with them—that we didn't back out, but stuck with the mothers as we had promised.

The larger student community responded in force to the Thursday arrests. Campus leaders planned a rally for the next day immediately after the arrests of Thursday evening. I believe it is significant that the student community began to mobilize while the mothers and the student "staff" were still in jail and out of communication with them. The Thursday jailing of demonstrators was also a crucial turning point in terms of media coverage. At this point national press arrived on the scene and stayed with the confrontation until the final settlement on Monday.

There was implicit in the sheriff's actions a specific attempt on the part of a law enforcement agency to determine the guilt of an individual before that person is brought to trial and an attempt to divide and displace the decision-making power of the group in a conflict situation. It has, perhaps, also a direct link with Judge Barnes' rumored remark that he had chosen to use the cases of the students who came up before his bench as "an example" to other students who became "involved" in local community affairs.

At a noon rally on Friday, students mobilized on campus and about 600 came down to the County Building to support the mothers in their meeting with the Board of Supervisors. A basic tactical agreement reached previously between the mothers and the student leaders still held—that the issue should remain that of school clothing, not turn into an issue of student power, police brutality or racism, although there were overtones of each of these considerations in the situation.

The students decided to sit-in throughout the building. The threat of arrest for "obstructing" and then an order for clearance of the second floor by the sheriff provoked discussion, debate and division among the participating students. Conflicting statements and the impending threat of arrest provoked many students to leave the County Building and to form picket lines outside.

The support inside and outside the building had a significant effect on the negotiations on the second floor. At the last minute Hanson called a special bargaining session in which the mothers were offered a package of a $60 flat grant plus the possibility of negotiation for a coat and a pair of boots in the future. By questioning Hanson, the ladies and their spokesmen found out that there was no real commitment by the Board to further action. They thus chose not to accept the Board's final offer and to have the demonstrators maintain their positions—at least on the main floor of the County Building. Again a confrontation developed with law enforcement officials. Removal from the building and arrest was handled pretty much as it had been the previous day—with six times as many law officers on hand.

The 192 arrests of Friday served to arouse the local community, to gain the support of sympathetic citizens and to mobilize students for a teach-in and a variety of other "educational" programs over the weekend.

The events of the weekend strengthened the support and interest of the group coalition which was loosely formed to help end the conflict between the ADC mothers and the supervisors. While university and community people telephoned and telegraphed supervisors their sentiments concerning the week of conflict, students held a weekend-long vigil in front of the County Building. The idea behind the vigil was twofold: (1) to act as a central information point from which to pass out leaflets, and (2) to keep the issue before the public.

The weekend was a welcomed rest period for many of the mothers. Some of the mothers came to the vigil, but most took care of homes and children they had been forced to neglect for the past week. The real fatigue which occurred among the mothers came on Monday.

Counterforces in action over the weekend were mostly linked to those set in motion by Mr. Dale. From Friday to Monday he attempted to undermine the positive line of negotiations by sending both his caseworkers and his resident advocates out to Howell to convince the residents of the benefits of the $60 offer. On Sunday, the local Housing Projects were buzzing with confused ADC recipients who were unclear about whether they could immediately obtain $60, were to wait for further negotiations, or whatever.

The Green City News ran a headline telling mothers to come to the Social Services office on Monday morning to pick up $60 per child. For Dale it was a very sophisticated tactic. It would have split the mothers into two groups. Their solidarity had been unanimous on their request that the county meet individual needs. However, the Social Services Board said publicly that *no* money would be given out on Monday morning. Dale's last maneuver had failed. At the same time, the County Board of Supervisors agreed to a meeting on Monday, beginning at 3:00 P.M., which would go on until a settlement was reached. There were to be no guns and no police in the County Building during the negotiations.

On Monday, 250 pickets clearly demonstrated broad community support for the mothers' demands. With Hanson chairing the meeting, the idea of a three-man fact-finding committee—consisting of a dean, the mayor of Howell and a corporate executive—was accepted by both sides. It was also agreed that their recommendations were not to be binding on either side. The ADC group then asked if anyone wished to say which clothing items on the list were not essential. There was no question as to the validity of the items. Finally, the mothers had achieved a hard bargaining position.

The mothers then met with the fact-finding committee to explain their position. They left the door open to negotiation on the items on the list, but refused to sacrifice their original concept of individual and minimum needs. The fact-finders were at this point well oriented to available dollar figures. This dollar orientation led them to the suggestion that $40 be mailed out to each recipient and the rest be distributed according to individual needs. When pushed, they admitted that a $70 ceiling would still have to be placed on what each person could receive. The mothers saw the committee was still not talking about enough money to meet their demands. The ladies made a counterproposal which was essentially the one which the fact-finding committee finally proposed:

1. $70 was to be given out immediately to each eligible child.
2. Mothers would be required to come to the office to obtain their checks.
3. After thirty days the mothers would negotiate with the Social Services Board to determine how the remaining funds from the pool (if any) would be administered.
4. The Fact-Finding Committee would have to determine the appropriate dollar figures for the proposal.

The fact-finding committee determined that $50,000 was to be appropriated from county funds, $4,500 from the Social Services Board, and the rest would be matched by the state (about $40,000). The final total was thus over $94,000. They also made it clear that a simple declaration by the mother would be sufficient to establish need.

It was 11:00 P.M. when Hanson reconvened the Board of Supervisors and the chairman of the fact-finding committee read the recommendations which had been accepted by the mothers. Hanson asked that all those opposed stand up and go on record. Since no one rose, a quorum of the entire Board of Supervisors had approved the special appropriation. The mothers had won a victory for minimum and individual needs which would lead to further actions in Indian County.

UNIT **9.**

Black Capitalism and Ethnic Economic Development: Portland Blacks Get Their Company Thing Together

One form of Black Power that has received acceptance and even support from the white establishment has been black capitalism. A basic plank in the generally conservative Nixon program on black issues has to do with the encouragement of business enterprises among blacks and other ethnic and racial groups. The program is seen favorably, of course, because of its congruence with essential features of the established order. Black capitalism constitutes a mechanism for "bringing blacks into the system" and permitting them to "get their share of the pie" without having to overturn the existing structure or question its basic premises.

Some militants see this as a "cooling out" and "buying off" technique. They contend that setting up black business ventures will not appreciably alter the structure of institutional racism in American society. Only a limited number of blacks stand to benefit and even those only in a limited way. The over-all power structure of the society, they contend, would not be penetrated or altered, and some of the steam may be taken out of the efforts to promote fundamental institutional change. However, even if one accepts the value of this form of ethnic economic development, a number of important issues arise—the accumulation of sufficient capital, the acquisition of experienced and capable personnel in management and skilled trades, the placing of governmental funds into private profit-making ventures, the training and utilization of "hardcore unemployables," the role of white consultants in black enterprises, and prejudicial stereotypes on the part of potential suppliers and consumers regarding a "Negro company."

Some of these problems are highlighted in the experience of the Albina Corporation, a black manufacturing firm in Portland, Oregon.

"It's been said black people can't do anything right," the short, bulky man in brown overalls said. "I felt if I got a job here at Albina it would be a step in the right direction."

"Portland Blacks Get Their Company Thing Together." *The Civil Rights Digest,* Spring, 1969, pp. 15-25.

A step in the right direction is Willie Garrett's appraisal—and perhaps the best one at the moment—of Albina Corporation, the Portland, Oregon, company for which he now works but which in time he may come to own with his fellow workers.

Garrett, an Alabama emigre, and some thirty other black on-the-job trainees, together with black owners and black managers, are the human factor in a radical economic equation being tested in the Portland mini-ghetto of Albina.

The venture is unique: the black enterprise incorporates the traditional forms and principles of business and industry but with an added measure—employee ownership and eventual employee control of the company.

The Albina Corporation, named after the ghetto district in which it is located, is a metal, plastics, and fiberglass manufacturing firm which has already processed a number of Government and commerical or private contracts. Albina is involved in negotiations and research for the fabrication of its own line of products. A top-flight black managerial team has been assembled and a black work force drawn from the nearby community is being trained to handle a broad range of manufacturing programs. By midyear, gross capitalization (buildings, equipment) will be about $2,000,000, and its payroll about $3,000,000 to $3,500,000.

At a time when national attention is turning to the economic development of the ghetto from within, a primary focus is on black entrepreneurship. The Albina Corporation is spearheading a most forward-looking venture which will extend to all employees the potential to earn incomes not only on the basis of their toil, but on the essential resource by which affluence is achieved in America—capital ownership, which entails a personal investment in the firm and a share in the community-wide enterprise.

The company is not yet a year old and still must prove itself—an achievement which may not be reached in terms of stabilized annual corporate growth for two or more years. Toward this goal, a $1,200,000 contract awarded Albina by the Department of Defense in February (to paint ammunition boxes by an electrocoating process) represents a major breakthrough and Albina's greatest challenge to date. As a trainee put it, "The ammo container job is the test; if we don't complete it, that may be it." With half a million dollars' worth of new equipment, revamping of plant facilities is under way to accommodate the Defense contract. Production force will be increased from the present 38 to 107 due to the Defense contract's manpower needs.

In another area, the company's efforts to develop its own products either through creating new lines—for example, in its fiberglass operation, or buying out already existing firms with established names and markets—indicate that managerial skills and production force capacity will be tested to the fullest. By the same token, new product development would increase the work force and in turn uplift the Albina community from which the company draws the majority of its employees.

Such is the potential for growth and the kind of odds facing Albina, a company which literally started from a bare concrete floor. The plant building at 3810 N. Mississippi Avenue is a former bowling alley whose high, cross-peaked roof contrasts with the one- or two-story wood frame buildings and homes which characterize the district. Creditors had foreclosed on the bowling establishment and had stripped all equipment from it, leaving only wall-to-wall concrete.

The prospects for the black firm are wide open; the pitfalls also that such a business starting from scratch faces are numerous, crop up unexpectedly, and can, at any given time, wipe out months of progress. The man most conscious of the promise that Albina holds as well as the problems it presents is Mayfield K. Webb, president and chairman of its Board of Directors. Born in Baltimore, Md., and a graduate of Morgan State College there, Webb moved to Portland after service as an infantry officer in Korea, earning a law degree in 1960 at Portland's Northwestern College of Law. He practiced law in the Albina ghetto until 1965 when he became director of the Albina Neighborhood Service Center, a project of the Office of Economic Opportunity. Two years later he was hired as executive director of the multimillion-dollar Portland Metropolitan Steering Committee, the local Community Action Agency.

Silhouetted by the incandescence of a welding torch behind him, the forty-two-year-old Webb stated:

"Albina is a form of institutional change, change of the normal corporate structure based on the concept of employee ownership. Many companies have bonus plans or stock programs for employees, but I don't believe there is another company, and certainly not a black one, committed to 100 per cent ownership by its employees.

"The concept of capital ownership is also being tried to determine if it will serve as a motivating factor, whether it will be meaningful to personnel to have a stake in the company. Frankly, it is too early to tell whether this will be an effect of the Albina plan," he admits. "Thirdly, the Albina Investment Trust is designed to provide a second income to employees. Actually, this is a retirement plan at this point. If the company is successful, employees could receive dividends.

"Through the second income plan," Webb said, "we hope to demonstrate that it is also an effective vehicle for a steady and measured system of corporate growth and that we can rely on the use of pre-tax dollars for continued growth each year."

Here is how the employee trust plan operates:

The Albina Investment Trust, a deferred-compensation trust, has been established in behalf of the employees of the Albina Corporation. The Office of Economic Opportunity made two outright grants totaling $586,000 to finance the creation of the trust and demonstrate the feasibility of employee ownership. The Investment Trust owns majority interest in the corporation and is responsible for educating employees in capital ownership.

The employee trust program (or Second Income Plan, SIP) is administered by both the corporation and the trust, each of which entails a board broadly representative of the company and the community.

At the end of each year of employment, the individual employee is vested or assigned by the trust 15 per cent of his total annual income in shares—his regular income is not touched: the 15 per cent is over and above what he ordinarily earns.

Under the Albina plan, after the first three years with the company, an employee will own outright 30 per cent of the total shares he has built up. He is vested with an additional 10 per cent each successive year until in ten years he will have 100 per cent ownership and control of his shares.

At any time he can retire his shares, that is, sell them to anyone he wishes to the percentage of shares he owns.

The corporation's Board of Directors is comprised of four representatives of the Albina Citizens' War on Poverty Committee; one each from the ADC Mothers, the Citizens' Improvement Association, Model Cities Planning Board and Eastern Star (The Masonic Lodge women's auxiliary); and five others representing the corporation's management. The trust's Board of Trustees consists of three persons from the Albina Citizens' War on Poverty Committee; one each from the Elks Club, the Masonic Lodge, and Model Cities; and three selected by corporate management.

On July 30, one of the three management representatives who now include Webb,

Ben L. Berry, and David M. Nero, Jr., will be replaced by an employee representative. The trust committee instructs the holder of the trust, the First National Bank in Portland, how to vote shares in the event of a stockholders' meeting. Along with built-in community involvement, the addition of an employee representative will also provide a voice and the initial sense of ownership control to the employees.

Not until the first week in April did Albina secure the Internal Revenue Service's approval to establish the employee trust. Because of the possibility that approval might be withheld, fulfilling the responsibility of fully instructing employees in depth about the trust plan has been delayed. With the IRS approval of the trust, the company can now introduce a formal program of instruction for employees and management, as well as directors and trustees according to Webb, since some of the intricacies of the plan must still be clarified for many people.

Providing a most articulate expression of his understanding of what Albina meant to him and particularly of the employee trust plan was Marion Blackburn, who left a job as a salesman for a bread company at the end of last September, started as a trainee in sales and marketing, and in March was named acting sales manager, "a big jump," his boss Mayfield Webb called it. Born in Huntsville, Alabama, Blackburn says of Albina:

"Albina was my first opportunity to move into management. I saw a chance for advancement in it and, frankly, I was tired of constantly dealing with Caucasians, didn't have a sense of confidence. It was a grin and bear it thing; the world isn't real to you: the conversations, the things they like to do, I didn't like. I was always subject to criticism, or worse, loss of my job, so I had to be reserved about my activities for my people. Albina is a chance to work with my own people.

"An important factor in my coming to Albina," Blackburn added, "was the ownership program. All we have to do is make the company go. To me the stock program will provide a substantial amount of reserves to borrow on. In ten years I'll have a kid ready for college. I haven't even entertained the idea of going any place else." The young executive concluded, "I'd rather be here than any place I know, like W. C. Handy said."

Blackburn is an individual, personal success story. Albina is making it possible, but the over-all effect of a successful Albina Corporation (failure isn't even contemplated—verbally—by most Albina staff) is that a ghetto-owned and controlled operation would have an impact far beyond its setting and far beyond its immediate beneficiaries.

Albina is also a testing ground to resolve other issues: the pooling of Government, private, and local funds in ghetto enterprise; the training of those usually considered "unemployable" or "hardcore"; and the functioning of white consultants among black entrepreneurs and workers.

These problem areas result directly from the ghetto and minority group foundation of the company and in turn generate conflicts or problems which the usual business or factory would not encounter. Albina and other black companies like it must handle not only the ordinary difficulties of private enterprise but face other unusual and often unique obstacles. It means that a black company starts with strikes against it.

One of the most immediate problems which Albina alone must resolve is how to make the ownership program meaningful. Webb and the brain trust of consultants and lawyers behind Albina are deliberating the establishment of a credit union or a yearly bonus plan, or some other means of putting that extra income into workers' pockets. The bonus idea, Webb points out, would be a concrete means, but that money would come out of profits and be taxable, whereas money kept in the employees' trust would not be taxed, would support the company's corporate growth, and simultaneously build up the stockholder's own capital base for future use. (Income on stock, or capital gains, derived in later years by the employee is taxable only to 25 per cent of the total.) The value of the deferred-compensation trust is difficult to communicate to most people, Webb says but much more so to an individual with little or no experience in saving, budgeting, or investing money.

That particular point of Webb's is especially relevant to Albina. Most of Albina's employees at the trainee level have been drawn from the ranks of the underemployed or unemployed. Under the Department of Labor Manpower training contract with Albina, the company must recruit its workers from the Model Cities area which includes the Albina district and other neighboring areas. The trainees also must meet certain limits of income, family size, and education or skills to qualify as trainees.

Because of the nature of the Albina commitment, the Labor Department has waived its regulation limiting the percentage of trainees in a company work force to 50 per cent. Albina can now have 100 per cent of its employees under training, which is very nearly the case. However, the reimbursement that Albina receives from the Department of Labor MA-3 programs for its training component is still at the level for 50 per cent of work force training. This means that Albina must accomplish twice as much in its training aspects for half the money. In terms of job costs, as Webb described it, "Labor is usually the factor that runs up the costs; if we figured in all labor costs, we would never be able to low-bid on contracts."

Because of the nature of the trainee, not only do labor costs mount, but the difficulty of getting maximum output is seriously affected. Absenteeism is the gravest shortcoming among the work force, a factor which management, from foremen to the president, indicates would be overcome as the worker gains industrial experience and as long as management is willing to persevere through the period of worker development.

Although the company does bend over backwards to keep some workers on the job, it could hardly be accused of being patronizing or soft in the face of the sheer reality of overcoming the workers' lack of industrial experience. Besides, the Albina president forecast, as production force increases, coupled with the demands and importance of the Defense contract, the company may have to become more selective in its hiring and maintenance of workers.

Aware, also, of the effects of the ghetto upon motivation and desire among its employees, a group of trainees have been enrolled in a Success Motivation Institute course sponsored by the Concentrated Employment Program (CEP), a training arm of the Department of Labor. Employees requiring further training or retraining could be remitted to the Portland CEP or the local Opportunities Industrialization Center.

Texas-born Matt Lockett, at twenty-five the shop foreman and an instructor for Albina, proudly relates that he was the first black man to complete the four-year apprenticeship welding course in Portland. A 1961 graduate of Benton Technical High School, Lockett was an apprentice at Willamette Iron and Steel Company but moonlighted for six weeks helping Albina finish its first contract before joining the black firm permanently last October. Exuding a self-confidence built up by his experience and knowledge of the trade, Lockett recalls: "When I first came to Albina I thought I was taking a chance, but I think the company will get on its feet. If you know your business," he stated, "you don't take a chance." Recalling his efforts in learning his trade, Lockett said something applicable to Albina's status: "Being the only Negro, you've gotta be a little bit better. I can go anywhere now and get a job. If we can get the thing together, the company will do fine." The youthful shop leader, by the way, also holds a part-time job as a city policeman.

Albina Corporation hardly had its office set up last year when Willie Garrett came in looking for a job. He had been a waiter at a restaurant in the North Center area of Portland, although he and his wife and five children live in the Albina ghetto. Still, he had to wait two weeks to be approved as "hardcore." The twenty-seven-year-old Garrett quit his former job, which meant, he relates, a cut in pay. But, he explains, "I want to learn a trade like welding or machine tools. I feel I'm progressing; every day I learn something new." Garett has had two pay increases since last May, worked on every contract in some way, and was recently made lead man on a small project for Western Electric which involves a number of stamping processess in producing brackets for wall telephones.

Garrett summed up for most of his fellow workers when he said his main reason for coming was that Albina was to be a "real black organization." "It's been said black people can't do anything right. I felt if I got a job at Albina, it would be a step in the right direction." Of the employee trust plan, he asserted that it would come in handy and that a "person will work harder if it's for himself."

Already apparent is the broad role of Government agencies in the formation of Albina. The Labor Department has various manpower training branches at work; the Internal Revenue Service and U.S. Treasury Department have carefully scrutinized the economic underpinnings of the corporation.

Two agencies which have had substantive roles to play this past year and a half are the Small Business Administration and the Office of Economic Opportunity. The SBA guaranteed a $350,000 loan through a Portland bank to Albina Corporation, which means that SBA can be counted upon to maintain close surveillance of the black company's progress. The SBA can also have continued effect because, as Webb pointed out, the agency has the legislative authority to negotiate with any Federal agency, declare these contracts "no bid," and award them to small businesses. In fact, Webb suggested that major contracts, for example, from the Defense Department, reach down into the smaller businesses through the granting of subcontracts. SBA could also extend its backing through negotiated contracts for two or three years instead of one as is now the case.

The most unique Government role has been undertaken by the Office of Economic Opportunity which in less than a year granted outright to Albina two grants totaling $586,000 to establish the trust. There was a slim possibility for a while because of the working of Government regulations that had the IRS not qualified Albina under Section 401 of the IRS Code governing "charitable trusts," OEO would have in effect become owner of the manufacturing firm since it would have owned all the shares of stock.

A contingency which Albina developers did not foresee but apparently was in the making due to those same regulations again was the IRS Code requirement that all funds placed in a trust must be allocated the same year: the $586,000 from OEO, in other words, must be divided among the shareholders in the first year. This could mean that an individual shareholder, an employee, would be credited with an amount of shares which would otherwise have taken him ten years to build. For example, if the OEO grant money were divided, a worker might be allocated $7,500 worth of shares after only one year of work, or more than he might earn over ten years. He would be entitled to cash in the stock to whatever percentage of value he was vested. The concept of creating long-term loyalty and long-term gains is jeopardized. Webb is sure that the complexity can be untangled by a special ruling from IRS either waiving the requirement to allocate all funds the first year or by establishing a special category of funds. Its qualification under Section 401 of the IRS Code at any rate is in no danger of being rescinded.

The money received through the OEO grants and the SBA guaranteed loan represented the capitalization with which the corporation was able to buy a plant, equipment, and supplies, establish a payroll, and revamp facilities. In fact, without this "unusual example of cooperation," as one Federal official described the OEO-SBA collaboration, Albina Corporation might never have developed. (Albina's directors are still seeking other sources of funds, including a sizable loan application to the Presbyterian Economic Development Corporation located in New York City.)

Dependence on Government agencies will continue for a time although the OEO grants will probably not be renewed but simply expire when the money is used up. Severance of such ties is part of the over-all goal of the Albina innovators. It will come more quickly the sooner Albina pays off its loans and develops its own product lines, stabilizes its work force, and is assured of more contracts.

The development of Albina products—that is, items of which Albina alone would be the producer or resource; for example, a new design of fiberglass boat or an electromechanical assembly—is severely cramped by a limited budget, reports Ben L. Berry, vice-president and chief engineer. Formerly with the consultant firm of TRW Systems in Redondo Beach, California, Berry insists that development of new product lines is "a necessary goal if we are to become a major company." A volunteer consultant and training director for Operation Bootstrap and other ghetto self-help projects in the Los Angeles area, Berry explains that "under a contract, the company has to meet competition by cutting into its profits to keep down costs, but if we have a patented product we can demand more profit; only a competitor's similar product could limit the price we could set."

Perhaps the most problematic internal concern in the company is the relationship between the black work force and the white consultants—every white man in the Albina Corporation at present is a consultant: he operates as a function of management but he cannot participate in the employee trust plan. Other companies attempting similar programs have experienced friction between black and white personnel. On the basis of interviews with employees at every level the situation at Albina in this regard has been exceptional.

Among trainees the criticism most often voiced is based on the hiring of four white welders to complete one of the early contracts; some of the black workers believe that Negro welders should and could have been recruited to do the job. It didn't help, the dissenting employees indicated, that the white welders demanded and obtained a dollar above scale for their work.

The role of the white consultant at this phase in the development of the Albina firm and for its duplication any place else is considered mandatory by the corporation's innovator, Linus J. Niedermeyer, a successful Portland businessman and executive consultant to Albina. Ability and a degree of empathy with the black man were prerequisites in the consultants he recruited for the firm. Niedermeyer points out that white consultants had to accept two major limitations: within a minimum of one year and no more than three years, they would no longer work for Albina— a black counterpart was to be found or trained within that time—and they could not share in the employee stock plan. Higher salaries than previous were offered as an incentive and compensation for exclusion from the trust program, Niedermeyer added.

Highly optimistic of Albina's own future, Niedermeyer also is confident that a team of Albina personnel could duplicate the firm in its basic conceptual framework in any city in America with sixty days. But Government and private business and industry, he asserted, will watch Albina for the time being as a pilot program before further commitments are made. The Portland lumber executive credits the state's U.S. Senators and Portland area Congressmen in particular for supporting the Albina project within the state and in Washington, D.C. According to Niedermeyer, "Without the Oregon legislators to overcome the reluctance among some Government officials to back an idea which is truly unique and innovative, Albina would not be in existence. After all, Albina is the first instance in which the Federal Government has funded a profit-making organization!"

Niedermeyer initiated his personal efforts to develop a ghetto enterprise along the lines of the Watts Manufacturing Company in 1967, but expanded the idea to include complete black ownership and operation as a necessary element. The concept of the Second Income Plan originated with Louis O. Kelso, of a San Francisco corporate law firm, with whom Niedermeyer also conferred in developing the economic structure for Albina. Kelso has advanced the Two-Factor Theory, which is a concept of economics he has proposed to create a system of "universal capitalism" in the United States, by which all persons will have the equal economic opportunity to own capital. His firm has established a number of SIP trusts which enable corporations to finance growth on the pre-tax dollar and build equity quickly among its employees and executives.

The idea of establishing a black firm in Portland began to germinate more than three years ago. James Woods, president and general manager of Watts Manufacturing Company in Los Angeles, a subsidiary of Aerojet General Corporation, but black-managed, originally suggested the venture to Niedermeyer. But Niedermeyer rejected the subsidiary aspect of developing such a firm and moved toward the creation of a black-owned company. Conferences toward drawing up an OEO proposal started in February 1967 between Niedermeyer, Woods, and a Portland resident, Clifford J. Campbell, Sr., a longtime leader in the Negro civil rights movement and at present a senior consultant to the Ford Foundation. To elicit community support Niedermeyer, Campbell, and national and regional OEO officials presented the idea before the Albina Citizens' War on Poverty in July 1967. The final proposal went to OEO in Washington in October 1967 with the support of every black organization of size and importance in Portland.

The necessary boards were organized, a thousand details worked out, and on July 1, 1968, the converted bowling alley's doors were reopened. Campbell was elected interim president until Webb succeeded him as permanent head of Albina Corporation in September.

Campbell is often quoted for having said in regard to the city where Albina is being tested: "Portland is small enough to be manageable, but big enough to be meaningful." Niedermeyer fully agrees with Campbell's view, adding that "we whites, who feel a portion of the collective guilt for the black man's situation, believe this is an honest approach and not one that will perpetuate the system of dependence."

Campbell's assessment of Portland's potential is remarkably salient. The state of Oregon contains nearly 1,900,000 people of whom 1.2 per cent, or 23,000 people, are Negro. In the city of Portland, about 5 per cent of the population is Negro, totaling about 20,000 persons, all but a tenth of the black people in the state. Most of the black Portlandites reside within the 20-square-block region of Albina. Clearly, then, Albina Corporation represents the firmest hope for excape from the ghetto for Oregon's black people. Its future is also Oregon's future in black-white relations.

From the business side, Webb states, the burden is on local businesses to support Albina's effort. In fact, he has told a meeting of the Portland City Club, "This corporation demands profitable business from our local industrialists. We can make anything in the steel or fiberglass line and we are entitled to a share of the local business. Frankly, it is embarrassing to tell an Eastern customer that we only have one order from a commercial establishment in our own local area. . . . Are you willing to share the responsibility which should be that of the total community by taking a first step to provide a last chance to those who still have hope?" he challenged.

The lack of local response of which he spoke in that February speech persists today, the Albina president reports. "We have to convince local industry that we can do the job," Webb says, adding that he believes companies with Defense contracts should subcontract with Albina for items they may now be getting from out of state. It doesn't help business, he admits, that the region itself is not a major manufacturing area. "Although we find sympathy from the community, when it comes to the nitty-gritty, we have to cut the mustard like everyone else. Well," Webb corrected himself, "maybe we have to do it more so." He does hope that despite the obstacles more black manufacturing companies will develop but sees little sign of any upsurge.

David Nero, formerly head of Procurement and Contract Administration for the Battelle-Northwest Project of the Atomic Energy Commission and now Albina's vice-president and marketing director, views the quality of Albina contracts to date with much reserve. An Army captain until 1955, Nero calls most of the private contracts awarded Albina "teasers."

"I recognize in the experience so far that people are victims of the stereotype Negro. I assure you, most of the contractors are imbued with the stereotype—that we can't deliver on time, for example—and it has to be overcome. How? We were given a stiff schedule by Texas Instruments (a contract for brass castings), but we beat the schedule by a week! When I flew down to the Texas office, I learned we could have had twice the order but the company had kept back half the order thinking they could at least depend on having half as many assured."

The stereotype has to be overcome within another of its victims—Government, Nero continued. If a contractor can show feasibility of his proposal, he believes that a Government agency should take another check among bidders to be sure that a company such as Albina isn't being overlooked. SBA should also lower its loan qualifications from 500 or less employees down to 100 or less or establish categories such as for a poverty pocket concern which might otherwise have the production capability but miss out because of its smaller size. "Under SBA regulations," Nero added, "subsidiaries of large companies have certain advantages which should not be denied companies such as Albina because of their independence."

"That's the nigger company," is the grossest instance of prejudice against Albina which Jack Perkins, consultant in charge of purchasing, traffic, and shipping, has experienced since joining Albina in its first months. The company represented by the voice on the phone has not been rung up again. Other than this one case, Perkins, previously administrative assistant at a local steel fabrication firm, reports "as good or better" service and terms from local firms in a number of brackets—discounting, training films, delivery, credit buying. A company representative had asked Perkins last year, "What can we do to help?" We need about a ton of scrap metal for trainees to practice on, he was told. A few days later, a truck drove onto the site and dumped a pile of scrap metal that seemed to mount up, Perkins recalled, to just about a ton.

Of the twenty-four active contracts that Perkins services, about half have been won on low bid. The rest have been negotiated; that is, the price was set with Albina the only company considered because of its specific nature as a ghetto enterprise. A contract was lost on the latter basis, Perkins related, to an Indian tribe in Montana, indicating a certain amount of competition even among ventures established to rehabilitate poverty areas.

Nothing will come easy for Albina Corporation during the next couple of years. Webb speaks of "turning corners every day" on the road to moving ahead in the profit margin, paying off its loans, establishing its independence from outright grant support, forming a cohesive work force. As an observer remarked, Albina must move through the entire industrial revolution. Having done so, it will have shown that people with no previous ownership can build economic power through ownership of capital and their human input.

The success of the employee trust program will develop gradually. Its greatest significance will be established if the black employees actually assume control of the company. They have the legal powers open to them. If they assume control of the firm, Albina will have achieved a status of momentous political and economic consequence. This will be its key contribution to minority people. Not the only way out as Webb, Niedermeyer, and others admit, but another way of achieving independence for minority peoples.

That's what Albina is really all about, getting to the point where it can "cut the mustard" on its own. It will have proven something to a lot of people, or to pick up where Willie Garrett left off, that "black people *can* do anything right."

The Effects of OEO and Other Local "Participatory" Programs: Oklahomans for Indian Opportunity

Mobilization for Youth was a kind of crucible in which contemporary community action strategies were initially tested. The assumption behind the Mobilization approach was that structural change was necessary—in particular, changes in the opportunity structure—before improvements could be made in the position of disadvantaged racial and ethnic groups. It was also assumed that programs of this character could be conducted under the sponsorship of governmental agencies. The Community Action Program of OEO was based on similar suppositions, in part informed and influenced by MFY. The crisis through which Mobilization passed, and the rough political sledding experienced by many of the more militant OEO programs, have led informed observers to question some of the early assumptions. While "maximum feasible participation" became a watchword, in most instances it served more as a slogan than a guide to actual performance. After all, it is now asked, can you realistically expect any establishment or bureaucracy to be serious in supporting insurgent tendencies which significantly threaten to challenge or destroy it? A fundamental imperative of organizational behavior is self-survival, and rare is the organization that will willingly implement its own demise or decline. In light of such a perspective, how much can one expect from OEO, Model Cities, Community Mental Health, and other programs which profess to foster the participation of racial and ethnic minorities in program activities? Can these programs be instrumental in supporting Black, Brown, and Red Power organizing efforts, or on the contrary, do they diffuse such efforts by neutralizing them, creaming off and co-opting leadership, and creating the facade of motion without the ingredient of movement? In the interplay of forces is the movement able to co-opt the establishment or is the establishment likely to co-opt the movement? Are there techniques that may be employed by movement groups to keep the upper hand, or conditions under which they are more likely to be successful? And if one is to discard these existing vehicles, what viable alternatives are available?

In Oklahoma, Oklahomans for Indian Opportunity is one of the few avenues for internal organization of the Native American community. How it is used and its impact on Indian solidarity and power can have an important effect on state politics and policies in the years ahead. The program is described in the following presentation.

Oklahomans for Indian Opportunity, Incorporated, is an educational, nonprofit corporation incorporated under the laws of the state of Oklahoma. The president of Oklahomans for Indian Opportunity is Mr. James Wahpepah of Jones, Oklahoma, a Kickapoo Indian. Mrs. Fred R. Harris is the honorary lifetime president of the corporation. The Board of Directors is composed of forty-one Oklahomans, including Indians from every section of the state; some interested non-Indians are also on the Board. Oklahomans for Indian Opportunity is the only representative, nongovernmental organization in Oklahoma capable of reaching a majority of the Indians of the sixty-odd tribes in Oklahoma.

Formed for the purpose of improving conditions for Oklahoma Indians and helping to draw them more fully into Oklahoma's economy and culture, Oklahomans for Indian Opportunity came into existence when it sponsored a statewide Indian Opportunity Conference at the University of Oklahoma on August 7, 1965. The conference was attended by over five hundred Oklahoma Indians, representing all tribes.

Although its Indian population is second only to that of Arizona, Oklahoma has no reservations. The fact that there are no reservations in the state means that the Indian people are increasingly being forced to make the transition into the total community of American life, even though they are often inadequately prepared to do so. Moreover, the non-Indian residents in many communities are often unwilling to accept Indians into community activities. Oklahoma, therefore, is the logical proving ground for new programs and approaches aimed at seeking solutions to the problems of off-reservation Indians. Oklahomans for Indian Opportunity feels that its experiences and ideas can be of value to all programs working with Indians and other minority groups, because after being tested in Oklahoma these new programs and approaches can become models for other states where there are large Indian populations.

Although some Oklahoma Indians are well-to-do and have adopted the patterns of the dominant culture, the majority of Indian people in Oklahoma are living in conditions of near or extreme poverty; many see little hope for improvement. Especially among the poor, many Indian people in Oklahoma appear to manifest no desire to enter into community affairs or to involve themselves with the institutions of their communities, partly because many Indian people are ambivalent about the extent to which they want to take part in "the white man's world." Oklahoma Indians must be assisted to develop an attitude of self-confidence which will enable them to find a place in the social, cultural, political, and educational aspects of the total community around them. As it is now, an accumulation of bad experiences, including disappointments with governmental and private agencies, has produced among many a kind of withdrawal and self-imposed isolation.

To see how widespread this attitude of resignation and withdrawal really is, one need only look at the small number of Indians who become involved in community or state activities. There are no legal discriminatory barriers that prohibit Indians from participating fully in the dominant social structure, but the fact remains that the number of Indians in community activities does not come close to comparing with their percentage of the state's population.

The various subgroups of Indians in Oklahoma simply have not developed the aggressive and universally respected leadership that some other ethnic groups have.

"Oklahomans for Indian Opportunity." Report presented to the annual Forum of the National Conference on Social Welfare in New York City on May 26, 1969, by Mrs. Iola Hayden, Director of OIO, and Mr. Bill Gover and Mr. William Hayden, members of the staff.

The jest that no Indian leader speaks for anyone but himself has all too often been true. Indian people will be unable to be equal partners with their non-Indian neighbors in any kind of community action until the Indian people have acquired the leadership skills which full participation in community affairs requires. It is essential, however, that these leadership skills be based on personal self-motivation and not on synthetic leadership imposed from outside the Indian community. Too many programs and agencies have sought to attack the problems of Indian people by imposing solutions and leadership from the outside; they have not seen that the basic need is the motivation and training of Indian people themselves for fuller participation in the larger society. Most of the talk about "Indian leaders" means so little because many people fail to realize that leadership must come from within the community, from people who live with and know the problems and are therefore the only ones qualified to propose solutions. This, more than anything else, is the reason behind Oklahomans for Indian Opportunity's existence.

Lack of education and inadequate income are two enormous barriers to the improvement of the quality of life for the Oklahoma Indian. The Bureau of Indian Affairs reports that approximately 90 per cent of the school-age Indian children in Oklahoma currently attend public schools; a study conducted by the University of Oklahoma found that the Indian dropout rate in public schools is sometimes three to four times that of the rate among non-Indian youngsters. In a recent study of the Indian school dropout rate in three counties in eastern Oklahoma (Wagoner, Cherokee, and Adair counties), the researchers found that approximately 70 per cent of the Cherokee Indian children left school before graduation. The average American child, as measured by the 1960 Census, completes between eleven and twelve grades of school; the median number of school years completed by Indians in Oklahoma is only 8.8.

Other than Oklahomans for Indian Opportunity, no agency addresses itself directly to the wide range of needs of the Indian people. Oklahoma, like most other states, has its share of community, state, and Federal agencies designed to meet the needs of special groups, but due to the structure of these agencies and the peculiar situation in Oklahoma non duplicate the past or proposed activities of Oklahomans for Indian Opportunity.

Although the Bureau of Indian Affairs has two offices in Oklahoma, it is important to remember that many of their programs were designed by Federal law especially for reservation Indians and are difficult to implement in Oklahoma, a state without reservations. Furthermore, the services provided generally do not offer solutions to the really basic causes of Indian people's problems. The Bureau of Indian Affairs often handicaps rather than helps Indian people, both because it continues the tradition of white paternalism and exclusion of the people themselves from decision-making roles, and because it reinforces the non-Indian belief that local communities and the state have little responsibility for the Indians because they are "taken care of by the government."

Although there is still some factionalism and disunity among Oklahoma Indians, OIO has been able to be a voice and an instrument of change for a broad base of Indian people. This is because OIO, unlike all other organizations and agencies in the state, is directed and operated by the people who live with the problems and who therefore can define the needs and devise ways of meeting them. All too often Indian leaders are powerful only because they make the non-Indian community comfortable, not because they have any real contact with the aspirations of the people. But they and distant white people are generally the people who in the past have made decisions *for* Indian people. Whatever effectiveness Oklahomans for Indian Opportunity has had is due to the wide range of the Oklahoma Indian population that is represented on the Board and in the staff. Rather than have a Board made up only of established "leaders," OIO has had the novel idea of having Indians running its affairs. The Board, which is nearly all Indian, has members from all parts of the state and representing all shades of opinion. Deliberate care has been taken to insure substantial representation of low-income Indians, who are often the people who are ignored by the established Indian and non-Indian power structure. The success of the various programs of OIO is due in large part to the fact that all programs stem directly from the needs of the Indian people and are solutions worked out by the people themselves.

Community Organization has had seven staff people during the past year, including a coordinator, an assistant coordinator, and five assistant field coordinators who are indigenous to the areas they serve. The assistant field coordinators are an important part of the staff. Not only are they local, nonprofessional people who are being trained for further advancement, they are also the most direct link possible with the feelings of the people in their areas. This is because they are *of* those areas.

The Youth Program is focused on a network of youth councils, which now number seventy-two and are located in all parts of the state. Well over 2,500 Indian young people are active participants in OIO youth activities. The state is divided geographically into ten youth districts; there are officers at the district level as well as statewide officers. Although the most important part of the youth program may be the day-to-day activities of each individual youth council, a good deal has happened on the district and state level. There have been fifteen district conferences over the past year, each one involving between sixty and one hundred and thirty young people. The programs of the youth conferences have varied, but most have included discussion groups on various issues, a panel of college students who talk directly with the young people, and a guest speaker. Care has been taken to hold the conferences on college campuses, partly because it gives the young people a chance to be exposed to a college and its students.

On March 29, 1969, Oklahomans for Indian Opportunity held its annual statewide youth conference, which was planned and executed with the active participation of young people at every stage. Activities included election of statewide officers, a keynote speech by former United States Attorney General Ramsey Clark, discussions with resource people from several organizations and educational institutions, and entertainment. More than 1,500 people were in attendance.

Emphasis has been placed on the use and training of local sponsors for the youth councils. Experience has shown us ever more clearly the absolute necessity of having parents and other interested adults actively involved in the work of the youth council and in the youth program as a whole. The youth councils are autonomous and all decisions are made by the young people themselves. Every youth council can use adults for transportation and other tasks, but the real importance of the sponsor is the effect his enthusiasm and guidance has on the young people. Too often an Indian youngster sees his parents uninvolved in local affairs, and many parents are unable to participate fully in the good and bad parts of a high school student's life at school.

The sponsor, then, serves several important functions. The young people have the advantage of working with Indian adults who show an enthusiastic interest in what they are doing, and if what they are doing is at all controversial this interest is of immeasurable importance. Secondly, the young people are able to call upon a person of perhaps greater experience who knows the local situation and who can act as a resource person for their activities. We have found that adults who become involved in youth activities will become involved in other community problems. They will take the lead in organizing a busing club, for example, or in speaking out about abuses at school, or in pressing for better facilities. Adult organization, or simply adult involvement, can grow directly out of involvement with the youth program.

In keeping with our increased awareness of the enormous importance of sponsor involvement, we have placed a great deal of emphasis over the past year on sponsor training and, as our proposed youth program shows, we will continue to do so. We have had intensive sponsor training sessions in various locations throughout the state, and have had sponsor workshops at most youth conferences during the discussion group period. The role of the sponsor has been discussed at the regional training sessions and at other meetings where adults have been present. Moreover, at the statewide youth conference a panel of four active sponsors—one board member, two parents, and an Indian teacher—presented their views of the sponsor's function to a sizable group of adults, many of whom had not previously taken part in the youth program.

The main value of the youth program, of course, is what it means to the young people themselves. The idea of the local youth councils emerged after quite a bit of experimentation; our experiences over this year in particular have shown us that the idea was a good one. The youth councils provide the young people, the OIO youth staff, and the communities with enormous flexibility in meeting local needs. Each youth council can work on projects relevant to the daily lives of its members. At the same time, district and statewide activities give young people with similar aspirations and interests a chance to exchange ideas and just to get to know one another. But the real test of the problem is not its theoretical acceptability or even how it looks from Norman; rather, it is the enthusiasm and interest of the young people themselves. We have seen that interest in every part of the state. The youth councils are developing strong, aware leaders who have been heartened by what they have done by themselves.

For many youngsters, especially some very bright ones, the youth council has been the one thing that has made school bearable. Many times principals or superintendents have said that a certian boy or girl would not be interested under any circumstances in youth councils; often it is just that boy or girl who emerges as the energetic leader of the youth council. This is because the councils, by their very nature as local groups run entirely by the young people, speak directly to the needs and desires of the Indian youth of the town. When we see the self-confident youngsters whose self-esteem has been developed through the youth councils, we feel heartened at the success of the youth program as a whole.

OIO has a very strong policy against becoming involved in tribal politics and against taking sides in factional disputes. Rather OIO personnel try to induce opposing parties to work together in a positive way on constructive projects.

In each community selected for an OIO effort the first step is for the OIO field representative or neighborhood worker or both to visit every Indian home for the purpose of: (1) explaining the OIO Rural Development Program; (2) attempting to find ways the particular family might become involved in the program; (3) to explore the possibility of holding a meeting in the near future so that the entire community might discuss the project together.

The next step is the actual organization of a community meeting. Usually the meeting will be held in a local Indian church, community center, or district school auditorium. Direct personal contact on a house-to-house basis is used to organize. Leaflets, newspaper and radio announcements are not used as a substitute for direct contact with the Indian community. Several types of meetings have developed with varying results. One type is the general information meeting—where the OIO program is explained and maybe other programs also. This type of meeting is generally not too productive although some results have come in later meetings called for a more specific purpose.

A second type would be a formal community development or industrial development type of meeting. Several Indian communities because of more sophisticated leadership have used OIO's help in organizing themselves, usually by incorporating for various purposes such as developing community recreational facilities and community-owned cooperative business enterprises.

The third and most important type of organization meeting has been the buying club meeting. To our way of thinking the buying club is a good fundamental test of community organization. They are not easy to organize. They involve sacrifice, development of trust in one another, and a high degree of cooperation on the part of the members for a very limited economic gain. Yet they prove to be very effective organizational tools in several parts of the project area. In many of these isolated rural areas the local grocery store is the center of economic life. Very frequently no prices are posted on goods. The local grocer extends credit on the basis of welfare or pay checks with the result that many of the local Indian population is in debt to the local store owner without knowing about how much or how long.

As a result of these organizational efforts a number of Indian-owned industries have been established. That is to say, because Indian communities were drawn together they were able to present ideas that could be profitably developed.

Buying clubs have been established in eleven communities with savings from 20 per cent to 30 per cent on food purchases. The following Indian-owned business establishments have been started: two service station-garages; one grocery store; two graphic arts and silk screening establishments; one feeder pig co-op; an artificial flower manufacturing company; a hauling and transport company; a plumbing company; and two community-owned laundry facilities. Of great local interest is the Cherokee Floats Operation which will operate during the spring and summer months. This project will provide a large employment for Indian young people. Also, OIO is giving assistance to an arts and crafts co-op that was already in existence.

Plans are in development for a large forest management program to be operated by Indian people. Also, in the early development stages is a fish farming cooperative and a tool handle factory.

The various Indian communities develop ideas for economic enterprises and the OIO staff attempts to give technical and financial assistance to make these ideas become successful Indian owned and controlled enterprises. Our program is only six months old but we feel that we have begun to demonstrate that it is possible to develop the resources of depressed rural areas and that Indian people can have an important and successful role in this effort if given the opportunity.

UNIT **11.**

Local Community Control in Social Work: A Community Services Project Director Seizes Brown Power

The notion of local community control has been well established as a phenomenon in the educational system. Ocean Hill-Brownsville was a daily household word among many American families for over a year. Local community control and school desegregation proposals have been put forth in hundreds of communities, sometimes on a competing basis. Local community control in the social welfare field has been discussed in a much more limited way. In part, this may be so because the welfare system is more peripheral to the lives of the bulk of people than is the educational system. Nevertheless, there are stirrings in the direction of local control in welfare as well as in the health field. A variety of problems arises with regard to this. First, the question of financing. How do low-income ethnic groups raise or command the monetary resources to fund indigenous welfare programs? Second, how do they gain the support and cooperation of the welfare establishment, which is likely to view such activity as divisive and illegitimate? Third, how does one staff programs such as this, which may require skilled professional people who are in low supply in the ethnic community? We will view some of these questions through a narrative describing the acquisition of "Brown Power."

When the director first arrived in San Jose to take over the Mexican-American Community Services Project, his first impressions were of a fully integrated community. It seemed, at least, that Mexican-Americans lived in all parts of the city and county, with some pockets of Mexican-American concentration.

To the average person the impression is that if people live freely in all sections of the community, then they must live free from segregation and discrimination. This first impression is immediately erased when one looks behind the façade that is customarily erected by the community power structure constructed to give such an appearance.

Among the items that are misleading are various indications of affluence. There are as many branch banks as there are supermarkets. The freeways are lined with shrubbery and trees, and one assumes that the total community lives in this kind of garden environment. But behind the branch banks and the supermarkets and behind the landscaped arterial ways there are slums, there are hovels, there are hungry people: the discards of society.

"Brown Power," From *Three-Year Report* on progress in a Mexican-American Service project by L. M. Lopez, Executive Director, Mexican-American Community Services Agency, San Jose, Calif.

131

In Santa Clara County the largest number of these hungry people are of Mexican-American ancestry. They are a people whose culture is different and therefore not properly understood by members of the majority society.

Their language is different (although quite often they may be fluent in English as well as Spanish). Their religious orientation is different. And because they belong to a minority culture as well as to a minority religion, until recently there was no hope of overcoming this sort of "double jeopardy."

There are many instances of thinly veiled discrimination against Mexican-Americans that the director discovered. In view of this problem the director, upon assuming the job, immediately took steps to organize community meetings with members of the Mexican-American community—professional, business, and lay, as well as members of organized labor. Each problem was aired for the benefit of these groups. The director received valuable feedback and advice from these groups.

Aggressive action was planned under the direction of Mexican-American community leaders. An advisory committee set up by the Community Council Board was not expected to engage in militant activities, for obvious reasons.

In fact, the director himself was told quite often by the director of the Community Council not to indulge in activities that would eventually expose practices that created and maintained social injustices. It appeared, however, that as the knowledge of these practices was gained by the Mexican-American leaders, groups that had heretofore been passive and not at all involved in protesting discriminatory treatment became concerned and at times moved even against their own bylaws. Such bylaws read, "We shall not participate in militant activities nor picket."

Many Mexican-Americans became convinced that it was their civic duty to voice some kind of protest in their own behalf, and in behalf of the minority community. They became vocal and militant protesters and surprised the defenders of the status quo. It was upsetting to the power structure to have people demanding equality and opportunity. Because these newly vocal members had never been involved in the planning of policies or programs, they were seen as rebels, wanting to take over. It was said they had no right to do these things; that the protest was the work of outside agitators; that the Mexican-American was happy where he was.

The practice of racial prejudice is an all-pervasive evil. In our particular "enlightened" society prejudice costs more than it is worth. It ought not to be tolerated; and yet human frailties are rooted deep and are difficult to weed out.

Concept and Conflict

The magnitude of the needs of the Mexican-American community as outlined in the preceding sections had to be tempered by the realities of budget and staff.

Research

There was no question but that one director and one meagerly paid secretary could do little alone. It is all well and good to speak of "research," "community organization," and "district councils," but meaningful liaison rests on a bond of trust and *esprit*. This director knew that the existing Mexican-American leadership in the community had to come to believe that the new project was to serve their interests first—or else he would be sitting alone in an East Side office with a secretary and some research papers.

Therefore, upon assuming the position as head of the project, the director opted for not initiating any research, if for no other reason then because it would have been time-consuming. Lacking the staff or the time for such a chore, he felt it would have dissipated not only the efforts of the staff but also the resources. Moreover, there was enough research available for other programs and agencies. This phase of the project as outlined to the Rosenberg Foundation therefore was abandoned (with some reluctance on the part of the Advisory Committee set up by the Board of the Community Council).

Organization

The second objective of the Rosenberg Proposal called for the organization of a District Council "composed of district residents and business and professional people with offices in the district." The director decided to substitute the advisory services of the affected group—in this case the Mexican-American—exclusively. He reasoned that if the professional people who had heretofore not understood the problem were to continue to prepare policies for the project, it would result in "more of the same kind" of direction that the Mexican-American already resisted—if not resented. On the other hand, the Mexican-Americans meeting with the director frequently suggested and advised him on things they themselves felt were necessary. Quite often, staff persons from agencies either have misunderstood such suggestions, or have been unwilling to listen.

Unnecessary conflict might have arisen if a "council" had been set up. As visualized in the proposal, this council would have consisted of "professional" persons meeting as a group with a handful of Mexicans of limited education. It ought not to be necessary to point out that in such instances the "professional" is always dominant. And why should this not be so? After all, he has mobility and verbal fluency. But all his merits aside, the net effect on the Mexican-American is that the latter soon would realize that he was the "window dressing." The Mexican-American is overwhelmed by such situations into either continuing his role of frustrated subservience—with a smile—or else, not participating.

In addition, by not organizing such a council, the director first had a direct line of communication with the group who had the problems; second, he had the opportunity to work intimately with a group who understood the needs of a client population; and third, he was able to put into effect a philosophy similar to that prevalent in the War on Poverty legislation. The affected group was to have "maximum feasible participation" in determing the kinds of programs that they desired and that they thought would alleviate their problems. The director has always practiced this kind of democracy.

Such a course was not a pleasant message to relate to the Advisory Committee. That committee felt, and justly so, that it was being bypassed. The director was reprimanded for not adhering to policies. He was further reprimanded for being insubordinate. He was judged incapable of maintaining working relationships with those who were to direct him. However, this did not deter him from his plan of action.

The director openly admits that in taking advice from a group that was not included by the planners of the project, he did something that a staff person ordinarily does not do. He did so because, in his judgment, the success of the demonstration project hinged on meaningful participation.

Obviously, the Advisory Committee did not understand the situation thoroughly. They knew there were problems. They had the statistics. They knew that the people

in need were not being provided with services. Yet they insisted that their traditional approach was correct, in spite of the fact that it had proved otherwise.

Further, the director had been chosen out of national recruitment. This was his
third demonstration project in the last twenty years in various parts of the county.
This background provided him the assurance that the suggested course by the planners and sponsors of the project was neither practical nor would it obtain the desired results.

Action and Service

The project was to serve as an intermediary or liaison between the Mexican-
American community and the majority community. Such an objective was very desirable because this was where the gap existed. The Mexican-American is a person
with a different culture, language, and religious orientation. He is unable to direct
himself to obtain services from agencies that normally provide them.

Therefore, a series of community referral programs was established whereby at
different times diverse groups would be provided with an understanding of where
services were available, who qualified for them, and how to obtain them.

At the same time, we attempted to provide the majority community with an understanding of the culture, the mores, the environment, the goals and the values of the
Mexican-American.

It is of value to note that our program has been able to emphasize the positive contribution the Mexican-American can make, not dwelling too much on the negative
effects of discrimination. After all, the Mexican-American *knows* he is discriminated
against, he needs no agency to tell him that.

Staffing the Project

Since the budget was meager and consequently the paid staff small, the director in
this project had to rely heavily on volunteers. People who are not paid in money
must be paid with a sense of accomplishment and/or social mobility.

Volunteers were essential from the very beginning. In order to seek out opinion
leaders in the community, in order to plan with them how best to utilize the basic
concept and limited budget of the project, the director needed "guides" as it were.
Men and women already a part of the established Mexican-American leadership
community were willing to introduce the director to individuals and groups. They
were able to point out explicit problems on an almost casework basis.

Two prominent citizens were most helpful in introducing the director to the community and in opening doors that otherwise might have remained closed for some
months. They expressed great hope and commitment to the project. More correctly,
their recommendations were to the greater possible benefit of the project.

There were more than 250 volunteers the first year who were exceptionally helpful and who should be accorded credit. The Mexican-American *sub rosa* advisory
committee, which the director referred to constantly, reads like a *Who's Who* in
Santa Clara County. *Ad hoc* committees were formed to deal with many important
problems.

Meetings were conducted among different segments of the minority community
to bring out leadership; different groups accepted responsibility for various projects.
The problems were defined and redefined; school dropouts, school motivation, employment, appointments to commissions, representation in city agencies, pre-school
programs, each became a task organized and staffed by volunteers.

The final result was that, altogether, hundreds of individuals from the community itself participated meaningfully in the execution of project objectives.

Administratively, one can complain that there was a lack of rigidity; that in many instances, policy and staff responsibilities were so hopelessly interwoven that an administrative analyst would have been dismayed. Advisers on policy quite often put into execution their own plans.

Justification for such criticism ultimately rests on the contention that order and structure are essential, and that domains must be divided and tasks made explicit in order that responsibility as well as authority can be intelligently assigned. If a certain task is not completed, it is imperative that a certain individual be responsible for an explanation. The United States Army runs quite successfully on such a hypothesis.

Counseling

The director, at the invitation of school principals and assisted by about thirty Mexican-Americans (mostly professional people), each year contacts approximately 1,200 Mexican-American high school students during the school year for counseling.

This program stresses cultural heritage—they are helped to understand the problems of a minority group in transition so they can comprehend the conflict, misunderstanding, and lack of rapport between themselves and thier parents or other members of their family.

A second point is the stressing of the value of a second language. Their insight into two cultures may be taken for granted by these young people; they may not even be aware of this as an asset. When they are shown how the possessor of two languages has increased his professional possibilities, proper preparation and education become more important to them.

There is opportunity to serve the government, or industry, or to teach. There are openings in many agencies, in welfare, in education, etc. Thus, concrete goals are shown in this counseling process rather then vague unspecified incentives.

Finally, these youngsters are helped to understand why the Mexican-American group in particular does not have the leaders necessary to help the group integrate.

This program was carried out inside the school building during school hours but away from a classroom situation. The young people made comments freely without being inhibited by the presence of teachers. They began to believe that they, too, could succeed, could accomplish, and that they, too, have a future.

MAYO was developed out of this program. To join MAYO is to say, "Si se puede." It can be done.

MAYO

MAYO spells the month of May, as well as the initials of Mexican-American Youth Organization. The group's motto is "Creators of a New Image." These young people accepted a challenge the moment they decided to organize.

Once a year they hold an all-day meeting to further improve their understanding of their problems, their needs, and the contribution they themselves can make.

The first annual meeting was held in 1964 at Santa Clara University (and hosted by the university) with 150 young Mexican-American men and women of high school age attending.

For the first time such a group was gathered at a campus, feeling comfortable and secure and with a purpose. The adult members of the Advisory Committee who had been invited to the conference were happily amazed by the tone and caliber of the talks, the facility of language, and the ability to express thoughts. The stereotyped image of the Mexican-American was indeed refuted that day by these youngsters.

This motivational program—MAYO—has gone far to erase the multiple misconceptions arising around the integration of the Mexican person into the American environment. It is not true that the Mexican-American's culture tends to inhibit him, or that isolation from the mainstream of society has produced a kind of behavior that will not allow him to participate on an equal basis with the average member of the majority community. The Mexican-American is not "the problem." These youngsters have demonstrated that "the problem" may lie in misconceptions and prejudices that prevent a true evaluation of the Mexican-American's potential contribution to the community around him.

In 1965 the second annual meeting was hosted by Stanford University. This time MAYO gathered 275 high school members to discuss plans and consider their role in society. Not only their own group problems and conditions were discussed. Members of other minorities were also invited: the Negro, Oriental, Jew, as well as members of the majority community.

Discussion centered on how the MAYO program helped them re-evaluate themselves and their future. Another topic was the understanding they obtained from their exchange of ideas with their own ethnic group, or from members of the other minorities that attended.

The MAYO program was stepped up in 1965-66. The director contacts nearly 1,200 Mexican-American youngsters yearly in the schools of Santa Clara County— from Gilroy to Mountain View, from one end of the county to the other.

The third-year conference of MAYO was held at the University of California at Berkeley. Present at this all-day meeting were 550 young men and women along with many school counselors.

Some concrete results of the MAYO programs: San Jose State College enrollment of Spanish-surnamed students has nearly doubled in the three years that the Mexican-American Community Services Project has been operating. According to school officials, many more Mexican-Americans are graduating from high school now.

The Mexican-American's sense of identity has become so strong that there is now an organization at San Jose State College called CSI (College Student Initiative) of Mexican-American students. They further their goals and intellectual development by promoting programs on campus and contributing to the college community. Many of these students were MAYO members before entering college. Originally, a college work-study was hired to organize CSI. They are now an independent organization.

There is also the Berkeley Mexican-American college campus group known as Quinto Sol—this group sponsored MAYO's conference in 1966. Again, it is an enthusiastic program that is quite stimulating and offers a proud sense of identity within the college community to the Mexican-American students.

Moving Ahead

A stated objective in the original request to the Rosenberg Foundation was that every effort would be made to continue the Project in one of several ways. "Additional demonstration or research" grants could be sought from a rather wide range of sources. Local financing (Non-United Fund) might be another source. Yet another possibility was that "the Community Council could include in its United Fund request . . . an additional professional position and another secretary in order to maintain a branch operation. . . ."

There was a point at which the continuance of the project was by no means guaranteed. It will be recalled that on more than one occasion the director acted without the consent of individuals or groups who felt themselves in one way or another responsible for his conduct.

A staff evaluation of the director by the Executive Director of the Community Council runs to eight pages. It opens with the observation that the Project is a success and that this director has contributed markedly to its success, ". . . that [the director] is extremely effective in initiating and developing a complex of varied activities . . ." because of his ". . . dedication, energy, creativity and general dynamism. . . ."

It then goes on to describe ". . . a systematic and chronic inability to operate within the structure and function of the Council."

There is a crucial question involved here. We dare not assume that there is only one way to run a project or to address a problem.

We very often assume an excessively defensive posture in guarding our administrative prerogatives. ("The Council cannot afford to operate with the responsibilities it has accepted and the community trust inherent in these responsibilities at the risk of relinquishing its authority to a Council employee. . . .")

There is a high probability that such a posture serves to isolate us from the very people we are supposed to serve.

There are many programs which, in order to succeed, must be accepted by the target group. Acceptance implies acceptability.

This project succeeded where others had failed because through his behavior, statements and style, the director convinced the Mexican-American community that this was *their* program and that *they* were primarily responsible for its success. In order to share honestly the possible burden of failure, it was necessary to share honestly the burdens of policy, planning, and operation.

Obviously, this kind of behavior on the part of the director did not make it easy for the Council to continue his sponsorship. In early October 1966 the Project received notice to make inventory and prepare to close at the end of that month since all available funds had been expended.

However, an independent Ad Hoc Committee of Mexican-American leaders had been meeting and planning for just such a contingency. Plans had been made to appeal, pressure, and, particularly, to picket in order that an aroused community insist that so valuable a vehicle as this project be allowed to continue.

A few days after the notice to close was received, the newspaper announced the availability of $18,000 for this project.

The final disposition was that the Project became a part of United Fund. It is now the Mexican-American Community Services Agency, Inc. And while as a separate agency it has many of the responsibilities and freedoms that it did not enjoy as a project, it is nonetheless very thankful to the Rosenberg Foundation for funding and the Community Council for its inception.

Summary

In testing the limits of authority, the director helped to redefine the relationships between the dominant and minority groups. In so doing, he also helped to define more realistically the possibilities and opportunities which exist for the Mexican-American in Santa Clara County:

1. Many more of the needs of the Mexican-American community are being met now then were met three years ago.

2. In part this is so because there is a Mexican-American Community Services Project.

It is very possible that the Mexican-American Community Services Project succeeded precisely because it digressed from what many might consider good social work practices and field techniques.

We have already alluded to differing concepts on the purpose and function of administration, the proper use of community advisory groups, and the use of volunteers.

Social work has developed, and indeed has inherited many of its ideas and techniques, from the psychological sciences. Thus, ideas of personal distance and non-involvement with the client are deemed necessary in order that a sound perspective of the problem be gained. This technique is often useful. It is useful if the client does indeed have difficulty in adjusting personally to some individual deviance.

But social evils—such as racial prejudice—ought not to be considered as an individual ill. Psychiatry is not designed to teach men how to remain at the very margins of society.

Prejudice and counterprejudice exist. There can be no denying this. These discriminatory practices must be abandoned by the community at large because they are immoral, because they are uneconomical, and finally, because the Mexican-American leadership will no longer tolerate the net results of racial segregation.

Major efforts are needed to avoid a violent confrontation between two seemingly peaceful coexistent societies. Time and the current interpretation of civil rights and civil liberties are on the side of the Mexican-American. The wise majority upper-middle-income group knows this and is, to a greater or lesser degree, content with the knowledge that we have made progress and that, in God's good time, things will be well.

The Mexican-American, on the other hand, is being educated to the fact that he cannot and must not wait any longer to become a fully participating citizen. His future and the future of his children depend on his contemporary actions.

Such opposing definitions of reality create a situation which is ripe for any demagogue or any spark to incite some larger conflagration.

One need not be a "Mexican" to work effectively among Mexican-Americans. Fred Ross, if no one else, has taught us that. One needs to choose sides, to agree with the segregated at the bottom of the heap that there are many things wrong. One needs to say in both word and deed that there is a fight to be fought—and that *this* social worker, this do-gooder is here to fight, and if need be, hang with the client group.

After all, the most naive of people know that no man can serve two masters. One serves somewhere through personal design and choice—or because one is pushed there. (The world will choose for those who cannot choose for themselves.)

This director—and thereby this project—chose the Mexican-American Community. Within a few short weeks after the project's inception there was no question in a

Mexican-American leader's mind—and certainly now there is no doubt—that this project belongs to the Mexican-American Community.

"Democracy," "America," "Freedom," and "Justice" must come to mean what they are supposed to mean to the oppressed Mexican-American who lives in terms of hunger, disease, welfare, ignorance, unemployment and despair. It is the full intent of this agency and the dozens of leaders and the hundreds of volunteers associated with it that this shall be so in our lifetime.

Frankly, the yet undeclared motto of this project could very well be: "This is the last generation which shall hear 'Mexican-American' in terms of opprobrium, shame, and ignorance."

UNIT 12.

Women's Lib New Power on Campus:
The Emergence of Group Consciousness

As part of the trend toward emerging group consciousness which has characterized the past half decade, a vigorous women's liberation movement has grown up. This movement is far different from past feminist reform programs in that it is not limited to specific gains, such as the vote or protection in the world of work. Rather, it aims at a basic restructuring of the roles of women and the elevation of their status in society. The women's liberation movement has ramifications which perhaps go beyond other group situations discussed in this volume in that women are not a minority in American society; rather, they constitute over 50 per cent of the population and many of the problems faced by women are not limited to any specific area but are instead concerned with the diverse roles played by women.

As of this writing, the women's liberation movement does not have—nor does it aim at having—a central organizational structure or a core of commonly agreed upon programmatic goals. The emphasis is on many groups, some with a national membership, some local—each, however, concerned with improving women's position in society in some way. Many groups focus on expanding and improving day care services and repealing and reforming abortion and birth control laws in order to allow women a greater choice of roles within the society. Other groups want to open channels for a more assertive role for women in social relations. Still others are pushing for greater political participation and influence for women. Better work positions with equal pay and authority is yet another thrust. Rap session and consciousness-raising groups also form an important part of the movement in many areas.

In the excitement of new political and personal activities and involvements, the rhetoric from women's lib groups ranges from the issue of equal pay to that of a separatist state. It is not surprising that many of the more militant women's organizations have developed on university campuses. In the following piece the reader will find the discussion of the activities of and the problems faced by one such campus group. The article covers the development of a new organization with new ideas and the inevitable clashing between the more conservative and radical factions within the group. The emergence of a sense of group oppression and of group identity is depicted.

140

It seems impossible to me that only two years ago I had never really thought about the constant oppression of women as women. I had had plenty of personal affronts on the job, but never connected a fraction of the elements of male chauvinist society with my experiences. I was a political person, "knowing" to look for the new forces of revolution in our time, but not really understanding why, at its formation in 1955, *News and Letters* designated women, along with workers, blacks, and youth, as a revolutionary category.

I first thought seriously about Women's Liberation about the time the new movement was starting, when a Puerto Rican friend told me about the treatment she and other women were receiving in some black and Puerto Rican leftist groups at the time: women not only limited to certain nonthinking work, but formally excluded from many meetings; a boyfriend telling her to shut up in public when she tried to express an idea; one CORE office at which, if you called up with anything but a simple factual question, you were told by a woman that she couldn't answer it, that you should call back "when a man is here." What was going on? It was part of the authoritarian tendencies blossoming in the New Left, but it was much more—it was the result of the lack of self-conscious, organized voices of women to fight the discrimination against them which so thoroughly saturates the dominant culture that we are *all* infected with it.

About a year ago, I became involved with the W.L. group at the University of Chicago. It was during the occupation of the Administration Building by several groups, including WRAP (Women's Radical Action Project). In a spring in which there was little new in the student movement, a reflection of the New Left's approaching dead end, the voice of W.L. was very new and very strong during that demonstration. The WRAP women were an organized, cohesive group. They met regularly on their own, formulated their own actions and ideas, and took part fully in the mass meetings with the men. For many women, it was the first time they had chaired a meeting, written a leaflet, or expressed their own ideas in front of a large group. Part of the impetus, of course, came from the fact that the event which triggered off the sit-in was the firing of Marlene Dixon, a radical woman professor who was active in W.L. But the women, including many who originally entered the building only because they liked Mrs. Dixon as a teacher, went beyond the single issue: They wrote and distributed analyses of male chauvinism in the university and the society, and convinced the larger group to add demands for more women professors and students, courses on women's history, and free child care to the rather standardized demands for student control and open admissions. They raised the issue of W.L. among *everyone* on that campus for the first time.

The Columbia University women had sparked an idea the year before, when they suddenly balked at being on the food committees during that occupation, and demanded that there be equal numbers of men and women on them. Now the University of Chicago women effectively applied the concept that women are equal to men in the realm of ideas. The women also shook up the "radical" men on a personal level. In addition to the women's example of self-organization and their full participation in every aspect of the occupation, from strategy to "sitting security," they also confronted the men with their male chauvinism during the long period of close contact. The following exchange, for example, must today be standard in such

"The New and the Newer Women on Campus," by Molly Jackson. From *Notes on Women's Liberation: We Speak in Many Voices,* a News and Letters publication, 1900 East Jefferson St., Detroit, Mich. 48207. Used by permission.

situations: Man—"If you're so liberated, how come you won't sleep with me?" Woman—"That's exactly the kind of thinking I'm liberated *from!*"

After the sit-in, large numbers of women began to attend the weekly WRAP meetings—often more than sixty. Almost every meeting consisted of several elements. There would be a business part to discuss requests for speakers around the city, demonstrations, other W.L. groups, etc. In a "personal" part we talked about our daily problems as women. I was surprised at the strength this gave many of the women to participate in the other activities, as well as giving them a whole new view of society when they discovered that *their* problems were common, and thus the fault of the society, not of themselves. Often, there was a "political" discussion. Again, I was surprised at the sophistication of the women. Most quickly stated, matter-of-factly, that capitalism oppresses women by using them as a reserve of cheap labor, that it uses men against them to prevent workers' solidarity, that part of women's mistreatment by their husbands is an outlet for the husbands' anger and frustration at *their* dehumanized jobs. Not so explicit, but surely in our attitudes, was the idea that women must be a force for liberation that will combine with other movements to tear down the existing society and create a totally new one, and must assure by our movement that the new one will be free of all aspects of male chauvinism.

We were fortunate to have a concrete women's struggle that crossed class and racial lines taking place on our own campus. The idea of a free child care center provided by the university for its employees and students was spreading among the employees. It became particularly important with the low-paid, unskilled university hospital workers, most of whom are black women. In the early spring these workers wildcatted against both the university and their corrupt, do-nothing union. Among their demands was the child care center. Students helped man the picket lines, and after it was over the wildcatters formed a permanent organization to try to change the union leadership and to press for the child care center. Shortly after that, another group of employees—secretaries and other office workers—formed a third group to fight for the center. These women did important research into the nonavailability of child care in the city and country, the cost and setup of good child care, etc., although they were later to be scorned by some SDS-WRAP women for lacking "militancy." I think it was good that any organization took place among these women, who are extremely isolated from each other and are trained to think of themselves as a part of their bosses, not as exploited employees.

The WRAP women took the lead in calling open mass meetings, coordinating, organizing, and arranging demonstrations. Some good ideas for the center, including the demand that it be controlled by the parents who use it, resulted. The university became scared enough at the thought of a joint movement by students and employees to send officials to rallies and set up a committee to "look into the feasibility" of the center. But the movement fizzled out by the end of the school year. One reason was that WRAP failed to press for a permanent steering committee or some body composed of both employee groups, who should have been leading the campaign, and who would have kept it up over the summer when the students were gone. Another—and related—reason was that the "most political" WRAP women abandoned work on the campaign to concentrate on the faction fights in SDS.

By this time, WRAP had ceased having the "personal" parts of meetings, and many women had dropped out as a result of that and of what it reflected about the leadership, the "most political" women. The women who dropped out said they "weren't ready" to do without the personal sessions and to "take the step into polit-ical work." What nearly all of the politicos failed to tell them is that you develop, *both* "personally" and "politically," through your own actions. This idea had been implicit earlier in the year, when one experienced and one inexperienced woman would always write a leaflet, go to speak to a new group, etc., together. But the vanguardist, authoritarian lines developing in SDS caused many SDS-WRAP women to begin to scorn their "less developed" sisters. WRAP shrank rapidly, and the women who were left stuck their heads in a cloud of rhetoric and no longer had time for what might have been a real movement of workers and students. (I might add that, from what I hear about compulsory group "lovemaking" in the Weather-men these days, some of the "political" women needed those personal sessions at least as much as the nonpoliticos needed help in organizing.)

A couple of illustrations of mistakes made by WRAP leadership are interesting to contrast with what their "constituency" was saying. For example, WRAP called a rally about the child care center and few people came. They proceeded with the speeches anyway. One of the women in the "secretaries" group turned to a few of us and said that if the hospital workers wouldn't come to a lunchtime rally across campus, we should go to them. She took her baby out of its carriage and carried it, and stuck a megaphone under the blankets. We wheeled the carriage right into the middle of the hospital cafeteria floor. She took the megaphone out of hiding and gave a whole speech about the center and a mass meeting at night before the campus cops came and threw us out. Another example was the WRAP meeting at which many politicos were saying we couldn't organize the students around the child care issue because they weren't thinking about having children. A student who had never been to a meeting before got up and said, "I haven't had any political experience, but I think you're wrong. *You* may not be thinking about having chil-dren, because you are the kind of woman who goes on to graduate school and a career, or is so active in organizations that you don't want children soon. But most of the women in college were sent there to get just enough education so they can make a little conversation with the professional husbands they will have. After these four years we may be stuck in the house for the next twenty. We are *very* interested in good, free child care."

It is no wonder, after being involved in or observing the mess the New Left is in, that many W.L. groups became so afraid of dogmatism that they spurned theory. Or after looking at the state powers that call themselves Marxist and the youth who want to repeat the same mistakes, that they spurned Marxism. Women have been told by men "theorists" of both the burgeoisie and the Left that Marxism is purely materialism. What is *really* new about the W.L. movement, I think, is its rejection of simple economic solutions to women's discontent. We are saying, not that we want to be like men, even rich men, in this society, but that we want to be whole human beings called women—beings who have many choices of how to live, many opportunities to create; beings who cannot exist without a total restructuring of society.

It is this Humanism that makes this movement different from the Suffragette or any other movement for equal rights with men in the past. And this Humanism *is* Marxism. Marx combined materialism and idealism to create a philosophy of libera-tion that can end class, racist, and sexist society. He scorned "vulgar communism," such as the change from private to state capitalism in Russia and China, as much as capitalism. He explained that it is who *controls* the means of production that deter-mines all human relations in the society, the relation of person to person including man to woman. If the end of your philosophy is not freedom for everyone, it is not Marxism.

Marxist-Humanism has been bursting out in the last two decades—in this country, in the mass black and student movements—and now it is a potential of the W.L. movement. This is even newer in the brand-new women's fight. I can see a change even since last year, when W.L. stressed statistics on job discrimination to spread their cause. Now they are talking about redefining *all* relationships in society. Even the "grandmother" organization of W.L., N.O.W., an organization of professional women itself only a few years old, is considered too conservative and too centralized in authority. And, I think, a serious search for theory—for a key to the self-development of our *own* movement—is starting. Hopefully, W.L. will overcome its fear of structure and philosophy, and meet up with *all* the different women in the country, so it can form a mass movement that will link up with the other forces for liberation and create a society in which women can be *whole women*.

PART III

INTERGROUP ATTITUDES AND RELATIONSHIPS

Fostering Positive Interrelations and Controlling Tensions and Hostilities

UNIT **13.**

Combating White Racism in Suburbia: The Interfaith Action Centers of Detroit

A shift in priority to organizing whites to fight racism among whites was given impetus by two events. One was the failure of the civil rights movement to make visible significant gains, and the other the concomitant emergence of Black Power as a force. White liberals and radicals found themselves expelled from the more militant black organizations with the admonishment to "go work with Whitey." Contemporaneously, the National Advisory Commission on Civil Disorders issued its precedent-shattering Kerner Report, which for the first time in an official Federal Government report, pointed a stern finger at "white racism" as the underlying cause of racial turmoil in the country. No longer was it the "Negro problem" of family breakdown or inadequate education or migration to urban areas that was to command our attention, but rather institutional white racism that infected the entire society.

Having agreed to make white communities a target population, how does one begin to undertake this new mode of action? Existing programs and organizational footholds were weak or nonexistent. The target population was likely to be apathetic, resistant, or hostile to the change efforts. The "client," reposing in a comfortable suburb, was feeling little pain. Should the major thrust of action be in the direction of changing attitudes or changing behavior? If the practitioner is aggressive in his approach, is he likely to be "tuned out" by the very people he is attempting to reach? But if he is a cautious and gradualistic can he hope to make a dent on a problem of such enormous proportions? And given the manifold, ubiquitous character of institutional racism, with what more specific subproblems or with what groups of people does the practitioner begin to work?

Shortly after the massive Detroit civil disorder in 1967, a group of religiously affiliated individuals turned their attention to what could be done to combat racism within suburban communities in a realistic way. In their Interfaith Action Centers they quickly began to encounter a myriad of basic problems associated with this programmatic approach. In the following interview, the first acting director recounts the experience.

Q: The first question that I'd have for you is how did it come about that a suburban action center program materialized in Detroit?

A: The suburban action centers is a project that was originally conceived and sponsored by the Interfaith Action Council of metropolitan Detroit. The Interfaith Action Council was formed by an emergency council created during the 1967 riot in Detroit. There was a conviction within the council that the problem was not in the ghetto in terms of the riot, but in the white community in terms of racist attitudes in white people. Members felt that the churches themselves had a responsibility to address their own constituencies within their own white communities. The suburban action centers idea was originally conceived about two or three months after the riot, in November 1967. At that time we began to develop a proposal which materialized in January of 1968 and was submitted in its draft form to the New Detroit Committee and to some of the member denominations who were interested in funding this kind of program. This got a kind of a push toward funding because at that particular time there were tremendous tensions in both the black and the white community around arming and there were all kinds of rumors such as that the blacks were going to go out into suburbia and knock off one child per ten blacks. There were vigilante groups and gun classes being held by whites at the same time. Within the power structure and religious leadership there was a conviction that we must do something to get out to that white community to quell the tension and alarm. There was concern within the ministerial groups in the black community: "We have racism in our community too!" Then in March of '68 this whole effort was propelled ahead by the Kerner Commission Report which identified white racism as being the basic cause that created the disorders. The proposal we had submitted received an immediate $12,000 from the New Detroit Committee. Churches began to ask, "How many people could we just spring loose from existing jobs to begin this program?" So we asked the churches to release people for a six-month period, either 50 per cent or 100 per cent of their time. This was greatly stimulated by the Catholic Archbishop's commitment of fifteen priests, eight of whom would be full-time. Then there was some "arm twisting" to get the Protestant and Jewish participants to measure up to the Archdiocesan commitment. With the original $12,500 and some seed money from denominations a director was sought during the summer of '68. I served as the interim director pending employment interviews with candidates until William Downs took over on August 15.

Q: Let me see if I've got that. The core group at the beginning then was an interfaith group of religiously affiliated individuals?

A: Actually the group that wrote the proposal was first called the Suburban Action Committee. Within the context of what was the Church and Synagogue Committee grew the idea of Suburban Action Centers which was proposed and submitted to the Inter-Action Council. The Interfaith Action Council now is incorporated and has a representation system. The Interfaith Action Centers are of course its biggest budget item right now in terms of personnel.

Structure

Q: Could you give me some idea of the structure of the Suburban Action Centers? From what you said before it's a program of the Interfaith Action Council.

A: Right. The committee of IAC that governs it is the Church and Synagogue Committee.

Interview by the editor with Mr. Frederick Brown, former Acting Director, Suburban Action Centers, and Professor of Community Organization, University of Illinois School of Social Work.

Q: Could you tell me a little more about that structure?

A: There's an Interfaith Council which has the three major religious bodies on it: the Protestants, the Jewish, and the Catholics and by denomination, they have so many representatives. They're appointed by their constituencies. In other words the Archdiocese decides how they will send the people to the Council. The Jewish Community Council plays a key role for that group. We don't tell them how they are to do it; they don't have to hold elections for instance. In addition there are at-large delegates and each community action center will send a delegate to the board. The Interfaith Action Council in its emerging status got into some quite controversial activity. I mean it supported militant Rev. Al Cleague in his initial Federation of Organizations for Self-Determination. After Martin Luther King's death it participated in silent marches in opposition to the governor's proclamation, which prohibited public assembly resulting in officers in the Interfaith Action Council being jailed. These actions tended to alienate some of the conservative groups and as the IAC became formally sanctioned, provision was made for member organizations to declare their nonsupport for IAC. In other words, any organization can demur from majority actions without withdrawal from the Action Council.

Q: In the sense of calling its delegate back . . .

A: No, they can say that in that given action we will not participate and that publicity releases have to include those organizations that are not participating. The minority cannot prevent the Council from acting but there is an agreement concerning a clear delineation of the organizations that have not agreed to an action being taken.

Q: The idea is that this is a federated structure rather than an independent, autonomous structure. And what's the main basis of funding now?

Funding

A: The constituent projects, like the Interfaith Action Centers, are funded, you know, by the denominations; whoever wants to participate in the projects funds those projects. The denominations and religious bodies funded the projects but the projects had to be approved by the Council. Funding is half from the denominations and half from the New Detroit Committee.

Q: What's the relationship between the Board of Directors of the local Interfaith Action Centers and the over-all sponsoring body?

A: Originally we conceived of two types of funding. One would be the metropolitan-level funding which would be for the metropolitan strategy in action. That would be funding that would be kind of a pool, a kitty, that the Action Centers could apply for but would need center board approval. And then there would be totally local funding which the central board would not try to act on at all, but which could be used autonomously by local operations. To date most funds have been metropolitan. The efforts to raise local money have not been substantial. This is unfortunate because we thought the most radical type projects in the local community would have to be locally funded. As an example, Dearborn came in and wanted to do an open housing petition drive and gave us a budget of $12,000 that they wanted us to provide for their drive. Well, we felt that open housing in Dearborn is a highly controversial project, and we asked them how much money they were going to come up with. They said they didn't have any. Well, where's the local commitment? You know, you can't really conceive of an open housing strategy being metropolitan because you have to enact the municipal ordinances locally, and outside funded efforts of this sort could be resented.

Local Centers

Q: How many centers are there now?

A: There are now six in existence; we are committed to nine. And these centers are located strategically. There's a whole list of criteria but essentially as I analyze it briefly, suburban communities that are seen as being visibly most racist, is one criterion. Also, we want centers in communities that are highly prestigious in terms of having people living there who are involved very much in the power structure of the metropolitan community. And then there is the criterion of heterogeneity—others just to have a kind of broad gauge kind of thing. But we knew we could never fund or even particularly administer an action center in every community since there are fifty-five separate units of government in the metropolitan Detroit area.

Q: So there is a principle of balance or spread involved here in selection.

A: Right, what we call a selective metropolitan action system. We feel that much of the problems of urban areas are metropolitan in scope, so we're trying to get some communication across community boundaries to where people begin to move in concert with each other, where they're not tied up only with the inadequacies of the local structure.

Q: How would you describe the local-oriented program for dealing with white racism as seen from the metropolitan office?

A: We see problem areas as being the focus; in other words, housing or education. We know that the racism that exists in the housing industry would not be solved in Dearborn if they were the perfect white community, you see, even though they completely turned themselves around. In some ways it's a Federal or national problem, but many of these things have their focus metropolitan-wise. I'll use an example: There is a large housing development being put up by the Chrysler Corporation in the suburb of Troy, which is right near our Birmingham-Troy Action Center, and in a sense four or five centers may be working on this in terms of working with Chrysler regarding their policy in this big development. How could they in the sense of being the financial sponsors of the program, insist on incorporation of not only racial mix, but economic mix?

Q: All right, as I see it, from the metropolitan standpoint, there are certain local problem areas, in a sense these are traditional areas in human relations . . . housing, employment, etc.

A: Right. And strategy-wise now, you see, it's important for the people in Troy to be involved in what those decisions are, but there also needs to be some access to the power structure that is making the decisions on these things. It's an attempt to develop a strategy that has the ability to operate at various levels and not be restricted to a simply local approach or simply a top power structure type of approach.

Programs

Q: What about the local centers . . . is there a general program or policy framework to guide them? Are there specific programs that centers are expected to follow? How about methods? Is there some understanding of the methods . . . how controversial or not they ought to be?

A: Well, the approach is to try to develop local potentiality or capacity to act on these things. Now part of developing the capacity to act on these matters is to become very closely acquainted with your community in terms of community analysis. Much of early staff efforts were geared just to community analysis of who's who, analysis of the power structure in a given community, what have been the historical issues . . . who have been the actors in these, who is going to have to be in any given organization for any given issue to succeed or fail, what are the inhibitions, the blocks of opposition, this kind of thing. Now, I was in close contact with the Warren center when it was working on the Macomb Community College issue. The college has two campuses and the south campus is very near the Detroit line and has become overcrowded. So they decided that they would close enrollment at that campus to out-county students—which really meant exclusion of a large number of black students who were coming from Wayne County. Well, this was aided by the Central Office in terms of putting local center people in touch with the Educational Task Force of the New Detroit Committee, linking them to the experience of some of the constitutional lawyers in town who had brought suits against certain kinds of public decisions by boards of trustees of community colleges like this to challenge the constitutionality of their actions. At the same time the Warren center was mobilizing local support—raising the question: Do we want our community college to be all white?

Structure

Q: All right, let's use that as a way of looking at the structure of a local center. Could you give us an idea? Is there a local board that's responsible for the Warren center? Is there staff? And then who decided to tackle this program? How did it come about?

A: Number one, we put the deployed priests and ministers into these centers, set them up in an office, gave them some training and told them how to start out. They came with a very mixed bag of skills. And even the input of training program including the School of Social Work faculty and others did not seem to significantly aid proficiency. You see, we found all kinds of contradictions . . . that some people wanted to create a structure that would be independent of the local church because they found the local church congregation impossible to work with. Some denominational officials were saying, these groups are just obviously racist, we can't work with them. Other people were saying, well, that's a tremendous constituency: it should be relevant and we should be able to shift it. There are a lot of these kinds of organizational decisions that we're just now resolving. We've decided to go the institutional route. Human relations councils used to essentially draw individuals who were committed ideologically rather than seek organizational commitments. IAC is moving toward organizational commitments to participate and support other organizations as they become involved.

Q: In other words, what you did was put a worker out in some kind of facility, an office or such.

A: Right, and he began to move around the community with some guidance in terms of whom you should contact and this kind of thing. And we suggested that he create what we called an Ad Hoc Advisory Committee to begin to consult with the community people in development of the Action Center. Obviously issues began to bubble to the surface and people wanted to get into action. This is how Macomb County Community College really involved people into the center once they got working on this. Another thing that was used opportunistically was the Kerner Commission Report. They developed a series of seminars, six weeks running, on the Report, where they used audiovisual and other rather sophisticated training tools for use with community groups.

Q: In Warren then, we have a situation where there is a worker who has been sent out there and his general directions are to form a kind of advisory committee which is made up of individuals in that community who would be interested in doing something on problems of white racism and moving eventually toward forming a board for a center.

A: This means obtaining organizational commitments to serve on a board, formal commitments that they get from churches from the official board, or whomever has authority to vote to belong to the center. This will be different from his organizing a protest as the first activity in the community and automatically alienating many of these same groups.

Q: Right. So you're saying that building this kind of base of support with the church as an important unit seems to be a good way to go.

A: This is a part of the organizational strategy on a metropolitan basis. We're asking people, before we tell them specifically what to do in action, to commit themselves to the idea of eliminating racism as an institution. As soon as you begin to be specific, you see, then immediately you get people saying, well it's not radical enough or it's too radical. You begin to divide the group.

Q: So you're trying to build an organization that's quite broad, that takes in quite a few people, and in which the programmatic directions are not too clear because in this way people can develop these directions themselves locally, and you don't turn away potential participants in the beginning. I wonder whether you could give an example.

A: O.K. The Ford Motor Company said that they were willing to develop fourteen hundred acres of land they owned in Dearborn for housing. The Dearborn Interfaith Action Center began to negotiate with them around the project. Professional expertise of city planners was recruited to technically develop suggestions for the 1,400 acres which would achieve IAC goals. These proposals were presented (and welcomed) by officials of Ford.

Q: What kind of staff works in the Dearborn operation?

A: The director, one of the few loaned clergymen who were hired as full-time staff, has a full-time secretary and two or three part-time deployed clergymen to work supportively to his efforts. He has a board of directors which has representatives from the churches that are contributing money to the center, as well as the Dearborn Human Relations Council. They tried to get the Kiwanis and some other groups who haven't committed themselves yet. They have developed task forces on each of the areas of education, housing and so on. They pulled off a protest during last fall's campaign when Georgia Governor Maddox came to campaign for Wallace. Two hundred and fifty people sat in on Maddox's political rally, sat up in front and simply said nothing. All dressed in good suburban middle-class style. (Unusual dress and beards were nonexistent.) They just sat there, and it was interesting, the kind of actions they were able to stimulate Wallace supporters to take against them, as well as the positive press they got from Dearborn and metropolitan papers. They showed some sophistication in terms of confrontation—willing to confront, but avoiding a "beatnik" image—attempting to project a suburbanite, middle-class, white, white-collar image.

Q: Well, one thing that interests me about this is that Dearborn has a reputation of being an exceedingly reactionary community, very bigoted and lily white. How was this center able to get that large a number of people who were committed to work against racism?

A: The situation here is that there are many people in Dearborn that are very restive under that negative image. They've labored a long time under that image and they would like to reverse it. And you see Mayor Hubbard, who has a reactionary reputation, has not controlled the Board of Education. The Dearborn Board of Education has been rather progressive in its attitude in this area. The other factor is that Mayor Hubbard did not originally gain his political strength from appeals to prejudice. He was elected mayor and he made his political mileage and developed his strength on the first thing he did—putting Ford Motor Company which had massive holdings in Dearborn on equalization of taxation. In other words, they had a privileged position and his action created for Dearborn the best tax base in the state. He acquired a kind of David and Goliath image, and since that time he has been able to provide all the funds necessary for excellent services and facilities. In the winter snowstorms, the sidewalks are plowed in Dearborn before the streets in the surrounding communities are plowed. Dearborn is a clean community, it's a well-run community, it's an efficient community, its Board of Education has a tremendously high record of producing in the area of curriculum and scholastic achievements. So excellence of community services has been what's really kept him there. In addition, he's played on people's fears. But there are a lot of liberal people there, for instance U of M has an Extension Campus in Dearborn, the Ford Motor Company itself is not happy with Dearborn's image, etc.

Q: What about the housing thing then? As I understand it, part of that bad image is that they have practically no blacks living there.

A: Well, when they came up with the 1,400-acre proposal, the Interfaith Action Center involved a knowledgeable city planner who came up with some of the components that could go into such a development, meaning how it could be more balanced and integrated both economically and racially and contribute to the total life of Dearborn. In a sense, by taking a constructive stance, IAC provided a community base upon which Ford could do some things in the community that would be difficult for Hubbard and some others to counter. If you line up the public image of Ford wanting to do the right thing along with fairly strong community support (which may not be a majority vote in an election to eliminate Hubbard) it's significant enough to neutralize Hubbard. It's a strategy built on the basis of providing a constructive program and then volunteering to do some of the community relations work to interpret what this project's about. To summarize, you have the Interfaith Action Center, you have Ford which wants to do something constructive, build some housing. Ordinarily Ford might do so within the pattern of community norms, and that would come out all white. But the Interfaith Action Center goes to Ford, has a plan, has some expertise and says, "Wouldn't it be a good thing to build this on an integrated basis?" In this sense they're short-circuiting the mayor. They're also beginning to line up local organizations, like Local 600, River Rouge Plant, of UAW, and some of the other political forces in Dearborn. The strategy is to get as many organizations as possible committed to a positive approach to those 1,400 acres. This permits Ford to do what they ought to do in the first place.

The Strategy of Involving the Local Community

Q: In a situation like Dearborn do you know what the general approach has been in attempting to get people to participate in such a center?

A: Well, you see, the original involvement came out of an Archdiocese project in which they tried to get people in every parish to have a human relations council in the parish itself. And initially, the Dearborn Interfaith Action Council involved primarily the people who had been active in these human relations councils and various Catholic churches as well as some Protestant churches. These were not powerful people in Dearborn. They took some rather immature or amateurish actions earlier, such as announcing they were going to integrate Dearborn. Finally they got some feedback from militants and some other people that this necessarily wasn't the appropriate thing to be doing at this particular stage. It's racist to invite black families to come into a racist community and to ask them to subject themselves to the bigotry that exists there. You should work on the racism first and if you can get that community straightened out then you can invite the black families in on the basis of its being a healthy community.

Q: In other words, work on attitudes first.

A: Well, no, institutional structures that are racist, in terms of how the police act, how people are acting in institutions in Dearborn. I don't think any of us are in the bag of trying to change people's attitudes. What we want to do is to create a structure by which people don't have to be so afraid, they have some organizational support to do some things they wouldn't do without that organizational support. But institutions, basically. I mean the focus is on institutional racism. We try to involve people in terms of institutional change and we would hope maybe some of them would change their attitudes in the process. Attitudinal aspects may be a kind of opening, softening-up approach, you know, that's what the whole Kerner Commission thing is trying to do. Even where Dearborn started was what they called an "Action Saturday." They had 250 people the first day, in all-day workshops, in which they divided up into housing, education, etc. But it was all related to what kind of action are we going to take? The whole idea of the confrontation with the Wallace rally came out of that first "Action Saturday."

Q: I'm going to put forth a criticism to see how you respond to it. It seems to me by taking that kind of approach what you're doing is largely working with those somewhat few people who already have a positive attitude, and who are willing therefore to put it into action. Aren't you therefore eliminating a large group of people who need to be changed too?

A: Well, there are two or three things that are going on. One is that we think that by dealing with the Wallace rallies a certain kind of communication begins to take place. Some of the people even in the Wallace organization perceive something differently. That this was not all a bunch of people who could be described as beatniks that might protest the way we're acting. These are our fellow Dearbornites that are doing this, you see. And this was very important. In addition, they're carrying out block-by-block coffee klatches . . . they're sitting down with neighbors and beginning to talk about these things. There have been a lot of exchanges, black and white couple exchanges, dialogue groups.

Q: Well, isn't a dialogue group related to attitude change?

A: Well, yes, but they wanted to *do* some things. One of the real tense things is that families exchanged children. Black middle-class families exchanged children with white middle-class families for two weeks and the white middle-class families tried to take their black kids to the local swimming pool and this created a real ruckus. We were able to win this out as long as there was a white Dearbornite family sponsoring the blacks. If they were guests of Dearbornite people, they could swim in that pool and they swam there. There were some tensions, but they swam there. We're trying to get away from the idea of outsiders creating these problems in Dearborn. We're trying to get Dearbornites to try to raise questions for themselves and in a sense work on organizational and institutional commitments to the point that there are a lot of people that are going to be shut up by the institution committed to the program. Now, a bank manager can't very well be openly bigoted in his public statements if his local chamber of commerce or banker associates support integration. If we get an open lending program going, we can go to talk to him and get him to support that open lending program even if he may personally be a racist. And then when we line up people to apply for mortgages or money for loans at that bank and there is a pattern of discrimination he's going to have to own up to his own fellow banks and businessmen about this.

General Problems in White Organizing

Q: Fred, you've probably had as much or more exposure in dealing with the problem of programs having to do with white racism as anybody else around. What do you see as some of the main problems in getting such programs going and in carrying them out?

A: Obviously, a difficult problem is funding. Well, two things: People that have a commitment to doing these kinds of things normally have inability to do the long-haul kinds of things necessary to pull off institutional change. You do not change institutions overnight, you know. It's still a long haul before that institution really produces nonracist practices. Meanwhile members may so isolate themselves ideologically that they're no longer effective. In other words, it's difficult to engage in institutional change while you're really committed to communicating with people of all views, without losing your own commitment in the process. The other problem is that once you begin to make real inroads, immediately somebody tries to cut off the funding. You know, when the schools are really under criticism and have to change, then somebody's going to try to find out where the source of agitation lies. We're hoping that by institutional commitments being high enough, actions will be sustained. This means we will need to be "responsible" in terms of the approaches that we use. That doesn't imply abstinence from confrontation strategy, but such approaches are used very strategically. I mean we think it's just as important to have professional testimony or proposals by professional planners. The Ford Motor Company institutionally is probably a more effective social change vehicle at a given moment than maybe a picket line in front of Ford Motor Company. We're trying to get people to be sophisticated about the strategies they use.

Q: What about problems in terms of participation? Are there these kinds of problems too?

A: Well, you know, in some ways you feel like an outpost in enemy territory. I've gotten this awful sense of isolation on the part of many of the staff that are functioning out there. Those of us at the metropolitan level are much more encouraged because we move in and out of those communities. But when you get stuck there with all the force of everybody looking askance at you, going by that store and thinking that's a bunch of subversives, it's hard to live with. This works at staff unless you give them a lot of constructive, positive support, and this is very difficult. Another problem is that staff in some senses do not realize how much personally they can do. They see the job as more than they can personally accomplish. Yes, the resources are not adequate to do the job decently, but staff members do not even see what they can do within the boundaries of their resources and time and energy. They just see the problem as so immense and the attitudes so rigid that this in itself is discouraging. You see, it's much easier for a person to go down to a community where there's felt need. A white suburban community doesn't say "We have felt need." Even the radicals, liberals, or whatever, don't ever see themselves as needing help.

Q: Well, what are you suggesting then for this staff guy? He's out there, he feels alone, he feels isolated. What are you suggesting? I mean, say he arrives Monday morning to start this job . . . what are some of the first things that he ought to do?

A: Well, my feeling is that he ought to really become as knowledgeable about that community as he can, to get to know as many people as possible in personal relationships, without getting committed to any strategies or any directions. He should start to build the relationships that later on are going to have to be tested in terms of commitments, pressures and strategies. He begins by calling on the telephone, sitting in offices and homes. Specifically we told staff to start with the churches, then get church people to suggest other people, and begin to isolate the issues . . . you know, determine who are the actors in the various issues. And we insist that they talk to both sides of the issue. And local residents are amazed that somebody from the Interfaith Action Center will come to the people that raised all the hell at a particular protest. You begin to demonstrate something by whom you're willing to talk to, the local union leader, the guy who's just a dumb nut that was out there throwing bricks, you know, whatever. This takes a lot of maturity on the part of staff to relate to the divergent types of personalities.

Q: Now when he speaks to these people, what would he talk about?

A: Well, we're usually very honest about the fact that with the Interfaith Action Center we're here to work on racial problems, but this is something that is going to be developed, to emerge out of the concerns of people in Warren for example. It's something that we try to get across . . . that all views are going to be considered. It's like introducing yourself and saying that we have a center here and we're interested in doing something, and right now there's no plan, and no strategies . . . what do *you* think the problem is? And who do you think needs to be involved? You might say it's along a traditional community development approach except that it's on a metropolitan basis with system ties. There's a local guy, but he's still tied into a vertical system. He's free to try to make contacts with, say, the New Detroit Committee to help with something he's doing locally. He's really trying to tie these two levels together, or a variety of levels depending on the situation.

Q: Thank you for your comments, Fred. This has been very helpful and informative and opens up a wide range of further questions regarding approaches to white organizing.

Background Information

The following is a summary of significant actions of the governing board of Interfaith Action Centers.

January 1968

The proposal for Suburban Action Centers orginated in the National Headquarters of the United Presbyterian Church, and was offered for Interfaith consideration.

April 1968

A subcommittee of the Interfaith Action Council prepared a finished draft of the proposal for Metorpolitan Detroit, and soundings were taken from denominational representatives and among church groups.

May 1968

Five (5) faith groups pledged support of a Central Office budget for the last six (6) months of 1968:

Episcopal Diocese of Michigan
Roman Catholic Archdiocese of Detroit
United Church of Christ
United Methodist Church
United Presbyterian Church

A request for funds was made to the New Detroit Committee.

June 1968
Informed of $12,500 grant from the New Detroit Committee.

As a consequence of limited funds and an urgent desire to get started it was decided to staff the centers entirely with released and loaned staff from participating denominations; such staff to receive continued compensation from the church or denomination releasing them, not from the center program funds.

Training sessions for loaned staff were scheduled to begin in July.

An Index to Major Actions of Church and Synagogue Committee

July 30, 1968
Appointment of Coordinator, and approval of three (3) year commitment to support of Action Centers program.

August 27, 1968
Policy of $2,000 per center start-up funds for each center authorized; areas authorized for centers: Dearborn, Warren, Royal Oak/Ferndale, Northwest Detroit, Downriver, Grosse Pointe, Birmingham, Central City.

September 27, 1968
Authorized Southfield as center area.

October 24, 1968
Approved and adopted revised proposal as superseding all previous documents. Established basis of computation for determining denominational allocations for 1969 at one cent per month per member. Instruction to Coordinator that his title is amended to include "Staff Director" with authority and responsibility for staff.

November 20, 1968
Established guidelines for receipt of funds by local centers and degree of central support. Defined "Operational Center." Resolution accepting provisions of revised proposal (pp. 8, 11) as defining relationship between Central Office and local centers. Authorized Coordinator to vary expenditures to 10 per cent from budget amounts at his discretion (except own salary).

December 12, 1968
Approval of revised request to New Detroit, Inc. Motion establishing bank account pursuant to authorization of Interfaith Action Council taken December 4; books to be kept at Coordinator's Office. Instruction to Coordinator to raise questions about proposed rules of Grosse Pointe Center. If grant is made by New Detroit for 1969, paid professional staff are to be phased in as loaned staff are terminated.

January 16, 1969
Approval of "Program Possibilities" document. Each denomination to be asked to confirm schedule of payments in 1969. Established Executive Committee.

February 20, 1969
Discussion of program budgets for 1970 and 1971, *no decision.*

March 20, 1969
Reaffirmance of $2,000 start-up allocation to Central City location. Approval of Coordinator's suggested funding level of $250 per center in addition to staff (assumption, $20,000 first year budget, 75 per cent or $15,000 centrally supplied in cash, staff, and services). All budget and financial information provided the Committee to be confidential and not released without Committee authorization.

April 17, 1969
Determination to reexamine structure, membership and function of Church and Synagogue Committee. Adoption of policy that staff loaned to program not eligible for employment in program. Preliminary decision for first annual meeting in August.

May 15, 1969
Decisions on six (6) dilemmas.

June 3, 1969 (Special Meeting)
Recommendations to separate Action Centers program from Church and Synagogue Committee, and to establish separate governing body known as "Action Center Commission."

The White Ethnic Backlash:
Electoral Campaigning in Lawrenceville

A source of consternation to group relations practitioners has been the growing polarization in the nation on racial and social issues. While racial and ethnic militancy has been viewed favorably by most as a useful and even necessary step on the path to social justice, the rising countermilitancy of the right and among white nationality ethnic groups (Irish, Polish, Czechs, Germans, Italians) takes on a disturbing and even dangerous cast. The Wallace election campaign of 1968 provided a rallying ground for this development, and Vice-President Spiro Agnew in the election of 1970 served as a spokesman to articulate many concerns of this group.

And their concerns are many. They feel themselves surrounded by lawlessness and anarchy on all sides, which ineffectual governmental leaders are incapable of containing. They are attempting to maintain their identity and position in the face of the pressure by other groups just below them in social scale to shift positions. Often blue-collar workers, they find themselves in an economic squeeze. While easily above the poverty level, taxes and high prices make their economic position uncomfortable and insecure. Meanwhile, the nationality ethnic finds what he considers unfair favoritism extended to blacks and other protest groups. Government programs such as OEO and Model Cities, expanding city services, political and industrial jobs he sees allocated in unequal proportions to these "self-seeking" power blocs. The white nationality member, like his black, brown, and red counterpart, feels himself to be powerless and overshadowed, a disregarded, disadvantaged minority. His modest educational level leaves him in an inadequate position to understand his and the nation's troubles perceptively and often brings him to the situation with a vulnerability to prejudicial rhetoric. He may start with an antipathy to blacks or migrants or Puerto Ricans and soon find himself swept into a political alliance with a more general form of organized political reaction.

What makes the situation particularly difficult professionally is that group relations agencies have tended to overlook or avoid this group, in part because it did not need special attention on a priority basis and in part because its attitudes were often inimical to the kinds of changes being promoted by the practitioners. Now that there is a more obvious need to reach the group, practitioners find themselves isolated, without points of contact. A first step, it is obvious, is a resolve to view the white nationality ethnic groups as targets of professional effort. Next, one is immediately confronted with finding means of making connections, especially in view of the fact that the practitioner comes with credentials that are likely to be suspect. Are there existing organizational bases within these groups that may be employed? Additionally, the practitioner needs to understand the particular cultural norms and structural forms of these groups so that meaningful and effective professional work with them can take place.

Practitioners are extremely handicapped in working with white nationality communities because these communities are often tight ethnic enclaves, resistant to outside influence, and because the practitioner is unfamiliar with how the groups are constituted and operate within their geographic regions. A graphic example is provided in a description of an attempt by liberal students to penetrate the Lawrenceville neighborhood in Pittsburgh. Here we find a community which is largely Polish Catholic, and containing as well sizable Italian and Irish population segments. While the action context is political organization for the McCarthy election campaign, the situation described is instructive for problems which the group relations practitioner is likely to encounter.

When evaluating the impact of students on politics in the phenomenal McCarthy for President movement of 1968, one important question is: What happens when the student drive hits old-style white ethnic machine-controlled wards? The Lawrenceville experience represents a revealing case study.

The Lawrenceville neighborhood of Pittsburgh encompasses the Sixth and Ninth wards. For decades these wards have been under the iron control to two of the city's strongest Democratic chairmen. There are nine voting districts in the Sixth and twelve in the Ninth. In each of these live several city and county employees who must help deliver the vote in order to retain their jobs. The regular Democratic organization in these wards has long been without competition and rolled up the best record in the city for the Democratic Party.

The residents of the wards are hardworking people employed in steel mill and fabricating plants, stores and hospitals, and in the fire, police, water and other departments of local government. Houses are small and for the most part neatly kept. Most children attend Catholic schools. Polish' surnames predominate, with a large number of Italian and Irish. The Sixth Ward has a sizable section of black voters.

These two wards are in the 14th Congressional District where the Citizens for McCarthy organization filed seventeen candidates for Delegate to the Democratic convention and endorsed the four who won the top places on the ballot for the April 23rd primary. Their principal competition was from the four Regular Democratic Organization (RDO) candidates, all of whom were well-known elected officials. This contest for delegates was the major battle of the Pennsylvania primary. Senator McCarthy was on the ballot for a Presidential preference poll, and the McCarthy workers sought to run up a big vote for him. However, the significance of this vote was reduced by his being the only name listed. The crucial battle was for delegates.

In mid-March the Citizens for McCarthy organization assigned two volunteers, a student and a teacher, to organize campaigns in the Sixth and Ninth wards.

They contacted the poverty office, churches, hospitals, recreation center, and Steelworkers Union office in Lawrenceville. Interest in McCarthy was expressed by

---

"The Lawrenceville Experience—1968," by William Rosendahl and James V. Cunningham, May, 1968. Report presented at Pittsburgh, Pa. Mimeographed.

some of the staff in these institutions, but even these said their support would have to be covert. Fear was expressed of crossing the Democratic organization. On first contact some promises were made to produce names of possible local volunteers for the McCarthy campaign. Few names were actually produced, and those that were produced proved to be either disinterested or fearful of participating. The campaign clearly had to begin with outsiders—and this meant students. Had the campaign gotten started earlier when more time could have been given to quietly searching out local neighborhood people with an independent interest in politics, and with time given to a relaxed cultivation of such contacts, it might have been possible to launch the public drive with local people involved.

At the same time local participants were being hurriedly sought, a search was made for an empty storefront to be rented for a Lawrenceville campaign office. Great difficulty was encountered here also. Realtors and owners were reluctant to displease the Sixth and Ninth ward chairmen.

First canvass was organized for Saturday, March 23. A Catholic pastor in the Sixth Ward was persuaded to lend his bingo hall. It was a cold, bitter, snowy day. Sixteen canvassers—mostly female students—showed up, were given training, and sent out. Most people in the two wards did not know much about McCarthy, but a few dozen pro-McCarthy voters were found. Each canvasser carried a part of a district voting list pasted on cardboard. The name of each voter talked to was marked with a plus, minus, or zero, indicating whether they were for, against or uncommitted on the candidate. A *Pittsburgh Press* reporter covered the canvass and his story identified the church whose hall was used. This resulted in "outside pressures" on the pastor and his refusal to allow further use of the bingo hall. It would have been well to have given better protection to this pastor.

For the next Saturday, a large auditorium in a hospital in the neighborhood was borrowed. The student among the two McCarthy volunteers operating the campaign was able to organize two busloads of students from Seton Hill and St. Vincent's Colleges, numbering about forty. Another dozen were recruited from Mt. Mercy, Pitt, and from high schools. The day before the second canvass the continued search for a headquarters to rent bore fruit with a widow living in the suburbs renting her old storefront at 4049 Penn Avenue for $125 for the month. This was a minor victory and resulted when the search was narrowed to attempting to find an owner or agent with no close ties with Lawrenceville so he would be free from the influence of the two ward chairmen.

The fifty students arriving on the second Saturday of canvassing were trained and fed in the hospital auditorium. Considerable attention was given to the training. Background was given on the neighborhood and what to expect. Issues were discussed so students knew where McCarthy stood. (Students later found few voters wanted to discuss issues, although several damned "the niggers.") Instructions were given on the techniques of canvassing, with the students taking part in practice skits. Students with long hair and sideburns were not excluded from the canvass, but later resident rumbling indicated it would have been wise to have done so.

The fifty canvassers fanned out through the entire neighborhood under sunny skies and talked to almost two thousand voters, finding a quarter of them seemingly favorable toward McCarthy. However, some of the students were too quick to mark a voter plus. A friendly reception was often mistaken for support for McCarthy. While an occasional householder was hostile—and many did not answer the door— most were friendly and could be talked to. The most friendly seemed to be those who had sons or daughters of their own in college. Such parents are growing in number in Lawrenceville, and they as well as their sons and daughters probably represent some of the best prospects for local workers.

When the canvassers were finished on the second Saturday they made their reports at the storefront headquarters which was in the process of being cleaned and decorated by volunteers. The sight of the HQ with its newly painted McCarthy signs was a source of encouragement to the canvassers as they returned. Cold pop was available amid a buzz of activity. On voters passing by, the HQ made visual impact. There was a disadvantage to this neighborhood HQ: it cost money to operate ($300 a month) and absorbed some valuable volunteer energy. The organizers continually had to make sure the number-one priority remained canvassing and organizing for Election Day. As a base of operations and foothold in the neighborhood for the organizers from the outside, the headquarters was essential, however.

The fifty exuberant young canvassers who had gone out from the hospital that second Saturday morning reported in with their voting lists ("handcards") well marked. This was the week prior to President Johnson's announcement that he would not stand for reelection. Students reported some resentment toward the President and his muddled war. They found more ignorance than interest about McCarthy. While one canvasser had been given thirty seconds to leave the neighborhood by a man who didn't like "these students from the outside," most reported a friendly reception, but voters still not having made up their minds. Great care was taken to insure that all the marked handcards were returned. These were fast becoming the basic voting tool of the campaign. For fear they might be stolen, they were not even left overnight in the headquarters.

Now the organizers turned to an attempt to recruit local people. Calls and letters went out to the plus voters inviting them to a Tuesday evening meeting. On Monday afternoon neighborhood children were hired to distribute several hundred flyers announcing the meeting. Five neighborhood people showed. It was an eerie meeting. Electricity had not yet been turned on in the headquarters, which was lighted with a camper's lantern and two candles. There was no heat. The five were mildly interested, and volunteered some help, but there was no leader among them able and willing to spearhead a Lawrenceville group. The need for time-consuming traditional organizing—utilization of every possible contact, patient home visits with every plus voter, a soaking into neighborhood life—was evident. But there was neither the time nor manpower for it before April 23.

Plans were made for a massive third student canvass to be held the following Saturday, with emphasis on the canvassers finding local workers, neighborhood people who would join the campaign and themselves become canvassers. The tragic assassination of Dr. Martin Luther King intervened and all canvassing was canceled. A dozen volunteers made telephone calls for another neighborhood meeting and found twenty neighborhood people who promised to attend. This also was canceled when civil disorders broke out in Pittsburgh and a 7 P.M. curfew was imposed on the city. During the week visits were made to several neighborhood people who had indicated the most interest. A dozen of these agreed to distribute literature, and three agreed to be canvassers. These visits confirmed that it was the student family that was interested. Most of those who agreed to help were either students themselves or parents of students. From the day it opened, the headquarters' window displayed a large VOLUNTEERS WANTED sign. This brought in eight or ten people, most of whom promised more than they delivered. Again, some of these no doubt represented good contacts—but there was no time for an organizer to build the relationship of involvement. The people of Lawrenceville are not accustomed or comfortable in the middle-class activity of independent politics. A careful and gentle introduction is needed.

The fourth Saturday was on Easter weekend and students were home on vacation. Still, the student among the two organizers was able to mobilize a dozen outside volunteers, who did some canvassing, and continued attempts to line up neighborhood people. By this time plans had been made for a major appearance of the candidate in Pittsburgh on the Wednesday after Easter (April 17) which would be only six days before the election. The Easter weekend was also used for promoting this rally. Neighborhood people who had agreed to help were given piles of rally flyers to distribute, and rally signs were posted around the neighborhood.

With only ten days left before the election, and a strong McCarthy impact still not made on Lawrenceville, the Sixth and Ninth ward organizers pressed the central McCarthy committee for a McCarthy stop at the campaign headquarters during his day in Pittsburgh. Reluctantly, the central committee agreed to do so—but with the stipulation he would stop only if a crowd was on hand. This challenge was taken up. Schools and other institutions and organizations in the neighborhood were visited and the argument pressed that the visit of a major Presidential candidate was an important educational experience, aside from partisanship. Reception was encouraging, particularly from the nuns in the Catholic schools and hospital. Flyers were distributed throughout the neighborhood. Another meeting of local people was attempted the Tuesday evening before McCarthy's visit. Again, many promised and few showed.

Wednesday afternoon arrived with sunshine (weather becomes crucial in an amateur political campaign). One organizer was driven through Lawrenceville with a bullhorn shouting word of the Senator's impending arrival (the horn was hidden whenever a police car approached).

The Senator was due at 3 P.M. By 2:30 there was only a handful of people out front. A borrowed rock and roll group arrived and began to set up their equipment. The group's amplifier and microphone were used to announce the coming Senator to the shopping street on which the headquarters was located. The needed crowd was not yet on hand.

Suddenly, far up the street there appeared a marching column: the nuns from St. Mary's School with the three upper grades. Soon a hundred noisy children and their teachers were gathered in front. The microphone was blaring, and the little crowd began to draw others. People came out of their stores and homes. Carloads of people began to arrive. Housewives walked over. As the Senator arrived in a plain little car, the street was in chaos, the rock and roll music was blasting, and the crowd was near 300. (The *Pittsburgh Point* has described the scene as "a bit devastating.") Senator McCarthy hopped out, shook a few hands, and was getting back in his car when the student organizer grabbed him by the arm and insisted he come to the microphone and say a few words. He did, and told the crowd when he was President he would tear down the fences around the White House and have picnics on the lawn "with music like this." Then he was off in his unobtrusive little car.

It was a great moment for Lawrenceville and two hundred kids went home wearing McCarthy buttons, and clutching notices of the night rally. From then on it was easier to talk about McCarthy in Lawrenceville. At the overflow evening rally Chairman Dan Berger mentioned the Lawrenceville happening and drew a response indicating Lawrenceville people in the audience. For a day, radio, TV, and front pages were filled with McCarthy and this was to show up in the final canvass on the weekend before Election Day.

Meantime, the Regular Organization workers who had been quiet up to then began to meet and move around the neighborhood with their literature which emphasized the Regular Organization delegates. Now was the time for a several-day massive effort—but the students, the only large manpower source, were able to pull away from studies only on Saturday and Sunday.

Most of the homes not previously visited were gone to on Saturday. Many persons were not home. The problem of the not-at-home remained throughout the campaign, in part because there was no evening canvassing and very little Sunday canvassing had been organized. On this final weekend voters knew much more about McCarthy and were more friendly toward him. Many of the formerly uncommitted voters were now ready to declare for McCarthy. It now appeared the McCarthy vote in the two wards could total over 1,000 in spite of the growing opposition of the RDO. The organization's workers swarmed throughout the neighborhood on this last weekend. For the first time McCarthy slating cards were given out, aimed at getting delegate votes.

About forty students canvassed on this final Saturday, going out for two hours before lunch and two hours after. Three were students who lived in Lawrenceville. Lunch was an important morale builder, and an expensive one as it was paid for out of the pockets of the two organizers. It also complicated transportation arrangements as students canvassing far-out voting districts had to be driven back and forth. But it was an essential activity, and offered a time for the organizers to obtain preliminary reports and adjust canvassing tactics.

These big canvass days could be much more effective if the training could begin earlier—say 8:30 A.M.—so canvassers could be in the field three hours (10 to 1) in the morning. Students are difficult to mobilize that early, but those that volunteer for political campaigns are dedicated people and will rise early if they feel it is part of a well-organized effort.

Students on this final Saturday made formal debriefing reports to one of the organizers, filling out a brief form in the process. This proved to be a valuable practice, systematically supplying fresh knowledge. It was a technique for assuring the canvasser that his work was important and appreciated. It is most important the student be treated with dignity, as a person and partner, and not as a thing. In such a campaign students should be involved also at policy levels.

Students reported: Many people ready to vote for McCarthy but largely confused about the complex delegate election; a substantial number of others said they would go with the Democratic organization, or were indifferent saying "all politics is dirty" or "I vote the way my husband tells me"; many aged persons were met who had little knowledge or concern about the campaign; harassment by RDO workers who told some canvassers they had no right to be in the neighborhood; even more harassment by dogs which were numerous; a few voters pleased and impressed that young people were interested in politics, while others seemed bothered and harassed by the canvass and some by the students' long hair; while the largest number showed no interest in any issue, there were several voters who discussed race or the war or both, with some bitter anti-black feelings expressed—along with support for Wallace; a few mentioned local issues including dirty streets; and there were voters who liked McCarthy because he was Irish Catholic and not particularly identified as pro-black.

A canvass was also organized on Sunday—the only large Sunday canvass of the campaign—and some voters were located who had never been home on Saturdays. Also, three more neighborhood people joined the canvassing. More Sunday and weekday evening canvassers clearly would have been valuable. As the canvassing ended on the Sunday before election, the five weeks of erratic canvassing had covered every street once and most streets twice.

Now the stage was set for Election Day. The organizers spent their time Sunday and Monday organizing workers for the critical Election Day work. Fifty persons were mobilized. Only a dozen could work the full day, however, most being able to volunteer only a few hours.

Polls opened at 7:00 A.M. A dozen of the all-day workers arrived between 6:30 and 7:00 A.M. at the headquarters where they were given some hurried instructions and each sent out to one of the twenty-one polling places like lambs to the slaughter. Throughout the day there was never more than one or two workers at a polling place, while the RDO had ten to fifteen experienced, determined, and disciplined workers in every voting district—men and women who spoke Polish, knew the voters personally, and instructed them in the intricacies of the delegate voting right up to entrance into the voting booth and sometimes beyond. The Ninth Ward RDO chairman met during the day expressed concern about the student canvass that had reached so many homes, and about the complexity of the candidate layout on the voting machine, which was a type of machine not long in use.

Only about half of the polling places had certified McCarthy poll watchers. In these places, if the watcher yelled loud enough, the instructions ended at the entranceway. But even the supposedly nonpartisan judges of election gave partisan instructions on the demonstration machines inside the polling place. RDO slate cards were supplied by members of the election boards. A single McCarthy worker at a polling place would often attempt to be watcher, then go out front and be a slate card passer, and at times would go out into the streets to try and bring in McCarthy plus voters.

Bagged lunches were delivered by car by organizers who journeyed from polling place to polling place to buoy up and back up the harassed workers. As the McCarthy organizers and workers became acquainted with the RDO workers (some of whom were most skillful organizers) it became clear that the RDO for years had been running the primary as a private affair and were shocked that anyone should challenge their traditional practices. Their efficiency in getting out the vote as the day wore on was a marvel, and indicated strongly the need for indigenous McCarthy workers in every district.

Of the four McCarthy candidates for delegate and two for alternate delegate, four had obviously Jewish names, with three named Cohen. RDO workers used this continually, showing voters the lists of names at the polling place, with anti-Semitic slurs.

During the afternoon and evening (polls close at 8:00 P.M.) the McCarthy workers concentrated on making sure the plus workers on the hardcards had voted, and on preparing these plus voters to withstand the barrage of pressures they were to receive at the polling place. As the polls closed some of the more pessimistic workers were predicting the McCarthy delegates would receive only 5 per cent of the vote. All McCarthy workers received a harsh lesson in machine politics.

The unofficial returns gathered by the workers showed McCarthy receiving 1,476 votes in the two wards out of a total of about 4,000 cast. The McCarthy delegates received votes ranging from 337 to 586 and the RDO candidates from 2,448 to

2,739; the McCarthy delegates won about 15 per cent of the vote. It was clear many plus voters felt they fulfilled their commitment to McCarthy by voting for him in the Presidential preference box, and then giving their delegate votes to their RDO neighbor who told them his job was at stake.

By the end of Election Day it was clear that any strong Election Day effort in the Sixth-Ninth wards had these minimum requirements, even if it were largely a student operation:

1. A strong and aggressive certified poll watcher in every polling place from 7 A.M. to 8 P.M. who would insist there be no campaigning and partisan instructions inside the polling place.

2. One or two workers outside the polling place from 7 A.M. to 8 P.M. who would take the initiative to greet all voters several feet from the polling place, in time to make a brief last-minute argument and present a slating card. There should be heavy postering to match the RDO.

3. At least one worker with car going out to bring in plus voters from morning until night in every district.

4. A simple and clear slate card with a full slate of candidates, differing from the RDO slate only where the independent campaign has its own endorsed candidates. (A slate card with only voting machine numbers of the endorsed delegates was used in Lawrenceville. It had no names. It was not successful.)

5. Election Day workers should receive careful training including detailed legal information on such matters as assisted voting and restrictions on workers and be given their assignment a day or two before Election Day so they can be familiar with the area, and fully prepared at 7 A.M. It would be much better if the Election Day workers meeting the voters would be local people, with students handling telephones and perhaps driving cars. This is the day familiar faces are most needed.

Conclusion

As stated, these Election Day recommendations are based on an effort which depends mainly on student manpower from outside the area. Such manpower can achieve a great deal. Had there been more of it, and had it been used more efficiently along the lines outlined in this report, the delegate vote probably could have been raised to almost 30 per cent. More efficiently also means starting earlier, and the same student canvasser sticking with a street week after week until he knows it well and working the same street on Election Day if there are no local volunteers by that time. If the slate of delegates would be a mixture of names indicating various nationality backgrounds, including a Pole, students could do even better than 30 per cent.

The overriding conclusion from all this, however, is the obvious one: Independent political triumph in Lawrenceville can come only with local people. A Lawrenceville campaign should be run by Lawrenceville citizens. Some were found. Many more could be found if there were more time and some incentive to offer. For example, if a couple of ambitious younger men could be promised important jobs if the candidate were elected, there would undoubtedly be a better chance to have strong local chairmen for the Sixth and Ninth wards.

A systematic search among the Pittsburgh area colleges and universities could be made to find all the college students from Lawrenceville. Both the students and their parents should then be seen in person, in their homes.

Any campaign is Lawrenceville has to have great respect for the people of the neighborhood. They are proud homeowners who have kept their area from becoming a slum. They desperately need political alternatives. They have been politically exploited for many years. Political alternatives cannot be handed to them, but they can be given help in creating their own alternatives, and in launching some of their own leadership. (Of twenty-five Democratic candidates for delegate and alternate, not one was from Lawrenceville.)

The self-interest of the people of Lawrenceville probably lies in their jobs, homes, fear of the Negro, and with their children. The sensitive nerves could be discovered much more readily by local leadership. A careful campaign begun early should provide for the getting together where these interests could be developed. Concerns about neighborhood conditions could be explored.

The March-April campaign described above might have recruited more local people had it assigned a couple of skilled volunteers to that task and no other from the beginning. Instead of attempting several small meetings, one large meeting could have been planned for the final week with the skilled volunteers taking plenty of time to organize it. It could have been held in a familiar place like the hospital auditorium, with a name speaker, door prizes, entertainment, and it would have been successful. It might even have been given an aura of political education rather than outright partisanship—at least in the premeeting publicity, which however would not hide the sponsorship.

If there is time a small series of well-planned meetings might be held using outside VIP speakers in a somewhat nonpartisan atmosphere speaking on the subjects selected by Lawrenceville people who would plan the meetings themselves. Also, Lawrenceville people themselves might develop so they could speak at some of the smaller meetings.

Entrenched in Lawrenceville is political despotism, exploitation of the voter, fear, and pressure as bad as any place in Chicago or any other machine-ruled city. The ward leaders of RDO politically and psychologically exploit the local government employees and the voters of these wards just as the Pittsburgh steel barons physically exploited the workers in the oppressive days of the late nineteenth century. The democratic spirit cannot breathe in such an environment, and it is little wonder the black man is used and promoted as a handy scapegoat to receive the bitterness that should be heaped on the white ward leaders. But also there is something else here—loyalty.

For the students and organizers—the outside change agents—there is the clear lesson that the ties of habit, family, friend, neighbors and nationality are not easily broken in the white ethnic neighborhood. The dilemma is to respect these ties and at the same time help people see they are not the best basis for political decisions if the community is to flourish.

All of these recommendations point to the need for a strong, year-round independent political organization in Pittsburgh which could do the planning and supply the initial manpower to carry out such recommendations and initiate a much more successful campaign in Lawrenceville than the McCarthy campaign of 1968.

Dealing with Youth Conflicts in the Schools:
Racial Flare-up at Williams High

The question of whether to concentrate on attitudes or on behavior has been with the field a long time, and changes in professional viewpoint have fluctuated with the times. There are fads in professional opinion just as there are in other spheres of social life, with the exception that the professional is committed to attempt to push beyond fashion to basic "truth." Perhaps in the past the kind of technology available and the prevailing concept of legitimate professional behavior led to a strong emphasis on attitudinal change. In part, it was felt that affecting changes in attitude leaves fewer residual wounds than does behavior modification that relies on law or pressure. The group relations practitioner has attempted to equip himself to employ group discussion techniques, educational materials, and mass media appeals. The cumulative results of these efforts have obviously been far from outstandingly successful. Together with a waning optimism about the potentialities of attitude change came the discovery that attitude change may follow rather than precede behavior change—that is to say when certain behaviors are prescribed by law or social norms, personal attitudes are likely to bend in order to conform with social practice. Some practitioners, especially those with strong civil rights orientations, take the position that attitude change may be immaterial. The important task is to eliminate discriminatory behavior and create structural mechanisms for equal opportunities, leaving attitudinal factors to be worked out naturally within a framework of formal justice.

A useful and balanced current position on this issue by practitioners has been set forth as follows:

> One of the most pressing needs at this time is to change the behavior of institutions. This must be done on the national, regional, state and local level. The Federal Government is increasingly facing up to the problem of using Federal funds—or the withholding of them—to bring about local institutional change, or a change in local institutional practices. Title VI of the Civil Rights Act of 1964 has been an invaluable tool in helping to change the practices of local institutions which receive Federal funds. Now the question is: How may that tool be used more effectively and with greater refinement? Another Federal program holding

168

great promise in bringing about change in local institutions is the Model Cities Act. Again the question: How can this tool be used more effectively and with greater refinement in bringing about the desired changes in local institutions? The Civil Rights Act of 1968, particularly its fair housing provisions, will tax the ingenuity and expertise of the Intergroup Relations field in seeking to bring about changes in the institution of housing.

While priority must be given to changing behavior—particularly institutional behavior—the nation can ill afford to ignore attitudes. As we know, from the field of social psychology, "what people think is true is often as important, and sometimes more important, than the truth in how they respond to a situation." It would be inappropriate for governmental agencies to work at changing the attitudes of citizens; not so for the private agencies. Governmental leaders may, of course, exhort citizens to obey the law and to accept the new situations for which they call. The private agencies, in contrast, may work to directly influence attitudinal change. This does not call for a massive "Madison Avenue" type program; rather it calls for a sophisticated use of knowledge from the field of social psychology to develop a climate of opinion which will support the changes now required. There is apprehension that if the public does not support the intent as well as obey the letter of the law, that the law will be ineffectual. The minimum level of attitudinal support to make the law effective is acquiescence.[1]

Racial tensions have become endemic to many high school situations. Group relations workers are called upon with increasing frequency by school authorities for guidance in responding to these events. In these situations one may find in microcosm the multifaceted question of attitudinal vs. institutional change. Some practitioners view these incidents as tragic occurrences, others as progressive steps. An illustrative episode is reported here. A series of fights and suspensions take place. The principal is not able to contain the situation, and the staff of a State Board Against Discrimination is called in to investigate and make recommendations.

Williams is a city of some 16,400 population located in the southeastern part of the state. There is a considerable amount of commuting and other forms of travel between three local cities which have become economically interdependent. Williams as a community qualifies for Federal funds for special projects under Title I of the National Education Act. Its School District enrolls some 5,631 students (as of October 1, 1968), approximately 12 per cent of whom are nonwhite, with the largest minority groups being Negro (7.4 per cent) and Spanish surnamed (4.4 per cent). Minority group students are (as of October 1, 1968) so distributed throughout the school system that no school has less than 2.6 per cent nonwhite nor more than 29.8 per cent nonwhite enrollment. The largest percentage of students from any one minority group at any school in Williams is 16.9 per cent Negro at Lowell Elementary School. (Lowell is also the school with the highest total percentage of nonwhite students, 29.8 per cent; 12.9 per cent of the total are Spanish surnamed.) There is one kindergarten for the entire district (10.7 per cent Negro and 16.9 per cent total nonwhite); there are six elementary schools (8.5 per cent Negro and 14.5 per cent total nonwhite); two junior high schools (6.6 per cent Negro and 10.7 per

[1]From "The Big Think Conference: A Working Conference of Intergroup Relations Practitioners and Social Scientists," sponsored by the National Association of Intergroup Relations Officials with the Community Relations Service of the United States Department of Justice, Foodergong Lodge, Ephrata, Pa., May 17-19, 1968.

cent total nonwhite); and there is one senior high school (5.1 per cent Negro and 8.0 per cent total nonwhite).

The people of Williams have followed a pattern of residential segregation (at least since World War II) with the result that a majority of the city's nonwhite residents (especially Negro citizens) live in an area known as "East Williams" which is physically separated from the remainder of the city by a railroad. In general, the East Williams area appears to contain very little of the total community's business and income. Few new homes (except for a Federally financed housing project) are being or have recently been built in East Williams, and most of the older homes appear to represent less of an investment than a majority of the homes elsewhere in the community. (Note that these observations were visually made, and no statistical evidence was sought to back them up. The reason for relying upon visual evidence is that what people *see* around them in the community where they live generally affects their self-concept more than cold statistics.) Racial and socioeconomic isolation is part of the residential pattern in the Williams community. Although there are a number of Negro and other nonwhite families living elsewhere in the community, and there are a number of low-income families (some of them living in housing projects) elsewhere also, the heaviest concentration of minority and low-income families still live in East Williams. This observation is important in assessing what the schools have done to provide equality of educational opportunity to all children and youth in Williams.

In January 1963, the Board of Directors of the Williams School District adopted a statement of objectives which reads (in part) as follows:

> The Board of Directors of the Williams School District acknowledges and subscribes to the statement in the Constitution of the State that it is the *paramount* duty of the state to provide for the education of *all* children. We construe this to mean that every child shall have educational opportunity from kindergarten through twelfth grade to the extent that his capabilities and personal interests will sustain his endeavors. . . .

At that time there existed a heavy concentration of Negro and other nonwhite students at Winston Elementary School in East Williams.

In March 1965, the Board of Directors of the Williams School District acted favorably on a motion,

> that the Board accept the Administration's recommendation that Winston School be closed as an elementary school as of July 1, 1965, with students and faculty being dispersed to other buildings in the District and the Winston School Building be utilized as a School District facility.

The Williams School District had always brought kindergarten, junior and senior high pupils from East Williams to schools located elsewhere in the city. Winston Elementary School, however, because of its location in East Williams, had a heavier concentration of pupils from minority and low-income families. When it was closed during the summer of 1965, students from that area were to be transported to other elementary schools with predominantly white enrollments. Over a three-year period students from East Williams were distributed among the six elementary schools in such a way that by the fall of 1968, all of the elementary schools had interracial stu-

---

From a report prepared by a State Anti-Discrimination Board. All names in the material have been changed in order to protect the identity of those concerned. Used by permission.

dent bodies with none less than 2.5 per cent nonwhite nor more than 30 per cent nonwhite. At the junior high level a redistribution of students between the relatively new Solo Junior High and the older Morton Junior High was accomplished in such a way that by the fall of 1968, Solo was approximately 7.1 per cent nonwhite and Morton 14.8 per cent nonwhite.

In summary, then, the Williams School District has acted positively to eliminate *de facto* segregation in all its schools, to provide a multiracial learning opportunity for all its students at every level, and to provide compensatory education and services for students from "culturally and economically deprived backgrounds." The District has tried to recruit additional staff (both certificated and classified) from minority groups, and this effort is beginning to bear fruit, especially at the high school. A new program called "Operation Motivation" promises to open up broader opportunities for vocational training to students who might not otherwise complete high school. Efforts to emphasize the contributions made by all racial groups to our country's growth are proceeding, though slowly and in a somewhat piecemeal fashion. And finally, a District Human Relations Committee has been formed and has developed a suitable set of objectives which will be implemented now that approval by the School Board has been obtained. With these efforts in mind, we now turn to the events of October 30 through November 12; what actually happened and why it happened, as far as we can determine.

The Events

The events of the two-week period from October 30 through November 12 will be more meaningful if set in a framework of incidents which appear to have had a major impact upon racial tension at the high school. These incidents are as follows:

October 31 (Thursday) A fight between Ellen Low and Millie Winter; Ellen Low suspended;

November 1 (Friday)   The suspension of Ellen took effect; a fight between Julia Gwen and Brenda Undale;

November 4 (Monday)   Several students wore a single black glove to school;

November 5 (Tuesday)   A fight between Dwight Dibbs and James Sill; the suspensions of three others;

November 6 (Wednesday)   The suspensions of Rhoda House and Cal Masters;

November 7 (Thursday)   Classes dismissed following rumor of dynamite in the building;

November 12 (Tuesday) The suspensions of James Sill and Dwight Dibbs.

Thursday, October 31: Where you begin in describing the events leading up to the fight between Ellen Low (black) and Millie Winter (white) depends upon whom you listen to in order to find out how it started. Certain events are fairly well verified, however, and do seem to be related to this fight. At some point, shortly before (and probably during the week of) the fight, Florence Mason and Millie Winter came upon Brenda Undal and Ellen Low in front of Florence's locker. (There may have been others present, but these four appear to have been most immediately involved.) Florence challenged Brenda's presence in front of her locker (apparently Brenda had her hand on the door of the locker), and Brenda responded with an explanation which apparently did not satisfy Florence who had her locker changed the same day. Later on (probably Wednesday, October 30) there was a fight between Brenda Undale and Florence Mason, which was broken up by James Winter without either girl being knocked down or hurt. The fight between Brenda and Florence was not immediately reported to anyone on the High School Administration staff.

On Thursday, October 31, Florence and Millie were sitting in Mrs. Hall's Latin class (7th period) on the second floor. Ellen Low (and perhaps Brenda Undale) walked by the door of the classroom, and Millie made a comment about this to Florence (the exact words used are in dispute, but some communication passed between them). At the end of the class Millie left the room and was confronted by Ellen in the hallway. Exactly what was said by the two girls to each other is disputed, but it appears to have had something to do with some very uncomplimentary things said by Millie about Ellen. Almost immediately a fight started between the two girls, and by the time Mrs. Hall reached them, they were down on the floor with Ellen on top striking at Millie and pulling her hair. Mrs. Hall re-entered her classroom to call the school office on the intercom—she felt that she could not break up the fight herself. She was unable to reach the office at first and turned the intercom over to one of her students while she returned to the hallway. By this time, Mr. Win, biology teacher with a classroom on the same floor, was breaking up the fight by pulling the two girls apart. When it was over, Millie was badly scratched and crying. She said: "Oh, I hate those Niggers!" Ellen went on outside the school building and got on the bus which would take her home.

Mr. Haines, vice-principal, asked Mrs. Hall to write out a statement of what she saw. Mr. Griggs, principal, went to the area where the fight occurred and saw Mr. Win leading Millie down the hall. He asked if anyone knew who else was involved. It is not clear what he found out at this time. He then went out to the bus which Ellen had just boarded, and stepped inside. He asked if anyone on the bus had been involved in the fight, and no one answered. Then he asked Ellen if she had been fighting, and she said that she had not. Them Mr. Griggs told the driver of the bus to wait until he returned, and he went back into the school building to get more information. When he returned to the bus he stepped inside again and told Ellen that she was suspended. Several students on the bus booed and hooted.

Later that afternoon, Mr. Griggs called Ellen's home to talk to her mother. Ellen answered the call and when she found out who it was hung up the phone. Later on Mrs. Low called Mr. Griggs, and he told her that Ellen was suspended (as of November 1) for ten days. (Later this suspension was extended for the remainder of the semester by the Superintendent at the request of Mr. Griggs.)

(From *City Herald,* November 5, 1968)

Williams High students have been warned.

Any violation of the ordinary rules of conduct and you place your educational future in jeopardy.

Implementation started Monday at the high school of what the Superintendent has described as a "firm but fair" warning policy following last week's two fights between white and Negro girls.

The school district's suspension policy was read to each class.

Moves have already been made to improve communication between the white and black students in an effort to avoid further incidents which take on special out-of-focus significance, not because of the incidents themselves but because of the color of the participants.

The High School Principal Bob Griggs says he will form groups of 10-12 white students and the same number of Negroes to sit down and thrash out problems.

The Superintendent said parents should realize that Williams High is experiencing nothing unique in a school with about 1,300 students and an enrollment of about 95 Negroes. He has asked school administrators and teachers to volunteer to form a human relations committee. The group would "evaluate the climate of human understanding and relations within the staff, students and patrons of the district; identify areas that merit further study, and prepare recommendations for action."

Two Negro advisers are already at work in the high school. One is a new student counselor. The other is checking attendance and supervising problem areas such as toilets, where parents of some white girls claim the girls can't go except in a gang.

To reduce likelihood of troublesome free time in the overcrowded school, lunch periods have been reduced from an hour to 30 minutes.

But there's still trouble.

Last year the Junior High's troubles were said to stem in the main from a hard core of 10 dissident Negro girls with about the same number of followers. This year they're in high school.

Are they going to be able to run wild?

The disciplinarian Griggs isn't about to let that happen. His suspension of one of the Negro girls last week has already brought threats that his home will be burned.

He knows that in certain quarters he's being labeled a bigot. He knows that within the high school his ability to communicate with Negro students is being questioned by some.

"But I've been in this high school long enough (28 years) for people of Williams to know me. If they have faith in me, I know I can straighten this out."

He hopes to do it by keeping a vigilant eye open for troublemakers, by picking them out, and by suspending them.

Regardless of color.

Griggs stresses that the present problem at the high school isn't caused only by blacks. The whites are also to blame. He stresses it's only a tiny minority of both blacks and whites causing problems.

He's anticipating the "firm but fair" policy of impartial enforcement of the school rules will probably cause more problems.

It's almost bound to when on one side you have a group of white students convinced that, "If you're black you can get away with anything."

And on the other side you have a group of Negroes equally convinced that, "If you're white you can get away with anything."

With such closed minds at work, should Griggs perform his task even with the wisdom and judgment of Solomon he's going to be in trouble.

According to the Superintendent, Griggs has "complete authority and backing of the school administration." Before the school year is out, Griggs may be needing it.

(From *City Herald,* November 7, 1968)

WILLIAMS HIGH EVACUATED AFTER DYNAMITE SCARE

Williams High School was emptied shortly after 10 A.M. today on the rumor there was a stick of dynamite in the building.

Principal Robert Griggs attributed the incident to rising racial tensions.

He said a teacher overheard a group of Negro students talking in the hallway about a stick of dynamite in the school and took two of them in to talk with the principal.

Griggs said students were worried and asked to go home.

"With the tension and all that is going on around the school I would have been foolish to keep them (all of the students) here," and he decided to close the school for the day.

Firemen made a spot check of the building but found no evidence of a bomb or stick of dynamite. He said guards and student monitors will be put on the door tomorrow and he also is considering asking parents to go to the school and help out.

Griggs said the "problem is part of a certain small group trying to disrupt the school. They are militant, their minds are closed and that's it. They feel the rules apply to others, not to them"

He explained the trouble now centers with a group of about 10 Negro students, although there are some "white militants."

Griggs said a group of Negro students suggested getting together with some of the white students and talking about their problems and differences.

The principal set up the meeting yesterday and it "ended up as a shouting match . . . no one was listening or thinking."

Emphasizing there wasn't a question of personal prejudice on his part, Griggs said the Negroes "didn't want to accept any reasons or do any serious thinking."

Griggs said he told the students after the meeting he would be glad to meet with individuals but would no longer have group meetings because they were totally unproductive.

He doesn't think the situation will cool off "until there is some change in their reasoning or they are removed from school."

Griggs admitted he's in a tough spot and "I'm damned if I do, and I'm damned if I don't."

He said since last Thursday there have been 8 students suspended—all of them Negroes—and some are part of the group of 10 that now appear to be the focal point of the trouble at the school.

He said a fight Tuesday between a white and Negro boy is still under investigation and he expects to "make up my mind by Monday or Tuesday. I expect to be crucified either way I go."

Neither student has been back at school since the fight, although neither has been suspended, he added.

Griggs said one of the accusations made against him by the Negro students is he is prejudiced and not giving equal treatment.

They cite his statement that if there is a fight then students involved will be suspended.

He noted there is quite a difference between suspending two students who get involved in a fight after accidentally bumping against one another and a student who, with premeditation, starts a fight.

"I'll just simply have to use my judgment on which students will be suspended when it's determined a fight is premeditated," he said.

Griggs said there is a proper way for students to present grievances to the administration and he's not going to tolerate any protests in the halls or open defiance of the faculty or administration.

Most of the problems have occurred when students are milling around in the halls before classes start or are out of class for one reason or another wandering around.

Griggs said there is going to be a "crackdown to get the kids out of the halls" and the administration, counselors and faculty will be involved in an effort to correct the situation.

(From *City Herald,* November 13, 1968)

WILLIAMS SCHOOLS MOVE TO EASE RACE TENSIONS

Williams School District will initiate a four-point program aimed at reducing and getting to the root of racial tensions.

Approval of the plan came at last night's board meeting in the Williams High School auditorium attended by more than 1,100 persons. The meeting saw principal Robert Griggs criticized and praised for his handling of the situation at the high school.

The program unanimously adopted by the board calls for:

• A survey of the situation by the State Board Against Discrimination.

• Appointment of a "blue-ribbon, top-level committee" to study the problems and come up with recommendations.

• Establishment of a district-wide Human Relations Committee made up initially of certificated and non-certificated employes in the district.

• Expansion of a program known as "Operation Motivation" to include girls.

Students will go to school a half-day and either work or return to the high school the balance of the day.

Most of last night's session of almost 2½ hours on the racial problem was devoted to comments from the audience. Overall, the meeting was orderly and punctuated with frequent applause for speakers. There were only occasional exhibitions of temper.

For the most part, the board and speakers—both black and white—seemed aware problems exist and showed signs of frustrations on how best to meet them.

It was also apparent from counter-statements that rumors, misinformation and lack of communication were major contributors to growing community concern.

Several speakers were critical of Griggs' handling of the tense situation at the high school and felt Negro students weren't getting the same consideration as white students.

They noted that out of 10 students suspended during the recent disciplinary crackdown, nine have been black.

Fair

Others defended Griggs as a fair and impartial administrator and supported equal disciplinary action for blacks and whites.

Tom Frich, president of the Teachers Education Association, read a letter approved "by an overwhelming majority of the teachers" that supported Griggs as "fair and firm." It said he only asks that the halls and restrooms be safe.

The letter also said there were white, as well as black, troublemakers in the school system.

Dr. Fall, Superintendent, repeatedly said it is a community problem as well as a school problem.

"We are going to use every method within our power to ensure the safety of kids without concern for color.

"When school is disrupted, we must put our foot down on the kids who are caus-ing the disruption," he said.

Suspended students have not been "forgotten" and two VISTA volunteers are tutoring them, Fall reported.

"We are making every effort to provide a safe school for education and to grow socially," he said.

Art Finch, Williams councilman, said a year ago he had urged the Community Action Committee recommend a program to the council to prevent racial problems such as those that developed in Williams last summer. No recommendation was made.

Plan

He also said he met with school administration in September, 1967, and offered to put together a plan "to prevent this sort of thing from happening."

He called for development of an "action program, not a policy, to put the resources when and where needed."

Finch declared that until he leaves Williams, he is "ready to help put together a definitive plan. I am sure you have Latin-American, black and white parents who are willing to help put together a definitive program."

Edward Jones opined that "the main thing the (Negro) kids are seeking is recognition," adding his 9-year-old grandson asks "what I or we have contributed. Teaching Negro history is as important as teaching the history of the State."

He said, "Kids get tired of reading books that say the white man did it. We want recognition."

Margaret Show said she had visited three Williams schools Tuesday and didn't see any unfair treatment. "There are problems but they aren't going to be solved in one day, one year. I think the administration is doing a good job."

Another woman suggested that "We should pick on parents instead of the administration. Start in with your own kids—don't expect them (the schools) to do all the job."

Problem

Paul Hatt, a high school teacher, declared "This is no school problem. It is a community problem. Instead of spreading rumors, we should sit down and set up channels to handle problems. It's too bad we had to wait until the problem developed."

John Jolson, chairman of the Community Action Committee, observed the word "discipline has been used quite frequently here this evening. Whatever action is taken by the board, it will have to include justice."

David Ball said "We don't condone what is wrong. The consensus of the Negro community is opposed (to the beating of a teacher) and to the suspension of black kids. I'm concerned about the racial overtones."

Jim Punter said the situation had been building up and there are some teachers who are prejudiced and more concerned about pay than the kids.

Conclusions of State Agency Staff

1. A pattern of increasing tension developed at Williams High School beginning with a fight between Brenda Undale and Florence Mason on or about 10/30/68, and ending with the suspension of James Sill and Dwight Dibbs on 11/12/68.

2. A pattern of punitive disciplinary action against black students developed from the suspension of Ellen Low on 10/31/68, and ended with the suspension of Dibbs and Sill which was constructive rather than punitive in maintaining discipline.

3. Relationships between the school administration and black students deteriorated beginning with the announcement of Ellen Low's suspension and a joint pro-

test by several black students in the hallway in front of the school office on the morning of 11/1/68. This deterioration continued until the all-school assembly on 11/12/68, at which Mr. Griggs asked the student body to work with him to restore sound human relationships with the school.

4. The Williams community became increasingly concerned and angered about the situation at the high school, and some of this anger was stimulated by the coverage given these events in the *Williams Herald,* which repeatedly emphasized the race of the participants. This public concern was partly met by the public meeting held by the School Board on 11/12/68 at the High School Auditorium, where the School Board acted to find out what brought about the crisis and to involve all segments of the community in seeking some solutions.

5. Members of the faculty and student body who were most acutely aware of the developing racial tension have placed considerable hope in the formation of a District Human Relations Committee, which has developed a meaningful set of objectives and some appropriate procedures for dealing with present and future intergroup and interpersonal tensions.

6. There are still several unresolved issues between the high school faculty and administration and many of the black students. These include:

a) the procedures for presenting grievances against any of the faculty or administration;

b) the disparity of treatment between students (white or black) who have developed special talents, and those whose talents have not been so well developed and whose behavior displeases the faculty and administration;

c) the continued use of threats and rumors by some students to disrupt the school program and keep the administration in a state of tension;

d) the introduction of Afro-American History and Culture into the curriculum;

e) the formation of a Black Student Union or similar organization representing the interests of black students, whether or not its membership is all black;

f) racial identification of so-called "troublemakers" at the high school in statements made to the news media.

7. There are still unresolved issues between black and white students at the high school. These include:

a) The acceptance of black students for their special talents (such as leadership, athletics, art, drama or music), and the nonacceptance of black students for themselves as persons;

b) the threats of bodily harm, express or implied, which have led many students to fear for their safety while in parts of the school building;

c) the use of name-calling and rumors of name-calling as a means of expressing anger in place of more honest confrontation of the feelings involved.

8. There are still unresolved issues within the Williams community which tend to create or aggravate racial tension at the high school. These include:

a) the growth of the community toward increasing involvement of minority groups in making decisions which will affect the whole community;

b) economic progress and increased employment for all groups within the community;

c) residential segregation vs. integrated living patterns;

d) interracial social contact, especially among youth;

e) the tension (which sometimes becomes conflict) between those who seek "law and order" as their top priority and those who seek "justice and equality" as their top priority.

General Remarks of Staff

Back-up data for some of the above conclusions are available in the State University Survey of Racial Attitudes at the High School. Some of this data supports the hypothesis that parental attitudes (sometimes hostility and sometimes anxiety) are being worked out through some of the youth involved in these and other incidents at the high school. That is, Caucasian parents have not resolved their anxiety concerning the trend toward integration among youth of different racial and socio-economic backgrounds. These parents are passing on their anxiety to their offspring who in turn have developed ambivalent feelings and behavior about their relationships with minority youth. Some minority parents have not resolved their hostility resulting from years of discrimination and exclusion, and this hostility is being passed on to their offspring without guidance or direction as to how these feelings should be worked out or expressed. The high school and related activity programs are affected by all of these unresolved parental feelings, and the youth are reflecting their recognition of some of these parental "hang-ups" when they say, "Stay out of our way and let us work this out for ourselves." In one way the youth are saying, "We don't want to be stuck with your hang-ups as adults"; and at the same time, these youth are saying, "But don't let us down when we need your best judgment and counsel."

Staff Recommendations

1. Institute mandatory human relations (sensitivity) training for all staff—both pre-service and in-service training in intergroup and interpersonal relations.

2. All courses in American History and Literature at every grade level should include Afro-American History and Literature as part of the curriculum (and part of the illustrations used in student textbooks).

3. Establish racially integrated staffs at every level of instruction (K through twelfth grade), and include more nonwhite counselors and teacher-aides.

4. Clarify the respective roles of counselors and attendance supervisors especially with regard to student problems and discipline.

5. a) Review grounds for student suspension and clarify what kinds of behavior will constitute good cause for disciplinary action.

   b) Establish procedures for investigating situations requiring disciplinary action, and clarify steps to be taken before a formal suspension is issued.

6. Establish a Student-Faculty Senate to hear complaints and charges against students and recommend disciplinary action for consideration of the school administration.

7. Establish guidelines for permissible and impermissible forms of communication and protest whenever grievances are felt to exist.

8. Revise District and High School Administration's policy regarding use of law enforcement officers to assist in maintaining school order, so that police are used only to enforce criminal statutes and not school rules.

9. Students, both individually and through their organizations, especially the Associated Student Body, take action to eliminate threats and rumors of violence and/or name-calling.

10. Establish program in cooperation with the Police Department to utilize articulate police officers to talk with students in classroom settings about the ways in which police work is carried on to maintain order and deal with law violations.

11. School District Administration and individual school administrators review their policies and practices regarding statements to the news media concerning tensions and/or conflict within a particular school, so as to avoid emphasis on racial identity in releasing information to the media.

12. a) Students and faculty work toward the acceptance of all students on an individual basis as persons, without regard to special talents or achievements; urge more minority student participation in extracurricular activities of their choice, and welcome those who respond and wish to join.

    b) Encourage an organization of black students to select representatives for purposes of communicating with the High School Administration and the Associated Student Body.

Dangers of a Retaliatory Police Response: Proposals for Riot Control

"Law and Order" has entered America's everyday vocabulary as a sloganistic antidote to "Crime in the Streets" or "Student Anarchy" or "Ghetto Riots." One reaction to urban disorders has been the program of social responsibility embedded in the Kerner Commission Report. Another has been the repressive, hard-nosed, punitive stance enunciated in the presidential campaign platform of George Wallace and by a number of mayoralty candidates in northern cities, and as implemented in caricature on college campuses at Kent State and in Jacksonville, Florida.

Civic disorders may be viewed symbolically as a form of language, an outcry of distress, frustration, and anger. At the same time, such disturbances may be depicted as threats to the social order, a danger to persons, and an assault on the rights of property. At what level should the group relations practitioner respond? As an advocate of the disadvantaged, he can easily comprehend the causes of disorders and appreciate the potentially beneficial consequences of these outbreaks in dramatically calling attention to social injustices. As a humanitarian and advocate of general community welfare he is alarmed by violence, dismayed by abrasive antagonisms, and especially disturbed by the potential peril to human life. Few practitioners would discount the necessity or at least the inevitability of public safety measures during times of great social upheaval. The crucial question would seem to be how to contain social turmoil within reasonable limits of safety and at the same time avoid the kind of repressive or retaliatory action which may curtail legitimate dissent and which in itself may constitute a threat to life.

In a sense, police have been placed unwittingly at the vortex of many critical contemporary social problems. They become society's agent of social control over situations which they, as law enforcement officials, had no part in creating. Policemen resent the ridicule and abuse contained in the "Pig" appellation and often feel themselves misunderstood and maligned, not only by the dissidents, but by society as a whole (low pay, low status, little community cooperation). The danger of overreaction is large under such circumstances, given encouragement by some unscrupulous political figures, intentional provocation, and brutalizing tendencies inherent in police work.

While preferring to emphasize preventive programs, group relations workers may find it necessary to intervene into police activity in order to mediate and control some of these repressive tendencies. Familiarity with police policies and techniques may become increasingly important as the general posture of the police moves in a hardened direction.

Judge George Edwards, former Police Commissioner in Detroit, reflects on two tense situations in that city, one of which led to a disorder and the other which did not. Based on the comparison he recommends a series of procedures for use by the police. These recommendations provide a useful point of departure for discussion of the issues involved in this subject.

Detroit: The Riot That Didn't Happen . . .

On August 9 and 10, 1966, Detroit met a major test. That summer had produced one race riot after another in city after city. Two much smaller Michigan cities had just been severely hit. At this point a routine arrest on Detroit's East Side, for loitering, prompted some young Negroes to call for riot. The resulting crowd quickly grew too big for the precinct officers on or near the scene to handle without additional help.

Police mobilization was prompt. Within an hour there were 200 men on the scene, including a specially trained Tactical Mobile Unit. The area was sealed off; high-ranking officers made a plan for police placement and tactics, and took charge on the scene.

The results of prior intelligence pertaining to riot-prone groups and individuals paid off. Carloads of activists, headed for the area with weapons in their cars, were arrested.

Where groups formed on the street, the police moved quickly to disperse them. Breaking in, looting and attempted fire bombing were met with prompt arrests.

The Negro community not only refused to rally to the rioters, it moved decisively to cool them off. As word of the trouble spread, leaders of block clubs came to the police station to check on the nature of the disturbances. From there, some went to the trouble spots and urged youngsters to go home. Other telephoned officers of block clubs asking them to get children off the street in their blocks, and to squelch rumors.

Some 150 Negro residents met at a church, pledged their support to the police, and organized two-man citizen "peace patrols" to walk the area. They also set up an information center where residents could check up on rumors.

For two nights, in a relatively small area around Kercheval Avenue, the trouble kept churning. But all it added up to was 43 arrests, some property damage and a few minor injuries. Businesses stayed open. There were no shots fired and no deaths. In short, the riot was not allowed to happen.

. . . and the One That Did

Another riot broke in Detroit in the early morning hours of Sunday, July 23, 1967. It was triggered by a police raid on a "blind pig"—an illegal after-hours drinking spot. The locale was Twelfth Street, the most explosive in the city; the time was

From *The Police on the Urban Frontier,* by George Edwards. Institute of Human Relations Press, New York, 1968, pp. 60-68.

2:30 A.M. on a hot summer night, in what was the worst summer of racial explosions thus far. The precinct that made the raid had not consulted with, or notified, central police headquarters.

The street reaction was immediate. Saturday night drinkers, pimps, prostitutes and numbers men supplied the active elements in the initial nighttime crowds. By dawn many others had arrived on the scene—among them advocates of violent "Black Power" who openly called for riot. Still later, Sunday morning churchgoers added numbers and complications to the Twelfth Street crowd.

Looting of stores on Twelfth Street began before dawn. At 8 A.M. the first fire bombing occurred.

At the time of the initial outbreak, the department was subsequently to reveal, only 193 policemen were on street patrol in the whole city—the lowest coverage in the entire week.

The police's initial response was weak in both manpower and effectiveness. No attempts were made to control the widespread looting. Police efforts concentrated on defending fire units, which came under attack as they arrived. Early in the morning one police squad in wedge formation attempted to regain control of Twelfth Street. A task which a trained force of 100 or more police might have accomplished was undertaken by fewer than twenty officers. The crowd recognized the show of weakness for what it was. No resistance to the progress of the squad was attempted, but rioters dispersed into doorways, alleys and side streets, and flowed back into Twelfth Street after the wedge had passed.

By midmorning the Mobile Task Unit had been partly mobilized. A trained commando platoon under experienced leadership, equipped with tear gas, bayonets and riot guns, was standing by on Twelfth Street.

At the same time, community leaders met at Grace Episcopal Church to seek ways of calming the spreading violence. The meeting decided (with some vigorous dissents) to ask for removal of the commando squad as the price of a civilian attempt to stop the quickly growing riot.

No top administrative city official and no top police administrator was on the scene at that time, nor at any time during the crucial first twelve hours on Sunday.

The civilian leaders, with Congressman John Conyers, Jr., as chief spokesman, attempted to talk to the crowds on Twelfth Street. Conyers made a brave attempt. He was hooted down.

The commando squad was never ordered to clear Twelfth Street. The Mobile Task Unit was "held in reserve" for other emergencies. The word spread on Twelfth Street, and thence through the entire city, that the police were not trying to stop looting. These facts led Detroit's leading Negro newspaper to headline its first post-riot front page "It Could Have Been Stopped."

Looting now spread far beyond the original riot area. Many persons of usually law-abiding disposition were caught up in the madness. Witnesses subsequently gave vivid descriptions of the carnival atmosphere attending some of the looting. There was ample evidence of anti-white bias in the selection of places to be looted and burned. But there was little or no evidence of any general lynch mob spirit toward white individuals as such. Negro and white looters mingled freely, and white bystanders were generally left unmolested.

But fire bombing spread throughout the city, and fire and police units seeking to respond found themselves under mob attack.

At 2 P.M., eleven and one-half hours after the "blind pig" raid, Mayor Jerome P. Cavanagh called Governor George W. Romney, reported that the rioting was beyond local control, and requested the dispatch of State Troopers and the National Guard.

In the four days that followed, widespread looting, fire bombing and sniping approximated guerrilla warfare conditions in many areas of the city. Of the three major forces involved in suppressing the mass violence, only the 82nd Airborne Division of the United States Army was to emerge with its reputation enhanced. The 82nd arrived late in the riot and was never committed to the worst of the riot areas. But its thorough integration, its cool-headed professional leadership and its completely disciplined response were major factors in ending the violence.

The Detroit Police and the Michigan National Guard bore the brunt of dealing with the worst of the mob violence. The courage and effectiveness of each unit undoubtedly served to restore order and to prevent an even worse holocaust. But in the aftermath of the riot, some actions by personnel of each command were subjected to bitter criticism. Lieutenant General John L. Throckmorton, who commanded the 82nd Airborne and was the ranking military officer on the scene, was later to characterize the National Guard troops as "green" and "trigger-happy." And the *Detroit Free Press*—a paper normally well disposed toward the police— published a lengthy analysis of the 43 riot deaths which plainly implied that a considerable number of them had been unnecessary. Post-riot investigation of the death of three young Negroes in the Algiers Motel resulted in the indictment of two Detroit police officers for murder.

The number of persons killed eventually mounted to 43—38 of them civilians. Damage to insured property totaled $38,000,000; uninsured and indirect losses reached still greater proportions.

The riot left a city which had made many vigorous efforts to prevent just this kind of catastrophe reeling from the impact of civic disaster. For days afterward, troops of the Michigan National Guard and the 82nd Airborne patrolled its streets.

Causes of the Disaster

National news media later emphasized almost unanimously that Detroit's efforts to solve its racial problems had been the most vigorous in the nation, but also that, in the process, the city had developed a complacent attitude of "it can't happen here."

The first of these two observations may be true, but what it principally illustrates is a lack of commitment among other cities to an attack on the problem of the ghetto. As to the second, much of Detroit, official and otherwise, presumably hoped for the best; yet neither public nor private circles doubted that explosive material was present and that the explosion, if it came, could be big.

While Detroit was still burning, *The New York Times* summed up the lessons of the outbreak:

> There are at least two conclusions to be drawn from the tragic events that have condemned forward-looking Detroit to the fate of less-deserving cities.
>
> One is, that if Detroit is an example of America's best efforts to solve the racial and other problems confronting its cities, the best is not nearly good enough.
>
> The other is, that even if progress is achieved on a broad front, the United States must be prepared to contend with serious turbulence in its cities for a long time to come.

As Dr. Kenneth Clark and other sociologists have pointed out, progress in its initial stages tends to generate expectations faster than they can be fulfilled. People who harbor frustrated hopes are more likely to rebel than those with no hope at all.

In this sense, Detroit may be viewed as a victim of its own limited success. But this is no reason to despair or quit. There can be no turning back, even if that were desirable. Detroit's anguish and that of other American cities will be relieved only when the promising social, economic and educational programs that have been initiated, and additional programs on a huge scale, are pressed to the point where they begin to fulfill the hopes they have rightly engendered.

But meanwhile, the absolute, prime requirement is the restoration of order to the beleaguered city and the application of as much force as is necessary to restore it. Without order there can be no progress.

Three explanations suggest themselves to account for the ferocity and extent of the Detroit riot of 1967. All three are important. All three are also true.

The most fundamental by all odds is society's failure to make the promise of equality for Negroes a reality. America has had 300 years and countless warnings to render equal justice to its Negro citizens. Yet the city of Detroit, the state of Michigan and the United States failed to do enough—in time.

A second, no less important, explanation is that the Detroit Police Department failed to employ its resources promptly enough and firmly enough when the trouble began. In the face of such a holocaust no one can be positive that a different response or tactic would have produced a better result. But if we compare the actual events to what are considered desirable tacts of riot control, the failures of the Police Department are all too obvious:

1. There was a complete failure of prior intelligence.

2. There was a failure to have a sufficient number of men on hand at the outbreak of the riot. (Recognizing that the riot broke at the time of the week when the assigned police manpower was lowest, we must still record this fact.)

3. There was a failure to mobilize quickly enough and to bring reserves into action at the critical moment of the developing riot.

4. There was a failure to apply massive, disciplined and effective force on Twelfth Street at any time during the critical hours—between 2 A.M. and 2 P.M. on the first day.

5. There was a failure to have high-ranking police supervision at the points where critical decisions had to be made in the early hours of the first day, before the riot became general.

Without trying to pinpoint the blame, the absolute least that must be done is to see that such failures of inaction do not recur. While doing so, however, it should be recognized that what is called for is disciplined, intelligent and effective police response. There are, unfortunately, those who would substitute for the indefensible inaction we have discussed an even more indefensible blood bath.

A third explanation of the severity of the disaster is the pattern of fire bombing, which turned a local riot into a city-wide conflagration. There is no hard evidence to prove that the Detroit riot as a whole was planned—either at the Kremlin in Moscow or at the Black Power Conference in Newark. And the way it actually started argues strongly against any prior plan as to timing. But Black Power activists did move into the riot in its early stage to intensify and to spread it. There is considerable reason to believe that at least part of the attendant havoc in the Cincinnati, Newark and Detroit outbreaks of 1967 was planned and organized. Indeed, it is possible that planned fire bombing was the added factor which put the Detroit riot of 1967 out of control and justified the term "rebellion" later applied to it by Black Power extremists.

The indications of planning are certainly sufficient to highlight the great need for prior police intelligence work. They also serve to highlight what a tragedy it is that Detroit has substantially dismantled its police intelligence unit—not many years ago regarded as one of the best in the nation.

Recommended Control Methods

A generally authoritative publication on riot control was distributed nationwide to local law enforcement officials by the Federal Bureau of Investigation in the spring of 1967. This booklet deals in depth with appropriate police training, intelligence work and planning prior to outbreaks of violence. It includes recommendations for alerting and seeking aid from state and national authorities if a disturbance exceeds local control.

We shall quote from two sections directly relevant to riot control by local police.

At the outset, according to the FBI, the police commander's best bet is a purposeful, disciplined display of force and a resolve to convince the mob that the police can and will maintain law and order—if necessary by force.

> The next step is for the police commander to give the order to disperse; such an order should not be given until the commander has sufficient force to back up his order. Never bluff! Officers who participate· in a show of force must be well disciplined so they will follow orders to the letter, stand firm in the face of abuse, and not lose their heads.

If the more law-abiding of the citizens momentarily caught up in the mob do not yield to a show of force, they may yield to actual force. Such action should be kept to the minimum necessary at any given moment, since unwarranted application of force may incite a mob to further violence. Depending on the need, force may be gradually intensified:

> Applying force by degrees insures that the maximum force employed to restore order is applied to the most violent and lawless individuals only. The degrees and the order of the application of force should be decided in advance. . . . All officers involved in the operation must be aware of these degrees and must know when each is to be applied and by whose authority. This is not meant to imply that police should not meet force with greater force; it does mean that unnecessary bloodshed must be avoided whenever possible.

Priorities in the use of force will depend on available weapons and equipment. Tear gas can serve to prevent threatened violence by rioters or to disperse them. When chemicals are used, there must be an avenue of escape; otherwise panic may result.

> Chemical agents, properly employed . . . can negate the numerical superiority the mob has over the police force. They are the most effective and most humane means of achieving temporary neutralization of a mob with a minimum of personal injury. Chemical agents should not be used or threatened to disperse demonstrators who are not in fact endangering public safety and security.

The baton, the FBI warns, must be judiciously used to be effective without inflicting unnecessary injury. Officers must be thoroughly trained in its use.

The baton should be used only in an emergency, and when blows are struck, it should be with the intention of stunning or temporarily disabling, rather than inflicting injury. Blows to the head should be avoided. The baton used as an extension of the arm is generally more effective than when used as a bludgeon or club.

The armed forces' order of priorities might serve as a model, the FBI suggests:
1. Unloaded rifles with bayonets fixed and sheathed.
2. Unloaded rifles with bare bayonets fixed.
3. Tear gas (CS and CN).
4. Loaded rifles with bare bayonets fixed.

The FBI recommendations emphasize that firearms are to be used only as a last resort:

The decision to resort to the use of firearms is indeed a grave one. . . . Among the important considerations, of course, are the protection of the officer's own life, as well as the lives of fellow officers, and the protection of innocent citizens. A basic rule in police firearms training is that a firearm is used only in self-defense or to protect the lives of others.

Officers should never fire indiscriminately into a crowd, the FBI stresses, lest they injure or kill innocent persons and thereby provoke a worse clash. Nor should they fire over the heads of crowds—a bluffing technique which may defeat itself or may take lives unnecessarily through poorly aimed or ricocheting bullets.

Snipers must be quickly and severely dealt with, the FBI recommendations continue, both because they pin down the police and because they endanger human lives.

It may be necessary to employ a countersniper, equipped and trained in the use of high-powered, telescopic-equipped rifles. Police officers, crouched behind any means of protection available and firing their service revolvers or shotguns aimlessly at a building or rooftop, are endangering lives and, at the same time, are prevented from accomplishing their mission.

As for other weapons, the bayonet can be an effective deterrent—used, not as a night stick or baton, but with the standard shotgun, especially in shows of force and standard riot control formations.

UNIT **17.**

Effects of Personal Contact and Cultural Exchange: "Summer in the City" and Monsignor Fox

Many group relations practitioners have turned away from the kinds of interpersonal contact programs that were once fashionable in the field. Such programs make little immediate impact on some of the big issues confronting us currently, such as institutional racism. It is surprising and interesting, therefore, to come upon an active and well-developed contemporary program having as its basic format the encouragement of intercultural and interpersonal exchange. This is the "Summer in the City" program conducted by the Very Reverend Monsignor Robert J. Fox in multi-ethnic neighborhoods in New York City.

How is one to respond to this programmatic approach? Fortunately this is one area in the field which has been subject to research by interested social scientists. As a consequence of these studies we may reasonably conclude that personal association across ethnic lines has higher probabilities of success when the following conditions are met: The individuals have approximately equal status in the situation; the individuals involved have similar interests and similar characteristics on at least some variables such as age or occupation; the circumstances of the situation tend to foster or favor cooperation; the mixed situation tends to enhance the goals of each party or at least not to impede or hinder them, and there is an opportunity to get to know one another as individuals. Thus, any situation of interpersonal association may be examined from the standpoint of the degree to which these predisposing conditions prevail. Further, the social climate of the situation in which the activity takes place may be important also. Thus, if a high school administration creates a climate which not only accepts but also encourages and rewards intergroup associations, this may contribute to a successful outcome of personal contact relationships.

Having established circumstances which maximize the success of these programs, the practitioner is forced to ask himself the question: Is it worth the effort? Is much or little in the long run accomplished by facilitating interpersonal attrition and improving attitudes? Might this effort be better directed into behavioral change activities? How long-lasting will attitude changes be once individuals leave the inter-

187

vention situation and return to more usual circumstances? Are these changes trans-
ferable to other situations? How do these programs articulate with efforts which
emphasize ingroup identity and separatism? On the other hand, one may ask, if we
are not in the business of improving the quality of relationship among people, then
what is our work all about anyway? The "Summer in the City" program appears to
emanate from a religious frame of reference which takes this last question very
seriously.

Everyone has inside himself—what shall I call it?—a piece of good news! UGO
BETTI. *Sign on a wall in the office of the Very Reverend Monsignor Robert J. Fox.*

A black dog wearing a bright-yellow crepe-paper collar wandered down the
sidewalk of 54th Street between Ninth and Tenth Avenues late one afternoon a few
days ago, past a hydrant that had been sprayed with orange and green Day-Glo
paint, under fire escapes strung with yellow balloons and flapping streamers, and
into a doorway where paper flowers had been twisted around rusted railings. Near
a "No Parking" signpost wrapped with bunting, several young girls were dancing
to music from a radio, and they waved when Monsignor Robert J. Fox came walking down the sidewalk behind the dog. Monsignor Fox, a tall, handsome man of
thirty-seven, is the director of an office of the Roman Catholic archdiocese called
Spanish Community Action in New York. He is also the originator of a nonsectarian program called Summer in the City, through which this past summer a staff of
about five hundred and eighty, financed by the federal Office of Economic Opportunity, attempted to draw people in slum areas of the Bronx and Manhattan into a
number of rather unusual community activities. Dressed in frayed black pants, dirty
shoes, and a black short-sleeved summer clerical shirt, Monsignor Fox looked to
me more like an off-duty fireman than a ranking priest. He was visiting some of the
activities being run by Summer in the City, now in its third season, and he had invited me to come along. We had spent the afternoon touring storefronts taken over
by the organization around East Harlem—where Monsignor Fox had led processions through the streets during the July riots—and then we had come over to the
West Side so that he could check on the preparations for a block party that was to
be held on 54th Street later that evening.

Two pretty girls in their early twenties hailed Monsignor Fox and hurried over. I
noticed that one of them had sprayed the toes of her shoes with green Day-Glo paint.

"We're going to feed everybody in the street tonight," she said. "All the women
are making sandwiches."

"We'll start with a dance," said the other girl. "And then let things evolve."

"We had fifteen hundred people at our block party on Fifty-sixth Street last
week," said the first girl. "It lasted till four in the morning."

Monsignor Fox told the girls, both of whom, I learned later, were artists working
out of a Summer in the City storefront on Tenth Avenue, that we'd come back when
the party started. As we walked along, Monsignor Fox exchanged greetings with
a succession of children and told me, "This block is a mixture of Puerto Rican,
Negro, and Irish. The last time there was a party out here on the street was twenty
years ago." He looked around. "Let's see what happens tonight." As we turned the
corner, he said, "We'll go pick up Judith, have dinner, and come back."

Sister Judith, a nun of the order of the Religious of the Sacred Heart of Mary, is a dynamic woman, in her twenties, who has charge of all graphic-design projects for Summer in the City; her own bold style is seen in publications, on posters, and on an abstract orange-and-pink Summer in the City button that is worn by workers in the program. A month earlier—the day after the first night of rioting in East Harlem—I had gone along with Sister Judith and Miss Sue Shapiro, another artist, on a tour of Summer in the City activities on the lower East and West Sides.

"The idea of Summer in the City," Sister Judith told me that day as we walked east from Tompkins Square, "is to try to make the city a place where people can live in a positive way, aware of its values and their own value. Once people realize their own value, the social structure is turned upside down. We try to create an air of celebration of the city, because most of the people in these blocks will always live here. We have twenty-six storefront centers in Manhattan this summer, and each has three paid artists. They may be poets, dramatists, dancers, photographers —anyone who is creative and can get other people to be creative, as a means to relationship. There's also a staff of workers from the neighborhood and a neighborhood board of directors. We have all kinds of activities, but everything we do is done, if possible, out on the street—not in the school, not in the church, but right on the sidewalk, where people can come along and see, and talk, and break down barriers. Each center also has a fiesta or a parade or a dance or some other kind of celebration at least once a week, always on a different block. This may do no more than get a group of Negro adults talking to a group of Puerto Rican adults, but it's a start." She waved a young man sitting on a stoop across the street, who was playing a harmonica. He removed one hand from the harmonica and waved back, still playing. "The hippies here are just great," Sister Judith said. "We had a big fiesta and the hippies came down and joined us, and one of them acted as m.c. for the whole thing."

I asked Miss Shapiro how she had become involved in the program. "Three years ago, I felt very hopeless," she said. "There were race riots threatened, and Vietnam was getting worse, and I felt I couldn't make a mark in any way. I was sort of tempted to stay in my studio and do nothing about it, but I got turned on by the idea of Summer in the City. It wasn't parochial or humdrum, and it was a chance to change something, at least in a little way. When I first went to our storefront, I made enormous puppets and walked around the street with them, just so I could meet the people. They were amazed. They'd say, 'How are you?'—adding, 'you nut,' to themselves—and I told them we were going to have a fiesta on Friday and did they have any kids who'd like to be in the potato-sack race? Who could help us paint the pinata? Did they know any musicians, because we'd be having a dance contest. As soon as you're in a storefront, people get curious. The result was they'd come in and get involved in it, and the contacts kept broadening, and their involvements in the neighborhood increased, and they were drawn into something larger. Festival times and spectacular events draw people into relationship with each other.

"We take paint out into the street to let people try it. Sometimes the old people pull back. So you say, 'O.K.—watch me,' and you start out, and then they'll try it, very carefully. We're trying to bring out the creativity that's in everybody. It's not always easy though. Last summer, I was in a storefront on Mulberry Street, right in the heart of Little Italy. When we went down there, they didn't want anything to do with us. They're very proud. 'We're not poor,' they said. None of the groups would speak to each other. The first time we made a banner, they burned it. It was like going through a jungle all summer, but we kept going. We scrounged materials from factories to make things, and we had a Space Parade, and a circus, and at the end of the summer we had a few Puerto Ricans speaking to Italians and some Italians speaking to Negroes. The teenagers were the hardest to involve, but it was the first summer in Little Italy they had no rumbles."

Sister Judith and Miss Shapiro and I visited some other centers and then headed uptown. As we passed Kelly Park, a playground on 17th Street between Eighth and Ninth Avenues, Sister Judith said that that playground used to have a reputation as a hangout for gangs and addicts and most mothers wouldn't let their children play there, so Summer in the City had tried to create events and activities inside the park to make it a place where the neighborhood people could feel secure. Sister Judith pointed out a huge mural on one wall of the park. "That was done by the people here last summer, and quite a few addicts worked on it," she said. The mural incorporated Mickey Mouse, palm trees, devils, stripes, a map of Puerto Rico, indescribable patterns, words ("Tootsie"), and slogans ("God Bless the People All the People").

I asked how they had settled on who would paint what where.

"You find out what a person feels secure about drawing, and you say, 'Johnny, you put your cat there,' " Miss Shapiro said. The whole thing seemed to hold together remarkably well. "They paint their world," said Miss Shapiro, "and if they have a clear conception of their world, how can it not work?"

A month later, early in the afternoon of the 54th Street block party, Monsignor Fox took me up to East Harlem in a green Volkswagen that he drives around the city. Monsignor Fox, who was born in the Bronx, has, among other things, worked as a parish priest on the Lower East Side, lectured on social work in Latin America, and marched in Selma, Alabama. He is easy to talk with, and laughs a lot. However, as we crossed 96th Street on Park Avenue and the wide, quiet, empty avenue suddenly became narrow, noisy, and cluttered, he was serious. "People here are afraid of the street," he said. "They're fearful of bringing their human qualities to it, and fearful of each other. It's a cold, hostile environment, and they're more and more turned off to it. Society keeps telling them that all this is not livable—it says 'Make something of yourself and get *out* of here.' Summer in the City is meant to help people believe in themselves—to reveal themselves and reconfirm each other's riches. If you can get people off balance—whether it's by a fiesta or a block party or a mock bullfight or a parade—fear is reduced and they rediscover themselves."

After turning east, Monsignor Fox parked across from a Summer in the City storefront at 110th Street and Lexington Avenue, and we got out. The July riots had started just around the corner, and I asked Monsignor Fox about the processions he had led through the area at that time.

"When I heard that trouble was brewing, I came up here to make sure that our storefronts stayed open," he said. "Mayor Lindsay was telling everybody to get off the streets, but I felt this would be counter-productive. We didn't want the people to surrender the streets to the cops and the rioters—the two groups that believe in force. That's why we marched."

We went across the street toward the storefront. "Hey, Foxy!" yelled a tall, cheerful young man. "I got people calling the Sanitation Department every half hour about this building on a Hundred and Eleventh. You want to see what they're calling about? Come on." The three of us started down the street, but both the young man—whose name turned out to be Jim Marin—and Monsignor Fox were frequently stopped by passersby who knew them and wanted to say something.

One girl greeted Monsignor Fox by saying grandly, "You're paying us a mayoral visit!" Everybody laughed.

"Listen, he was here when they were throwing the bottles—not after!" Marin said, and they laughed again.

As we moved on, Marin talked about the day of the first riot, and how the sudden appearance on the block of thirty-five policemen in full riot gear had built pressure rather than eased it. "I was never here in my life until a few weeks ago," he said, "but now I know the first names of maybe three hundred people."

A disheveled man approached Marin. "Listen, I talked to that guy that hit you," Marin said, and the two had a brief discussion.

Marin told me that he was returning to the Harvard Graduate School in the fall. "I should probably stay here," he said. "I'll learn more in East Harlem than I'll ever learn in Graduate School. And yet at the beginning I was ready to walk out of here. I was up to my eyebrows. I'm a teacher, and I'm used to results. That's what the O.E.O. wants—statistical results. They always want to know 'How *many* people have you serviced?' But it's not like that here. A lot of the poverty program is locked inside a possession ethic that says what makes a man significant in our society is that he has *things*. The poverty program is saying that's what it means to be a person. It's perpetuating a myth. Poverty is not lovable, but you've got to find what it means to be a man. If a person can't find his manhood here, he can't find it anywhere." We stopped in front of an abandoned building. "That's what we're calling Sanitation about," Marin said, pointing to a large mound of garbage and junk. There were half-burned mattresses, and bedsteads, and dozens of beer cans. "We want them to take it away," Marin said. "It's a perfect place for the bandstand for our block party on Friday."

Later, as Monsignor Fox and I were driving along 103rd Street between Lexington and Third, an old man in a blue shirt waved enthusiastically. "*Como esta?*" Monsignor Fox yelled back. "There are fantastic people on this block," he said. "He's Don Andres, superintendent of three buildings here, and in the midst of all this he keeps his buildings and sidewalks spotless. People here experienced their own power in the riots. Now there's a chance they can use their power for the problems in their blocks. Don Andres is part of a group that's going to mobilize the people on this block to try to do something very visible and immediate. They're going to have five hundred people—including middle-class people from the suburbs, who will come not as paternalistic white fathers but just as people willing to work—and they'll start redeeming space. Taking away junk and garbage in back yards and basements to make room for classes and art and games. Even though it will benefit the landlords, it will demonstrate that human development and interaction are not dependent on outside power."

A small girl of about eight ran up to the car and asked for a ride down to 100th Street. Monsignor Fox got out and opened the door for her. "This is Guillermina," he said. "Otherwise known as Mami."

We drove to 100th Street and Second Avenue. "Right here!" said Guillermina. She climbed out. "Thank you, Father!" she called, skipping east into the block.

Monsignor Fox let the car idle and gazed down toward First Avenue. "I run out of words for this street," he said after a moment. The block, which newspapers have sometimes called the city's worst, did not look much different from many others we had seen. It had the same tenements, the same garbage, the same noise. "It's got narcotics, gambling—everything—right on the street," said Monsignor Fox. "But it's so *alive.*" He parked the car near the corner. "It's always been considered a problem street," he said. "But it's never had people approaching it with the idea of believing in the street—the idea that the Kingdom of Heaven is here. Not 'Can we bring it here?' but 'Can we recognize it, and open ourselves to its reality?' If there's going to be growth here, it'll be the result of people knowing they don't have power, and doing things at the risk of being laughed at and ineffectual—being vulnerable but willing to take on the whole environment. They've got to see it all, and see themselves. A creative response. Until people come to that kind of awareness of their scene, there'll be no solutions. The planners are paternalistic, and they use the same old hackneyed approach. Unless people start looking at themselves, there can be no response that is relevant. When people pull down the shade on rats, narcotics, garbage, prostitutes, and roaches, they become alienated—just the way the middle class loses touch with itself when *those* people pull down *their* shade on superficiality, lack of integrity, graft. It's the same process. There isn't a problem on this street that isn't a reflection of parallel problems shot through the whole society. They use narcotics on this block so they won't be vulnerable to reality, but the middle class has its narcotics, too—success, lawns, flowers, boats, collecting things— so *they* won't be vulnerable to reality. The arguments you hear in shaftways here, the drinking on the steps—they're doing the same thing in Larchmont in different forms. There's the same alienation out there, but in a ten-room house the people don't have to be aware of how isolated they really are from each other. Middle-class people who have worked and saved to get out of these blocks have established the premise that this is the bottom of the world. But helplessness and powerlessness exist on all levels. Look at President Johnson—look at his agonizing powerlessness." Monsignor Fox paused. "People either accept powerlessness as a premise, and move on, or else they turn to illusions. Some people accept the illusion of power—like buying things, collecting things, acquiring prestige objects instead of objects of discovery—and others turn to destruction: 'If I can destroy what I feel powerless in front of, then I have power.' There's a tremendous drive to destroy now. We have a preoccupation with so many forms of death. The media come in on the riots with cameras rolling, wallowing in it; it's what the middle class is interested in. Another illusion is withdrawal: 'They won't let me do anything, so I'm pulling out. I'm going to sit and watch it crumble.' "

Monsignor Fox got out of the car. "Do you want to visit some friends of mine on this block?" he asked. I followed him, and halfway down the block we entered a tenement and climbed three flights. The halls were dark, but through the windows, in back yards and alleys, we saw an incredible landscape of despair, in which everything seemed thrown away, abandoned, neglected, blending together in an absence of value. We knocked on a door in a dark hallway, and a few moments later were having iced tea with three young, pretty, and very cheerful Maryknoll nuns. The nuns, who wore gray skirts and white blouses, had no special mission on the block where they lived—only to get to know the people there and to do whatever they could to help them. They were extraordinarily joyful, and the twenty minutes we spent with them were full of laughter. There was no solemn talk about motives or purpose, and the stories they told were about what the neighborhood bookie had said about the addicts, or about trying to kill cockroaches, or about taking a bath in a large kitchen sink. Several children came in and out, and the only note of sadness I was aware of during the visit came when one the the nuns said that they had been ordered to return to their college in the fall. It was clearly a grave matter to them, a true loss, but in a moment they were laughing again.

Monsignor Fox and I visited some other places in East Harlem, including a storefront on 97th Street between Second and Third Avenues where children had painted a picture on the sidewalk depicting an ark with "WELCOME" written on it and a procession of animals extending fifty or sixty yards down the pavement. As we headed south again, Monsignor Fox said, "We're trying to get Summer in the City projects to carry over into winter activities. We've started credit unions and adult education, and we're getting kids to teach Spanish to the policemen in their precincts. Three hundred and seventy-five cops said they wanted to participate, but it's taken a year and a half to get the program through the bureaucracy. A thing like that could make a real dent in the neighborhoods."

Around nine-thirty that evening, Monsignor Fox, Sister Judith, and I drove over to West 54th Street to see how the block party was going. There was a big crowd in the street, under a floodlight, and a lot of people were dancing. Rock 'n' roll music was blasting from a loudspeaker, and people were milling around on the sidewalks or sitting on stoops watching and talking. I saw the artist with Day-Glo toes and asked her how the party was. "It's *O.K.!*" she exclaimed enthusiastically. A small boy approached her, sobbing. "What's the matter, Junio?" she asked, bending down to him. He pulled the front of his shirt from his pants and wiped his eyes on it, shaking. The girl put her arm around him and walked him down toward Tenth Avenue, listening to his trouble.

Monsignor Fox and Sister Judith and I watched the dancers for a while. Near us, a man in dark glasses with a cigarette held in his teeth was Frugging with a child who might have been four. Children on bicycles circled the floodlit area, and people moved through the crowd calling to each other. Monsignor Fox introduced me to a short, stocky man named Antonio Lizaso, the director of the Summer in the City storefront that was responsible for the party. He said that the party was going fine. "It may seem foolish to spend Federal money on a party," he said, "but the last time there was a party on this block was in 1947, and people are speaking to each other who haven't spoken in years." He looked up at the balloons on the fire escapes. "The kids had to ask to go through the apartments to decorate the fire escapes, and sometimes it was Yes, sometimes No. But when one man sees his neighbor's fires escape decorated, then he says, 'Hey, what about mine?' " Lizaso paused. "I'm head of the Music Department at Manhattan College in the winter," he told me. "I'm a Cuban refugee, and I have no family or anything, so it is hard for me to relate to many people in the United States. But I have come to the streets, and—well, just look around here. There's five Negroes, there's two Puerto Ricans, this man here is Irish. What I think is important is that the block has realized it has people in it with different values that we can share—a celebration of life."

"Hey, Tony!" a young man yelled to Lizaso. "Come out here and dance!" Lizaso excused himself and joined the dancers.

I went over and said hello to the man Lizaso had said was Irish. We shook hands, and he told me his name was Barney Sharkey. He said he had let them plug the floodlight into his building. "They're using my juice," he said. "It was my party here twenty years ago," he added. "It was when I came out of the service. What a party! I had thirty-six beers!" He grinned. "The block was Irish, Italian, German, and Yugoslavian then. I've seen all the changes."

"Come on, Barney!" called a man nearby. "Have a beer!" Sharkey walked away, and a few minutes later I saw him talking with Monsignor Fox and Sister Judith.

I walked up the street, away from the bright light. A number of people who are not attending the party were sitting on chairs on the sidewalk looking toward the dancers, and I could see some of them tapping their feet in time to the music.

Mediating Conflicts Among Minority Groups:
A Jewish-Black Confrontation

Group conflicts involve not only antagonism and competition between "minority" groups and "majority" groups, but also sometimes hostile interaction among racial and ethnic minorities. A pluralistic social structure suggests a fluid, dynamic field of group interaction, involving ongoing shifts in relative position, status, resources, prestige, etc. "Outs" battle with "ins" for a better place in the sun. When the "ins" move over and relinquish a piece of the turf, "outs" contend with one another for location and possession. Often internecine warfare among the dispossessed for small gains permits the elite groups to maintain their hegemony.

Ocean Hill-Brownsville exemplified aspects of complications in contemporary Jewish-black relations. Jewish schoolteachers and administrators were in direct conflict with black parents and militants concerning policy and authority in the school system. The Jewish teachers, having recently made it professionally, were not about to give up their hard-earned advances. The black group, straining for self-assertion and utterly disenchanted with the educational experience of its children, was not going to stand for someone else controlling the education of black youngsters. A disruptive clash of significant proportions resulted.

Despite prominent Jewish participation in the civil rights movement in the past and support of liberal programs conducive to black progress, many areas of tension and friction exist between these two groups that have historically shared a common fate of extreme discrimination. There are the exploitative practices of some Jewish merchants and slum landlords in the ghetto. There is the succession-flight relationship of blacks and Jews in urban neighborhoods. There are the anti-Zionist and anti-Semitic utterances of some black nationalists. There is the competition for professional and administrative jobs in the social welfare-education-civil service complex. Complicating it all is the high level of sensitivity of each group to prejudicial attack, particularly by the other group.

A group relations practitioner involved in Jewish-black issues would be well advised to keep in mind that he is not dealing solely with a "human relations" problem, but that there also are real differences in group interests at stake that must be accommodated. On the other hand, emotional reactions on both sides may seriously impede the resolution of the more objective issues.

Several of these matters are reflected in the discussion here which is based on an actual incident but has been disguised for purposes of anonymity.

The Jewish community of Warrenton, a city of about 85,000 in a border state, has become agitated over an unprecedented incident involving a confrontation between Negroes and Jews. An industrial city, it has been characterized by the rapid growth over the past decade of its nonwhite population which now comprises about 30 per cent of the total population. Most of the increase has come from Negroes moving into Warrenton from rural and semirural areas in search of employment in the city's industrial plants. Jews, numbering about 5 per cent of the population, are highly active in civic life and some are very influential. Densely populated, Warrenton has little vacant land; the question of open housing is becoming an increasingly sensitive issue.

For some months Warrenton has been seriously divided over finding a way to implement a court order requiring that an acceptable plan ending *de facto* school segregation be submitted by April 1. Now, with the deadline only one month away, feelings are high over a plan proposed by the Warrenton School Board calling for the experimental pairing of two elementary schools, one predominantly Negro in an adjacent low-income area, the first of what would be a series of such pairings of schools of different racial composition. As presently conceived, the proposed plan would require busing pupils beyond neighborhood boundaries to both schools and the reassignment of members of the two faculties.

Within a few days after the first public announcement of the proposal, a new organization, Parents for Neighborhood Schools, was initiated with the stated purpose of rallying opposition to the plan. Its chairman, Harvey Goldberg, a prominent Jewish merchant, issued the following statement to the *Warrenton Bugle* on behalf of the group:

> As concerned parents, we support the proposition that quality public education should be made available to every child on equal terms. But we seriously question whether quality education can be secured by transporting children far from home into unfamiliar surroundings. The neighborhood school concept has been the backbone of our free educational system. While no one would deny that there is room for improvement in curriculum, in teaching techniques and equipment, we cannot shunt aside what is still the best educational system in the world for the mere sake of achieving racial balance. Negro children no more than white will benefit from such an unreasoned disruption of neighborhood patterns as is being proposed. The result would be, not improved educational achievement at all, but *two* culturally and educationally disadvantaged schools instead of one.

Numerous letters to the *Bugle* and public pronouncements followed the statement of the Parents for Neighborhood Schools, most of them agreeing vigorously with its stand. One spokesman, Mrs. Vera O'Donnell, president of the Warrenton Public Affairs Association, an influential organization of prominent women concerned with the breakdown of law and order in our society, announced that a petition her group was circulating had in just two days obtained over 1,000 signatures of persons opposed to the School Board plan.

Opposition was also angrily expressed, but for different reasons, by the Warren-

Case study prepared for American Jewish Committee, Leadership Training Institute, Waxahachie, Texas, 1969. The names of individuals, organizations and places mentioned in this case study are fictitious, and the circumstances here presented were composed for the purposes of discussion only.

ton Committee for Freedom Now, a chapter of a national Negro civil rights group. Claude Johnson, chairman of Freedom Now's Education Committee, who had previously led a series of disruptive sit-ins at School Board meetings to protest the Board's "white racist policy of savage and systematic destruction of the minds of our black children," denounced the plan as absurdly inadequate and "a typical product of our degenerate and inept School Board."

Alarmed over the unanticipated rise in the community's temperature over the proposal, William Harkins, School Board president, quickly conferred with Board members, the Superintendent of Schools and the Mayor. After a two-hour closed session, Mr. Harkins announced to the press that "in view of the misunderstanding and misrepresentations of our plan to pair the Lakeview and Whittier schools, we have decided to hold a public meeting on the plan next week at which our interested citizens can get a firsthand, objective, dispassionate and factual report on what is really being proposed. Our plan was the result of months of careful study and research. We consulted with some of the foremost educators and social scientists in this part of the country. We are firmly convinced that the plan, while admittedly unable to solve all of our educational deficiencies, offers us a model for meaningful progress toward our goal of quality education for all of Warrenton's children, white and black."

The meeting, held in the auditorium of Northside High School, drew about 200 persons, and the atmosphere was palpably charged with tension. As Mr. Harkins began his presentation, he was interrupted by Mrs. Rose Craig, local president of Freedom Now, who, with Claude Johnson at her side, shouted "We are here to demand our rights!" At this a white man in the second row jumped up and yelled at Mrs. Craig to "sit down or go home." Immediately several other persons began to shout at one another while Mr. Harkins futilely banged his gavel and called for order. Striding to the front of the room, Johnson, obviously enraged, pointed a finger at Harvey Goldberg and screamed "Hitler made one mistake when he didn't kill enough of you Jews."

After a moment of shocked silence, angry outcries began to be directed at Johnson; a young Jewish salesman, recently transferred to Warrenton from his firm's headquarters in Newark, had to be restrained from striking Johnson. Mr. Goldberg and most of the other Jews in the audience walked out as Mr. Harkins tried again to resume the meeting. The *Bugle,* covering the incident on the front page of the morning edition, reported that later in the meeting, which had been adjourned early, Johnson took the floor again to make a "public apology." He explained that he had been "reacting impulsively to the degrading insults being hurled at us by the whites in attendance. It's true that I pointed at the Jew who is head of the reactionary Parents for Neighborhood Schools, but I am against genocide in any form whatsoever." Next to the article appeared a statement issued by the Warrenton Chapter of the American Jewish Association deploring Johnson's "deviation from decency" in the Hitler remark. Conceding the "bitter frustration" of the city's civil rights battle, the statement said that nevertheless "Mr. Johnson's remark must earn him the condemnation of all people of goodwill." Earlier in the day, Mayor John P. Reynolds barred Johnson from City Hall as a rights representative and said, "I will not recognize anyone from Freedom Now as long as Mr. Johnson remains a member." These sentiments were applauded in a strong editorial statement by the *Bugle.*

Called at his New York office for comment, Freedom Now's national director, Wilton Foster, issued a statement to the media announcing that an investigation was under way "to ascertain the context of Mr. Johnson's remark before determining what action to take."

Two days later, these new developments took place: It was announced by Mrs. Craig that Johnson had resigned from his post and his membership in Freedom Now "so as not to impede the progress of organizational goals" and Freedom Now's director disavowed Johnson's remarks. "In our investigation over the last few days," the *Bugle* quoted Wilton Foster as saying, "we have ascertained many facts. . . . The investigation has in no way excused Mr. Johnson's remark, which we unequivocally disavow, but it does serve to help us understand its provocation. Mr. Johnson's comment was intolerable, but the Warrenton School Board's delaying tactics on school integration were also intolerable. . . ."

The evening edition carried two additional items on the continuing controversy, a letter from Mr. Johnson and one from Michael Bernstein, executive director of the National Jewish Council in New York City.

In his letter, Mr. Johnson admitted that he had made "a cruel and excessive remark" but noted that he had already apologized publicly for it. He added, "Why are anti-white remarks so shocking? The white man has abused black people since 1619, but whites don't attack that. . . . Why is the *Bugle* so anxious to defend the Jews, Italians, Irish or anyone else, and why do whites always hide behind such labels as anti-Semitism? . . . At this point I feel that if the Jewish community is so fragile as not to be able to accept this apology, then perhaps it should reflect upon itself. . . ."

Mr. Bernstein's letter, released to the national press, announced his resignation as a member of the National Advisory Board of Freedom Now which includes distinguished leaders of national civil rights and religious bodies. A letterhead group, it had not met in two years. His action, Mr. Bernstein stated, was prompted, not by the "horrifying" remark about Hitler, but by Freedom Now's "tepid and ambiguous response to it. . . . I cannot continue an association with a group whose moral fiber is so flabby. . . ." Called for his reaction, Mr. Foster, Freedom Now's national director, stated that Mr. Bernstein's letter of resignation had not been received. He expressed regret that it "was sent to the press before it was sent to us, and that he saw fit to resign before investigating the facts." He announced that he was calling a meeting of the National Advisory Board of Freedom Now for the following week in response to a telegram received that day from Daniel Frankel, a Jewish labor leader and one of the thirty-eight members of the Advisory Board, which urged an immediate meeting to "eradicate all taint of anti-Semitism within Freedom Now."

That night a special meeting of the Executive Committee of the Warrenton Jewish Welfare Federation was held, called by its president, Jacob Berg. All the officers were present, including Harvey Goldberg, a Federation vice-president.

Mr. Berg explained that he had called the meeting in response to many urgent requests; there was, he thought—on the basis of the tenor of the calls he had received—considerable concern in the Jewish community over this incident and a demand that the Federation "do something about it." *What* to do was the purpose of this session.

He went on:

"I confess to some confusion over what the Federation should do in this very unfortunate situation. We seem to be the only Jewish organization which has remained officially silent—the local chapter of the American Jewish Association issued a statement, the national agencies have seen fit to speak out presumably on our behalf, although their offices are hundreds of miles away from the scene, but we who represent the Jewish community of Warrenton, the targets of Johnson's abominable remark, have said nothing. Should we? Or should we now let the matter rest?"

Mr. Goldberg spoke:

"Jake, since I'm one of the ones who called you right away, I must say now what I said then—that I'm furious that the Federation wasn't the first to respond to this vile attack. Why did the national agencies have to rush in? Who asked them to? This was our responsibility and we flunked it. Of all the people in this city, we have been the most active in trying to help Negroes. I myself was among the first to hire Negro saleswomen in my store. Johnson pointed at me but he was ranting against all Jews. We can't take this piece of anti-Semitic bigotry lying down, just because some self-interested groups muscle in. I have been a contributor in the past to Freedom Now and some of the other Negro organizations. I assure you that I'm going to withhold any further contributions until they clean their houses of such rabble-rousers and I would urge all the rest of you to do likewise. I also urge that the Federation go on record to denounce Johnson and his ilk."

Philip Aaron, the young director of research and development of a large electronics firm and a new Federation officer, said in a quiet tone husky with emotion, "Mr. Goldberg, with all due respect to your feelings—I can certainly understand and share them—I cannot see what further good a resolution or statement from us could do. The man has been dropped from Freedom Now; he even has—in his peculiar fashion—apologized. What would we be accomplishing?

"But there's really another element involved. How free are we ourselves of racism? Look at the membership and leadership of Parents for Neighborhood Schools; we Jews are very prominently represented. Why shouldn't the black community resent our torpedoing the only plan that has been advanced so far to secure at least some integration in our schools? Parents for Neighborhood Schools and Mrs. O'Donnell's little old ladies in tennis shoes make quite a pair."

A chorus of protest followed. "Phil," said Mr. Goldberg evenly, "I'm going to assume that you didn't mean to call me a racist; I don't have to defend my long years of service to this community. The fact is busing is wrong and it hasn't worked. That's what I'm opposed to, not integration. I deeply resent your comment." Other members vigorously supported Goldberg's position. In the din, Mr. Berg recognized David Weiss, a respected attorney:

"Mr. Chairman, aren't we really confusing two issues? We started out be reacting to how Negroes behave toward Jews and we're now talking about how Jews behave toward Negroes. Phil has a point, though perhaps he might have made it differently, but I don't think it's relevant to our purpose this evening. I should like to propose that we focus on what our response should be to the Johnson incident and hold for future discussion larger questions of Jewish-Negro relations."

Mr. Berg replied: "Thanks Dave. All right, ladies and gentlemen. Let's get back to where we were before. What should we do?"

Effects of Educational Programs:
A Catholic "Commitment" Project

Religious groups have a potentially powerful part to play in group relations activities. First of all, they have legitimation—it is basic to their mission as an institution to be concerned about the ethics of group relationships. Second, religious groups may have considerable authority with respect to their members, especially those churches which have a fairly strong hierarchical structure. Additionally, through the clergy the church has available a potential cadre of staff who can be drawn upon if motivated or directed to promote group relations programs. Religious groups also have direct contact with large numbers of individuals who participate as congregants and parishioners in church and synagogue rituals and programs. Furthermore, there exists an administrative and financial structure by means of which appropriate programs may be expedited.

Through its Committee on Human Relations, the Archdiocese of Detroit has conducted a vigorous educational program on racial matters. This program, "Project Commitment," had the objective of communicating to members the dedication of the church, on an official basis, to the ideal of racial justice and equality. In the account of Project Commitment the reader will be able to discern the unique organizational factors and modes of influence that a devoted clerical structure can bring to bear on race. The question of the relevance and effectiveness of an educational vs. a behavioral approach has been discussed elsewhere, particularly in Unit 15, but would be well worth considering again in this instance. The "structure" of Project Commitment is presented here. The reader may want to consider also the "process" by which such an educational program may best be carried out.

Project Commitment is an Archdiocesan Program in Human Relations designed to communicate the teachings of the Church and the needs of society for racial justice to a leadership group in every parish of the Archdiocese in the most practical way, and in a minimum of time. It is educational and motivational.

In 1943, '58 and '63, the Bishops of the United States dedicated their annual Statement to the subject of racial justice. In 1963, the Bishops of Michigan made a

"Project Commitment" Report, Archbishop's Committee on Human Relations, Archdiocese of Detroit, 305 Michigan Avenue, Detroit, Michigan 48226. Used by permission.

ten-point statement on racial justice which was farsighted and far ahead of any-thing yet done. With the passage of months and years, it has become apparent that high-level statements are far from enough; they must also be taught, preached and implemented on the parish level. The vast majority of Catholics still feel no strain on their consciences from the existence of segregation and discrimination in Amer-ican society. Christ's words about our being the "salt of the earth," the "light of the world" and the "leaven of society" are not seen to apply to the area of interracial justice—although in this area perhaps more than any other, light and positive leaven-ing action are needed.

In the Archdiocese of Detroit, Archbishop Dearden established his Committee on Human Relations, in 1960. The Education Department of this committee has developed and presented one of the better educational programs in race relations being done in this country. While these programs have experienced some failures they have in the main been successful, sometimes spectacularly so. In the five years this program has been carried on, fewer than 25 per cent of our 346 parishes have been covered. Something more is needed. Project Commitment is designed as a major tool which will help to meet this need by communicating the theological positions of the Church on race.

A well-formed conscience, however, makes morally right decisions only when based on a well-informed intellect. Project Commitment, therefore, is also designed to remove misconceptions about race, and about human relations in the field of ed-ucation, employment, crime, housing and other areas of the society in which we live.

Project Commitment aims to:

1. Create in each parish a core of committed Catholics, informed and active in human relations, who will work within their own parish and community.

2. Create a group of Catholic leaders who individually and in groups act as a leaven in our business and professional communities.

3. Create a broad sense of community responsibility and solidarity among the people working in human relations in all the parishes in the diocese.

4. To establish greater communications between the separate groups in the Arch-diocese, particularly between white and Negro Catholics.

Archbishop Dearden opened the Pilot Program of Project Commitment on February 2, 1966, in the Wayne Northcentral Deanery. In the ensuing weeks, seven sessions on human relations were presented using a variety of formats each of which was designed to create two-way communication. Some 465 people from the twenty-seven parishes in the deanery regularly attended these programs. The participants were assigned to small discussion groups which not only heard the presentations, but also had group discussions and opportunities for questioning the speakers and making reports.

On the basis of the experiences gained through the Pilot Program, we are now extending Project Commitment to the other deaneries. One of the keys to the success of Project Commitment in the Wayne Northcentral Deanery was the development of a team of highly responsible people, all in a volunteer capacity, who by careful division of labor and constant communication and follow-up, were able to handle the massive detail of this program. In the fourteen remaining deaneries in the Arch-diocese, this same team approach will be used. Since Project Commitment requires two full months for its presentation, the only times of the year which lend themselves to it are the periods from late September to Thanksgiving, and after Christmas to Easter. In the eight counties which compose the Archdiocese there is the heavily urbanized metropolitan area of Detroit, some population centers of considerable size which are apart from the metropolitan area, and some rural areas.

SUBJECT: Status Report—Special Project   DATE: December 10, 1965
           Archbishop's Committee on Human
               Relations
FROM: Joseph L. Hansknecht, Jr.
           Project General Chairman

The initial planning involved in determining goals, techniques, organizational structure, etc., for our Project is almost completed.

We now have facilities arranged (Gesu Parish), and an organizational structure to take care of training a staff of 70 to 80 moderators and recorders. Staff members will be trained by a professional in the field of group dynamics, Cecil Crews, Director of Education, Michigan Credit Union League.

Cooperation from the Chancery and the Deanery has been excellent. All 73 Pastors and Assistant Pastors in the Wayne Northcentral Deanery have received an individually typed and signed letter from the Vice-Chancellor, Monsignor Gumbleton.

We have already held a meeting with lay representatives from the 27 parishes in the Deanery. Their reactions to the Project were excellent. We have also had a personal visit with each pastor to explain the program and the Dean hosted a dinner at which we had the opportunity of giving them additional information and answering their questions.

A professional public relations firm, Stone & Simons, has agreed to handle news releases for the metropolitan and local newspapers and parish bulletins, as well as arranging radio and television news coverages, and news conferences for some of the speakers.

As we see the Project, it is an Archdiocesan-wide major program conducted on a deanery basis. Participants are selected on the basis of their membership within the community power structure. By the use of prestige building activities, we are most hopeful that the participants will, in fact, include most of the Catholics in the Archdiocese who form a part of Detroit's power structure. Invitations to them will go out from the Chancery. Newspaper publicity will emphasize the high caliber of the speakers during the series, and the selectiveness in the granting of invitations to attend. Archbishop Dearden himself will open the series. Speakers will be well-known community leaders who are acknowledged experts in the area of their talk. One national speaker will be invited. The competence of the speakers alone should do much to create a desire on the part of the participants to attend the entire series.

We also are inviting the Jewish and Protestant communities to send observers to the series. Five to ten leaders from three other deaneries will be invited to participate in the entire series so that they can form the core around which their own deanery programs will be developed. Each of these deaneries in turn will follow the same procedure, so that we can have as many as three and four programs occurring simultaneously within a year after the initial Project '66 program is presented.

We will have special committees to take care of facilities, registrations, staff, background materials and displays, speaker coordinations and audiovisuals, and finances.

We anticipate that our cost will be approximately $750 for facilities, printed material, programs, etc.; $200 to $500 for public relations; and $1,000 for misc. Total costs, therefore, will be approximately $2,250. We anticipate raising these funds through the parishes within the deanery, with the ACHR underwriting that part of the cost which is not raised within the deanery.

The goal of the Project is to arouse a sense of personal responsibility and commitment in the field of race relations among the 70 per cent of the participants who are not active in the ranks of civil rights workers, nor in the ranks of the bigots.

To the extent that we are successful, it is most important that the participants have knowledge of ways and means to carry out their desires to fulfill their own personal responsibility. I believe that the Archbishop's Committee has a very important role in developing materials listing and explaining the many ways in which race relations can be improved (e.g., educational series within *each* parish; programs by management or labor organizations for all employees on the meaning and effects of the Civil Rights Act of 1964 and the new Michigan Constitution; integrating Negroes and whites in every activity in which they are engaged, including parish organizations, bowling leagues, professional associations, bridge clubs, etc.). Without such follow-up activities, much of the impact of the Project will be lost within a year. This material should be completed prior to February 1, 1966.

Suggested Staff Recruiting and Training Technique

Recruit qualified personnel. One moderator and recorder per table of six participants plus ten to twenty on reserve staff to fill in for absentees and dropouts.

A. *Sources of potential staff members*
  1. Christian Family Movement
  2. Cursillo
  3. Gabriel Richard Institute
  4. National Council of Catholic Women
  5. Community Councils
  6. Pastor referral.
Obtain at least two names for every staff member needed.

B. *Training Sessions*
Two training sessions for staff members are recommended. This is to ensure a thorough understanding of the goals and mechanics of Project Commitment and the role of the staff in the program. There is also a greater possibility of achieving among the staff an early commitment which hopefully will be transmitted to participants.

Another advantage is that the members of the personnel committee can get to know the staff and use this knowledge in making assignments.

Content
  1. Thoroughly explain the goals and format of the project.
  2. Explain the role of the moderator and recorder. Commitment through discussion is also explained.
  3. Demonstrate techniques. Opportunity should be provided for the staff to

hear speakers and to participate in discussion groups to experience the role of the participants in subsequent sessions, while gaining valuable background in the field of human relations.

4. Sample materials should be available to staff, i.e., program dates, time, and speakers if available; discussion guides; recorder's report form.

5. Emphasize importance of moderator and recorder working as a team to achieve discussion in depth by participants. If possible, they should prepare for each session together.

C. *Staff Discussion Meetings*

It was found helpful to meet with the staff for 10 or 15 minutes immediately following the sessions to discuss mutual problems, to reinforce training or to pass on pertinent information.

A large staff can be broken into smaller groups with two members of the personnel committee meeting with each group. Personnel committee members can compare notes following these short meetings. Recorders' reports are collected at these meetings for evaluation before the next session.

Tentative Program and Outline
1st Series — Archdiocesan Human Relations Program

I. *Morality of the Race Issue*
Archbishop Deardon
Concelebrated Mass—Sermon on morality of the race issue

II. *History of Race Relations*
Outline —Civil Rights efforts of years past
U.S.A. —Dominant role of white society
  —Law enforcement primarily to maintain white supremacy
  —Prejudice in USA—other than anti-Negro
  —Long history of efforts
  —Law over the years
Detroit —Race Riot '42
  —Follow-up actions by community
  —Current organizations and problems

III. *Detroit Today*
Outline —Crime in metro area
U.S.A. —Broad sociological history of industrialization and urbanization of our society
  —Problems with Core Cities, transportation, old schools, too few and too small parks
  —Strong on city development apart from Negro
  —To what extent have we followed the patterns where unique problems called for unique solutions?
Detroit —Negro and white attitudes
  —Reflections on attitudes of Negroes today

IV. *Housing*—Rights and Wrongs
Outline —Answer fears regarding property values, criminal elements, low-

ered school standards, block-busting, pattern of change and effect on Deanery residents
—Big picture in pressure, pre-change deterioration
—Absolute necessity of open housing . . . this Deanery being hurt by discriminatory practices elsewhere
—Poor housing, crowded conditions

V. *Education*
Outline —Broad picture of the educational needs of the twentieth century
—Education in urban society, pluralistic
—School's role in aiding in acculturation of rural peoples to city demands
—Breaking down of barriers of cultural differences. Do parochial schools do this?
—Need to find solution to de facto segregation in schools
Reactors—Why are Negroes mad?
—How Negroes feel about segregated education today
—Needs in Catholic schools
—How both Catholic and public schools are in trouble if all white or all Negro
—Catholic's responsibility for personal involvement in de facto segregation problems of public schools
—When child attends segregated school, parents have added job of equipping child for life in integrated society

VI. *Role of Government*
Outline —Federal laws—in force
—Rights of everyone
—Conflict of rights
—Role of Government
—Limitations of the law . . . what are they?
—Where does law reach a point of diminishing return?

VII. *Neighborhood Self-Help*
Outline —You do have some control over your destiny
—From big metropolitan community to block clubs, community or human relations councils, CORE, NAACP, Urban League, SNICC
—Neighborhood—old concept of the "neighbor" is gone . . . people live for years without knowing the neighbor's name

VIII. *Parish Responsibility*
Outline —How does an institution serve its community?
—Is your Parish organized for bingo or involvement?
—How does the Parish (a group of people) see itself, the community . . . is it a ghetto or a leaven?

Criteria for Participant Selection

Please try to select parishioners who:
—Hold an executive or middle management position in business, finance or government (in factory or office), or
—Hold a policy-making office in a union or professional association, and/or

—Have a record of demonstrated leadership in civic, fraternal or religious organizations.

Suggested Categories

(1) Superintendents, managers, personnel directors of major industrial firms or plants.

(2) Officials of banks, savings and loan, credit union, and other financial institutions.

(3) Local or international officials of labor unions.

(4) Presidents, managers, owners of smaller businesses, offices, firms.

(5) Managers or owners of larger retail stores.

(6) Insurance, real estate, and other professional group leaders.

(7) Editors, columnists, reporters of newspapers, radio, TV, etc.

(8) Officials of voluntary organizations (such as Rotary, Kiwanis, Cotillion Club, American Legion, owners and Community Councils, etc.)

(9) Officials of organizations such as K of C, DCCM, DCCW, CFM, Guild, PTA, Scouts, Cursillo, etc.

List of fifteen (15) participants selected from the parish should be *returned before January 14, 1966.*

Sample Letter Inviting Clergy Participation

ARCHDIOCESE OF DETROIT
1234 Washington Boulevard
Detroit, Michigan 48226

OFFICE OF THE CHANCELLOR

September 29, 1965

Reverend Nicholas Rieman
Gesu Parish
17204 Oak Drive
Detroit, Michigan 48221

Dear Father Rieman:

One of the major objectives of the Archbishop's Committee on Human Relations Education Department has been to provide our people with background information which will enable them to make enlightened moral judgments on racial matters. In establishing the Committee, you will recall, it was the wish of the Archbishop that there be a core of informed people in each parish.

In order to achieve this objective with greater dispatch, a deanery-wide program has been developed with the approval of Archbishop Dearden. The first such program will be conducted for the Wayne Northcentral Deanery with the full cooperation of Msgr. Fedewa. The program will be presented in February and March, 1966, for 10-15 people from each parish, along with representatives of lay organizations and the colleges.

We are sending this letter to pastors, assistant pastors and to the officers of the deanery lay organizations.

In order that your people may share in the planning and presentation of the program, two of your parishioners are invited to serve on the steering committee. Each pastor is asked to select two people to represent his parish and send their names to Mr. Joseph Hansknecht, Jr., 18255 Fairfield, Detroit, Michigan 48221.

A preliminary brochure on the program is enclosed for your information.

Sincerely yours in Christ,

Vice-Chancellor

Sample Letter Inviting Lay Participation

CHURCH OF THE PRECIOUS BLOOD
13305 Grove Avenue
Detroit 35, Michigan

RT. REV. MSGR. WM. L. HERMES

January 21, 1966

Mr. Dennis Dundon
16614 Washburn
Detroit, Michigan 48221

Dear Dennis:

The diocesan as well as the daily papers carry many articles on the topic of "Human Relations," particularly concerning the Negro-white relationship in our city.

The "Archbishop's Committee on Human Relations" has arranged an excellent and informative as well as unique program on this topic. This program, known as "Project Commitment," is for hand-picked representatives from the parishes of Northwest Detroit.

I have personally selected you from Precious Blood Parish. You will soon receive detailed information and an invitation to participate in this important project. I am certain you will give "Project Commitment" serious consideration. I hope you will be able to make arrangements to attend the sessions.

I would not ask you to give of your time and ability if I did not feel that this program will be enlightening for yourself as well as of great value to the Church and the community.

Sincerely in Christ,

(Rt. Rev. Msgr.) William L. Hermes
Pastor

PART IV

GROUP WELFARE

Providing Services for Disadvantaged Racial and Ethnic Groups

Changing the Minority Individual vs. Changing Society: Gang Workers Link Youths to Community Resources

The major problem faced by minority groups is their disadvantagedness—the lack of sufficient resources allocated by society for their use and development. Double jeopardy enters into that; because of lack of information or social isolation, disadvantaged groups fail to maximize utilization of the resources which are, in fact, made available to them. Providing direct personal services entails two dilemmas. Somehow there is the implication conveyed that the individual himself is at fault in the situation, thus the service is aimed at the racial or ethnic group member himself rather than at society or its institutions, which essentially produce these problems for individuals. Second, allocating resources toward service for persons may divert money or manpower from the broader task of institutional change, thus delaying or reducing the impact of social reform efforts. As an aspect of this second point, as the individual finds his personal discomfort or difficulty accommodated he may be less likely to ally himself with change activities which seek preventive outcomes. In the two narratives that follow, gang workers attempt to link up young blacks with community resources and to prepare them for employment.

GROUP: Unorganized teens
WORKER: James Johnson
SUBJECT: Launching a new program: a new worker, who is new to the community, interprets a new agency and a new service to the agencies, the adults, and the teen-agers. At the same time he begins his working relationship with groups.

Background: This is an independent street work agency that is part of a research program. It is housed at Durham Boys Club where the Project has rented office. The

"Unorganized Teens Group," in *Neighborhood Gangs: A Case Book for Youth Workers.* National Federation of Settlements and Neighborhood Centers, New York, 1967, pp. 5-7. Used by permission.

Project is designed to work with delinquent groups of teen-agers in an old, run-down, all-Negro neighborhood of a northern industrial city. One of the criteria for selection of groups to work with is that the boys are not active members of existing agencies.

Mr. James Johnson is a trained and experienced worker but is new to this community. He will direct the Project and is now making contacts with the community and particularly with teen-agers who may join the Project.

Worker's Report

Lining up the Community Resources

Sept. 25. I had met with Mr. Waddell, director of Durham Boys' Club, last week to arrange for offices and for other procedural matters. I had suggested that since his staff must be very curious as to the relationship of his agency to the Project, it might be wise for me to appear at a staff meeting soon. He agreed, and a special meeting was set up for today.

Fortunately, I had met most of the staff earlier so that they knew who I was. After I had described the program, they started to ask questions indicating that they were very apprehensive.

I went over with them that we would be working with youngsters who were not members of their program. I also emphasized that they would be coming to the offices as individuals. When we had the need for using agency facilities, we would make special arrangements for this with the specific worker in charge, and if a group wanted to use this particular agency on a regular basis, it would have to be on a membership basis. This would also apply to individuals who might want to join. I made it clear that when one of our boys wanted to join their agency, we would provide the money for it, but the agency had the right to turn down the youngster if they didn't think he fitted in or didn't meet their membership requirements.

They were also very apprehensive about controls. And although our offices were on one wing of the building, they raised the logical question of who could keep these boys in control in their goings to and from our offices. I really didn't know the answer, and we put this down as something we would watch very carefully and see what had to be done.

Sept. 26. I met with Mr. Woodruff, Chief Probation Officer of the Juvenile Court, and described our Project. I emphasized that we were interested in direct referrals of boys and groups of boys who lived in the "Valley" that he thought might meet our interests and could benefit from our services.

He introduced me to his other staff members and explained the Project to them. Mr. Smith, one of the probation officers, suggested that I come back that afternoon as he had a 3 o'clock appointment with Richard Arthur who might be of concern to the Project. I expressed interest in seeing Richard Arthur alone since he no doubt would have lots of questions about anyone suggested by a probation officer. My appointment with him was scheduled for 3:30 P.M. later that day.

The next morning I talked with Mr. Robert McHenry, in charge of the special teen programs in the public schools. Several helpful things came out of our discussion, and I anticipate seeing a lot of him in the future.

A couple of days later I attended a staff meeting at the Bell Community Center to meet the staff and to pass out a statement regarding the purpose of the Project. I am scheduled to talk with them at length soon.

Making First Contacts with the Kids

At 3:30 on Sept. 26 I met with Richard Arthur, age sixteen, described the Project to him, and indicated our interest in him. I made it clear that we had no connection with any existing agency or with the police. We were interested in working with people like him to help them find things to do with other kids that kept them out of jail, that were O.K. to do—such as basketball, swimming, trips; that we were also interested in helping them figure out what they wanted to do, what they wanted to be, and helping them to do it.

Richard still seemed suspicious, and I went over again that our job was to be of help to them and that although we were meeting in the probation office, whether he wanted to work with me or not made absolutely no difference to the Probation Department. We would see that the fellows got a fair shake with the police or with the school, but we were not police nor were we anti-police.

Richard seemed to be interested, and I suggested that he meet me at my office. I gave him my card, and he agreed to come down the following day. He said he didn't have carfare, so I told him I'd drop around and pick him up about 1 o'clock.

As I finished talking to Richard, Mr. Smith introduced me to James Mason.

Sept. 27. About 1 P.M. I went to Richard Arthur's house. Richard was not at home, and I talked with his mother through the window. She said that she didn't know where he was but suggested that I come back in about half an hour. I told her that I had met Richard the day before and had been introduced to him by Mr. Smith.

When I returned to his house about 1:30 P.M., Richard said that he had just called me at the office. He also said that he saw me when I left his house and had been waiting for me ever since. Richard and I then drove to the office and talked there about the possibilities of his becoming involved in the Project and some of the things which might stem from his involvement . . . the use of the YMCA's pool . . . Durham gym . . . also the possibility of going to camp . . . and helping boys to find jobs.

So we left the office and drove down Main Street. We saw Joe, a friend of Richard's, and stopped to pick him up. He said that he had worked the night before and was also going to work that day, and asked Richard whether he wanted a job. Richard hesitated and asked, "What kind of job?" Joe explained that he unloaded trucks for a produce company. He was paid ten dollars per truck. Joe said that he was sixteen years old and out of school. He has also had contact with the Juvenile Court. I later learned that Joe is theoretically attending school, when he feels like it.

I explained the Project to Joe and promised to get some written material about it for their friends. I mentioned that Mr. Blackstone would join the staff later on. Both boys knew him and seemed to like him. They also knew several probation officers at the Juvenile Court. They indicated that they "hung around" at Richard's house or on the streets until 2 or 3 A.M. . . . both boys like basketball very much. Before leaving I suggested that we might be able to get together with some of their friends in order to talk about the Project. Both said they would talk to other boys, and we agreed to make contact early next week. Richard didn't have a phone but could be reached at an upstairs neighbor's phone.

Next I went to James Mason's house. When I drove down the street, James called me from his window. As I went into the house, his mother, who was talking with someone across the street, looked curiously at me, wondering what we were talking about. When she came into the house, I explained the Project and our interest in working with youth. She seemed pleased that someone was interested in working with James and trying to help him get a job or learn to do something well. I gave her one of my cards and invited her to visit the office or call me at any time. I also told her that I was in the process of writing a brief description of the Project and would give her a copy when it was done. (I intend to write up a description of the Project, playing down "work with delinquents.")

James and I agreed to meet the following day at noon at the Ephriam basketball court. He promised to talk with his friends before then about getting together and discussing the possibilities of the Project. In spite of the fact that Richard and James live nearby, I talked with each boy separately because I believe that their personalities are different.

Sept. 28. I went to the outdoor basketball court on Ephriam, to keep the appointment with James. He was not there. I decided to go by his house. I blew my horn and motioned for him to come outside. After a short time he came outside, and his mother came to the window. She kept her head out of the window while I talked with him. I asked if he had told anyone about our conversation yesterday. He had talked with several boys, but none of them wanted to be a part of Durham because Durham did not buy uniforms. Most of the boys were in school. After he mentioned the names of three boys who were not in school, I suggested that we get together with them to talk about the Project. I wanted them to understand what was involved and the kinds of things that we could do together. We finally agreed that Tuesday, about 1:15 P.M., would be a good time for the other three and us to get together. I could meet them any place he thought would be good, or they could come to Durham and "chew the fat." I said that I would have something written about the program by Tuesday. I left after saying "so long" to Mrs. Mason.

Driving away, I saw Richard Arthur with three other boys so I stopped the car. Richard immediately got into the car with me, saying that he had been working.

I inquired whether he had talked with any of the boys about the Project and whether a time was set for me to meet other boys. Richard said he had talked with several and pointed toward the boys standing on the corner. I said that I would like to meet them, and Richard started to call the boys over. But I suggested that we go across the street to meet them. We did, and I was introduced as "that man I told you about." The boys' names were Jim, Mike and Bradley. I explained the Project to them. Richard was enjoying his knowledge of me and the Project and took over answering questions.

They agreed to meet with me as soon as they could get some other friends together—like 4:30 tomorrow.

Setting the Ground Rules

Sept. 29. About 4 o'clock Richard called to tell me that the boys had been waiting on the "corner" for fifteen minutes. I thought that we were to meet at 4:30; however, I said that I would be right down.

When I arrived, six boys ran toward my car to get a seat by the window. All three boys I had met earlier with Richard were there plus Bennie and Ronald. We drove to my office at Durham.

Apologizing for possible repetition, I discussed the Project and suggested they ask questions about their concerns. I mentioned I had written down some possible interests and proceeded to talk about sports, weekend and overnight camping, job counseling, job training, organizing small groups, etc. There were various responses of likes and dislikes from several boys.

Ronald, who was reading a comic book, had been relatively quiet. I attempted to involve him in the discussion by asking what he wanted to do "other than get a job," since he had stated this over and over again. When he repeated that he wanted a job, I said, "Well, recognizing that you don't have a job and that you have lots of time to do many things or to do nothing during the day, what kind of things would you like to do?" Ronald said he might like to play basketball. I suggested we could get a gym period any time they wanted one. This kind of conversation went on for some time, with an agreement that we would meet here at Durham on Wednesday at noon and go to the gym. I then told the boys that under ordinary circumstances I would not pick them up every time they came to Durham, but since this was our first trip and I was really anxious to help them get organized, I would pick them up on Richard's street at noon on Wednesday. I also told them "there might be some other guys with whom I have contact at the gym on Wednesday."

Oct. 2. I talked with the principal and a home and school visitor at Logan School. We concerned ourselves with the Project and ways in which we might work together to help youth of the community. I was introduced to several boys at the school and talked with three of them briefly, setting up appointments with them for next week. I could have met more boys but declined, indicating that I wanted to see what could be developed among the boys to whom I had been introduced.

Went to James' street looking for the boys who hang out in that area; found no one I knew.

Spent most of the evening around the Atlantic Service Station talking with Kenny and Earl. Also talked with several other boys who stopped by the station. Invited them to the gym on Wednesday afternoon. Kenny said he knew a couple of boys he wanted to bring. Left the station about 10:30.

Spent about an hour in the pool parlor of Herron. The "rack man" asked my name and where I worked. Told two boys about the gym period Wednesday at noon. Left there around midnight.

GROUP: The Oblongs
WORKER: Roger White
SUBJECT: The worker helps the boys prepare to apply for jobs.

Background: The Oblongs are an in-building group of twelve boys, seventeen to nineteen years of age. They were first contacted by the agency three years ago as part of a street gang. They come mainly from working-class homes but there are some members in fatherless homes where the family is on ADC. Many members have served time for strong-arm robbery, purse snatching and fighting. Within the past year, however, no member has been in court. There is an obvious effort by members of the group to change. One expression of this has been its basketball team. At this time three of the members are still in high school, while two others have graduated; the rest dropped out before completing.

This is primarily a working-class Negro neighborhood. A heavy proportion of the children were born in the South, as were practically all of the parents. However, most of these boys, and most of their neighbors, have lived in the neighborhood for more than three years. The main street of the Negro community, solidly lined with taverns, liquor stores, resale shops, and pawnshops, is only four blocks away.

"The Oblongs," in *Neighborhood Gangs: A Case Book for Youth Workers.* National Federation of Settlements and Neighborhood Centers, New York, 1967, pp. 36-37. Used by permission.

The agency is a settlement house serving an exclusively Negro clientele. It has utilized street workers for the past five years.

Roger White, twenty-eight years old, Negro, is a college graduate with a major in physical education. He was a member of his college basketball team. Mr. White is a very sensitive man who worked as a street worker for two years; he is now assigned to in-building groups who have histories of antisocial acts.

Worker's Report

It was about fifteen minutes before the Oblongs' meeting was to start when Kennedy Blake came into the agency. Kennedy had told me he was going for a job at the Chevy Plant, where his dad worked, and that it had all been "fixed." I asked Kennedy if he had gotten the job, and he responded in his usual joking manner, "Yea, I went up there, man, and walked into that office, and looked at that white stud behind the desk. He looked at me, gave me a piece of paper and he said, 'Fill this out.' I didn't like the way he talked so I grabbed the paper, said I won't do it, and left."

In Kennedy's way of talking, this meant he had walked in, gotten scared, and walked out, so I tried to get him to tell me realistically what happened. He finally let me know that he had gone into the employment office, had been given a form he didn't know how to fill out, and had just left. I didn't know whether it was that he didn't understand the questions or whether he was just too scared, because Kennedy is not a stupid person. So I got out some application forms that the agency uses and began going over them with him.

As Kennedy and I were working on this, more of the Oblongs came into the agency. As it was time for the group meeting to start, I told Kennedy that we would come back to it, and left the office.

Governor Barnes asked me what Kennedy and I had been working on and I told him. Governor Barnes and the others started to ridicule Kennedy, saying that he was too rough and ragged for anybody to hire even if he had enough sense to write his name, let alone fill out a form. Ronnel Smith particularly picked on his "process." While we were talking the rest of the Oblongs came in so we went to the meeting room and continued our conversation.

I noticed that the boys were kidding Kennedy quite heavily and wondered out loud if this wasn't a problem they all had, meaning being scared of going into personnel offices because they didn't know how to act and they were scared of the strange forms. I turned to Tommy, who had recently been job hunting, and asked him what his experience was. Tommy said that he had done real well. He had gone into the office at Shay's Department Store, filled out his form, walked up to the desk, given the form to the man, and the man thanked him and told him they would call him later. Tommy had said this with a feeling of accomplishment and was greeted with a roar of alughter from the kids. And someone said, "Yea, he'll call you later!"

With this start we began talking about the problem of job hunting. I got the forms from the office, had the boys fill them out, and they began freely asking questions about what the terms meant, whether you write over or under the word, who do you use as references, etc.

After we got through with the form I brought them back to attitude and appearance when you go looking for a job, and Jim this time brought up Kennedy's "process." I had to protect Kennedy by saying people have a right to experiment with different hair styles. I suspect what they were saying is he was aping the white man by having his hair smoothed out.

I then went back to how did this affect the job hunt, and the boys pitched in with the effect of appearance and dress, where they again picked up on Kennedy's "gouster"-like dress—belted black raincoat with big metal snaps on it, fedora hat, narrow trousers, pleats, etc. All the members joined in on saying that it was important to dress neatly and not to look like a hoodlum if you expected someone to consider you for a job.

As we talked about approach and mannerisms and fears, the boys started acting out a job interview, with first one and then the other taking the role of the employment manager and criticizing the role of the job applicant that each one took in turn—sometimes not in turn.

I was impressed with the amount of knowledge that they had to share regarding job interviews, and really flabbergasted at the amount of difficulty they had in facing a written form although all but Ronnel Smith, with help, could fill them out.

UNIT 21.

Value of Compensatory Educational Programs:
A Visit to P.S. 165

Material on the "disadvantaged child" has greatly increased in the professional and popular literature on education in the last few years. Special techniques and services, including compensatory programs of all sorts, have been advocated to meet his needs. The Head Start program of OEO was oriented in that direction and was perhaps the most widely approved activity entered into by this often controversial agency. At the same time, little hard evidence points to success from these efforts and a variety of complex problems are associated with their implementation.

At the crux of the educational process is the classroom teacher. Can enough dedicated, sensitive, creative teachers with appropriate skills and attitudes be found to meet the challenges presented by inner-city schools? Can such skills and attitudes be acquired through training? How can individuals with the basic personal prerequisites be recruited into the teaching profession? Can white teachers reach or communicate effectively with racial and ethnic populations in the current period? If not, how is it possible to cope with the situation in the light of a shortage of qualified teachers from racial and ethnic communities? Is the extensive use of indigenous paraprofessionals a viable answer to this problem?

Besides personnel matters, other technical factors must be considered. What special materials and curriculum requirements are necessary to meet educational needs and support cultural forms of such populations? How may such materials be produced? How does one deal with student apathy and resistance to educational routines? Can the family be usefully enlisted to reinforce the educational values and goals of the school? May certain structural or institutional changes in the school system facilitate urban education? In what way would these changes facilitate educational goals?

Come along on a visit to P.S. 165 in Manhattan to see how one school is grappling with these issues.

216

P.S. 165 is a New York City elementary school with classes ranging from kindergarten to the sixth grade. A five-story, gray stone building surmounted by a stubby Gothic tower in the late Victorian mode, it stands in the middle of the block between Broadway and Amsterdam Avenues on Manhattan's upper West Side. Short wings enclose and protect a small playground. Built in 1898, its exterior is grimly institutional—though no more so than the sterile facades of its more modern sisters. The building's first four floors were renovated in 1952 and shortly thereafter twelve additional classrooms were carved out of the fifth floor to accommodate P.S. 165's share of the population explosion.

The interior of the school is also uninspiring at first glance. The narrow corridors are dim and deeply scarred and exude the unmistakable odor of that disinfectant that seems to be used in American public schools and nowhere else. Nevertheless, the halls are clean and brightened at the major intersections by student bulletin boards which display drawings, accompanied by laboriously lettered captions, of eminent figures—both contemporary (L. Gordon Cooper) and historical (Amelia Earhart). The classrooms to which these corridors lead are well-lighted and determinedly cheerful, despite the Board of Education's inordinate fondness for a particularly nasty shade of green paint. One gets the impression of an old building, but a building that is constantly being fussed over.

Besides being a "K-6" (kindergarten to the sixth grade), P.S. 165 is also a "special service" school, which means that it is called upon to perform a whole range of functions over and above those assigned to public elementary schools in other neighborhoods. P.S. 165's district covers an area that runs north and south from 106th to 116th Street and east and west from the Hudson River to Central Park. Almost all of the white middle-class children who are to be found here are drawn from the district's outer boundaries—from the roomy old apartment buildings of Riverside Drive and Central Park West and from the Columbia University area to the north. These children account for somewhat less than a quarter of P.S. 165's population of 1,600 to 1,700; a similar percentage is Negro, and there are about one hundred Oriental children. One-half of the school population is Puerto Rican.

Most of the services are related to the teaching of language. The bulk of the Puerto Rican children come from homes where no English is spoken and a sizable number have spent a considerable portion of their young lives shuttling back and forth between Puerto Rico and the mainland, picking up a smattering of both English and Spanish. To cope with this problem, the faculty of P.S. 165 includes a "corrective reading" teacher, a "reading improvement" teacher, a "coordinator of programs for non-English-speaking children," and an auxiliary teacher "for social guidance" to Spanish-speaking children and their parents—all of whom try to carry out the basic policy of the school system, which is to integrate the Spanish-speaking pupils into the rest of the student body as quickly as possible. There is an orientation class lasting from one to ten weeks for new students who are transferred out as quickly as individual reading skill permits. Still another class is taught entirely in Spanish, for children who are poor readers of their native tongue, the theory being that reading deficiencies are usually psychological in origin, and that the children will therefore be better able to cope with English when they can read Spanish more easily. But most of the Puerto Rican "language learners" are scattered through the school's regular classes, where they receive individual help.

"P.S. 165," by Richard Schickel. *Commentary* Magazine, Vol. 37, no. 1 (January, 1964), pp. 43-51. Reprinted from *Commentary* by permission. Copyright © 1964 by the American Jewish Committee.

In addition to these services, P.S. 165 has specialized classes for other kinds of children. There are two classes for intellectually gifted students, two "health" classes for those with physical problems, and several "opportunity" classes for slow learners. The term "opportunity" is not altogether a euphemism, for the more relaxed and patient atmosphere of these classes does enable at least a small number of the children to develop sufficiently to return—after a semester or two—to regular classes. Finally, the school acquired last year its first full-time guidance counselor, who deals with all manner of emotional disturbances. While the counselor has still not fully appraised the situation, she believes—and most teachers at the school agree—that in recent years there has been a definite rise in the number of children with emotional problems. She also cites Federal statistics indicating that one out of twelve children in the U.S. is measurably disturbed. Applied to P.S. 165, this percentage would mean that theoretically something like one hundred and fifty children attending the school (and, almost inevitably, their parents) are in need of her help.

This list of "special services" does not convey the special spirit of P.S. 165, whose staff is forever called upon to deal with matters that no one ever wrote about in education textbooks. It is a common practice for individual teachers to dig into their own pockets to provide treats for the children. The guidance teacher collects outgrown clothing still in good condition and distributes it to kids who feel put down by their own shabby clothes. Last year a number of teachers, tracing a certain midmorning restlessness among their pupils to the fact that they had had nothing to eat before coming to school, organized a daily "breakfast club." Another of the teachers, aware that fresh meat and vegetables are scarce, expensive, and low-grade in Puerto Rico and that this has encouraged a dependence on canned goods, has introduced a midafternoon snack of vegetables and fruit, word of which she hopes the children will carry home.

It is clear that P.S. 165's pragmatic approach to the special problems it faces, and its atmosphere of bustling concern for children as individuals, originate with its principal, Dr. Edward Gottlieb, a short, broad-faced man of undaunted energy and curiosity. Unlike the chill, orderly office that one associates with school principals, Gottlieb's is cluttered with books, pamphlets, reports, and the paper detritus of a creative man involved, whether he likes it or not, in a bureaucracy. During our interview I learned that along with running this large and complicated school, he was also taking a course in the new mathematics at Columbia, serving on a committee attempting to establish a Summerhill School in New York City, drafting reports for various educational study groups, and serving as unofficial adviser to a number of conscientious objectors. Last fall his picture appeared in *Life,* manning a sound truck at a rally of the teachers' union, which at the time was contemplating a school strike.

Gottlieb has, to be sure, a tendency to discourse in a somewhat eccentric fashion on educational philosophy ("I think it was Shaw who said that schools and prisons were invented by society at the same time—they'll probably disappear at the same time too," or, "Kids have a problem—they want to be nice and happy and we lock them up in a school all day"). But any doubts his theories might raise about Gottlieb's competence as an administrator of a real school with real problems are quickly dispelled when one accompanies him on his moring rounds. Stopping to chat with an assistant about teacher assignments for the next semester, he evidences a gift for quick, shrewd, human judgments of the talents and weaknesses of his faculty. Encountering a second-grader who has been banished to the corridor for disci-

plinary action ("What happened to you?" "I laughed too funny"), Gottlieb sup-
presses a grin, hands out a quick man-to-man lecture devoid of the usual moral
uplift, and moves along. Passing through the gym on the fifth floor, he pauses to
chin himself a few times, much to the amusement of teachers and children alike.

The last stop is a large room equipped with a conference table, where Gottlieb
joins an assistant principal and the guidance counselor to administer tests in reading ability to half a dozen sixth-graders who failed on a previous try. It is a crucial
business, for placement of pupils in slow, average, or bright sections in the New York
City schools—as in those of many other cities—is based exclusively on reading
ability, and so too is promotion of sixth-graders to junior high. Having failed the
first test the children are aware that this is their last chance. "You try to disguise
how important this is," Gottlieb says, "but the kids can't help but know."

One by one they come up to the table, and are given a multiple-choice vocabulary
test. Following that, Gottlieb distributes seventh-grade-level readers and asks each
pupil to read a paragraph aloud. "You've got to be cool when you take the test,"
he advises Angel, a Puerto Rican boy who hadn't done well on the vocabulary test.
To another, struggling through a description of a basketball game, he finally says:
"Would you cheer if you saw that play?" "I don't know," the boy answers
sadly. No one at the table betrays any emotion, but everyone present is obviously
trying to will the kids to pass. A girl, reading a story about a cat, reads "pounce"
as "bounce" and all the adults chime in with an explanation of the difference. "These
kids nearly always score higher on general comprehension than vocabulary," Gottlieb explains after she has returned to her seat. "They've got nobody at home to
ask what a word means." Reading problems frequently have nothing to do with I.
Q. One boy, obviously overfed and overprotected, tells the teachers that he wants
to be a doctor, but Gottleib has no doubt that the ambition stems from his mother
and that undue pressure at home is what causes the boy to do poorly in reading.
Another boy rejects Gottlieb's suggestion that he take more books out of the library.
"I have my own books at home," he lies proudly.

In the end, five of the six children are passed. As Gottlieb put it, "These kids
are defeated too much of the time. Give one of them a defeat like not letting him
go to junior high and you literally mar him for the rest of his life."

The two great themes in the very mixed world of P.S. 165 are brotherhood and
community. They are punched home at every conceivable opportunity, and are
staple features of Gottlieb's twice-a-week talk which is piped into every classroom
over the P.A. system. One that I heard began with speculations on the reasons for
the defeat of the teachers' team in a recent field-day tug-of-war against a tem made
up of sixth-graders ("Maybe we lost to the sixth-grade boys and girls because they
were a team and worked together while the teachers each pulled separately"), and
concluded, after some routine announcements, with an excerpt from that morning's
Herald Tribune—a statement by Dean Rusk. Emphasizing that Rusk "has the third
highest position in the United States and represents us in talks and dealings with
other countries," Gottlieb informed his school that Rusk "solemnly warned congressional leaders that racial strife was gravely crippling the United States in its
dealings with other countries. Our voice is crippled and we are running this race
with one leg in a cast."

Following this talk, I attended a play put on by third-graders in the school auditorium. It was about a Princess "who has no feeling," and is spirited away by a
group of elves to the kingdom of "Musicland," where she is sung back to health:
"There's feelings, yet there's feelings in that land called Musicland . . . work to-

gether, for each other, onward we go." At the climax of the play, thanks to her exposure to Musicland's citizens and their indestructible good will, the Princess learns to have emotions. "Oh, I feel like shouting in my heart, I have so many feelings in my heart," she trills, while her elfin friends, in costumes made mostly out of old bedsheets, cavort around her.

The message of the play as well as the other messages about brotherhood and teamwork which bombard the pubpils of P.S. 165, are not so different from the rhetoric to which millions of other American kids are subjected daily. The difference is that interracial harmony is a live issue at P.S. 165. The teachers are not aimlessly reiterating our conventional social wisdom; there is an intensity in their voices and manners that stems from the reality of the immediate situation. And this is communicated to the kids.

The pedagogical emphasis at P.S. 165, as in most grade schools, is on reading and writing. In an interview with Mrs. Joan Abrams, assistant principal in charge of the reading curriculum, I learned that there is a wide range of teaching choices within the curriculum outlined by the Board of Education. At the present time, she says, the general trend in elementary school education seems to be away from strict reliance on the traditional "basal reader," and toward more individualized books, in the hope that this emphasis will lead to more reading outside the classroom. There is, however, a good deal of controversy on this matter in educational circles. Mrs. Abrams has come to believe that the slower students need the structure which the basal reader provides. On the other hand, she recognizes that the bright children and even a sizable percentage of the average students can hardly wait to pass on to more stimulating books, and she is currently experimenting with a program that takes the second-graders off the basal reader entirely.

All of which comes to seem typical of the pragmatic, flexible approach of P.S. 165 and of its grounding in the one educational tenet that Gottlieb repeatedly affirms—the importance, especially in a school of this kind, of enhancing the "self-image" of the child. Similarly, Mrs. Abrams has chosen to teach reading on an individualized basis and to be eclectic in her methods, believing as she does that reading is "the key to everything" and, further, that no one really knows exactly what will best awaken the desire and ability to read in a child. Thus, P.S. 165 does not take a dogmatic position on the current controversy between the "look-say" method of teaching reading and the phonetic or "sound-it-out" style which is advocated by the radical revisionists. Some children, she explains patiently, are more visual in the way they learn, while others tend to hear a word better than they see it, and in practice most teachers at the school usually combine the two methods.

Once in a classroom, however, these problems become concrete and one soon realizes that the flexible and individual orientation toward learning is nothing to take for granted in a public school. In a typical first-grade class, the kids were struggling through a basal reader recounting the adventures of Benjamin B., Mary, a baby named Susan Jane, and a kitten named Smarty Cat. No one called upon during this period was really a poor reader and many were quite proficient. The teacher was doing a perfectly sound job of relating the use of words in the stroy to the ways in which the children will use them in writing or talking; moreover, she was scrupulous in taking time out to discuss such pitifully few overtones of meaning as the story contained ("How old is the baby?" . . . "What color is his hair?" . . . "What's the baby doing to poor Smarty Cat?"). Yet the whole enterprise was, somehow, a disaster. The teacher's pleasant face was firmly set, as though she were determined not to let the kids have any unprogrammed fun or to allow them, even for a moment, to drag her in undignified fashion down to their level. The result was that rebellion seethed relentlessly in the class, and almost half her time was spent on the wrong side of the barricades: "I think we're just going to have to march Table One right out of here." . . . "Rodney, I hear you without even turning around." . . . "Now everyone in Group One is sitting up *verry* tall." . . . "Is your reader open, Willy? Your mouth *is* open." In short, the traditional dispiriting litany.

It would be impossible to determine to what degree the pain present in this room was caused by a querulous teacher, how much by the methods and materials she was using, and how much by the fact that the pupils were afflicted by the minute attention spans of the very young. Still, that the absence of imaginative teaching did account for some of the problems in the first-grade room is suggested by the contrasting atmosphere in two of the "special" calsses—"the opportunity class" for slow students, the IGC [Intellectually Gifted Children] class for bright ones. Both offer challenges (of vastly different kinds) to their teachers, and both seem to have attracted exceptionally competent teachers who work at the top of their bent.

The "op class" inhabits the most battered room in the school. Even the students' art work seems more somber in tone than displayed in the other classrooms. And though the orderly rows of desks, standard in the classrooms of our childhood, have been abandoned throughout P.S. 165 in favor of furniture that can be easily rearranged, no classroom presents quite the shambles at the end of the day that is found in Room 503. As long as the rearrangement is not overly noisy, the teacher, Donald Jackson, will probably not say anything, not even when a student undertakes to drag a chair or desk to the opposite corner of the room in the middle of the lesson. A slender, quite-spoken Negro who in his spare time has an interest in a Greenwich Village art gallery, Jackson presides over a class of about a dozen eleven-, twelve-, and thirteen-year-old children working at the fourth-grade level. Their manner ranges from the elaborately bored to the excruciatingly restless. They have all been over and over it, but they still have not learned to master the intricacies of subjects like long division.

Throughout P.S. 165 a teacher who has asked a question can count on a number of eagerly waving hands, or on triumphant cries mixed with dubious, but at least interested, murmurs. Jackson, however, can't count on anything. His questions may elicit startling irrelevancies, sullen silences, elaborate hoaxes, or overt hostility. Yet Jackson altogether avoids the disciplinary approach of the first-grade classroom. He chooses to keep the noise down to a dull roar, and to single out each child in his turn for intensive work. If a few of the others, for want of something better to do, also attend, well and good; if not, their turn, as they well know, will come. Once it arrives, Jackson is implacable. He does not lose his temper, but he will not be distracted from his pursuit of the answer, and he seems never to give up. The only way off the hook is to think and think until you give the right answer.

A typical encounter during arithmetic period: Ruby, a large, dull-eyed Negro girl wearing an enormous bow in her hair, is called to the blackboard and faced with the problem of dividing 124 by 9. She stares lengthily at the offending digits. "What's the first step, Ruby?" Jackson asks. "Estimate?" she asks doubtfully. "Right. How many 9's do you think there are in 124?" A long silence ensues before she dubiously guesses: "Fifteen?"

"Try it," says Jackson. Another period of agony. It develops that Ruby has forgotten how to check her estimate. Jackson relents to the point of advising her to multiply.

"What's multiplying, Mr. Jackson?"

It is a concept to which she has undoubtedly been exposed for at least three years. She knows it if she knows anything, but Jackson's expression does not change. "What's two 4's?" he asks. "Eight," she replies with surprising quickness. "You just multiplied to get that answer," Jackson informs her. "That's adding," she shoots back, thinking she's topped him. "Multiplication is a form of adding," he replies calmly.

But, for the moment at least, Ruby is completely blocked on multiplication, and at last Jackson allows her to add. Very slowly she writes fifteen 9's on blackboard and begins to add them up. Whatever interest her performance had for the audience is by this time dissipated. A boy gets up and turns the alarm clock on Jackson's desk around so that it faces him. There are at least thirty minutes of the school day left, but he is prepared to watch each of them tick by. In the back of room another boy flips a paper airplane uncertainly through the air. A bright-looking, freckle-faced kid, Hughie, who has been quietly reading a bubble-gum cartoon in the opposite corner, now rises and starts wandering aimlessly around the room. Finally he darts into the hall. Jackson lets him go.

Ruby has by now discovered that fifteen 9's add up to 135, and reports sadly: "It's too much. What do I do now?" "Try a smaller number," Jackson advises. Without much hesitation Ruby picks thirteen as the correct number of 9's in 124. Has she known all along? Has it all been just a way of holding Jackson's attention?

Suddenly the wandering boy returns to class, an event which Jackson ignores. It is too much for Hughie. "You want to hit me," he charges. Jackson quietly denies it. But the incident has obviously distracted him from Ruby who has, in the meantime, erased all fifteen of her previous 9's and carefully replaced them with thirteen new ones. She turns on Hughie and starts chasing him, whereupon Jackson must actively intervene. He seats Hughie firmly in a chair, and orders Ruby back to the blackboard, where she begins printing her name. Since she has forgotten the problem by this time, it is necessary to begin at the beginning. "What's the first step?" "Estimate," she replies, tacking on a diversionary request for the word's spelling. No one in the class responds to Jackson's bid for assistance, so he writes "yes" on the board, erases the y, and proceeds from there. Now the whole class helps him sound out the word and a full seven minutes are devoted to this cooperative spelling effort.

"Now," says Ruby as the word gradually appears in full on the blackboard, "I can tell my mother the teacher said to estimate." Jackson tells her to start adding up her column of 9's. She sets to work. But in the meantime Hughie is once more on the loose. Stopping long enough to pick up his jacket, he starts out of the room again. Jackson tells him to come back. Hughie hesitates, then disappears. Jackson shouts a warning which is met with silence. But in a minute or two Hughie is back, just as Ruby miraculously gets a total of 117 from her thirteen 9's, and perceives that it is easy coasting from there on in. In two or three more minutes Jackson has gotten the answer from her in proper form. She has been at the blackboard for something like half an hour, but she has solved the problem.

Jackson retires, unruffled, to his desk. He can hardly praise Ruby's performance, but he doesn't condemn it either. He reads out a four-problem homework assignment in long division and allows the class the last fifteen minutes of the day to get a running start on it. Ruby spends the time singing tunelessly to herself. The rest of the class relieve their boredom by kicking, poking, and punching one another.

I cannot remember a more agonizing half-hour than this one with Ruby and

Hughie and Mr. Donald Jackson. But I was also forcefully reminded of Gottlieb's words: "These kids are defeated too much of the time." The opportunity class houses the most defeated of the defeated, but I left it feeling I had witnessed a kind of victory, I do not wish to attach any illusions to it. Ruby's ordeal at the blackboard will not be the beginning of some magical transformation, and it is difficult to imagine that she will ever be anything but one of society's most luckless members. Yet her school has refused to be part of the general gang-up on her. True, she will never belong to that more fortunate one-quarter of his group that Jackson manages to return to the general school population each year, but it is conceivable that she is at least learning from him the value of endurance; perhaps in future she will not give up on a problem—or on life—quite so easily as she might have otherwise. Does this mean that her self-image is being "enhanced"? There is no way of knowing, of course, but one cannot escape the feeling that Donald Jackson daily adds a tiny measure to the possibility that it will happen. One hopes—and in the meantime so does Jackson, who refuses to deal in finalities. "Listen," he says, "you came at the end of the day when the kids are restless. You should have seen them this morning. They spent an hour concentrating on their reading—there wasn't a bit of fooling around. They can do it when they want to."

The second-grade class for gifted children offers, of course, the greatest possible contrast to the "op class." But the more significant contrast is with the first-graders described earlier. The teacher is far less experienced than her first-grade colleague and still occasionally betrays awkwardness and insecurity. But what she lacks in technique is more than compensated for by her enthusiasm, by her willingness to try anything, and by the obvious pleasure she derives from her students which she in turn communicates back to them. Though many younger teachers are frightened at the thought of departing from the security of the curriculum outline, or of the basal reader, this girl seems genuinely exhilarated by the possibilities of freedom.

She is not a forceful disciplinarian and wields her authority as if she were amazed by it. Nevertheless, hers is the quietest room in P.S. 165. When I came in she was busy with some paper work at her desk, while the pupils were occupied with all sorts of projects of their own. Four girls were off in a corner planning a dramatic adaptation of a book they had read; three were busy looking up new words in the dictionary and copying down their meanings; still others were engaged in writing what I believe used to be called "compositions," while the remainder sat quietly reading books of their own choosing, ranging from fairy tales to a study of astronomy written at least at the sixth-grade level, which was being studied by a little Korean boy with the utmost concentration. Those whose projects required talking were murmuring together, those who were reading and writing wriggled not, neither did they squirm. I commented on this remarkable concentration. "I try to get the children to realize that they're not working for me, but for themselves," the teacher replied. "I tell them that their main job is to please themselves." It sounded like a fairly routine remark—except that I cannot recall anyone at any point in an educational career spent entirely in public schools, ever saying it to me.

During the work period I was given a guided tour of the class bulletin board, sectioned-off to correspond to the children's diverse interests—science, art, and writing. Back at her desk the teacher showed me excerpts from some ten pages of a work in progress entitled *Summer in Alaska with John Bobby Reilly,* a complex narrative to which the following hasty plot summary can scarcely do justice. It begins with the hero's concoction of an explosive "out of dynamite, sulfuric acid, firecrackers, cherry bombs, two quarts of Ajax, some turpentine, and a dash of Ivory Snow." In storage the stuff unexpectedly begins to turn bad, becoming transformed in the process into a "hepto-poison." Whereupon the author deftly shifts the scene to the suite of rooms occupied by John Bobby Reilly's girlfriend, Alice, at the Pyjama Hotel. Alice telephones down to room service for some caviar, which is in due course followed by a mound of lemon sherbet "72 inches high." "She told the maid," writes the author, "that she was very happy with the service she was getting." But Alice pays her bill with counterfeit money and moreover gives the maid only a fifteen-cent tip. At this point the scene shifts back again to John Bobby Reilly in his laboratory.

The teacher's response to the story is model. Unlike a number of well-intentioned adults, she does not inform the author that his story is "unrealistic," nor does she take issue with his invention of words. Her obvious delight in the tale is unmanufactured and uncondescending, and her interest in how it is going to come out, the eagerness with which she presses the creations of her pupils on the observer, all bespeak a genuine enthusiasm, unspoiled by the usual gush about "creativity."

This same enthusiasm animates the discussion period, where each child contributes words he has recently acquired to a kind of community vocabulary fund: *cherub, fond, investigate, disposition, presentable* were the new words on the day of my visit, while *nebulae* and *algae* (contributed by the young Korean scientist) were postponed for consideration at some future time. The new words were then used in a sentence by various members of the class, defined, conjugated, grammatically identified. For this group, language and its usage has ceased to be a private agony; words are handled with easy familiarity. ("I'm *fond* of cake" draws a laugh during the session of practice usage; "I'm *fond* of school" elicits the expected groan.)

Does this mean that only the exceptionally bright and the exceptionally slow students get the best teaching P.S. 165 has to offer? A visit to a "typical" sixth-grade class composed of what could be called average students testified to the contrary. Led by a teacher whose manner was brisk but never forbidding, the class moved easily from subject to subject. Following a talk of a few minutes about art criticism—which she also used as an occasion for praising some abstract paintings the kids had done—the teacher, in an apparent *non sequitur,* asked the class to list for her those things which could be seen, heard, or felt in Central Park in the springtime, but could not be found there in winter. The column headed "See" on the blackboard was the fastest to be filled. In this column they noted flowers and grass, new leaves on the trees, and "animals coming out of their holes." "What kind of animals?" the teacher asked, and a girl named Carmel was the first to reply: "Foxes." The class laughed. The teacher did not. "Carmel comes from Haiti," she reminded the others. "They may have different names for animals there, they may even have different animals." After carefully questioning Carmel about the fox under discussion, then drawing a picture on the blackboard and comparing it with a similar likeness in a picture book, it was established that what Carmel had seen in the park was a squirrel. The atmosphere was one of triumphant communication.

Since the "See" list was by then amply filled, the children were asked what they could expect either to feel or hear in the park. "Fresh air," "the sounds of birds," "the breeze and the bees," were some of the replies. This led naturally into a discussion of insect life and a dispute about the number of eyes insects have, adjudicated in the traditional manner: "When we're not sure of a fact, where do we look it up?" The most persistent questioner was dispatched to the bookshelf, and the teacher then asked how many of the children had encyclopedias at home and where they had got them.

"This man, he come to my house," one boy volunteers.

"This man *came* to my house," she corrects.

Another boy suddenly remarks: "My father wouldn't buy encyclopedias when the man came. He wasn't working." He pauses, embarrassed at the admission.

The teacher says quickly: "But your father is working now, isn't he?"

He is, the awkward moment is forgotten, some information on sight among the lower phyla is imparted, and the teacher resumes the pursuit of items for the "Feel" column, but with a shift in emphasis. She now wants not a discussion of physical sensations, but of emotional ones. "How does going to the park make you feel different than if you were walking down Broadway?" she asks.

Garry says that when you go to the park you feel as if you want to do everything. Cynthia says it make her feel bigger and that it also makes her "feel like thinking about the future." "It's peaceful," another girl adds, "because of the birds and the flowers blooming." Carlos begins to free-associate: "When you sit next to the ocean. . . ." He gestures vaguely and is unable to finish. José says the park makes him feel free. Another child, a large, rather rawboned girl, contributes a sober coda: "If you have a big decision to make it's easier to do it in the park—you don't have to stay in the house."

The teacher presses forward, and now it becomes clear why the discussion began with the pictures the children had drawn. She points out that there are pictures other than those you draw; there are also "word pictures." That, she informs them, is what they have just been drawing as they talked about the park.

"What makes *Charlotte's Web* such an interesting story?" she asks.

"Because when you read it you feel like you're there," Garry volunteers.

"Yes. Now what did he write with?"

"A pencil," someone says. It is not a smart-alecky remark—but merely an example of the concreteness of a child's viewpoint. "But what did the pencil write?" the teacher persists. "Words," come the chorus.

"Now, those are what we've been using to describe the park. We could write them down instead of just saying them, and then we might have a word picture"—the creation of which then comprises the homework assignment.

The intention behind the discussion is clear. In the course of it, the class has been gently encouraged to speculate upon all manner of things: life in a different culture, nature lore, the research process, the process of communication, and, most important, the immediate world in whcih they live and their experience of it. Not once have they betrayed the slightest boredom or restlessness. One senses that, for the majority, the performing of that night's homework assignment will be more than an irrelevant chore. If so, the teacher will have accomplished something quite rare in our society: the realization by her students that writing is not some exotic or tedious undertaking, but rather another form of an activity in which they are constantly engaged—the definition of the world around them.

Later, I remarked to Gottlieb about the skill of this teacher. "She's always telling me that teaching is just a temporary job," he replied. "I don't worry. She's one of those people who will never find anything more rewarding. Once you're good, there's no job that's better." Ironically enough, the skill and spirit of such teachers point up how much more P.S. 165 could do, given really good conditions instead of merely passable ones. Gottlieb, with his almost obsessive emphasis upon "raising the aspirations" of the children in his charge, cannot put enough stress on the magnitude of what is yet to be done in broadening the educational experiences of these kids—and, more specifically, in enriching the school curriculum. "We need more science," he says, "more physical education, more art—we don't have a trained, full-time art instructor in the school. We don't have enough good literature for the children to read. We don't even have readers that show Negro and white kids living together in the world."

Enrichment is the key problem not only in a school like P.S. 165 but also throughout the public school system. Gottlieb and a large number of his teachers, perhaps a majority of them, are keenly aware of it, and one cannot fault their efforts—they are, after all, far above and beyond the call of duty. The pupil at P.S. 165, if he is handicapped or if he is especially bright, will receive special aid as good as he can obtain anywhere. If he is an average student, his chance of encountering a brilliant, mind-quickening teacher is also as good as it is anywhere. And if, through the luck of the draw, he misses all of them, he will at least be taught by reasonably competent teachers using pedagogical techniques that meet generally accepted standards.

Given the patent inadequacies of our society's attitudes toward education, this seems to me the best that one can realistically hope for from a school, be it public or private. And I have no doubt that P.S. 165 provides at least as good an education as I received in a suburban system on which a great deal of money, concern, and pride were lavished.

Why is it, then that white middle-class parents are withdrawing their children from the public schools in such numbers that, in New York City at least, thoughtful educators believe that the whole concept of free, universal education may be threatened? The excuse for these removals is generally that parents are seeking a better education for their children, and indeed, it is entirely possible that there are poor elementary schools on the West Side of New York, and more than possible that there are some highly undesirable junior and senior high schools. But the business of an elementary school is, after all, elementary. The teaching of reading, writing and arithmetic to small children is not a task requiring rare genius. Instead, it calls for patience, perseverence, practicality, and, most of all, an open mind. These qualities abound at P.S. 165 and, by the admittedly fuzzy standards a layman applies to elementary pedagogy, it is hard to imagine that the best private school or the most favored public school would have a higher level of competence or a lower level of incompetence on its faculty. Given the quirky, chancy ways in which parents, when they have the opportunity, go about selecting a school for their children, it is hard to see how they could come up with a place markedly superior to P.S. 165. Yet in spite of this clearly observable reality, a fiercely biased set of attitudes toward Manhattan's public schools has reached such a generality of acceptance that in recent years we have begun to witness a natural reaction on the part of Negro organizations, who suggest that racial imbalance in schools like P.S. 165 be corrected either by the enforced transfer of more white students from other districts, or by the transfer of Negro and Puerto Rican students to predominantly white districts. The reason for this campaign is clear enough: spokesmen for the Negro community have become convinced that schools with predominantly white populations offer a better level of education and service then do those with predominantly Negro or Puerto Rican populations. Considering the way the middle-class whites have been carrying on, their assumption is understandable.

But both the Negroes and the white middle class might well heed the finding of

Joseph P. Lyford of the Center for the Study of Democratic Institutions, who has made an exhaustive study of schools on Manhattan's West Side. Lyford points out that the "totally exclusive preoccupation of some civil rights groups with the question of racial percentages . . . is going to have damaging effects on some of the good schools." Reshuffling, he points out, is likely to damage the morale of everyone, from the principals to the students, and make it difficult to justify those special services which, as we have seen, are the chief glory and inspiration of these schools.

The answer, both to the complaints of the Negro leaders and to the white middle-class parents who are withdrawing their children in increasing numbers from the public schools, might be precisely the cultural enrichment for which Dr. Gottlieb pleads. In general, the kids who least need such enrichment at P.S. 165 are from the wihte middle-class homes. Yet it is their parents who are most conscious of the school's cultural failures and most likely to withdraw them when they find that cultural enrichment is not one of the special services offered by a special-service school. The draining away of the white middle classes from the public schools could probably be slowed down by the addition of more cultural opportunities to the curriculum. This, in turn, would still the fears of Negro leaders about racial imbalance. Indeed, it may well be that, in order to preserve their role of educating children for a pluralist society, the overburdened public schools of New York City will at last have to add the art and music teachers, the expanded libraries, and the foreign-language programs that advanced educators like Gottlieb would like. In the meantime schools like P.S. 165 require the faith of the educated white middle class if they are to continue to provide the excellent basic education that I witnessed there.

UNIT **22.**

The Place and Importance of Cultural Factors in Group Relations Work: Serving an Indian Village in Alaska

To what degree does the practitioner need to relate to cultural factors in his work with a group? Do certain problems, because of their inner construction and dynamics, need to be attacked in uniform ways or do problems become defined and acted upon differentially depending on cultural forms and values of those affected? Who indeed defines a given problem as a problem? How specifically can culture be taken into account by the practitioner? Do people participate in programs or problem-solving ventures in accordance with differing cultural norms? How does the practitioner learn these if he is not part of the group? Do such norms lead to different strategies by the practitioner and different styles of participation on the part of clients? Does indigenous leadership vary according to cultural conditioning and how does this affect the ways in which the practitioner connects with and engages such leadership? These kinds of issues will be explored in a description of a service program to American Indians.

Occasionally service programs involve periodic field visits by a staff member from a central agency to an outlying district in the role of a detached worker or expert. This is reflected in the report that follows, which consists of a summary of the activities in the Indian village of "Yutat" of a social worker employed by the Bureau of Indian Affairs. The record is an actual verbatim administrative report from the agency files. Only the names of the village and of individuals have been changed on request for purposes of confidentiality.

The following is a summary of the report prepared by Mr. Warren Day, Supervisory Social Worker, Southeast District Office, Bureau of Indian Affairs, on his activities during 12 months when he made 23 visits to the community of Yutat with each visit averaging about three days.

Mr. Day had joined the Bureau of Indian Affairs in July, 1964. He had no experience in community development. He was given materials to read and the prob-

---

Summary Report on Community Development Project in Yutat, by Warren Day. Administrative Report, Bureau of Indian Affairs, United States Department of the Interior, Washington, D. C.

lems and questions that arose during each visit were reviewed with him to help him gain perspective.

Before beginning the summary, it is important to know that Yutat in April, 1966, had a population of 300 with 40 families, 30 of whom had income of less than $3,000 per year. There were 150 persons under 21 years of age, 16 persons age 65 and over, 95 males age 14 and over who were employable, and 60 males and 20 females who were unable to work. Only 11 cases received Old Age Assistance, 20 children received Aid to Families with Dependent Children, and 21 families received help from the Bureau of Indian Affairs during the month of greatest need. It was considered that 80 of 110 houses were substandard.

It is noteworthy that the Bureau of Indian Affairs was selected by the young mayor as the culprit who caused the people to drink and not work. The financial assistance program, designed to help those in need, was the instrument used by the Bureau that received the blame. Interestingly enough, the Bureau assistance to Yutat had been by fiscal year: 1960—$4,726; 1961—$6,413; 1962—$5,006; 1963—$4,636; 1964—$7,764; 1965—$8,822; and 1966—$12,456. The number of cases receiving aid on the average each month were: 1963—4; 1964—8; 1965—8. The number of separate, individual cases receiving aid each year were: 1963—17; 1963—14; 1964—25; 1965—29; and 1966—24.

The State of Alaska has extended assistance each month as follows:

NUMBER OF CASES

Year	Adult	AFDC	Total	Amount
1960	14	11	25	$2370
1961	NA	NA	NA	NA
1962	13	11	24	2245
1963	13	8	21	1665
1964	13	5	18	1445
1965	11	5	16	1040
1966	12	4	16	955

A very casual study of the assistance expenditures reveals an uninterrupted decrease in state assistance over the years due entirely to a 30 per cent reduction in AFDC cases.

Perhaps these data will be helpful as the summary of the report is read.

Summary by Worker

Yutat is a predominantly Native village which appears to have an abundance of natural resources. While there are a good deal of social problems including breakdown in family living, weak governmental structure and educational problems, there are some people in the community with the desire and ability to upgrade and stabilize village life. Finally, Yutat's 250 population is of manageable size which should allow me to learn the community and know the people more quickly.

Attempts will be made to visit Yutat every other week and for the winter schedule —arriving on Monday and leaving on Thursday. Visits will begin on October 26, 1964, and initially the time spent will be in becoming acquainted and learning the village and knowing the people. Reports of the progress of this project will be included in a monthly narrative to the Area Social Worker. In addition, this narration will include a more detailed and comprehensive record of activities primarily for my own use in promoting the project.

The following is from a previous village report describing the physical description of Yutat. Yutat is situated near the southern mouth of Yutat Bay, which is located on the Gulf of Alaska. It is extremely isolated from all other communities, the closest being more than 100 miles away.

Yutat has a protected harbor and is located on a lowland peninsula covering an area of close to 2,000 square miles. In the background are the Evan Mountains, making a most picturesque setting on clear days. Unfortunately, these clear days do not occur frequently, inasmuch as the rainfall is in excess of 100 inches annually and they receive from 200 to 300 inches per year in the form of snow. The weather conditions make living at Yutat rather difficult, but they ordinarily do not have severely cold temperatures.

Yutat has a population of approximately 250 people residing in the village. There are perhaps an additional 100 people residing at the nearby airport, Wyatt Station, and Coast Guard Morgan station. All of these are about five or six miles away from the village proper.

"The village is extended in two main portions along approximately a mile of beach. Houses are rundown, the road through the village is poorly kept, and generally the village is unattractive. There are two general stores in the community, the one being located in connection with an old salmon cannery, which no longer operates. However, they do have a crab and salmon freezing operation. There are reasonably good docking facilities at the cannery store and about a year ago [1963] a small boat float was constructed about a mile from the village. There is a fairly extensive network of roads within the immediate area, but it is completely isolated from the outside except by air or water."

The winter air schedule for Yutat involves arrivals from Juneau on Monday, Wednesday and Friday and departures from Yutat for Juneau on Thursdays and Sundays.

This was my second visit to the village of Yutat so I knew a few people from brief previous introductions. The following paragraphs give some facts and observations about various areas of community concern.

Yutat's only school is located in the central part of the village in a rather rundown but currently adequate building. At present there are 71 pupils in the school with 13 in junior high (seventh, eighth, and ninth). In addition, there are two pupils for the tenth and eleventh grades who are not enrolled in regular classes, but are being helped by the staff with correspondence courses. Yutat operates as an independent school district and receives 91 per cent of its financing through the state. There has been a large change in staff over the last year.

The Federal Aeronautics Administration (FAA) maintains its own school (grades one through eight) at the FAA site about six miles from the village. Last year there were considerable attempts to unite these two schools into a single system. I have heard conflicting reports as to why this was not done including resistance on the part of FAA personnel and on the part of some people in the village.

There are two churches in Yutat. One is the Presbyterian Church. There is an Assembly of God Church which is reasonably active in making some progress in the community.

The primary factor in the economy in the village is fishing. In the Yutat area fishing is generally accomplished through setnets at the mouths of the various rivers located in the area. During the summer, entire families go to the fish camps at these rivers and usually return for the weekend or on days when fishing is closed. Low overhead in this type of operation allows a fairly large margin of take-home pay from the fishing earnings which allows many of the people to remain financially independent year after year. A few fishermen gillnet in Yutat Bay.

A cannery operated by the Will Canning Company operates during the fishing season. Although they no longer can fish at the cannery, they do tie up a floating cannery and operate it. In addition, they have a freezing operation and crab processing activity which employs a number of the villagers.

The FAA maintains the airport and weather station in Yutat. While twenty to thirty men are employed there, probably not more than three or four are native. The Coast Guard Morgan Station and Wyatt Station account for about twenty-five men, but none of these are Native employees.

Connected with the cannery is the cannery store which operates the year around. The other store in town is operated by the widow of a former mayor in the village. He was non-Native. A small restaurant known as "Pop's Place" is located centrally in the village. There is a garage (filling station and repair) at the edge of town. The owner is a former Coast Guard Caucasian who married an Indian woman.

Several years ago a Community Cooperative Corporation was formed in the village. This corporation owns and maintains a liquor store with the profits to be used for community betterment. The liquor store opened on July 13, 1963. The directors were chosen to represent various aspects and organizations in the community.

The Yutat area has potential for extensive tourism. The area is one of the prime moose-hunting sections of the state.

There is no doctor in Yutat. The community has a Public Health nurse position that is presently unfilled. This would be of an itinerant nature and the nurse would be shared with another area. In addition, a physician from the Public Health Service Hospital, Mt. Ellening, visits the village about four times a year. Occasional dental services are provided in the same manner although I am not aware how extensive dental services can be given in the field. There are three registered nurses in the community who provide informal unpaid health care when requested.

The Alaska Native Brotherhood (ANB) and the Alaska Native Sisterhood (ANS) are relatively active, but do not seem to be as strong a force in the community as they could be. The president of the ANB has submitted his resignation (not yet accepted) because of what he calls jealousy and bickering. I attended an ANB-ANS meeting and explained my function in community development. This took no more than fifteen minutes and the rest of the time from 8:00 P.M. to 12:15 A.M. was taken in choosing delegates for the ANB Encampment from November 9 through November 13, 1964. The meeting progressed agonizingly slowly with many pauses of fully ten minutes with nobody speaking. The ANB sponsors movies once or twice a week, but the use of this income is rather nebulous. I feel I know very little about the dynamics of the Yutat ANB-ANS as yet, but it must be kept in mind for its potential for action in the community.

The Five Chiefs organization was founded in the 1950's for the purpose of representing the people with the Concord Oil and Gas Company.

A deputy magistrate court sits in Yutat, but the incumbent is leaving. The one police officer is in the process of being replaced. The jail is inadequate and seldom used.

Yutat is organized as a second-class city. Its government has had many ups and downs and is currently in dire fiscal difficulty. The mayor is the former postmaster deposed because of inefficiency. The village's source of revenue includes the following:

Two per cent sales tax from stores. This is collected four times a year and the only dependable revenue.

Property Tax. This has not been collected for two or three years. A new property assessment is required, but the village cannot afford it, consequently, they cannot tax. In addition, about half of the property is owned by persons with restricted deeds which means that they do not have to pay property taxes.

Water. Currently, the bill is $5.76 per month, but it is not being collected from all persons. The water system was put in a year or two ago by the Public Health Service and each person was required to pay $120. The Public Health Service is still owed $2,400.

Electricity. The village has its own "cat" generators for which they have a bond indebtedness. They do collect revenue for electricity.

It is my impression that the local government is a sorely needed area for development.

The city has a good water system thanks to the aforementioned PHS project a couple of years ago. However, there is no general sewer system and sewage and waste is handled via septic tanks, outdoor privies and throwing debris and garbage onto the shore for the tide to take care of.

Yutat now has a telephone system with approximately fifty telephones in town and thirty out of town. Administrative services are contracted to Will Canning Company.

Second Field Visit
(November 16, 1964, to November 20, 1964)

The Coast Guard Station is located about eight miles south-southeast of the village. It is considered an isolated station so that families are not with the men. The Wyatt RCA Station Site is owned by the Air Force and operated under contract through RCA.

The airport at Yutat is owned and operated by FAA. There are two or three Natives who work part-time for FAA and the high turnover rate may have implications for hiring more.

The Weather Bureau employs six men, all non-Native.

Regarding previous questions, Yutat has chlorination and fluorination.

I attended another meeting of the ANB and ANS.

With the mayor's permission, I spent part of one day in the city offices (above the Health Center) reviewing the material they have. I have obtained copies of most of their ordinances. In the evening, I attended a council meeting which lasted from seven until after midnight. The meeting was interesting, dynamically, in that quite a formal procedure was used. Parliamentary procedure was strictly adhered to. Business, however, moves in a slow manner.

The new Chief of Police was sworn in that evening. His salary is $100 a month and paid by the local liquor store. The city, supposed to match this with another $100, is not able to afford it, but the Chief of Police accepted the position anyway. I rather admired the mayor when he told the police chief that he would be considered a representative of the police twenty-four hours a day and emphasized his need to conduct himself in that manner. He has had a drinking problem in the past.

The city has a truck and if the car is fixed, would have other equipment for rent. I was asked to find the going rental prices in Juneau.

I was also asked to check on whether a legal opinion is necessary before an ordinance is passed in the village. It has been the pattern for the village to send their ordinances to an attorney in Juneau for a legal opinion, but at the present time, two ordinances (water and garbage) are pending and are not passed because they have not been able to afford to buy this service.

I contacted the Field Solicitor for the Department of the Interior, who stated that it was not necessary to have a legal opinion or audit of ordinances.

I shared with Tribal Operations my activities so far and "sparks" flew when they found out that I had contacted the solicitor about the ordinance problem. They think that this is their realm and are resentful about anybody else getting into the act . . . or at least it appears so.

Third Field Visit
(November 30, 1964, to December 2, 1964)

On the evening I arrived, the city water system froze up because the heat tapes on the intake pipe disintegrated so the community was out of water for about twenty-four hours. It is interesting to note that one fellow assumed a great deal of responsibility in this matter by calling the Public Health Service representative in Anchorage and getting instructions on how to go about correcting this situation. The following day I went to call on the mayor whom I found trying to thaw out his pipes thinking that they were frozen. When I informed him that the city had been out of water for a day, it was news to him. I was rather appalled that he, as the mayor, had not been informed and this kind of illustrates the problem of communication there.

Fourth Field Visit
(December 28, 1964, to December 31, 1964)

The purpose of this visit was to begin acquainting the community with the new Economic Opportunity Act and the possibilities it might have for improvement in Yutat. One evening I gathered together some of the leaders in the community to talk about the Economic Opportunity Act. We discussed the types of things they felt were needed in the community and the following is a list of those that were mentioned: relocation of the village, more people in the town, a sewer system, a grocery co-op, a project in which carpenters would build houses using village help and they would be sold at cost to the village, a co-op manager, a housing co-op like Cedar Park in Juneau, teaching the people more about living off the land as they have in the past—putting up fish, berries, etc., city planning, shrimp fishing, a central meeting place, shipbuilding, more medical facilities, a cold storage for king salmon and halibut, an area for children to play, a tribal house to attract tourists, recreation facilities to take the place of drinking, and training for loggers anticipating further logging developments in the area.

As we talked about these things, we explored each one somewhat as to feasibility. It was decided that the village would certainly have to agree (as many had different ideas) as to what type of program they would like to obtain through the Office of Economic Opportunity. I suggested they have an ANS meeting (which they plan to do) to talk this over with the village as a whole and get their ideas and see if they can come to some consensus about various programs.

On this visit, I began calling on the houses individually without knowing who was in them to discuss what their ideas were about community development and the needs they felt for Yutat. These persons, for the most part, have not been really brought into community affairs before because they are not considered community leaders. They are all quite taken with the idea of the village grocery co-op.

Fifth Field Visit
(January 11, 1965, to January 14, 1965)

One evening I met with the City council for their regular meeting which started in its routine fashion until disturbed by a drinking citizen. I had a meeting with six or seven people concerning self-help housing.

I met with the Health Committee. This committee primarily raises funds for supplies and other activities such as paying the dentist's transportation to Yutat. The purpose in getting them together for a meeting was to have them act for a solution of the medical emergency. All of the members seemed very unsure of themselves about anything they could do and required much support. They finally decided that they would write two letters. One would be to the Director of Health and Welfare outlining and detailing the medical needs and services that Yutat has with the idea of pressure being brought to bear for a Public Health nurse in Yutat. The other will be to the hospital submitting two names (which they will select) for "Health Aide" training which is a program where Native people are taken to the hospital and given a week's training primarily in how to report symptoms.

Sixth Field Visit
(January 25, 1965, through January 28, 1965)

Increased drinking on the part of the teen-agers in town was discussed. It appears that quite a few of this age group have returned to Yutat as school dropouts.

To provide an outlet and diversion for these youths, the liquor store has arranged for Pally's Restaurant and Pool Hall to be leased as a teen-age center. One citizen is the prime mover behind this and organized the group in such a way that the teen-agers themselves are running the center.

I contacted a few members of the Health Committee. Nothing has been done in the way of letter writing as planned during the previous visit.

My previous contacts concerning the Economic Opportunity Act were culminated in an ANB meeting. The response of the people seemed more one of interest than enthusiasm and a committee was not formed to work out a community action plan as I had hoped. This may have been due to the fact that the meeting was taken over by one of the citizens toward the end and he is not a very effective leader. Hopefully, on my next visit I can rekindle some interest in this.

Seventh Field Visit
(February 8, 1965, to February 11, 1965)

I was informed that the Chief of Police had resigned. A new magistrate will have to be appointed.

I had another meeting with the people interested in the self-help housing project. Only about twelve people showed up.

The Health Committee had a meeting which I attended and they decided they would send five people to the Health Aide Training Program.

It is becoming increasingly more difficult to get the Community Action Program off the ground. I think part of the problem is that the city has other interests that are more important to them such as Mutual Self-Help Housing, a sawmill, etc. I am afraid that by participating in the Economic Opportunity Act interest in all programs will be diluted and although I will still keep them in mind of it, I am not going to push as hard as I have on this in the past.

Eighth Field Visit
(March 3, 1965, to March 7, 1965)

This visit was made Wednesday through Sunday which gave me an opportunity to observe the community on a weekend. I noticed a significantly greater amount of drinking in the village this visit than ever before.

Ironically, I took a movie on drinking problems to the village this time. It was shown twice in the high school and developed a reasonably good discussion. It was also shown before the regular movie on Friday night and held over again on the following Monday. I think this movie was particularly well done, but if it did any good to show it, it is anyone's guess. The ANB president and movie shower, told me after the movie on Friday night that he was very impressed by the movie and felt that the other people were too. About an hour later, the president of the ANB was among a number of us who visited the Coast Guard Station. He proceeded to get completely drunk and had to be carried to the car and then to his house. So much for movies.

There are too many persons that go on binges that last for days and sometimes weeks. For instance, at this visit, when I visited the mayor's house, his wife who is usually among the nicest people I have known, held up the bottle from the kitchen to show me that she was drinking. I saw her numerous times while I was there and she was drunk continuously.

The Chief of Police job has been rotated like musical chairs. Finally, the Council said that they had to do something about it and the job just could not be passed from one man to another.

A contact or two was made for the Division of Public Welfare. Talked to a gentleman at length about his efforts in obtaining a boat. Passing on messages from the Branch of Industrial Development. Met emergency needs for a client. Played basketball with the 49'ers against the ANB team and lost. A man injured his arm. I returned to Juneau with a woman recently discharged from the Alaska Psychiatric Institute who intends to live in Juneau. A boat trip was taken up the bay with a couple of men which was a very interesting trip. We saw deer and seal, checked crab pots, halibut lines, etc.

Ninth Field Visit
(March 22 to March 25, 1965)

Social conditions are about the same, but I made attempts to talk to various people more specifically about how the drinking problem compared to a few years ago. I really question whether the village is ready to attack the alcohol problem from the village approach. No one is very judgmental nor deplores drinking conditions in the village.

Other Visits

Tenth Field Visit (April 5 to April 9, 1965) &
Eleventh Field Visit (April 14 and 15, 1965)

The primary purpose of this visit was a meeting with those persons interested in the Mutual Self-Help Housing Program.

Twelfth Field Visit (April 19 to April 22, 1965) &
Thirteenth Field Visit (May 17 to May 20, 1965)

Two meetings were held during this visit relating to the development of a sawmill.

Fourteenth Field Visit (June 2 to June 4, 1965);
Fifteenth Field Visit (July 13 through July 16, 1965);
Sixteenth Field Visit (August 25 to August 27, 1965)

This trip concerned Community Development.

Seventeenth Field Visit (September 27 to October 1, 1965) &
Eighteenth Field Visit (October 19 through October 21, 1965

The big news of this visit was the election which occurred while I was there.

Nineteenth Field Visit
(November 3 through November 6, 1965)

Considerable time was spent in discussing FHA loans.

Twentieth Field Visit
(January 3 through January 6, 1966)

I attended a council meeting under the new administration for the first time.

Twenty-first Field Visit
(February 14 to February 17, 1966)

While nothing specific has happened in the area of municipal government, I am much more optimistic for the prospects of getting this in order. The mayor wrote to the Governor and the Alaska Delegation outlining the need for a city dock in Yutat.
The Presbyterian Church burned to the ground in January.
I had a long talk with the new VISTA volunteer in Yutat.

Twenty-second Field Visit
(March 14 to March 17, 1966)

I attended a council meeting. I am impressed by the way the mayor carries on the business. He is somewhat forceful in getting the council to go along with his proposals, but would be overwhelmed by apathy if he did not proceed this way.
Drinking continues to be quite high in Yutat during this visit.
As mentioned, a hot lunch program is being tried with some success.

Twenty-third Field Visit
(April 18 to April 20, 1966)

The conclusion of the Community Development approach was discussed with the mayor. This followed a discussion between the Assistant Area Social Worker and myself essentially deciding to drop the experiment on the basis of its having been tried for nearly two years as originally proposed and the fact that results were not as progressive as we had hoped. The mayor felt that the biggest advantage to my function had been as a liaison person between the village and other agencies. We agreed that there also was stimulation on the part of some people to be concerned with the community, although this is not affecting a large segment of the population nor were they particularly able to follow up on their concern with action. Hopefully, the change in administration was due to the people being aware of the ineffective previous administration.

Termination of the Project

This concluding statement is an excerpt from the Community Development worker's letter to the mayor of Yutat, dated April 27, 1966.

"Regarding my regular activity in Yutat and following our last discussion on the value and success of the Community Development attempt over the last year and a half, I will be discontinuing my visits. From the practical standpoint, this is advisable for a number of reasons. First, the Community Development goals of enlisting total and grass-roots involvement of all members of the community in concern and decision making has not been successful. I believe that some of the people have become more thoughtful about their community but still do not see themselves as possessing influence or ability to actively participate in the community affairs.

"Secondly, the city government is stronger and better organized. However, I cannot emphasize enough the need for leadership to be expanded so that all the reliance is not to one or a few men when their continuing availability is tenuous. I think the newsletter proposal is great and may be a way to develop awareness from which additional leadership can emerge. It might be well if this communication device could be considered a forum of expression from the bottom up as well as an information device of the council.

"Finally, the presence of John Smart, the VISTA worker, suggests an overlapping of efforts on my part. The fact that he is a permanent resident and apart from the Bureau of Indian Affairs allows a greater chance of effectiveness than in my situation.

"It may be that the Advisory Welfare Council Proposal will require some discussion with the council. If it does, I may come at least once again. On the other hand, Joe Hoit will be providing welfare services to Yutat and it might be better for him to be the one involved in the final development of this plan.

"My interests and hopes for Yutat will in no way be diminished by my lack of contacts with the community. I am sure you know that anything I can do from this end will always be given a strong and enthusiastic effort. Please never hesitate to contact me if I can be helpful.

"I have a great deal of personal regret in not having the chance to visit Yutat frequently from now on. I began visiting there about the same time I came to Alaska so that I feel my friendships there are nearly as well developed as in Juneau. There are a good many fine people I will miss very much. I hope you will share this thought with them."

Group Relations As a Primary or Secondary Agency Function: A Church Helps Out in a Civil Disorder

Group relations objectives and programs may be the primary or secondary function of an agency. For the NAACP, it is clear that racial and civil rights matters are the "raison d'etre" for the organization's very existence. On the other hand, for a labor union or a church denomination, the civil rights or race relations department is often in a more peripheral position—in a minor key in the scheme of things.

The saliency of group relations in an organization's goals may have an important impact on selection of program activities and their effectiveness. If it is the primary function, it has high legitimacy within the organization and perhaps in the outside community. In addition, the organization is likely to acquire specialists who are qualified to meet personnel requirements. Further, there is likely to be sustained continuity of concern and action with respect to group relations matters. If group relations has a secondary position there may still be valid outcomes. For example, this function will have lower visibility in the agency and community, and may achieve objectives without calling too much attention to itself. This posture may have certain advantages, especially when issues are controversial within the organization. Also, there may be an opportunity for greater flexibility and experimentation in programs when such approaches do not tie up the major resources of the organization. It can tolerate a risk of failure when such failure does not damage what it considers to be its central mission. In addition, permitting group relations "add ons" to a great number of existing programs in the community is a way of expanding the scope of involvement and activity in this area.

On Sunday, July 23, 1967, Detroit police raided an upstairs speakeasy, or "blind pig," as local citizens call it. Reports quickly spread that police had clubbed a man and kicked a woman. Crowds gathered and began to stone the police, then turned to looting, setting fires and sniping. It was Wednesday night before more than 14,000 paratroopers, guardsmen and state and local police could quell the revolt. Worst hit of all the American cities which exploded into riot in the summer of 1967,

Detroit's toll was 39 dead, about 2,000 injured, more than 1,250 fires, and some 5,000 arrests, with damage from fire and looting above $200,000,000.

The report that follows tell how the churches helped the people of Detroit in their time of crisis, both during and after the disorder.

A few hours after the riot had erupted on that summer Sunday in Detroit, it was apparent that the city faced grave trouble. The Church wanted to know how it might most creatively participate in serving the total community as well as the areas where the disturbances were occurring. On Sunday evening, I stationed myself at the Diocesan Center and regularly called as many of the churches as possible in the affected areas, seeking to learn what was going on and to discover if there were any specific ways in which the diocese could be of assistance. By this time the east side clergy were on the streets and unavailable for any conversation. The west side clergy reported that even as they talked on the telephone they were observing looting, the setting of fires, and wild disorder. All of them were to report that at this stage no threats had been made to church buildings.

How Can We Help?

During Monday morning, July 24, the Rt. Rev. Archie H. Crowley made a telephone survey of the churches in the affected areas and visited several of them. At 10:00 A.M., having failed in my attempts to contact urban officials of other denominations, I attended a meeting of the Interdenominational Ministerial Alliance (IMA) at St. Paul's African Methodist Episcopal Church on Dexter Boulevard. This group of Negro pastors was attempting to plan for the moment and for the future, and my role was to listen to what they said. Afterward, I toured the affected areas of the city, including the downtown area which had also sustained damage. at 3:00 P.M. a meeting of urban executives and others with similar interests was convened at the Archdiocese of Detroit by the Rev. James Bristah. All the IMA representatives were there. This was essentially a meeting of the mainline white denominations. The fundamental question which the group asked itself was this: What is the most helpful service we can render the city of Detroit at this point?

The first answer was phrased in the negative: The least helpful thing we could do would be to pontificate on the causes of the riot and to issue gratuitous calls for law and order. The second answer said in effect: We will offer ourselves to the IMA and other community groups whose people are very much affected by and in many instances participating in the disturbance. We will make no public statements but rather will seek to be of assistance.

By 4:30 P.M. on Monday, the participants had decided that the most practical way of assisting was to offer an information service—a communication nerve center—a place where people could call for information and offer their services. I offered the facilities of the Diocesan Center, which were accepted, and a news release was prepared which went on the six o'clock news to the effect that the telephone number TE 2-4400 would put citizens in contact with "Interfaith Emergency Center."

At the same time the full group constituted itself as the Interfaith Emergency

Violence in Detroit: How Community Churches Responded to a City in Flames. Report by Rev. William S. Logan, Executive Director of Program for the Episcopal Diocese of Michigan and Chairman of the Emergency Center of the Interfaith Emergency Council. *Church in Metropolis,* Spring 1970 issue. A former publication of Joint Strategy and Action Committee, 475 Riverside Drive, New York, N.Y. 10027. Used by permission.

Council with four committees, one of which was responsible for the above Center, the others being entitled Needs, Finances, and Long-range Plans. The Rev. Arlie Porter was elected chairman of the Interfaith Emergency Council, and I was named chairman of the Emergency Center.

A switchboard was set in operation, and many clergy began immediately to volunteer their services. By 7:00 P.M. the switchboard was jammed with incoming calls and remained so for five days, twenty-four hours a day. Every office in the Cathedral Center was occupied by the volunteer workers who were setting up and operating this information center.

Emergency Services

The first assumption was that people would want information and the Center tried to provide it. This assumption proved true for only a few hours at which time it became apparent that the bulk of calls from the suburbs were offers of assistance. "What can we do?" "Where shall we send money?" "Can you use volunteers?" "Shall we collect food?" Other calls set forth needs. "I'm an elderly person trapped in my own neighborhood. I'm terrified and I need my heart medicine. Can you get it for me?" "Where is a drugstore still open?" "Is there a grocery store not yet burned down where we can get dietetic food?" Other questions came from churches which wanted to meet emergency needs of food, clothing, and shelter. They asked, "Can you get us some word as to how we may serve and help?"

Therefore, even before the first midnight shift was complete, it became apparent that there were five major categories of need which the Center could meet:

1. Locating and encouraging food collection centers in the suburban ring of churches.
2. Locating and supplying the food pipeline with food for distribution centers in the affected areas.
3. Registering volunteers and seeking to find places where they might be used.
4. Taking and responding to calls for meeting human need.
5. Supplying community information.

Volunteers came from many sources. Social workers, for example, came both from the private agencies and from their homes and they began to make orderly plans for those who called in with personal needs. College students, high school students, hippies, lay men and women from the suburbs and the city began to register as volunteers and also went on personal visits in response to the needs mentioned above. Those who had offered the use of station wagons or trucks were dispatched to food collection centers to pick up food and told to which food distribution center to deliver it. A major information-gathering group made regular telephone surveys of food collection centers to determine the availability of supplies, and surveyed food distribution centers to determine the most important points of need.

It became evident that a major need was trucking. The AFL-CIO Council, through its officers, Russell Leach, Tom Turner, and Dave Dancey, volunteered to supply the trucking services. Using volunteer drivers and trucks donated by large and small firms, they set up a dispatching service as an adjunct to the Interfaith Emergency Center to carry out the vital function of transporting food supplies.

We knew that clothing would also emerge as a major need, but it was impossible for the Center to take direct responsibility for this. The quantities of clothing needed were too great as were the complexities of repair, laundering, sizing, and distribution. Therefore, all clothing was referred to St. Vincent de Paul, the Salvation Army, the Purple Heart Organization, and ultimately to a city-operated warehouse.

Operation of the Center

It became apparent that several of the volunteers would have to commit almost their entire time and energy to the operation of the Center. St. Paul's Cathedral lent two assistant clergy, the Rev. Robert Wollard and the Rev. Eugene Montague, who alternated the day and night shifts. The Rev. Robert Wills of the First Congregational Church (United Church of Christ), Dearborn, served full time as did the Rev. Harry Cook, assistant minister of Christ Church, Detroit, and I gave my full time. In this way the basic supervision and operating management of the Center was provided.

Under Mrs. Lucille Cantoni (of the Metropolitan Detroit Family Service Society) and Mrs. Betty Kalichman, both of whom are professional social workers, the social work section was set up and manned by volunteers whom they recruited and scheduled. Harry Cook and his assistants managed the food distribution section in close walkie-talkie communication with the United Automobile Workers' dispatching group. The volunteer section was structured under Miss Ruth Belew, a Detroit schoolteacher, and Miss Myra Barron, a retired schoolteacher and Detroit Teachers' Credit Union employee. This latter group had to procure telephone switchboard operators, home visitors, drivers, dispatchers, truck loaders, helpers and cooks to prepare food to feed the volunteers lunch and dinner and for the small number who required breakfast. The actual assignment of volunteers in the social work section was the responsibility of the social workers.

By the end of the first week the Center slowly began to phase out of the food distribution program, although it continued in operation for another five days, as community resources, both secular and private, began to accept their tasks of distribution of welfare checks, emergency loans, housing and relocation services, and the location of kin among those who had been shipped out of town by the thousands for temporary detention by the police (Project Find). Our Needs section began to develop an information section which referred more and more people to appropriate agencies.

On Saturday, July 29, eighty people were convened from the major food collection and food distribution centers to reflect on their experience, to identify needs, to talk of ongoing plans, to evaluate critically the functioning of the Interfaith Emergency Center as their communication channel. They were divided into ten small groups, each staffed by a professional social worker, including the dean and assistant dean of the Wayne State University School of Social Work. The social workers later compiled a summary of their information and analyzed it in terms both of the effectiveness of the Center and the problems faced by the food distribution and collection points.

Future Plans

Where would be go from here? Certain needs were still not being met, so on a small, professionally staffed basis, the Interfaith Emergency Center continued to operate through Labor Day. Three full-time social workers were provided respectively by the Protestant Community Services, the Catholic Social Services, and the Jewish Family Welfare Services. Vista Volunteers were also assigned to assist and served by following up on all referrals made by the Center on which they had records to see if the needs were being met, by assisting the Finance Committee in determining valid individual financial relief needs which might be met through the funds collected, and by inventorying the services offered by public and private agencies to see if the performance was in accord with the claims. It was felt that in this way the agency could act as a conscience and gadfly to the public sector without supplanting the public sector's work.

The new relationships between the IMA and the larger white denominations and the Jewish community have been pursued so that a new version of the Interfaith Council could be established which would integrate the two groups. This Council has been meeting several times a week to work on both immediate and long-range problems. The Interfaith Emergency Center is still operating as a subcommittee of this major committee. The faiths, having come together, are determined to stay together.

The riot is over but recovery and rehabilitation still go on. It is crucial that the Interfaith Council serve as one of the major conscience groups of the community, seeking to insure the participation of the poor, the dispossessed and the target area residents in planning for the rebuilding of the new Detroit.

Bibliography

BLACKS

BAILEY, B. L. "Toward a New Perspective in Negro English Dialectology," *American Speech,* 40:171-173 (October, 1965).

BALDWIN, JAMES. *Nobody Knows My Name,* New York: Dell, 1961.

BALTZELL, E. DIGBY. *The Search for Community in Modern America,* "The Need for Community Among Negroes," New York: Harper & Row, 1968.

BENNETT, LERON. "Passion: A Certain Dark Joy," *Ebony,* XXIV (December, 1968).

BERNARD, JESSIE. *Marriage and Family Among Negroes,* Englewood Cliffs, N.J.: Prentice-Hall, 1965.

BILLINGSLEY, A. *Black Families in White America,* Englewood Cliffs, N.J.: Prentice-Hall, 1968.

BLACK, I. "Race and Unreason: Anti-Negro Opinion in Professional and Scientific Literature Since 1954," *Phylon,* 24, 1 (Spring, 1965).

BLOCK, JULIA. "The White Worker and the Negro Client in Psychotherapy," *Social Work,* 13:2 (April, 1968).

BROWN, CLAUDE. *Manchild in the Promised Land,* New York: Macmillan, 1965.

BULLOUGH, B. "Alienation in the Ghetto," *American Journal of Sociology,* 72:469-478 (March, 1967).

CAYTON, H. and ST. CLARI, DRAKE. *Black Metropolis,* Vol. 1, New York: Harper & Row, 1962.

CLARK, KENNETH. *Dark Ghetto,* New York: Harper & Row, 1965.

CLEAVER, ELDRIDGE. *Soul on Ice,* New York: McGraw-Hill, 1968.

CURRY, ANDREW E. "The Negro Worker and the White Client: A Commentary on the Treatment Relationships," *Social Casework,* 45:131-136 (March, 1964).

DELANY, LLOYD. "Some Psychological Factors in the Development of Black Identity," *Black Caucus,* Vol. 11 (Fall, 1969).

DERBYSHIRE, R. L. "U.S. Negro Identity Conflict," *Sociology and Social Research,* 51:63-77 (October, 1966).

DRIMMER, MELVIN, ed. *Black History: A Reappraisal,* New York: Doubleday, 1968.

FEBUSH, ESTER. "The White Worker and Negro Client," *Social Casework,* 46:271-277 (May, 1965).

FINE, SIDNEY, and BROWN, GERALD S. *The American Past, Conflicting Interpretations of the Great Issues,* University of Michigan, Vol. II, pp. 574-562.

FRANKLIN, JOHN HOPE. "A Brief History of Negroes in the U.S.," in J. P. Davis, ed., *The American Negro Reference Book,* Englewood Cliffs, N.J.: Prentice-Hall, 1966.

GLASGLOW, DOUGLAS. "The Emerging Black Community: The Challenge to Professional Social Work," A paper presented at the NASW Symposium, San Francisco, California, May 25, 1968.

GRIER, WILLIAM, and COBBS, PRICE. *Black Rage,* New York: Basic Books, 1968.

HENRY, JULES. "White Time Colored Time," *Transaction,* March/April, 1965.

HERSKOVITZ, MELVILLE J. *The Myth of the Negro Past,* Boston: Beacon Press, 1958.

HERZOG, ELIZABETH. "Is There a Breakdown of Negro Family?" *Social Work* January, 1966, pp. 3-9.

JONES, LEROI. *Blues People,* New York: William Morrow, 1963.

KEIL, CHARLES. *Urban Blues,* Chicago: University of Chicago Press, 1966.

LEWIS, HYLAN. *Culture, Class and Poverty,* Washington: Cross-Terrell, 1967.

LIEBOW, ELIOT. *Tally's Corner,* Boston: Little, Brown and Co., 1967.

MALCOM X. *Autobiography,* New York: Grove Press, 1965.

MARX, GARY T. *Protest and Prejudices: A Study of Beliefs in the Black Community,* New York: Harper & Row, Harper Torchbooks, 1967.

————. "Religion: Opiate of Inspiration of Civil Rights Militancy Among Negroes?" *American Sociological Review,* 32:64-72 (February, 1967).

MCCORD, WILLIAM, *et. al. Life Styles in the Black Ghetto,* New York: Norton, 1969.

MILLER, HENRY. "Social Work in the Black Community: The New Colonialism," *Social Work,* 14:65-76 (July, 1969).

PETTIT, LOIS. "Some Observations on Negro Culture in the United States," *Social Work,* 5:3 (July, 1960).

PINKNEY, ALPHONSO. *Black Americans,* Englewood Cliffs, N.J.: Prentice-Hall, 1969.

PROSHANSKY, H., and NEWTON, P. "The Nature and Meaning of Negro Self Identity," in Deutsch, Katz, and Jensen, eds., *Social Class, Race and Psychological Development,* New York: Holt, Rinehart & Winston, 1968.

QUARLES, B. *The Negro in the Making of America,* New York: Macmillan, 1964.

RAINWATER, LEE. "Crucible of Identity: The Negro Lower Class Family," in *The Negro American,* Parsons and Clark, eds., Boston: Houghton-Mifflin, 1965.

ROSENTHAL, ROBERT, and JACOBSON, L. E. "Teacher Expectations for the Disadvantaged," *Scientific American,* 218:4 (April, 1968).

SANDERS, CHARLES L. "The Negro Worker in the Dark Ghetto," *Black Caucus,* Fall, 1968, pp. 12-21.

SAUNDERS, MARIE SIMMONS. "The Ghetto: Some Perceptions of a Black Social Worker," *Social Work,* 14:84-88 (October, 1969).

SILBERMAN, CHARLES. *Crisis in Black and White,* New York: Random House, 1964.

SLAWSON, JOHN. "Mutual Aid and the Negro," *Commentary,* April, 1966.

WELLMAN, DAVID. "The Wrong Way to Find Jobs for Negroes," *Transaction,* April, 1968.

WOODS, FRANCES J. *Cultural Values of American Ethnic Groups,* New York: Harper & Row, 1956.

CHICANOS

ADAIR, DOUGLAS. "Cesar Chavez's Biggest Battle," *The Nation,* 205:627-628 (December 11, 1967).

ALISKY, MARVIN. "The Mexican-Americans Make Themselves Heard," *The Reporter,* 36:45-60 (February 9, 1967).

BEALS, RALPH L., and HUMPHREYS, NORMAN D. *No Frontier to Learning,* Minnesota: University of Minnesota Press, 1957.

BOGARDUS, EMORY S. *The Mexican in the United States,* Los Angeles: University of Southern California Press, 1934.

BONGARTZ, ROY. "The Chicano Rebellion," *The Nation,* 4:208-271 (March 3, 1969).

CAMPA, ARTHUR L. "Language Barriers in Intercultural Relations," *Journal of Communications,* 1:41-46 (November, 1951).

————. "Manana Is Today," *Southwestern Write,* T. M. Pearce and A. P. Thomason, eds., Albuquerque, N. Mex.: The University of New Mexico Press, 1964.

CLARK, MARGARET. *Health in the Mexican-American Culture,* Berkeley and Los Angeles: University of California Press, 1959.

COLES, ROBERT, and HUGH, HARRY. "Thorns on the Yellow Rose of Texas," *The New Republic,* 160:13-17 (April 19, 1969).

DE LEON, MARCOS. "Wanted: A New Educational Philosophy for the Mexican-American," *California Journal of Secondary Education,* 34:398-402 (November, 1959).

EDUCATIONAL POLICIES COMMISSION. *Education and the Disadvantaged American,* Washington, D.C.: National Education Association, 1962.

FAIR EMPLOYMENT PRACTICES COMMISSION. *Californians of Spansih Surname: Population, Education, Employment, Income,* San Francisco: 1964.

FREEMAN, DON M. "A Note on Interviewing Mexican-Americans," *Social Science Quarterly,* 49:909-918 (March, 1969).

GAMINO, MANUEL. *Mexican Immigration to the United States: A Study of Human Migration and Adjustment,* Chicago: University of Chicago Press, 1930.

GITTLER, JOSEPH D., ed. *Understanding Minority Groups,* New York: John Wiley, 1956.

GONZALEZ, HENRY B. "The Mexican-American: An Awakening Giant," *Employment Service Review,* July, 1967, pp. 10-13.

GONZALEZ, NANCIE L. *The Spanish Americans of New Mexico: A Distinctive Heritage,* Los Angeles: University of California at Los Angeles, Graduate School of Business Administration, Division of Research, 1967.

GREBLER, LEO. *Mexican Immigration to the United States: The Record and Its Implications,* Los Angeles: University of California at Los Angeles, Graduate School of Business Administration, Division of Research, 1966.

GRIFFITY, BEATRICE. *American Me,* Cambridge, Mass.' The Riverside Press, 1947.

HARWARD, NAOMI. *Socio-Economic and Other Variations Related to Rehabilitation of Mexican-Americans in Arizona,* Temple, Ariz.: Arizona State University, 1969.

HAYNER, NORMAN S. "Notes on the Changing Mexican Family," *American Sociological Review,* 7:489-497 (August, 1942).

HELLER, CELIA S. *Mexican-American Youth: Forgotten Youth at the Crossroads,* New York: Random House, 1966.

HUMPHREY, NORMAN DAYMOND. "The Education and Language of Detroit Mexicans," *Journal of Educational Sociology,* 17:534-542 (May 1944).

_____ "The.Cultural Background of the Mexican Immigrant," *Rural Sociology,* 13:239-255 (1948).

HUMPHREY, NORMAN D. "The Generic Folk Culture of Mexico," *Rural Sociology,* 8:364-377 (December, 1943).

Invisible Minority, The, Washington, D.C.: Department of Rural Education, National Education Association, 1966.

JONES, LAMAR B. *Education and Training of Mexican-Americans: Problems and Prospects,* Baton Rouge, La.: Louisiana State University Press.

JONES, ROBERT C. "Ethnic Family Patterns: The Mexican Family in the United States," *American Journal of Sociology,* 53:450-542 (May, 1948).

_____ "Mexican American Youth," *Sociology and Social Research,* 32:793-797 (March-April, 1948).

KIBBE, PAULINE R. *Latin Americans in Texas,* Albuquerque, N. Mex.: The University of New Mexico Press, 1946.

KNOWLTON, CLARK. "Tijerina: Hero of the Militants," *The Texas Observer,* March 28, 1969.

MADSEN, WILLIAM. *The Mexican-American of South Texas,* New York: Holt, Rinehart & Winston, 1964.

MANUEL, HERSCHEL T. *Spanish Speaking Children of the Southwest,* Austin, Tex.: University of Texas Press, 1956.

MASAR, EVELYN P. "Comparison of Personality Characteristics of Junior High Students from American Indian, Mexican and Caucasian Ethnic Backgrounds," *Journal of Social Psychology,* December, 1967, pp. 145-155.

MCWILLIAMS, CAREY. *North From Mexico: The Spanish-Speaking People of the United States,* New York: Greenwood Press, 1968.

REDFIELD, ROBERT. *Tepoztlan, A Mexican Village,* Chicago: University of Chicago Press, 1930.

RIESSMAN, FRANK. *The Culturally Deprived Child,* New York: Harper and Brothers, 1962.

ROMANO, OCTAVIO IGNACIO. "The Anthropology and Sociology of the Mexican-Americans: The Distortion of Mexican-American History," *El Grito,* 2:13-26 (Fall, 1968).

SAMORA, JULIAN. *La Raza: Forgotten Americans,* South Bend, Ind.: Universtiy of Notre Dame Press, 1966.

SAUNDERS, LYLE. *Cultural Differences and Medical Care,* New York: Russell Sage Foundation, 1954.

_____ *The Spanish Speaking Population of Texas,* Inter-American Education Occasional Papers, Austin: Universtiy of Texas Press, 1949.

SAVETH, EDWARD N. *American Historians and European Immigration,* 1875-1925, New York: Columbia University Press, 1948.

SENTER, DONOVAN. "Acculturation Among New Mexican Villagers in Comparison to Adjustment Patterns of Other Spanish Speaking Americans," *Rural Sociology*, 10:1-47 (March, 1945).

STEINER, STAN. *The Mexican Americans*, New York: Harper & Row, 1970.

WATSON, JAMES B., and SAMORA, JULIAN. "Subordinate Leadership in a Bicultural Community," *American Sociological Review*, 19:413-421 (August, 1954).

WOODS, SISTER FRANCES JEROME. *Cultural Values of American Ethnic Groups*, New York: Harper and Brothers, 1956.

JEWS

ALEICHEM, SHOLOM. *Some Laughter, Some Tears*, New York: Putnam, 1968.

BERGER, MILTON, *et al.*, eds. *Roads to Jewish Survival*, New York: Bloch, 1967.

BISGYER, MAURICE. *Challenge and Encounter: Behind the Scenes in the Struggle for Jewish Survival*, New York: Crown, 1967.

COHEN, HENRY. *Justice, Justice: A Jewish View of the Negro Revolt*, New York: Union of American Hebrew Congregations, 1968.

DAWIDOWICZ, LUCY S., and HIMMELFARB, MILTON, eds. *Conference on Jewish Identity Here and Now*, American Jewish Committee, 1967.

DEAN, JOHN PEEBLES. "Jewish Participation in the Life of Middle-Sized American Communities," *The Jews: Social Patterns of an American Group*, Marshall Sklare, ed., Glencoe, Ill.: The Free Press (1958), pp. 304-320.

DUCKAT, WALTER. *Beggar to King: All the Occupations of Biblical Times*, New York: Doubleday, 1968.

DUKER, ABRAHAM G. *Jewish Community Relations: An Analysis of the MacIver Report*, New York: The Reconstruction Press, 1952.

FELDMAN, LEON A. "Resources for Jewish Living in American Society," *Journal of Jewish Communal Service*, 31:148-291 (Spring, 1955).

FIEDLER, LESLIE A. "Negro and Jew—Encounter in America," *Midstream*, Summer, 1956, pp. 5-17.

FINE, M., and HIMMELFARB, eds. *American Jewish Year Book: Volume 68*, Philadelphia: Jewish Publication Society, 1968.

FRIED, JACOB, ed. *Judaism and the Community: New Directions in Jewish Social Work*, New York: Yoseloff, 1968.

GAMSEY, ROBERT. *Covenant*, New York: Yoseloff, 1967.

GANS, HERBERT J. "Park Forest: Birth of a Jewish Community," *Commentary*, 11:330-339 (April, 1951).

GERSH, HARRY. *The Sacred Books of the Jews*, New York: Stein and Day, 1968.

GLAZER, NATHAN. "The Jewish Revival in America," *Commentary*, 20:493-499 (December, 1955).

————. "Jews and Poverty," *Midstream*, January, 1966, pp. 30-36.

GORDIS, ROBERT. *Sex and the Family in the Jewish Tradition*, New York: Burning Bush Press, 1967.

GREENBERG, CLEMENT. "Self-Hatred and Jewish Chauvinism," *Commentary*, 10:426-433 (November, 1950).

GUTSTEIN, MORRIS A. *Profiles of Freedom*, Chicago: College of Jewish Studies Press, New York: Bloch, 1967.

JANOWSKY, OSCAR I. *The JWB Survey*, New York: Dial Press, 1948.

————, ed. *The American Jew: A Reappraisal*, Philadelphia: Jewish Publication Society of America, 1964.

KAPLAN, BENJAMIN. *The Jew and His Family*, Baton Rouge, La.: Louisiana State University Press, 1967.

KERTZER, MORRIS N. *Today's American Jew*, New York: McGraw-Hill, 1967.

LEVIN, NORA. *The Holocaust: The Destruction of European Jewry, 1933-1945*, New York: Cromwell, 1968.

LEWIN, KURT. *Resolving Social Conflicts*, New York: Harper and Brothers, 1948.

MACIVER, ROBERT. *Report on the Jewish Community Relations Agencies*, New York: National Community Relations Advisory Council, 1951.

MARTIN, BERNARD, ed. *Contemporary Reform Jewish Thought*, Chicago: Quadrangle, 1968.

MASLOW, WILL. "Negro-Jewish Relations," *Freedom Now: The Civil Rights Struggle in America*, Alan F. Westin, ed., Basic Books, 1964.

Negro-Jewish Relations in the United States, The Citadel Press, 1966.

PODHORETZ, NORMAN. "My Negro Problem—and Ours," *Commentary,* February, 1963, pp. 93-101.

POLIER, SHAD. *The Jew and the Racial Crisis,* American Jewish Congress, 1964.

RINGER, BENJAMIN B. *The Edge of Friendliness,* New York: Basic Books, 1967.

ROSENBERG, HAROLD. "Jewish Identity in a Free Society," *Commentary,* 9:508-514 (June, 1950).

RUBENSTEIN, RICHARD L. *The Religious Imagination,* New York: Bobbs-Merrill, 1968.

SANDMEL, SAMUEL. *We Jews and You Christians: An Inquiry Into Attitudes,* New York: Lippincott, 1967.

SCHOENER, ALLAN, ed. *Portal to America: The Lower East Side, 1870-1925,* New York: Holt, Rinehart and Winston, 1967.

SKLARE, MARSHALL, ed. *The Jews, Social Patterns of an American Group,* Glencoe, Ill.: The Free Press, 1958.

———— and GREENBLUM, JOSEPH. *Jewish Identity on the Suburban Frontier,* New York: Basic Books, 1967.

———— and RINGER, BENJAMIN. *Not Quite at Home: How an American Jewish Community Lives with Itself and Its Neighbors,* American Jewish Committee, 1969.

SLAWSON, JOHN. *Toward a Community Program for Jewish Identity,* American Jewish Committee, 1967.

———— and SHAPIRO, MANHEIM S. *Trends in the American Jewish Community,* American Jewish Committee, revised edition, 1962.

STEINBERG, MILTON. *Basic Judaism,* New York: Harcourt, Brace and Co., 1947.

STEMBER, CHARLES HERBERT, and others. *Jews in the Mind of America,* New York: Basic Books, 1966.

WIRTH, LOUIS. "Education for Survival—The Jews," *American Journal of Sociology,* 48:682-691 (May, 1943).

NATIVE AMERICANS

"American Indians and American Life," *Annals,* AAPSS, May, 1957.

ASTROV, MARGARET. *American Indian Prose and Poetry: An Anthology,* New York: Capricorn Books, 1962.

BLUMENTHAL, WALTER HART. *American Indians Dispossessed,* Philadelphia: MacManus Co., 1955.

COHEN, FELIX S. "Indian Self Government," *ABC,* Vol. II, No. 5 (June, 1965).

COLLIER, JOHN. *Indians of the Americas,* New York: North American Library, Mentor Books, 1961.

DANIELS, WALTER M. *American Indians,* New York: Wilson, 1967.

DEXTER, EARLE F. *Doors Toward the Sunrise,* New York: Friendship Press, 1955.

DOCKSTADER, FREDERICK. *Indian Art in America,* New York: New York Graphic Society, 1962.

EDMONSON, MUNRO S. *Status Terminology and the Social Structure of North American Indians,* Seattle: University of Washington Press, 1958.

EGGAN, FREDERICK RUSSEL. *The American Indian: Perspectives for the Study of Social Change,* Chicago: Aldine Publishing Company, 1966.

———— *Social Anthropology of North American Tribes,* Chicago: University of Chicago Press, 1955.

FEY, HAROLD E., and McNICKLES, D'ARCY. *Indians and Other Americans,* New York: Harper & Row, 1959.

FRIEDL, ERNESTINE. "Persistence in Chippewa Culture and Personality," *American Anthropologist,* 58 (1956).

HALLOWELL, ALFRED IRVING. *Culture and Experience,* Philadelphia: University of Pennsylvania Press, 1955.

———— *Backwash of the Frontier: The Impact of the Indian on American Culture,* Washington, D.C.: Smithsonian Institution, 1958.

HOUGH, HENRY W. *Development of Indian Resources,* Denver, Colorado: National Congress of American Indians Fund, 1968.

Indian, The: America's Unfinished Business, Commission on the Rights, Liberties and Responsibilities of the American Indian, Norman, Oklahoma: University of Oklahoma Press, 1966.

Indian Health Program, A Review, Hearings, Subcommittee on Indian Affairs, House Interior and Insular Affairs Committee, 88th Congress, GPO (May 23, 1963).

JACKSON, HELEN H. *A Century of Dishonor,* New York: Harper & Row, Torchbooks, 1965.

JONES, LOUIS THOMAS. *Indian Cultures of the Southwest,* San Antonio, Texas: Naylor, 1967.

KROEBER, ALFRED LOUIS. *Cultural and Natural Areas of Native North America,* Berkeley: University of California Press, 1963.

LA FARGE, OLIVER. *As Long as the Grass Shall Grow,* Alliance Book Corporation, 1940.

LANDY, DAVID. "Tuscarora Tribalism and National Identity," *Ethnohistory,* V, 3 (Summer, 1958).

LINTON, RALPH. *Acculturation in Seven American Indian Tribes,* Gloucester, Mass.: P. Smith, 1963.

MARRIOTT, ALICE LEE. *Greener Fields: Experience Among the American Indians,* New York: Crowell, 1953.

McNICKLES, D'ARCY. *The Indian Tribes of the United States: Ethnic and Cultural Survival,* New York: Oxford Universtiy Press, 1964.

———— "Indian Tests the Mainstream," *The Nation,* September 26, 1966.

MOONEY, JAMES. *Ghost Dance Religion and the Sioux Outbreak of 1890,* Chicago: University of Chicago Press, 1965.

New Interpretations of Aboriginal American Culture History, Anthropological Society of Washington, Washington, D.C., 1955.

OLD PERSON, EARL. "Indians as Human Beings," *Indian Voices,* December, 1966-January, 1967.

OWEN, ROGER C., DEXTOR, J. F., and FISHER, A. D., eds. *The North American Indians: A Source Book,* New York: Macmillan, 1967.

SAPIR, EDWARD. *Selected Writings in Language, Culture and Personality,* David G. Mandelbahm, ed., Berkeley: University of California Press, 1949.

Smoke Signals, Publication of Indian Arts and Crafts Board of U.S. Department of Interior. Frederick Dockstader, Chairman, Washington, D.C.

STEINER, STAN. *The New Indians,* New York: Harper & Row, 1968.

THOM, MEL. "For a Greater Indian America," *The American Indian,* San Francisco (March, 1964); *ABC,* VI, 4 (December, 1964); *ABC,* II, 5 (June, 1965).

THOMAS, ROBERT. "Powerless Politics," *New University Thought,* 4, 4 (Winter, 1966-1967).

TROTTER, GEORGE A. *From Feather, Blanket and Teepee,* New York: Vintage Press, 1955.

United States Indian Service, The, A Sketch of the Development of the BIA and Indian Policy, BIA, 1962.

WAHRHAFTIG, ALBERT. "Community and the Caretakers," *New University Thought,* 4, 4 (Winter, 1966-1967).

WARRIOR, CLYDE. "How Should an Indian Act?" *ABC,* II, 5.

———— "Which One Are You? Five Types of Young Indians," *ABC,* 2, 4 (December, 1964).

WILLOYA, WILLIAM, and BROWN, VINSON. *Warriors of the Rainbow: Strange and Prophetic Indian Dreams,* Healdburgh, Calif.: Naturegraph Co., 1962.

WISSLER, CLARK. *Indians of the U. S.,* Garden City: Doubleday, 1967.

YOUNG, ROBERT. *The Navajo Yearbook,* Window Rock, Arizona: Navajo Agency, 1961.

PUERTO RICANS

BERBUSSE, EDWARD J. *The United States in Puerto Rico, 1898-1900,* Durham, N.C.: University of North Carolina Press, 1966.

BERGER, JOSEPH. *Poppo,* New York: Simon & Schuster, 1962.

BERLE, BEATRICE BISHOP. *Eighty Puerto Rican Families in Sickness and in Health,* New York: Columbia University Press, 1958.

BOARD OF EDUCATION, New York City, *Puerto Rican Profiles,* Resource Material for Teachers, 1964.

BOUVINE, DOROTHY N. Thirty Years of Change in Puerto Rico, New York: F. A. Praeger, 1966.

COLON, JESUS. *A Puerto Rican in New York,* New York: Mainstream, 1961.

DIAZ, ELLEN. "A Puerto Rican in New York," *Dissent,* VIII:3 (Summer, 1961).

FISHMAN, JOSHUA, COOPER, ROBERT L., and MA, ROXANA. *Bilingualism in the Barrio,*

U.S. Department of Health, Education and Welfare, New York: Yeshiva University, 1968.

FITZPATRICK, JOSEPH P. "Attitudes of Puerto Ricans Toward Color," *American Catholic Sociological Review,* 20:3:219-233 (Fall, 1959).

_____. "Puerto Ricans in Perspective: The Meaning of Migration to the Mainland," *Int. Migration Rev.,* II:2:7-19 (Spring, 1968).

_____, BURNS, MARY LOU, and MURPHY, JOHN. *Educational Experience of the Puerto Rican Community in New York City: A Review Paper,* Unpublished paper, Center for Urban Education, 1969.

GLAZER, NATHAN, and MOYNIHAN, DANIEL PATRICK. *Beyond the Melting Pot,* Cambridge, Mass.: M.I.T. Press, 1965.

GRUBER, RUTH. *Puerto Rico: Island of Promise,* New York: Hill and Wang, 1960.

HANLIN, OSCAR. *The Newcomers: Negroes and Puerto Ricans in a Changing Metropolis,* Cambridge, Mass.: Harvard University Press, 1959, also 1962.

HANSON, EARL PARKER. *Puerto Rico: Land of Wonders,* New York: Knopf, 1960.

HATT, PAUL K. *Background of Human Fertility in Puerto Rico,* Princeton, N.J.: Princeton University Press, 1952.

HERNANDEZ ALVAREZ, JOSE. "The Movement and Settlement of Puerto Rican Migrants within the United States," *Int. Migration Rev.,* 2:2:40-51 (Spring, 1968).

JAFFE, A. J., ed. "The Puerto Rican Population of New York," Bureau of Applied Social Research, Columbia University, January, 1954.

KANTROWITZ, NATHAN. "Social Mobility of Puerto Ricans: Education, Occupation and Income Changes Among Children of Migrants, New York 1950-1960," *Int. Migration Rev.,* 2:2:53-70 (Spring, 1968).

KATZMAN, M.T. "Discrimination, Subculture, and the Economic Performance of Negroes, Puerto Ricans and Mexican Americans," *American Journal of Economics,* 27:371-5 (October, 1968).

KLEIN, Woody. *Let in the Sun,* New York, 1965. (Newspaper account of reporter living in a slum apartment.)

LEWIS, GORDON K. *Puerto Rico: Freedom and Power in the Caribbean,* New York: Monthly Review, 1964.

LEWIS, OSCAR. *La Vida: A Puerto Rican Family in the Culture of Poverty—San Juan and New York,* New York: Random House, 1966.

MALZBERG, BENJAMIN. "Mental Disease Among Puerto Ricans in New York City," *Journal of Nervous and Mental Disease,* 123:263-269 (March, 1956).

MAYERSON, CHARLOTTE LEON, ed. *Two Blocks Apart,* New York: Avon Paperback, 1967.

MILLS, C. WRIGHT, SENIOR, CLARENCE, and GOLDSON, ROSE KAHN. *The Puerto Rican Journey,* New York: Harper and Brothers, 1950, and Russell and Russell, 1967.

MINTZ, SIDNEY. *Worker in the Cane,* New Haven: Yale University Press, 1960.

MOZER, ROBERT. "Victims of Exploitation, New York's Puerto Ricans," *Catholic World,* 189:441-6 (September, 1959).

ORITZ, RITA. "A study of Well-Adjusted Puerto Rican Families in New York City . . ." student project No. 3173, 1947; and Wilson Gonzalez, "A Study of Ten Self-Sufficient Puerto Rican Families in New York City," student project No. 4595, 1956, both New York School of Social Work.

PADILLA, ELENA, *Up From Puerto Rico,* New York: Columbia University Press, 1958.

PAGE, HOMER. *Puerto Rico: The Quiet Revolution,* New York: Viking Press, 1963.

RAND, CHRISTOPHER. *The Puerto Ricans,* New York: Oxford University Press, 1968.

SENIOR, CLARENCE. *Strangers—Then Neighbors: From Pilgrims to Puerto Ricans,* New York: Freedom Books, 1961.

_____ *The Puerto Ricans,* Chicago: Quadrangle Books, 1965.

SEXTON, PATRICIA C. *Spanish Harlem: An Anatomy of Poverty,* New York: Harper & Row, 1965.

STEWARD, JULIAN M. *The People of Puerto Rico: A Study in Social Anthropology,* Urbana, Ill.: University of Illinois Press, 1957.

TAEUBER, IRENE B. "Migration and Transformation: Spanish Surname Populations and Puerto Ricans," *Population Index,* 32:30-34 (January, 1966).

THOMAS, PIRI. *Down These Mean Streets,* New York: Knopf, 1967.

TUGWELL, REXFORD G. *The Stricken Land, The Story of Puerto Rico,* New York: Doubleday, 1947.

TUNIN, MELVIN, and FELDMAN, A. *Social Class and Social Change in Puerto Rico*, Princeton: Princeton University Press, 1961.

United States-Puerto Rico Commission on the Status of Puerto Rico: Status of Puerto Rico, *Report of the United States-Puerto Rico Commission on the Status of Puerto Rico*, Washington, D.C.: U.S. Government Printing Office, 1966.

WAKEFIELD, DAN. *Island in the City: The World of Spanish Harlem* (also entitled, *Island in the City: Puerto Ricans in New York*). New York: Citadel Press, 1960.

WELLS, HENRY. *The Modernization of Puerto Rico: A Political Study of Changing Values and Institutions*, Cambridge, Mass.: Harvard University Press, 1969.

WHITE ETHNIC

ABBOTT, DAVID W., GOLD, LOUIS H., and ROGOWSKY, EDWARD T. *Police, Politics and Race: The New York City Referendum on Civilian Review*, Boston: Harvard-MIT Joint Center for Urban Studies and The American Jewish Committee.

AIKEN, MICHAEL, and FERMAN, LOUIS. *Economic Failure, Alienation and Extremism*, Ann Arbor: University of Michigan Press, 1967.

BALTZELL, E. DIGBY. *The Protestant Establishment: Aristocracy and Caste in America*, New York: Random House, 1964.

BELL, DANIEL. *The Radical Right*, Garden City: Doubleday and Co., 1963.

BERGER, BENNET M. *Working Class Suburb*, Berkeley: University of California Press, 1968.

BETTELHEIM, BRUNO, and JANOWITZ, MORRIS. *Social Change and Prejudice*, New York: The Free Press, 1964.

BRESLIN, JIMMY. "The Last of the Irish Immigrants," *New York*, March 17, 1969, pp. 29-31.

DANZIG, DAVID. *The Social Framework of Ethnic Conflict in America*, Unpublished paper presented at the National Consultation on Ethnic America, June, 1968. Available from the American Jewish Committee.

FRIEDMAN, MURRAY. "Kensington, U.S.A.," *La Salle Quarterly*, Fall, 1967, pp. 5-9.

GANS, HERBERT J. "Anxiety and Anger in the White Working Class: Some Hypotheses and Research Suggestions," unpublished paper, Fall, 1969.

GLAZER, NATHAN, and MOYNIHAN, DANIEL P. *Beyond the Melting Pot: The Negroes, Puerto Ricans, Jews, Italians, and Irish of New York City*, Cambridge, Mass.: MIT Press, 1963.

GRAHAM, HUGH DAVIS, and GURR, TED ROBERT. *Violence in America: Historical and Comparative Perspectives*, A report submitted to the National Commission on the Causes and Prevention of Violence, New York: Bantam Books, 1969.

GREENE, VICTOR. *The Slavic Community on Strike*, Notre Dame: University of Notre Dame Press, 1968.

HAMILL, PETE. "The Revolt of the White Lower Middle Class," *New York*, April 14, 1969, pp. 24-29.

HAMILTON, RICHARD F. "The Marginal Middle Class: A Reconsideration," *American Sociological Review*, April, 1966, pp. 192-199.

HUEBENER, THEODORE. *The Germans in America*, Philadelphia: Chilton, 1962.

JACOBS, PAUL, and LANDAU, SAUL. "To Serve the Devil: Minority Groups in American History," *The Center Magazine*, March, 1969, pp. 41-48.

KARMIN, MONROE W. "Polish Hill: The White Ethnic's Complaint," *The Washington Monthly*, August, 1969, pp. 35-39.

KOLODNY, RALPH L. "Ethnic Cleavages in the United States," *Social Work*, January, 1969, pp. 13-23.

KOMAROVSKY, MIRA. *Blue Collar Marriage*, New York: Random House, 1964.

LANE, ROBERT. *Political Ideology: Why The American Common Man Believes What He Does*, New York: The Free Press, 1962.

LEGGETT, JOHN C. *Class, Race, and Labor: Working-Class Consciousness in Detroit*, New York: Oxford University Press, 1968.

LENSKI, GERHARD. "Status Crystallization: A Non-vertical Dimension of Social Status," *American Sociological Review*, 19:405-413.

LEVINE, EDWARD M. *The Irish and Irish Politicians: A Study of Cultural and Social Alienation*, Notre Dame, Ind.: University of Notre Dame Press, 1966.

LEVINE, IRVING M. *A Strategy for White Ethnic America*, unpublished paper, The American Jewish Committee.

LIEBERSON, STANLEY. *Ethnic Patterns in American Cities,* Glencoe, Ill.: The Free Press, 1963.

MILLER, SEYMOUR M. "Sharing the Burden of Change," *New Generation,* Spring, 1969.

MILLER, S.M., and REISSMAN, FRANK. "The Working Class Subculture: A New View," *Social Problems,* Summer, 1961, pp. 86-97.

MOYNIHAN, DANIEL P. "The New Racism," *Atlantic,* August, 1968, pp. 35-40.

Newsweek Magazine, "The Troubled American," October 6, 1969.

NOVAK, MICHAEL. "Politicizing the Lower-Middle," *Commonwealth,* June 6, 1969, pp. 341-343.

PARENTI, M. "Ethnic Politics and the Persistence of Ethnic Identification," *American Political Science Review,* 61:717-26 (September, 1967).

PERLMUTTER, NATHAN. "We Don't Help Blacks by Hurting Whites," *New York Times Magazine,* October 6, 1968, pp. 30+.

PISANI, LAWRENCE F. *The Italian in America,* New York: Exposition Press, 1957.

Proceedings of the Philadelphia Conference on the Problems of White Ethnic America, "Diffusing the White Backlash," sponsored by Greenfield Center for Human Relations American Jewish Committee, Wellsprings Ecumenical Center, The Lighthouse Settlement with Philadelphia Board of Education Office of Integration and Intergroup Education, 1968.

RAAB, EARL. *Religious Conflict in America: Studies of the Problem Beyond Bigotry,* Garden City, N.Y.: Doubleday, 1964.

SCHRAG, PETER. "The Forgotten American," *Harper's,* August, 1969, pp. 27-34.

SEXTON, BRENDAN. " 'Middle-Class' Workers and the New Politics," *Dissent,* May-June, 1969, pp. 231-238.

SHANNON, WILLIAM V. *The American Irish,* New York: Macmillan, 1966.

SHOSTAK, ARTHUR B., and GOMBERG, WILLIAM. *Blue Collar World: Studies of the American Worker,* Englewood Cliffs, N.J.: Prentice-Hall, 1964.

SUTTLES, GERALD D. *The Social Order of the Slum: Ethnicity and Territory in the Inner City,* Chicago: University of Chicago Press, 1968.

TYLER, GUS. "The Working Class Rediscovered," *New Leader,* July 21, 1969, pp. 11-13.

WILENSKY, HAROLD L. "The Professionalization of Everyone?" *American Journal of Sociology,* 70:137-158 (September, 1964).

WILEY, N. F. "Ethnic Mobility Trap and Stratification Theory," *Social Problems,* 15:147-50 (Fall, 1967).

WITTKE, CARL F. *We Who Built America: The Saga of the Immigrant,* Cleveland: Western Reserve University Press, 1964.

WOOD, ARTHUR E. *Hamtramck: A Sociological Study of a Polish-American Community,* New Haven: College and University Press, 1955.

WOMEN

Aphra, A Feminist Journal. Available, Elizabeth Fisher, 22 Cornelia Street, New York, New York 10014.

BEARD, MARY E. *Woman as Force in History,* New York: Macmillan, 1946.

BERNARD, JESSIE. *Academic Woman,* University Park, Pa.: Pennsylvania State University Press, 1964.

_____. *The Sex Game,* Englewood Cliffs, N.J.: Prentice-Hall, 1968.

BIRD, CAROLINE. *Born Female: The High Cost of Keeping Women Down,* New York: McKay, 1968.

CARSON, JOSEPHINE. *Silent Voices: The Southern Negro Woman Today,* New York: Delacorte Press, 1969.

COSER, ROSE. *The Family: Its Structure and Functions,* New York: St. Martins, 1964.

CUSSLER, MARGARET. *The Woman Executive,* New York: Harcourt, Brace and World, 1958.

DALY, MARY. *The Church and the Second Sex,* New York: Harper & Row, 1968.

DEBEAUVOIR, SIMONE. *The Second Sex,* New York: A. Knopf, 1952.

DEUTSCH, HELENE. *The Psychology of Women, A Psychoanalytic Interpretation,* New York: Grune and Stratton, 1945, two volumes.

DITZION, SIDNEY. *Marriage, Morals and Sex in America, A History of Ideas,* New York: Bookman Associates, 1953.

DUNBAR, ROXANNE. *Female Liberation as the Basis for Social Revolution,* Southern Female Rights Union, Box 30087, Lafayette Sq. Station, New Orleans, Louisiana.

ELLMAN, MARY. *Thinking About Women,* New York: Harcourt, Brace, 1968.

FAVA, SYLVIA. "The Status of Women in Professional Sociology," *American Sociological Review,* April, 1960.

Female Liberation Journal, Fall, 1968, Spring, 1969. Available from Female Liberation, 371 Sommerville Avenue, Somerville, Mass. 02143.

FLEXNER, ELEANOR. *A Century of Struggle,* Cambridge: Harvard University Press, 1959.

FREUD, SIGMUND "Feminity," in *New Introductory Lectures on Psychoanalysis,* New York: W. W. Norton, 1965.

FRIEDAN, BETTY. *The Feminine Mystique,* New York: Dell, 1963.

GINSBERG, ELI, and YOHALEM, MARIE. *Educated American Women: Self Portraits,* New York: Columbia University Press, 1966.

HACKER, HELEN. *Women as a Minority Group,* New York: Bobbs-Merrill, Reprint Series.

HERNTON, CALVIN. *Sex and Racism in America,* New York: Grove Press, 1965.

KANOWITZ, LEO. *Women and the Law. The Unfinished Revolution,* Albuquerque: University of New Mexico, 1969.

KLEIN, VIOLA. *The Feminine Character, History of an Ideology,* New York: International Universities Press, 1946, 1948.

KOEDT, ANNE. "The Myth of the Vaginal Orgasm," Anne Koedt, 97 Second Avenue, New York, New York 10003.

KRICH, ARON, ed. *The Sexual Revolution, Pioneer Writing on Sex,* in two volumes, New York: *Fell,* 1963, 1965.

LERNER, GERDA "The Feminists: A Second Look," *Columbia Forum,* A Quarterly Journal of Fact and Opinion. Vol. XIII, No. 3 (Fall, 1970).

————. *The Woman in American History.* In press, Addison-Wesley. Scheduled publication date May, 1971.

LIFTON, ROBERT JAY. *The Women in America,* Boston: Houghton Mifflin, 1965.

MALINOWSKI, BRONISLAW. *Sex, Culture and Myth,* New York: Harcourt, Brace, 1962.

MANNES, MARYA. *More in Anger,* Philadelphia: Lippincott, 1958.

MEAD, MARGARET. *Male and Female,* New York: Mentor Books, 1955.

————. *Sex and Temperament,* New York: Morrow, 1935.

————, et. al. *The Peaceful Revolution: Birth Control and the Changing Status of Women,* Planned Parenthood-World Population, 1967.

MILLETT, KATE. *Sexual Politics,* New York: Doubleday, 1970.

MONTAGUE, ASHLEY. *The Natural Superiority of Women,* New York: MacMillan Co., 1953.

MORGAN, ROBIN, ed. *Sisterhood Is Powerful: An Anthology of Writings from the Women's Liberation Movement,* New York: Vintage Books, 1970.

MURRAY, PAULI, and EASTWOOD, MARY. "Jane Crow and the Law: Sex Discrimination and the Title VII," *George Washington Law Review,* 2 (1965).

NEW YORK RADICAL WOMEN, *Notes from the First Year,* New York: NYRW, 799 Broadway, Room 412, June, 1968.

Off Our Backs, Women's Liberation Newspaper, 2318 Ashmead Place, N.W., Washington, D.C. 20009.

O'NEILL, WILLIAM L. *Everyone Was Brave, The Rise and Fall of Feminism in America,* Chicago: Quadrangle Books, 1969.

————. *The Woman Movement: Feminism in the United States and England,* New York: Barnes & Noble, 1969.

PATAI, RAPHAEL, ed. *Women in the Modern World,* New York: Free Press, 1967.

PUTNAM, EMILY JONES. *The Lady: Studies of Certain Significant Phases of Her History,* Chicago: University of Chicago, Press, 1970.

REICH, WILHELM. *The Sexual Revolution,* New York: Farrar, Straus and Giroux, revised, 1969.

RHAM, EDITH DE. *The Love Fraud,* New York: Clarkson N. Potter, Inc., 1965.

RIEGEL, ROBERT E. *American Feminists,* Lawrence, Kansas: University of Kansas Press, 1968.

RUDERMAN, FLORENCE. *Child Care and Working Mothers,* New York: Child Welfare League of America.

RUITENBECK, HENDRIK M. *The Male Myth,* New York: Dell Books, 1967.

SEATTLE RADICAL WOMEN (SRW), *Radical Women: Program and Structure,* SRW, c/o
Severn, 2940 Thirty-sixth Avenue, Seattle, Washington 98144.

"Sex and the Contemporary American Scene," special issue of the *Annals of American
Academy of Political and Social Science,* Volume 376 (March, 1968).

SINCLAIR, ANDREW. *The Better Half: The Emancipation of the American Woman,* New
York: Harper & Row, 1965.

SMITH, GEORGINA. *Help Wanted: Female,* New Brunswick, N.J.: Rutgers, The State University Press, 1964.

STOLLER, ROBERT J. *Sex and Gender,* New York: Science House, 1968.

Up From Under, Woman's Liberation Magazine, 339 Lafayette Street, New York, New
York 10012.

DATE DUE